Digital Histories

Emergent Approaches within the New Digital History

Edited by
Mats Fridlund, Mila Oiva & Petri Paju

HUP HELSINKI UNIVERSITY PRESS

Published by
Helsinki University Press
www.hup.fi

First published in 2020

Cover design by Ville Karppanen
Cover photo: iStockphoto

Print and digital versions typeset by Siliconchips Services Ltd.

ISBN (Paperback): 978-952-369-020-2
ISBN (PDF): 978-952-369-021-9
ISBN (EPUB): 978-952-369-022-6
ISBN (Mobi): 978-952-369-023-3

https://doi.org/10.33134/HUP-5

The full text of this book has been peer reviewed to ensure high academic standards. For full review policies, see http://www.hup.fi/

VERTAISARVIOITU
KOLLEGIALT GRANSKAD
PEER-REVIEWED
www.tsv.fi/tunnus

Suggested citation:
Fridlund, M., Oiva, M., & Paju, P. (Eds.). (2020). *Digital histories: Emergent approaches within the new digital history*. Helsinki University Press. https://doi.org/10.33134/HUP-5.

Table of Contents

Acknowledgements vii

Contributors ix

Foreword xvii

Part I: The Beginning **1**

Chapter 1: Digital and Distant Histories: Emergent Approaches within the New Digital History **3**
Petri Paju, Mila Oiva and Mats Fridlund

Part II: Making Sense of Digital History **19**

Chapter 2: The Long Road to 'Digital History': History of Computer-Assisted Research of the Past in Finland since the 1960s **21**
Petri Paju

Chapter 3: Towards Big Data: Digitising Economic and Business History **45**
Jari Eloranta, Pasi Nevalainen and Jari Ojala

Chapter 4: Digital History 1.5: A Middle Way between Normal and Paradigmatic Digital Historical Research **69**
Mats Fridlund

Chapter 5: Building Historical Knowledge Byte by Byte: Infrastructures and Data Management in Modern Scholarship **89**
Jessica Parland-von Essen

Chapter 6: Big Data, Bad Metadata: A Methodological Note on the Importance of Good Metadata in the Age of Digital History **103**
Kimmo Elo

Chapter 7: All the Work that Makes It Work: Digital Methods and Manual Labour **113**
Johan Jarlbrink

Part III: Distant Reading, Public Discussions and Movements in the Past 127

Chapter 8: The Resettlement and Subsequent Assimilation of Evacuees from Finnish Karelia during and after the Second World War 129
Mirkka Danielsbacka, Lauri Aho, Robert Lynch, Jenni Pettay, Virpi Lummaa and John Loehr

Chapter 9: Towards Digital Histories of Women's Suffrage Movements: A Feminist Historian's Journey to the World of Digital Humanities 149
Heidi Kurvinen

Chapter 10: Of Great Men and Eurovision Songs: Studying the Finnish Audio-Visual Heritage through NER-based Analysis on Metadata 165
Maiju Kannisto and Pekka Kauppinen

Chapter 11: Tracing the Emergence of Nordic *Allemansrätten* through Digitised Parliamentary Sources 181
Matti La Mela

Chapter 12: Evolving Conceptualisations of Internationalism in the UK Parliament: Collocation Analyses from the League to Brexit 199
Pasi Ihalainen and Aleksi Sahala

Chapter 13: Picturing the Politics of Resistance: Using Image Metadata and Historical Network Analysis to Map the East German Opposition Movement, 1975–1990 221
Melanie Conroy and Kimmo Elo

Chapter 14: The Many Ways to Talk about the Transits of Venus: Astronomical Discourses in *Philosophical Transactions*, 1753–1777 237
Reetta Sippola

Chapter 15: The Many Themes of Humanism: Topic Modelling Humanism Discourse in Early 19th-Century German-Language Press 259
Heidi Hakkarainen and Zuhair Iftikhar

Chapter 16: Manuscripts, Qualitative Analysis and Features on Vectors: An Attempt for a Synthesis of Conventional and Computational Methods in the Attribution of Late Medieval Anti-Heretical Treatises 279
Reima Välimäki, Aleksi Vesanto, Anni Hella, Adam Poznański and Filip Ginter

Chapter 17: Macroscoping the Sun of Socialism: Distant Readings of Temporality in Finnish Labour Newspapers, 1895–1917 303
Risto Turunen

Part IV: Conclusions 325

Chapter 18: The Common Landscape of Digital History: Universal Methods, Global Borderlands, *Longue-Durée* History, and Critical Thinking about Approaches and Institutions 327
Jo Guldi

Index 347

Acknowledgements

With the publication of this book a more than five year long journey is reaching an end and new beginnings. In 2015 a group of historians met up in Helsinki to discuss how we could best promote the development of digital history. Our first heartfelt thanks therefore go to Anu Lahtinen, Hannu Salmi, Ilkka Mäkinen, Jaakko Suominen, Jessica Parland-von Essen, Marko Tikka, Mikko Tolonen and Visa Immonen, who came up with the idea for the research project that started this process. Their work led to a survey of digital history projects, then a digital history demonstration roadshow that travelled across Finland, and, now, this book—much of which draws on conversations that developed over the course of the roadshow.

In addition to the more than hundred historians who in 2018 participated in our digital history roadshow to six Finnish universities, we would especially like to thank Antti Härkönen, Heli Paalumäki, Henri Hannula, Jo Guldi, Johan Jarlbrink, Kaisa Vehkalahti, Pasi Nevalainen, Risto Turunen, Tero Aalto, and Virva Liski for helping to realise the tour. Many colleagues have provided support, resources, insights, and advice during this process, and some of them deserves a special thanks, especially Aaro Sahari, Bernard Geoghegan, Dagmar Schäfer, Ilkka Jokipii, Juho Savela, Justine Cassell, Kati Katajisto, Lisa Onaga, Maiju Wuokko, Martina Schlünder, Nina Lerman, Pekka Kyrenius, Saara Matala, Sami Suodenjoki, Shi-Pei Chen and the University of Turku IT services.

The funding that made it possible to bring together all the digital historians and let us editors work together on this book has come through two research grants from the Kone Foundation and with additional funding and support from Aalto University, the Academy of Finland, the Centre for Digital Humanities at the University of Gothenburg, the Emil Aaltonen Foundation, the Max Planck Institute for the History of Science in Berlin, and the University of Turku. At Helsinki University Press, we received helpful advice and constructive comments from two anonymous reviewers. Our editor Aino Rajala—who steered us through the material realization of our book—deserves our warmest thanks, as does the Helsinki University Press Academic Board, who found our book worthy to be published as one of the first open access books of the press.

Outside the historical community, the very humanist computer scientist Timo Honkela was one of the earliest supporters of our project. We were delighted when he accepted our invitation to write the book's foreword, and we are deeply saddened that he has not lived to see its publication. Timo passed away in May 2020, following a long struggle with a serious illness. To commemorate his professional achievements in the digital humanities and his personal generosity both to us and to other digital and analogue humanists, we—the editors and the authors of this volume—dedicate this book to his memory.

Gothenburg, Helsinki and Turku in the viral summer of 2020
Mats Fridlund, Mila Oiva, Petri Paju

Contributors

Lauri Aho has a master's degree from the Department of Biology of the University of Turku, Finland. He is currently a biology and geography teacher in Helsinki, Finland.

Melanie Conroy is Associate Professor of French at the University of Memphis, United States. She received her doctorate from Stanford University and master's degrees from the University of Buffalo and the University of Paris, VIII. Her research explores the intersection of networks with literature, cultural history and visual studies in modern European culture. She is currently working on a cultural history of European salons as sites of literary production and a digital humanities survey on literary geography in the French realist and post-realist novel.
ORCID: https://orcid.org/0000-0003-0410-1610

Mirkka Danielsbacka is Assistant Professor of Sociology in the Department of Social Research at the University of Turku, Finland. She holds a PhD in Finnish and Nordic history and second PhD in Social and Public Policy, both from the University of Helsinki. Her research focuses on the Second World War, the welfare state and intergenerational family relations.
ORCID: https://orcid.org/0000-0002-8547-9502

Kimmo Elo is Associate Professor and Senior Researcher at the Centre for Parliamentary Studies at the University of Turku, Finland. He holds a PhD in Political Science from the University of Turku. His current research interests include text/data mining, network analysis, knowledge visualisation, computational history and German and European history since 1945, as well as intelligence studies.
ORCID: https://orcid.org/0000-0002-3223-5221

Jari Eloranta is Professor of Economic History at the University of Helsinki, Finland. He holds a PhD in History from the European University Institute, Italy. His research focuses on comparative economic and business history, especially the fiscal transformation of states, and he is currently involved in projects that use digital humanities methods and data.
ORCID: https://orcid.org/0000-0002-8572-5902

Mats Fridlund is Associate Professor in History of Science and Ideas and Deputy Director for the Centre for Digital Humanities at the University of Gothenburg, Sweden. He has a PhD in History of Technology from KTH Royal Institute of Technology, Sweden. His research focuses on cultural and political history of science, technology and materiality. He has been Principal Investigator for two Kone Foundation projects to strengthen digital history in Finland and has published on topic modelling in historical studies and used digital methodologies to study history of terrorism and Chinese industrialisation.
ORCID: https://orcid.org/0000-0002-5759-0027

Filip Ginter is Associate Professor of Language and Speech Technology at the Department of Future Technologies at the University of Turku, Finland. He has a PhD in Computer Science from the University of Turku. His research area is natural language processing and its various applications. His is a member of the Turku NLP Group.
ORCID: https://orcid.org/0000-0002-5484-6103

Jo Guldi is Associate Professor of Britain and Its Empire at Southern Methodist University, United States. She has a PhD in History from the University of California, Berkeley. She was the inaugural Mellon Postdoctoral Fellow in Digital History at University of Chicago and is currently Principal Investigator of a $1 million NSF grant, 'The Unaffordable World', which uses digital methods, among others, to inquire into the history of property rights and affordability.
ORCID: https://orcid.org/0000-0002-5085-0738

Heidi Hakkarainen is postdoctoral researcher at the University of Turku, Finland. She has a PhD in Cultural History from the University of Turku and currently works in a research project entitled 'Viral Culture in Early Nineteenth-Century Europe'. Her research interests include cultural history,

history of the press, urban history, 19th-century studies, history of emotions, popular culture and digital history.
ORCID: https://orcid.org/0000-0003-2110-6907

Anni Hella is doctoral candidate at the Department of Cultural History at the University of Turku, Finland. She has a master's degree in Cultural History from the University of Turku. Her dissertation deals with the use and authority of manuscripts in the Council of Ferrara-Florence (1438–1439) and the impact of the Council on humanism. She is also interested in digital humanities and especially the authorship attribution of pre-modern Latin texts.
ORCID: https://orcid.org/0000-0002-2433-8618

Timo Honkela (1962–2020) was Professor Emeritus of Research in Digital Resources at the University of Helsinki, Finland. He had a PhD in Information Technology from Helsinki University of Technology. Honkela was a pioneer in applying digital methods to humanities, social science and the arts, and a generous supporter of projects in digital humanities. A truly humanist scientist, his last research was devoted to the 'peace machine' concept, in which artificial intelligence and machine learning were applied to provide tools for improved human communication, better understanding of one's own and others' emotions, and societal themes such as economy and democracy.
ORCID: https://orcid.org/0000-0003-0917-2020

Zuhair Iftikhar is a research student at the Department of Mathematics and Statistics at the University of Turku, Finland. He has a master's degree in Mathematics and Computer Science from the University of Turku and enjoys collaborations with digital humanities researchers. His other research interests include machine learning, natural language processing, digital signal processing, image processing and optimisation.

Pasi Ihalainen is Professor of Comparative European History at the Department of History and Ethnology at the University of Jyväskylä, Finland. He has a PhD in History from the University of Jyväskylä and has published widely on the history of political discourse, nationalism, democracy and parliamentarism since the 18th century, applying comparative and transnational perspectives. He is currently working on the conceptual history of internationalisms and on the history of the concept of 'politician' and is preparing a study combining distant and close reading to analyse parliamentary speaking in several European countries.
ORCID: https://orcid.org/0000-0002-5468-4829

Johan Jarlbrink is Associate Professor in Media History and Senior Lecturer in Media Studies at Umeå University, Sweden. He has a PhD in Culture and Society from Linköping University, Sweden. His research has mainly focused

on the history of journalism, media technologies and information management. He is currently involved in the project 'Welfare State Analytics: Text Mining and Modeling Swedish Politics, Media & Culture, 1945–1989'.
ORCID: https://orcid.org/0000-0002-1167-046X

Maiju Kannisto is a cultural historian and media scholar with experience in Finnish media history, media industries and digital humanities. She received her PhD in Cultural History from the University of Turku, Finland, and has worked as a postdoctoral researcher at the John Morton Center for North American Studies at the University of Turku. Kannisto's research interests include national popular culture, media companies and media ethics.
ORCID: https://orcid.org/0000-0003-1722-6850

Pekka Kauppinen is a former technical assistant at the University of Helsinki, Finland. He has a master's degree in language technology from the University of Helsinki. His primary research topics included finite-state applications such as automatic post-processing of Finnish and Swedish historical texts digitised by the means of optical character recognition. In 2017, Kauppinen was tasked with improving and expanding the Finnish rule-based named-entity recogniser FiNER.
ORCID: https://orcid.org/0000-0003-2071-5110

Heidi Kurvinen is a postdoctoral researcher affiliated with the Department of Cultural History at the University of Turku, Finland. She has a PhD in History from the University of Oulu, Finland. She is specialised in the history of feminism and media history in the Nordic countries and currently works as an Academy of Finland postdoctoral fellow in her project 'The Travelling Image of Bra-Burners: Negotiating Meanings of Feminism in the Finnish Mainstream Media from the 1960s to 2007'. She is a board member of the Nordic Media History Network (NOMEH) and head of the editorial board of Kulttuurihistoria—Cultural History book series published by the Finnish Society for Cultural History.
ORCID: https://orcid.org/0000-0002-1056-0701

John Loehr is a researcher and research coordinator at the University of Helsinki's Lammi Biological Station, Finland. He has a PhD in evolutionary ecology from the University of Jyväskylä, Finland, and he currently heads the project on Karelian evacuee research (project website: http://www.helsinki.fi/en/projects/learning-from-our-past).

Robert Lynch is a bio-cultural anthropologist and currently has a position as a postdoctoral researcher in the sociology and biology departments at the University of Turku, Finland. He holds a PhD in evolutionary anthropology from Rutgers University, United States, and his research focuses on how biology,

the environment and culture come together to shape behaviour, life histories and health outcomes. His research questions have ranged from the predictors of self-sacrifice and how exposure to stress in childhood affects reproduction to the impact of immigration on social mobility and reproduction and its effects on voting behaviour.
ORCID: https://orcid.org/0000-0002-2477-6204

Virpi Lummaa is an evolutionary biologist and ecologist. She holds an Academy of Finland Professorship at the University of Turku, Finland. She received her PhD in Biology from the University of Turku, thereafter holding positions in Cambridge and Sheffield in the UK and Berlin, Germany, before returning to Finland. Her research interests include ageing, lifespan and natural selection in contemporary human populations.
ORCID: https://orcid.org/0000-0002-2128-7587

Matti La Mela is a visiting researcher at the Department of Business Studies at Uppsala University, Sweden. He has a PhD in History and Civilization from the European University Institute, Italy, and was previously a post-doctoral scholar at Aalto University, Finland. La Mela has a background in social science history and his research focuses on themes such as (intellectual) property rights, commodification of nature and transnational relations. He has extensive experience in multidisciplinary digital humanities research and has published on Nordic patenting and innovation networks and the use of large digitised textual data in historical research.
ORCID: https://orcid.org/0000-0003-0340-9269

Pasi Nevalainen is postdoctoral researcher in business history at the University of Jyväskylä, Finland. He has a PhD in Finnish History from University of Jyväskylä. He is interested in a number of 20th- and 21st-century themes related to structural changes in the economy, society and business organisation. His research interests include state-owned companies, telecommunications and management history. He uses digitised source databases and working methods as tools for qualitative history research.
ORCID: https://orcid.org/0000-0003-1172-9537

Mila Oiva is a cultural historian, digital humanist and an expert on Russian and Polish history. She has a PhD in Cultural History from the University of Turku, Finland, and has worked as post-doctoral scholar at Aalto University and the University of Turku. Currently she works as a post-doctoral Research Fellow at CUDAN Open Lab at the Tallinn University, Estonia. Her main research interest focuses on circulation of information which she has studied in research projects on 19th-century global news flows and contemporary Finnish and Russian internet forum discussions on medieval history.
ORCID: https://orcid.org/0000-0002-5241-7436

Jari Ojala is Professor of Comparative Business History at the University of Jyväskylä, Finland. He has a PhD in History from University of Jyväskylä and specialises in economic, business and maritime history and has used digital humanities data and methods in his studies for two decades. He has published his research in main journals in the field, including *Business History*, *Explorations in Economic History* and *European Review of Economic History*.
ORCID: https://orcid.org/0000-0002-4348-8857

Petri Paju is a cultural historian with research interests in the development of digital history and its uses, and in history of technology. He has a PhD in Cultural History from the University of Turku, Finland. He has previously worked in two Kone Foundation-funded projects based at Aalto University which studied and advanced digital history research in Finland since 2016, and in the Academy of Finland research project 'Computational History and the Transformation of Public Discourse in Finland, 1640–1910'. He has written broadly on the history of technology in Finland and on computing history in the Nordic countries, as well as on the IBM Company in postwar Europe.
ORCID: https://orcid.org/0000-0002-2486-2364

Jessica Parland-von Essen is development manager at CSC—IT Center for Science, Finland. She holds a PhD in History from the University of Helsinki, Finland, and has studied book history, library and information science and worked with digitisation and digitalisation within the cultural heritage sector and research data management. She is a member of Open Knowledge Finland and has been a proponent for open scholarship on both the national and international levels. Recently, she has studied research data management and is working to find solutions for promoting and supporting well-documented and managed publication of research outputs, especially different types of data.
ORCID: https://orcid.org/0000-0003-4460-3906

Jenni Pettay is a Senior Researcher in the Department of Social Research at the University of Turku, Finland. She has a PhD in biology from the University of Turku. Her research focus is on evolution of human life history traits and family dynamics.

Adam Poznański is a librarian at the Department of Manuscripts of the Wrocław University Library and teaches Latin at the Wrocław University of Life and Environmental Sciences, Poland. He has a PhD in classics from Wrocław University. His main research interests are persuasion and argumentation in medieval anti-heretical texts and theoretical aspects of rhetoric and composition in the Middle Ages, as well as codicology and Latin paleography.

Aleksi Sahala is a doctoral candidate in Language Technology at the Department of Modern Languages at the University of Helsinki, Finland.

He is currently a member of the Digital Humanities team in the Center of Excellence in the Ancient Near Eastern Empires at University of Helsinki. He has a combined master's degree in Language Technology and Assyriology with a focus on computational Assyriology and the Sumerian language from the University of Helsinki. His research interests include Computational Assyriology and distributional semantics.
ORCID: https://orcid.org/0000-0002-4255-3872

Reetta Sippola is a doctoral candidate in Cultural History at the University of Turku, Finland. She has a master's degree in Cultural History from the University of Turku. Her dissertation explores spatiality, embodiment and the relationship of humans and the non-human in the British scientific travel narratives of the 18th century. In her research she is using digital humanities methods to provide new perspectives on the voyages of Captain James Cook. In addition, her recent publications include work on text reuse and public discourse in historical Finnish newspapers and text mining with Blast.
ORCID: https://orcid.org/0000-0002-7703-196X

Risto Turunen is a doctoral candidate in history at Tampere University, Finland. He has a master's degree in History from the University of Tampere. He is currently finishing his thesis on the origins, structure and evolution of Finnish socialism as a political language from the 1860s until 1917. Turunen has published articles on labour history, conceptual history and digital humanities.
ORCID: https://orcid.org/0000-0002-8898-1274

Aleksi Vesanto has a master's degree in Computer Science with a focus on Natural Language Processing (NLP) from the University of Turku, Finland. His research interests include various applications of NLP, such as text reuse detection and authorship attribution, as well as several areas in speech technology.

Reima Välimäki is a postdoctoral research fellow at the Turku Institute for Advanced Studies (TIAS) and the Department of Cultural History at the University of Turku, Finland. He has a PhD in Cultural History from University of Turku. His research interests include heresy and inquisition, polemical literature, manuscript studies, medievalism and history politics, as well as authorship attribution.
ORCID: https://orcid.org/0000-0002-8301-6563

Foreword

Timo Honkela

Do historians need computers for more than writing? What could be the other uses? Does the use of computers pose a threat to history by bringing in a reductionist approach? Perhaps surprisingly to some, I would say that historians are dealing with phenomena that may be characterised as much more complex than those studied by scholars in natural sciences. This has meant that historians have had to work using educated human interpretation rather than machines or algorithms as their methodological basis. In natural sciences, it is commonplace to look for underlying simple causes even for phenomena that appear to be highly complex on the surface. Such a reductionist approach is neither wise nor productive in many areas and topics within history, because human behaviour and social organisation includes complexities like phenomena's instability as they change over time. The reliance on words of written languages and human-made images and less on numbers based on measurements, and the non-linear dependence of context and complex feedback mechanisms between society, individuals and their times further increase the intricacy of a historical study. An example of the latter is that a written document on history may itself influence the track of future events and thus history can change history. These kinds of connections are not known to exist within the natural sciences. History is different.

I have for a long time followed, participated in and had aspirations for connecting history and computer science. In the 1980s, I as a computer scientist

How to cite this book chapter:
Honkela, T. (2020). Foreword. In M. Fridlund, M. Oiva, & P. Paju (Eds.), *Digital histories: Emergent approaches within the new digital history* (pp. xvii–xix). Helsinki: Helsinki University Press. https://doi.org/10.33134/HUP-5-19

was using rule-based artificial intelligence (AI) methods in particular in the area of natural language processing. Thanks to my personal contacts, I had often a chance to discuss with historians their work, results and methodologies. Soon the idea came up of finding ways to build a bridge between historians and AI researchers, but after some consideration this did not seem feasible or relevant. With the rule-based AI methods, it was not possible to approach phenomena that were relevant for historians. Computer science was not sufficiently developed for historians. The challenge was both quantitative and qualitative. However, as history tells us, and this volume gives many examples of, our tools and our times change. Since the 1990s, my experience of using and developing neural networks and statistical machine learning methods has been quite different. My personal experience of applying these methods since 1991 led to the conclusion that important opportunities were available, in which the expertise of the historians was a central asset. In the 2000s, I entered into a joint research project using neural networks on digital history with a historian that succeeded in producing results of mutual interest to me, the computer scientist, as well as to the historian. Computer science had caught up with history.

Today, the situation to some degree has been reversed, in that historians have started to seek out the advanced methodologies of computer science. Historians, like all researchers in the humanities and social sciences, wish to work in an analytically and methodologically solid manner. Occasionally, the success of natural sciences has led historians to find research questions where the borrowing of methods of natural sciences would be suitable and sufficient. This might be for wishes to achieve a wider generalisability and predictive power may be sought. However, in many cases, this leads to reductionism that prevents the results to be relevant within the complex world of humans as individuals and as social constellations. The challenges of how to account for symbol function, human intentionality and the role of artifacts are just some of the many factors that still render history a very challenging field for computer science. But the development within computational analysis, modelling and visualisation methods and tools are changing this situation, which is exemplified by the research in this volume.

The current research illustrates the state-of-the-art nature of this collaboration and when looking even further ahead there are new challenging opportunities related to history that stem from possible collaboration among history, other disciplines in humanities and computer science. From the point of view of cognitive linguistics, the meaning of meaning could be studied more carefully than what is usually done within the study of history. The meaning of linguistic expressions is dependent on the historical, societal and linguistic context in which they were written. Qualitative nuances can further be obtained by studying how items such as words, names, events, periods of time, individual persons or institutions are related to one other through some data than can be studied using statistical machine learning methods. These results can further be studied using the historian's expert considerations. Although this line of research is already being conducted today, the studies are usually limited by focusing on time series or so-called matrix data.

If one would try to predict what the future might offer for the next generation of digital historians, one mathematical concept in particular could be considered relevant for historians, that of the *tensor*. In order to explain what a tensor is about, one can consider Excel spreadsheets. As a mathematical structure, a matrix is like an Excel spreadsheet. A kind of plate of numbers on a table. A tensor is an extension of this structure. In the case of a tensor, there are several layers on top of each other. For instance, in the traditional matrix ('on the table'), the number of people in the different neighbouring areas may be stored as numbers. In a tensor, layers of different years may be added so that the number of people in the different years can be conveniently stored and analysed. Tensors are essential extended data structures that could be highly useful in, for example, studying conceptual change in history, varieties of interpretations of the same word or item by different people, the development of some phenomenon over time within a complex context, or filling in gaps in history with hypothetical data to be searched for. This potential of the tensor remains for future historians and computer scientists to realise. Naturally, it is not the only promising direction from the methodological point of view.

The works in this collection provide a view on how history can be simultaneously studied with analytical rigour and without the need to straightforwardly accept the need of reductionism. The developments of studying human behaviour, culture and history with computational modelling, data science and complexity science and thus to engage with and better understand the new tools of our digital times is also a promise of an increasingly better ability and central societal role for history to help us understand our digital present and future.

PART I

The Beginning

CHAPTER 1

Digital and Distant Histories

Emergent Approaches within the New Digital History

Petri Paju, Mila Oiva and Mats Fridlund

Half a century ago, historian Emmanuel Le Roy Ladurie, when surveying the progress of quantitative history, prophesised that 'tomorrow's historian will have to be able to programme a computer in order to survive'.[1] Since then, computers and programming have indeed profoundly changed historians' practice through such digital tools as word processing, the internet, email, PowerPoint, Google, JSTOR, Facebook, Twitter and Zoom. They have made all of us historians into digital historians in one way or another. As these digital tools used by most historians illustrate, there are many ways that the digital has transformed the historian's craft beyond mere practical and administrative improvements. During the new millennium, the computer together with the internet have begun to change also the historian's research tools and methods in new and previously unforeseen ways into a novel kind of digital history. It is this new emerging digital history, together with some ever-significant approaches of the 'old' quantitative digital history, that is the subject of this book.

Digital history encompasses diverse historical practices, such as digitisation efforts at archives, libraries and museums, computer-assisted research, web-based teaching and professional and public dissemination of historical knowledge, as well as research on the history of 'the digital', computers and

How to cite this book chapter:

Paju, P., Oiva, M., & Fridlund, M. (2020). Digital and distant histories: Emergent approaches within the new digital history. In M. Fridlund, M. Oiva, & P. Paju (Eds.), *Digital histories: Emergent approaches within the new digital history* (pp. 3–18). Helsinki: Helsinki University Press. https://doi.org/10.33134/HUP-5-1

digital technologies. One comprehensive definition capturing this diversity of practices was suggested more than a decade ago in a discussion between digital historians in the *Journal of American History*:

> Digital history is an approach to examining and representing the past that works with the new communication technologies of the computer, the Internet network, and software systems. On one level, digital history is an open arena of scholarly production and communication, encompassing the development of new course materials and scholarly data collections. On another, it is a methodological approach framed by the hypertextual power of these technologies to make, define, query, and annotate associations in the human record of the past. To do digital history, then, is to create a framework, an ontology, through the technology for people to experience, read, and follow an argument about a historical problem.[2]

While the digital embraces the whole spectrum of the historian's craft, this volume focuses on digital history as a form of scholarly research that uses digital sources and tools to produce new historical knowledge. This form of digital history research is part of the larger digital turn in academia, identified as digital humanities, culture analytics, computational social sciences and other concepts related to utilisation of computer-assisted methods for research.[3] By bringing together research contributions to the new digital history from historians, computer scientists, computational linguists and other scholars producing new empirical historical knowledge using digital methodologies, as well as conceptually focused perspectives on critical issues of the field's past, present and future development, this book provides digital histories that we hope will be read as laudable exemplars from within the emergent digital history research community. The digital histories collected here simultaneously represent various methodological applications of and themes within digital history research and thus an attempt to take stock of current research rather than providing a pedagogical textbook or programmatic manifesto. The new digital history has matured enough for us to instead be able to present historical work currently furthering historical research. Thus, the studies in this book take digital history beyond discussions of its future potential, proofs of concept and pedagogical examples to instead focus on digital history 'in action', to the making of new historical knowledge.

Through this focus on presenting results from digital history research projects, this book breaks new ground within the current wave of digital history. Other digital history books published so far have mainly been monographs focused on discussing how historians could use digital sources or methods to conduct and present research such as the pioneering *Digital history: a guide to gathering, preserving, and presenting the past on the web* (2006) by Daniel J. Cohen and Roy Rosenzweig, or anthologies such as *History in the digital age* (2013) contributing discussions of the problems and possibilities of doing the new digital history, rather than research results of historical studies using new digital methodologies.[4] This is as expected, as it is only during the last couple of years that we have seen the first research publications using digital history research methodologies within mainstream academic historical publishing outlets. Matthew Jockers' *Macroanalysis* (2013) appears to be the first research monograph published by a university press, and Cameron Blevins' 'Space, nation, and the triumph of region' (2014) is the first peer-reviewed research article published in the *Journal of American History*.[5] In this way, this book aspires to pioneer and promote work within the new digital history by being a timely research anthology from the current third generation of digital historians that,[6] outside of digital spatial history,[7] focuses on contributing new historical knowledge from research using digital research methodologies.

Emergence of the New Digital History

The roots of exploiting modern data-processing equipment in humanities research date back at least to the 1950s, when Josephine Miles started using punch cards for literary analysis.[8] The development was continued in the 1950s with Father Roberto Busa utilising IBM mainframe computers and John W. Ellison using the UNIVAC I to produce lexical concordances.[9] Since then, computer-assisted history research has produced three 'generations', roughly following the advancement of computers and internet technologies. Simultaneously, there are continuities of parallel developments borrowed from, or developed together with, sister disciplines, such as text analysis in literary studies, statistical analyses in economic and social history, Geographic Information System (GIS) within geography, and digital image analysis in art history and visual studies. Allegedly, 'the first published work by an historian involving actual computerized research' came in 1963 with a 'scalogram analysis of voting patterns' in the British Parliament in the 1840s by William Aydelotte at the State University of Iowa.[10] A few years later, Viljo Rasila (Paju, this volume) did somewhat similar work in Finland. The first larger and more widespread application of computers was by the cliometricians of the 1960s, who were recognised as constituting the first generation of digital historians. They were followed by a second generation centred around the new 'personal' computers in the 1990s and were often seen as a part of the wider humanistic research field of 'humanities computing'.

The current third generation of digital history can be said to begin to emerge in the late 1990s and the early 2000s with the appearance of the first large digitised full text databases, such as Early English Books Online (EEBO) and Project Gutenberg,[11] and with the rebranding and expansion of humanities computing to digital humanities in the mid-2000s. Since the early 2000s, contemporary historians' toolkit has been expanded by an increasing volume of digitised sources and the swift development of computational analysis methods. This was taking place at the same time as geographical history was going through a development from historical GIS (HGIS) to spatial history.

The snowballing growth in the amount of digital sources and the development of new research approaches and concepts has gradually increased the number of humanists using computational methods. One of the most frequently used concepts is *distant reading*, a perspective pioneered by the literary historian Franco Moretti. Distant reading can be understood as a counterpart to *close reading* that has been used extensively in humanities for distilling meanings from texts from the 1970s onwards. Distant reading has been used to extract meaningful patterns from textual sources, particularly when the number of texts are so numerous that it is impossible for a human to read them in a consistent manner.[12] The examples in this volume show that distant reading can also be a useful approach for exploring smaller amounts of text, as it provides another kind of approach to the texts in focus. Such machine or algorithmic reading provides 'another pair of scholarly glasses' and allows examining the sources from new perspectives. In the best case, close and distant readings complement each other.

Characteristic for this potentially paradigmatic digital history (Fridlund, this volume) is not just the introduction of new conceptualisations, such as 'distant reading', 'macroanalysis' or 'algorithmic reading', or the application of methodological tools such as topic modelling, but also the utilisation of novel practices for historians, new digitally augmented ways of working. Digital research brings along the collaborations of larger multidisciplinary group projects, the use of centralised technical infrastructures and machines. The changes that are taking place in history today are in several ways reminiscent of the changes that natural science disciplines such as physics and biology went through earlier with changeover from individuals' 'small science' tabletop experiments to interdisciplinary large team 'big science' collaborations.

The origin of this volume lays in an initiative to strengthen digital history research proposed by a collective of historians in Finland in 2015. That ambition was generously funded by the Kone Foundation through two interconnected projects 2016–2018, which brought together the majority of the authors in this volume. The first project, Towards a Roadmap for Digital History in Finland, aimed at identifying practical, professional and institutional obstacles and possibilities for developing digital history research. The second project, From Roadmap to Roadshow, built on the first one by bringing together digital historians to shape the best practices for disseminating knowledge about digital methods to historians so that in the end these would facilitate new digital history research. This was accomplished through a road tour to six major Finnish research universities, where the project organised presentations and workshops on emerging research and methodological developments within digital history.

Originally, the aim of the project was to end after the roadshow and to conclude with the subsequent publication of articles by the three main project researchers. However, the enthusiasm among the participants at the various universities promised new digital research results in a not-so-distant future. Thus, towards the end of their shared work, the team decided to extend the project towards its logical conclusion by organising a workshop during the spring of 2018 that invited historians and specialists in digital research methods to come together to work collaboratively on formulating and answering a number of specific and concrete historical research questions. The historians who responded to the invitation brought their source materials and historical research questions, while the digital specialists contributed with their methodological expertise to jointly find answers to the research questions. At the workshop, the research teams analysed the sources to come up with preliminary solutions and answers and afterwards the teams were encouraged to keep working on their projects, and in this book, several of those projects are now brought to completion in the form of peer-reviewed research articles. They are complemented by articles from other digital historians, presenting results from a selection of the other recent research projects.

The majority of the research presented here is by digital historians active at Finnish universities. The rationale behind this is, in addition to the books' specific historical origins as explained above, that the emerging Finnish digital history community is both a representative and in many ways exemplary part of the larger international development of digital history. It is representative in that the used methodological research approaches correspond to the predominant directions of current digital history and thus the diversity and breadth of the studies presented in this volume, representing digital history research in a wide range of topics, from diverse disciplines from political, economic, cultural, intellectual and feminist history to history of science and technology and periods going from the Early Modern to the recent past. Taken together they provide a representative overview of the state-of-the-art of not just Finnish digital history research, but also of emerging digital history overall. Like most other research communities, the digital history landscape in Finland is diverse and dispersed, including bigger research groups, individual researchers and interdisciplinary and collaborative projects with national and foreign colleagues in Finland and abroad. This volume is exemplary in that digital history in Finland as a community and practice can be said to be more developed and institutionalised than in many other countries. In addition to several digital historians working at all levels of academic seniority, there are designated doctoral positions and professorships, textbooks, a regular digital history conference series and seminars and a digital history section within the national historical society. Compared to most other countries, the stage of digitisation of newspapers and archival documents is very advanced, which encourages digital history research. The common understanding of digital historians in Finland is that the focus of digital history research should be in finding answers to the research questions rather than utilisation of digital research tools just for their own sake. The contributions to this book, we feel, exemplify that critical evaluation of digital sources, metadata and research methods, and the results they provide, are the basic components of good digital history research. Thus, the Finnish digital history research, together with the other contributions presented in this volume, should be a good representation of some of the most widely shared research practices emerging within the new digital history.

The New Digital and Distant Histories

This book contributes to advancing the field of history in primarily two ways, through new conceptual explorations of the past, present and future of digital history research and with new empirical historical knowledge coming out of research using digital methods. Through this, we aim to illuminate the new digital history's potential and pitfalls. We have divided the book into four parts. Part I 'The Beginning' consists of this introduction. Part II 'Making Sense of Digital History' starts with discussing the historical and methodological roots of digital history and contributes conceptual and contextual explorations of the current state of digital histories. Part III 'Distant Reading, Public Discussions and Movements in the Past' presents empirical case studies from various time periods that through the application of digital tools, primarily various forms of distant reading methodologies, demonstrate the further potential for expanding historical knowledge. The final Part IV 'Conclusions' draws the volume to an end by an exposition of the landscape of digital history and its future potential.

In the foreword, the late computer scientist and pioneering digital humanist Timo Honkela, draws on his wide experience of multidisciplinary cooperation using computational tools, to offer his thoughts on the digital future of history. In Chapter 2, providing a longer historical context for the new digital history, Petri Paju examines the history of computer-assisted history research from the 1960s until the 2010s. By focusing on one particular national development, that of historians' use of computers in Finland, he recognises how, although a particular national story, it was part of a larger, international and transnational pattern of development within digital history research.

After the overview of the roots of digital history, the subsequent chapters in Part II shed light on the fundamental components of digital history research: data, metadata and the mundane, often manual, work enabling the operation of our digital tools and resources. In Chapter 3, Jari Eloranta, Pasi Nevalainen and Jari Ojala exemplify how economic and business historians in many ways have been forerunners of digital history with computerised analysis of numerical and event code databases. They also share their experiences of the challenges to historical research of digitisation and uses of databases. Chapter 4 by Mats Fridlund attempts to conceptualise emerging historical practice by exploring the present state of digital history research according to two ideal types of digital history. Following Thomas Kuhn's theory of scientific revolutions, he describes them as 'normal' and 'paradigmatic' digital history. Further, as a middle way between the two, he proposes one that is beyond the normal but still a less revolutionary form of semi-automatic digital history, described as 'digital history 1.5'.

This is followed by Chapter 5, which concerns research infrastructures, where Jessica Parland-von Essen calls for better data management and increasing the openness of data. She presents the FAIR (Findable, Accessible, Interoperable and Re-usable) approach to data, which would not only improve the efficiency, but also increase the trustworthiness and quality of historical research. The critical theme of the role of metadata in digital history research is taken up in Chapter 6 by Kimmo Elo, who points out that when focusing on data, we often neglect metadata, although it is a crucial part of the whole. In his chapter, he explores ways of improving the quality of the historian's metadata. Following this is a valuable reminder offered by Johan Jarlbrink in Chapter 7 on the importance of manual work to digital machine processing. In his chapter, he shows how digital research is far from automated, and that it actually requires countless hours of manual work which most of the time stays invisible and thus its problems and possibilities are often unnoticed and neglected.

The subsequent chapters offer a wide array of empirical case studies using a selection of digital research methods that exemplify how they can help us to reach for new understandings of the past. Beginning this series, in Chapter 8, Mirkka Danielsbacka, Lauri Aho, Robert Lynch, Jenni Pettay, Virpi Lummaa and John Loehr use statistical quantitative analysis to explore migration of Finnish individuals in the 20th century. Using a database that they have digitised and complemented with other historical data, they explore socio-demographic and environmental factors that can be combined with the domestic relocation and settlement of migrants. In Chapter 9, Heidi Kurvinen, in the vein of feminist history methodology, uses her personal experience of getting acquainted with historical text mining to explore traditional and not so traditional historians' experiences in encountering the new digital history methods. She notes that entering the field of digital history 'requires cultural and technological capital which marginalises researchers who do not have the skills to conduct digital analyses by themselves or do not have access to the organisational support'. Among the factors influencing the ability of researchers to participate, she identifies their gender. The next case study by Maiju Kannisto and Pekka Kauppinen in Chapter 10 illustrates the use of Named Entity Recognition (NER) to explore Finnish audio-visual history as it is presented in the public radio and television online archives. Their metadata analysis reveals interesting peculiarities in what kind of audio-visual imaginary of the past is provided by the dataset, and which elements of the national history it hides. In Chapter 11, Matti La Mela gives an excellent example of the opportunities of text analysis by tracing the history of the concept of *allemansrätten* (freedom to roam) in the Finnish parliamentary debates and argues counterintuitively to common knowledge that the present understanding of the concept has a surprisingly short history. His article also takes extra care in making the methodological steps transparent to readers. In Chapter 12, Pasi Ihalainen, with the assistance of Aleksi Sahala, uses collocation analysis to study changes of the concept of 'internationalism' in 20th-century British parliamentary debates. By reconstructing the meanings attached to foreign political issues in the British Parliament from the early 19th century, they show that the 'international' has been associated in different ways during the various deliberations on the United Kingdom's membership in international organisations.

In Chapter 13, Melanie Conroy and Kimmo Elo, with the help of network analysis of the metadata of a large picture archive, explore the structure and temporal dynamics of the geospatial social networks of the East German opposition movement. They show how the network method can be used for exploring and visualising, as well as analysing, quantitative historical data. Reetta Sippola's contribution in Chapter 14 uses topic modelling to explore the evolution of the scientific discourse in the pioneering British scientific journal *Philosophical Transactions* in the mid-18th century. In her study, the method of arranging the data makes topic modelling reveal previously neglected themes and unnoticed temporal changes in the discourse. Heidi Hakkarainen and Zuhair Iftikhar also use this methodology in Chapter 15, in the expanded form of dynamic topic modelling, to focus on the formation of the concept of 'humanism' in the early 19th-century German-language press. They show how reaching reliable analysis results demands a deep understanding of the context, skills and time, but how the method has the potential to challenge established patterns of thought and underlying presumptions by providing a novel perspective on the sources. In Chapter 16, Reima Välimäki, Aleksi Vesanto, Anni Hella, Adam Poznański and Filip Ginter study author attribution and apply methods based on neural networks to explore their medieval cases of authorship recognition. Their intriguing results show how the uses of 'black-boxed' computational methods can potentially help us to solve centuries-long debates on the attribution of authorship. In the final case study in Chapter 17, Risto Turunen uses advanced collocation analysis to study Finnish labour newspapers during the late 19th and the early 20th centuries. With that material, he takes a macroscopic approach to study expressed temporality of the papers and especially the 'sun of socialism', which differed from the biblical sun shining on all and in this 'highlighted earthly problems'. Towards the end of his chapter, Turunen turns his discussion to the present situation and to future aims of digital history.

Jo Guldi concludes the volume in Chapter 18 by drawing a wide picture of the potential game-changing nature of digital history. She stresses the universal character and widely applicable nature of digital research methods: researchers of Chinese industrialisation can find a method used by a medievalist also useful to their research and vice versa. She also predicts that with the increasing number of digitised sources and utilisation of digital methods, we may see a rise of *longue durée* in history, which as she puts it could provide new findings that 'border on the breathtaking'.

New Historical Challenges and Criticisms

Digitisation and computer-assisted research tools open new possibilities, but also bring novel challenges and criticisms to the history discipline. There is a need for a wider methodological discussion on how digital research methods could and should be used in history research. To be able to take part in interdisciplinary collaboration, it is important for historians to have a discussion on what digital methods mean, and where they can lead us. The ambition is that the studies in this book will contribute to foster this discussion. Among the critical components of digital history research that are addressed in the following chapters are digitisation of sources, creating metadata for digital source materials, human–computer interaction and digital research methods. These are only a few of the critical issues troubling current digital history.

One of the most pressing questions in digital history research is access to and problems of *digitised sources*. Although also important to scholars in other disciplines, they are fundamental to historians. The availability of consistent digitised collections with long time series is one of the critical prerequisites of digital research. Simultaneously, the existing digitised sources invoke discussions of their availability and usability, and what overall should be digitised. Furthermore, digitisation also changes the object of research, as a digitised newspaper is not the same as the physical object of a newspaper. When digitising sources, we, as Mikko Tolonen and Leo Lahti have pointed out, also lose important elements of the physical objects.[13] The consensus of the scholars contributing to this book is that the readily available digitised sources should be used with the same or even higher level of source criticism than before. While the existence of easily accessible digitised sources is a crucial requirement of digital history research, non-problematised use of data—a kind of 'source myopia'—has the potential to skew the historiography towards the most readily available databases and source material, rather than the most important or representative, and thus possibly motivate researchers to study them instead of the sources that, digitised or not, would provide the best answers to the research question (Chapter 3, this volume). For example, the very popular usage of newspapers as sources, especially for historical studies before the 20th century, is not necessarily because they are the most relevant historical sources, but is rather due to the simple fact that newspaper collections have in many countries been extensively digitised.

In digitising historical sources, the digitiser faces several practical choices that have extensive effects on historical research. The first major question is what to digitise. In making such basic selections, there is a threat of repeating and amplifying the biases of the past knowledge constructions, leaving less prominent and marginalised topics aside. The sources chosen to be digitised, the ways in which they are digitised and shared, have far-reaching consequences.[14] Memory organisations, such as archives and libraries, often begin their digitising efforts from sources that are most often used by the general public and researchers, and are thus considered to be more important. This common practice creates a threat to further marginalise less prominent topics and to exclude less studied materials. Therefore, alongside the use of digitised sources in readily available collections, the ability for historians to digitise their own sources is becoming an increasingly important skill. Learning how to digitise, and setting the best practices for digitising, data life cycles, and sharing digitised sources among historians are emerging important additions to the historian's toolbox. To increase the variety of the available digitised sources, it is valuable that historians learn to digitise sources on their own, and whenever possible, share their new data. The authors of this volume use both readily available databases and sources that they themselves have digitised. Digitisation is time consuming, and therefore the sharing of data is an important means of widening the base of digitised sources.

In addition to digitised sources, a key issue for digital history research is *metadata*, the data that describes and gives information about the digital data (sources), and especially concerning its varying quality. As Kimmo Elo points out in Chapter 6, 'more attention should be paid and more resources should be invested in metadata creation'. From this perspective, the real problem is not the structure of a data system itself (its 'ontology'), but rather the process of creating source material's metadata. The principles of adding metadata to the documents are often rather unsystematic and not transparent, and only too often the usefulness of (meta)data depends on the person creating and inserting the metadata. For example, at the workshop described above, one research team planned to work on metadata of images from a public source database (www.finna.fi). After some trials with that material, they ended up terminating their project because of the overly scattered and random character of the metadata collection. The large amount of processing necessary to enable digital methods to be applied would not have made it possible to finalise their project within a reasonable timeframe. However, this attempted project was not in vain, as it partly inspired one of its participants (Elo) to write a chapter on metadata and digital history for this volume.

The new kind of source material for historians in the form of digital data and metadata makes it important for digital historians to develop a new *digital source criticism*. Compared to the pre-digital era with large amounts of data in non-digital forms, the contributions in this volume demonstrate how digitisation instead of selective sampling allows historians to use all the available data in their analysis, and thus more systematic analysis. Interestingly, distant reading of large datasets often exposes the used databases' borders and restrictions better than traditional sampling for close reading. For example, the analysis of Kannisto and Kauppinen revealed the biases and partiality of the studied dataset. Using digitised sources demands deep understanding of what the data consists of because, as Eloranta, Nevalainen and Ojala point out in Chapter 3, straightforward and non-problematising data usage may lead to missing the key issues of the data and misleading interpretations of the historical processes. In big data lie opportunities also for significant misinterpretations and falsifications.

As the contributions in this volume demonstrate, undertaking digital history research is often more time consuming and demands perhaps more conscious methodological choices than the traditional history approach. When one is undertaking digital history research, it becomes evident that alongside the algorithms used, the selection, creation, cleaning and filtering of the data heavily influence the results of the computer-assisted analysis. As Johan Jarlbrink shows, the digital research process at many stages demands manual work to be done, such as data cleaning. He demonstrates that this work is not only a necessary precondition for the analysis, but is actually in itself an important part of the analysis, as the researcher gets to work on and read through the material several times, and in this way learns to know the data in depth. While the quantitative digital analysis makes the conclusions more convincing, the in-depth knowledge of the data provides crucial qualitative understandings that guide the interpretations of the quantitative analysis.

Connected to this new source criticism, there is also a need to develop what has been described as a *digital resource criticism* (Chapter 4, this volume). This refers to the need, in order not to draw false conclusions, to be better aware of the internal technological logics of the digital resources used by historians, such as that of a database or a search engine. Similar questions of an awareness of the opportunities and limitations of the available resources and methods have lately been raised in reference to representation and visualisation of historical data.[15] One example of this is how Maiju Kannisto and Pekka Kauppinen in their study (see Chapter 10, this volume) found out that the frequencies of the search terms in the metadata did not reflect the actual frequencies of the audio-visual material to which the metadata referred, but that they were more an artifact of the processes of how the metadata had been produced. Both Elo (Chapter 6) and Kannisto and Kauppinen (Chapter 10) suggest in this book that archivists and historians should collaborate more and in this openly discuss the principles and practices of metadata formation, and how they could best serve all the parties.

Furthermore, the chapters of this book point out the methodological zigzag between distant and close reading of data, the repetitious adjustment of the algorithmic parameters, the evaluation of the means of the data formation, its broader context and preceding research, all involved in an overall research process of trial and error. Sippola, Kurvinen, and Hakkarainen and Iftikhar all show how the choices of the researcher influence the outcomes of the research. For example, when using topic modelling, the testing of the results with varying numbers of topics is a very important step in the process of analysis. Simultaneously, the scholar's understanding of the context is essential in identifying the meaningful results, and to be able to differentiate them from the potential nonsense produced by the computer, to discern the historical signal from the data noise. Usage of digital research methods amplifies the research findings, but they also amplify the potential of false results. Computers and algorithms are important helpers, but they cannot operate on their own: they always require human guidance.

Despite all these challenges, the contributions to this volume demonstrate how computational analysis can disclose new and previously unnoticed patterns in history. For example, in Chapter 12, Ihalainen summarises the benefits of computer-assisted analysis for his study on conceptual history by stating that it revealed associations between the studied concepts, which made it possible to estimate trends in political attitudes and revealed particular and peculiar political issues that would have been very difficult to find with traditional methods. Along the same lines, Kurvinen states, in Chapter 9, that combining digital analysis and close reading allowed her to identify topics that might have remained unnoticed otherwise and exposed new ways of perceiving the material, ways that could prompt novel and previously unresearched questions.

The new digital history might also foster a wider rethinking of the parameters of historians' professional practice. Digital research methods create new and at times more stringent demands on accuracy, methodological thinking, self-organisation and collaboration than traditional historical research. As Kurvinen points out, digital environments could encourage historians to conduct their research in 'a more self-aware manner when every step of the process needs more thought than a traditional day with paper archives'. Similarly, Eloranta, Nevalainen and Ojala point out in Chapter 3 that collaborative research on digital data can lead to more efficient and accurate research, but it requires the development of a different professionalism from researchers. Jessica Parland-von Essen shows in Chapter 5 the importance of historians starting to manage their data in a more qualified manner to themselves so they become more like data curators and archivists, and including thinking about the preservation and reusability of research data from a longer-term perspective. To support the development of such new practices in historical disciplines, there is a need for historians to participate in developing new joint practices that support FAIR data and thus better research. This calls for collaboration among historians and memory organisation specialists, and for historians to reach outside of history to seek out ideas from other disciplines facing similar challenges.

Most of the chapters in this volume were written collaboratively. Along the process of our project, it was confirmed that digital history research demands interdisciplinary collaboration, since it is rare that a historian manages to combine in him- or herself both the skills of the historian and of the programmer. That said, it is not necessary for the historian to become a programmer. What is needed is the ability to collaborate and work together in an interdisciplinary manner with collaborators who bring expertise from the domains of computer and information science.[16] The above-mentioned workshop proved that fruitful collaboration with IT professionals is not only needed, but also feasible and beneficial. And this book proves that it can bring new knowledge, as well as conceptual developments, to the field of history.

One basic challenge, nevertheless, is that although multidisciplinarity is much-needed in the realm of digital humanities research, it is well known that not all computer-related questions or tasks carried out in digital history research are challenging enough to peak the interests of computer scientists. For example, the application of a ready code to a dataset is for a traditionally trained historian often too challenging a task, but rather trivial for a computer scientist. Thus, there is an increasing importance for universities and research institutions to be able to provide more mundane and routine technical support to historical researchers through their libraries, IT support facilities or other means, much like before the widespread availability of easily accessible online databases and online sources such institutional structures were central in assisting historians in finding research literature and source materials.

Conclusion

It seems evident that history research has been and will continue to be increasingly influenced by society's overall digitalisation. Still, the historians in general would benefit from being more aware than before of the interaction between historical research and the digitising world around them in order to stay both critical and constructive towards the changes and continuities of today. This includes taking advantage of the latest tools, as well as exploring their limitations to be able to keep our methods up to date and to gain a better understanding of the possibilities and pitfalls of historical research in the digital era.

As always, the future holds both promises and threats for historians, digital and otherwise. Although it is essentially an older condition, the skills and resources needed for digital history research could broaden the gap between history departments that are better positioned and those that are not, and consequently create more divisions among historians. One key issue for the digital historians is how to succeed to excel in using and developing new methods, while simultaneously avoiding overlooking the values of more traditional research. Doing and succeeding with the new explorations, while also respecting the older known and tried ways, has often shown to be the best working path towards the future.

In a similar vein as the encouragement by Jo Guldi and others in this book, one lesson from sociologists and historians of technology has been that users matter, that they, rather than being passive adopters of new technology delivered in black boxes, can have their say in influencing the direction of technological change, and at times even open up and reconstruct their tools so they better fit their particular needs and desires.[17] Historians as a group can and should be active in making choices and guiding their discipline towards an ever-more digital world of tomorrow, a tomorrow that soon will be a past and needs its born-digital history researched.

After almost 50 years, perhaps we have finally arrived at Emmanuel Le Roy Ladurie's 'tomorrow'. Or maybe we are already far beyond that—not least as most of the authors in this collection would not identify themselves as doing the quantitative kind of history Le Roy Ladurie expected future historians to be doing. As historians, we can recognise how difficult it is for history's actors to foresee future developments, and that while Le Roy Ladurie correctly predicted that historians needed to learn to harness computer technology for their work, neither he nor his colleagues could hardly have imagined the possibilities of the information technology at historians' disposal in the early 2020s. However, in the sense that historians should learn how to make the most of the 'computer', we feel that the historians in this book with their new digital and distant histories have tried to live up to his hopes by going towards and away from his tomorrow to reach our today and its past, present and future digital histories.

Notes

1 Le Roy Ladurie 1979: 6. Rabb wrote: 'In 1967, the basic posture of quantitative historians was a mixture of brashness and defensiveness. Le Roy Ladurie was sufficiently impressed by the discussions at Ann Arbor to predict that "the historian will be a programmer or he will be nothing"' (Rabb 1983: 591).

2 William G. Thomas III quoted in Cohen et al. 2008: 454.

3 See Jones 2014.

4 For some of the major books published within the new digital history, see: Staley 2002; Cohen & Rosenzweig 2006; Galgano et al. 2008; Schmale 2010; Gantert 2011; Genet & Zorzi 2011; Haber 2011; Rosenzweig 2011; Clavert & Noiret 2013; Dougherty & Nawrotzki 2013; Jockers 2013; Weller 2013; Graham, Milligan & Weingart 2015; Bozic et al. 2016; Koller 2016; Brügger 2018.

5 Jockers 2013; Blevins 2014. See also Guldi & Armitage 2014.

6 As we well know, historical 'firsts' are often contested and contextual.

7 The field of spatial history evolved from within Historical Geographic Information Systems research starting in the 2000s. See Gregory & Geddes 2014: x, xii, xiv–xv.

8 Sagner Buurma & Heffernan 2018.

9 Jockers 2013: 3; Vanhoutte 2013: 127–128.

10 Swierenga 1970: 5.

11 Although these collections also have much longer histories. See Lebert 2008.

12 Moretti 2000, 2005, 2013. See also Underwood 2017.

13 Tolonen & Lahti 2018.

14 See, for instance, Jarlbrink & Snickars 2017.

15 Foka, Westin & Chapman 2018.

16 See also Fickers & van der Heijden 2020.

17 See Oudshoorn & Pinch 2003.

References

Blevins, C. (2014). Space, nation, and the triumph of region: a view of the world from Houston. *Journal of American History, 101*(6), 122–147.

Bozic, B., Mendel-Gleason, G., Debruyne, C., & O'Sullivan, D. (2016, 25 May). *Computational history and data-driven humanities: second IFIP WG 12.7 international workshop, CHDDH 2016, Dublin, Ireland, revised selected papers*. Berlin and Heidelberg: Springer.

Brügger, N. (2018). *The archived web: doing history in the digital age*. Cambridge, MA: MIT Press.

Clavert, F., & Noiret, S. (Eds.). (2013). *L'histoire contemporaine à l'ère numérique—Contemporary History in the Digital Age*. Brussels: Peter Lang.

Cohen, D. J., & Rosenzweig, R. (2006). *Digital history: a guide to gathering, preserving, and presenting the past on the web*. Philadelphia, PA: University of Pennsylvania Press.

Cohen, D. J., Frisch, M., Gallagher, P., Mintz, S., Sword, K., Taylor, A. M., Thomas, III, W. G., & Turkel. W. J. (2008). Interchange: the promise of digital history. *Journal of American History, 95*(2), 452–491.

Dougherty, J., & Nawrotzki, K. (Eds.). (2013). *Writing history in the digital age*. Ann Arbor, MI: University of Michigan Press.

Fickers, A., & van der Heijden, T. (2020). Inside the trading zone: thinkering in a digital history lab. *Digital Humanities Quarterly, 14*(3). In M. Oiva & U. Pawlicka-Deger (Eds.), *Lab and slack: situated research practices in digital humanities*, special issue.

Foka, A., Westin, J., & Chapman, A. (Eds.). (2018). Technology in the study of the past. *Digital Humanities Quarterly, 12*(3), special issue. Retrieved from http://www.digitalhumanities.org/dhq/vol/12/3/index.html

Galgano, M. J., Arndt, C., & Hyser, R. M. (2008). *Doing history: research and writing in the digital age*. Boston, MA: Thomson Wadsworth.

Gantert, K. (2011). *Elektronische Informationsressourcen für Historiker*. Berlin: de Gruyter.

Genet, J.-P., & Zorzi, A. (Eds.). (2011). *Les historiens et l'informatique: un métier à réinventer*. Rome: École française de Rome.

Graham, S., Milligan, I., & Weingart, S. (2015). *Exploring big historical data: the historian's macroscope*. London: Imperial College Press.

Gregory, I. N., & Geddes, A. (2014). Introduction: from historical GIS to spatial humanities: deepening scholarship and broadening technology. In I. N. Gregory & A. Geddes (Eds.), *Toward spatial humanities: historical GIS & spatial history*. Bloomington, IN: Indiana University Press.

Guldi, J., & Armitage, D. (2014). *The history manifesto*. Cambridge: Cambridge University Press.

Haber, P. (2011). *Digital Past: Geschichtswissenschaft im digitalen Zeitalter*. Munich: Oldenbourg.

Jarlbrink, J., & Snickars, P. (2017). Cultural heritage as digital noise: nineteenth century newspapers in the digital archive. *Journal of Documentation, 77*(6), 1228–1243.

Jockers, M. L. (2013). *Macroanalysis: digital methods and literary history.* Urbana, IL: University of Illinois Press.

Jones, S. E. (2014). *The emergence of the digital humanities.* London: Routledge.

Koller, G. (2016). *Geschichte digital: historische Welten neu vermessen.* Stuttgart: Kohlhammer Verlag.

Lebert, M. (2008). *Project Gutenberg (1971–2008).* University of Toronto and Project Gutenberg. Retrieved from http://www.gutenberg.org/ebooks/27045

Le Roy Ladurie, E. (1979). *The territory of the historian.* Translated from the French original (in 1973) by B. Reynolds and S. Reynolds. Brighton: The Harvester Press.

Moretti, F. (2000). Conjectures on world literature. *New Left Review, 1*(1), 54–68.

Moretti, F. (2005). *Graphs, maps, trees: abstract models for literary history.* London and New York, NY: Verso Books.

Moretti, F. (2013). *Distant reading.* London and New York, NY: Verso Books.

Oudshoorn, N., & Pinch, T. (Eds.). (2003). *How users matter: the co-construction of users and technologies.* Cambridge, MA: MIT Press.

Rabb, T. (1983). The development of quantification in historical research. *Journal of Interdisciplinary History, 13*(4), 591–601.

Rosenzweig, R. (2011). *Clio wired: the future of the past in the digital age.* New York, NY: Columbia University Press.

Sagner Buurma, R., & Heffernan, L. (2018, 11 April). Search and replace: Josephine Miles and the origins of distant reading. *Modernism/Modernity Print Plus.* Retrieved from https://modernismmodernity.org/forums/posts/search-and-replace

Schmale, W. (2010). *Digitale Geschichtswissenschaft.* Vienna: Böhlau Verlag.

Staley, D. J. (2002). *Computers, visualization and history: how new technology will transform our understanding of the past.* London and New York, NY: Routledge.

Swierenga, R. P. (1970). Clio and computers: a survey of computerized research in history. *Computers and the Humanities, 5*(1), 1–21.

Tolonen, M., & Lahti, L. (2018). Digitaaliset ihmistieteet ja historiantutkimus. In M. O. Hannikainen, M. Danielsbacka, & T. Tepora (Eds.), *Menneisyyden rakentajat: teoriat historiantutkimuksessa.* Helsinki: Gaudeamus.

Underwood, T. (2017). A genealogy of distant reading. *Digital Humanities Quarterly, 11(2).*

Vanhoutte, E. (2013). The gates of hell: history and digital | humanities | computing. In M. Terras, J. Nyhan & E. Vanhoutte (Eds.), *Defining digital humanities: a reader.* Farnham and Burlington, VT: Ashgate.

Weller, T. (Ed.). (2013). *History in the digital age.* London and New York, NY: Routledge.

PART II

Making Sense of Digital History

CHAPTER 2

The Long Road to 'Digital History'

History of Computer-Assisted Research of the Past in Finland since the 1960s

Petri Paju

> Kranzberg's First Law reads as follows: Technology is neither good nor bad; nor is it neutral.[1]

Historians have rarely been associated with the latest IT, or the other way around. In broad terms, the same applies to all IT, both old and new, and history research; they seem a world apart, unless one counts things such as pens and books. In their publications, most historians make it look like their use of information technologies is unbiased and unproblematic. However, Melvin Kranzberg, who was a veteran historian of technology, reminded us that technologies always come with consequences. With digital history, and the growing use of computational methods in historical research, this practice and performance of neutrality vis-à-vis technological tools, as well as the old stereotype, could be changing.

In reality, IT such as computers has been utilised in history research since the 1960s, as in most other walks of life. At that time, a few historians in the United States (and elsewhere) started to explore the usability of mainframe computers for their work.[2] In over 50 years, computer-assisted history research has evolved, or graduated, from the tests of a very few scholars into an emerging

How to cite this book chapter:
Paju, P. (2020). The long road to 'digital history': History of computer-assisted research of the past in Finland since the 1960s. In M. Fridlund, M. Oiva, & P. Paju (Eds.), *Digital histories: Emergent approaches within the new digital history* (pp. 21–44). Helsinki: Helsinki University Press. https://doi.org/10.33134/HUP-5-2

field of computational history, also called more broadly digital history research. Of course, one should inquire if those are phases and part of the same continuum or rather separate developments with no tangible influence from the former to the latter. In any case, this development seems to be something else than a straightforward progression.

This chapter focuses on the history of computer use by historians, drawing its evidence mostly from Finland, but with an emphasis on the researchers' transnational influences. To explore this evolution, this chapter asks: What have historians been doing professionally with computer technology, and when did that begin in Finland? What were their international influences in developing the use of computers in history research?

Here, 'computer technology' refers to the technological developments connected to computers and IT during the research period: in this case, its evolution from the relatively large mainframe computers to microcomputers, to internet and beyond. The focus in this chapter is on historical research, thus mostly excluding teaching history with the help of or via IT, as well as technological changes related to publishing.

Interviews and memoirs, various written documents, especially digitised history journals, and observations (since the late 1990s) are used in answering these questions.[3] With these materials, the chapter aims to examine this development from several different levels and viewpoints. These range from the individual scholar(s) to their collaboration and extend into libraries and archives, and institutional use and support of digital means to advance research in the field of history.

One important motivation behind these questions is to distance the researcher and readers from the present terminology concerning digital humanities and digital or computational history, which often seem to make studying their own development very confusing. Without these concepts, I hypothesise, we can better approach and understand historical events and trends on their own terms.

While research in historiography had tended to value and focus on the theoretical aspects of historical thinking and research, this chapter highlights the more practical side of carrying out historical research and thus contributes to a more balanced idea of how historians conduct their work. A better, increased understanding of the now mundane technologies and practices of historians is especially appropriate now that the discipline is facing yet another change towards an increasingly electronic and more digitised research process, with new and more powerful computational tools, which present challenges to historians themselves, but also to teaching and outreach to the public.[4]

Further, for the international discussion, this chapter serves as a reminder of and correction to the US-centric or Anglo-American view of history of computing-assisted history. This too was an international and transnational development.[5] In international comparison, the number of Finnish historians was fairly limited. After rapid growth in the 1960s, there were, in 1970, historical research units in six Finnish universities, employing a total of 32 professors.

Since then, the community grown to the extent that, in 2015, there were 56 history professorships in eight research units, but the profession has expanded greatly, especially when one counts all historians with doctoral education.[6] Nevertheless, from early on, this community of historians in Finland took part in most if not all transnational trends and developments in their field and adopted major new technologies used by historians in industrialised countries. In general, then, Finnish historians' experience of using computers can be thought of as rather representative of other Western countries. The few untypical aspects will be highlighted.

Computer Usage Starts in the Late 1960s

According to the digitised version of the *Historiallinen Aikakauskirja* (*Historical Journal*) in Finland, the word 'computer' (*tietokone*) was first mentioned on its pages in a book review in 1964.[7] One early Finnish historian to make use of computers, Pertti Huttunen, later wrote that he became interested in using computers during that same year, in 1964, while extending his studies and planning his doctoral dissertation in Rome, Italy. There, he first talked about such an option with a Finnish physicist and also visited a local computing centre.[8]

Following examples abroad, a small number of historians had started to familiarise themselves with mainframe computers in the mid-1960s. The first public discussion about computers by historians in Finland took place in the spring of 1967. At that time, the Historiallinen Yhdistys ry. (Historical Association), or younger generation of historians, had invited historians Kaarlo Wirilander and Pertti Huttunen, a well-known senior researcher and a doctoral candidate respectively, to talk about 'The historian and the computer'. At the meeting, an IT specialist from the Helsinki University's computing centre, Jorma Torppa, offered technical expertise.[9]

Before this seminar in Helsinki, historian Viljo Rasila had joined the first short, introductory course given by the new computing centre at Tampere University. The centre had installed its first computer in 1966. The following year, Rasila became the first historian in Finland to publish an article about using computers in the national *Historiallinen Aikakauskirja*. In it, he mentioned the work of Wirilander, Huttunen, the 'brick group' studying Roman brick stamps and his own as examples of history research involving computers in Finland. According to Rasila, this computer use by historians was just beginning.[10]

This use so far included collecting and inserting data into (punched) cards, which were meant for building databases (to create tables and to compile statistics) and performing calculations. Rasila himself was applying multivariable analysis, and specifically factor analysis, to weigh up the various reasons for the civil war in Finland. That same year (1967), Pertti Huttunen published an article outlining his ideas about how to use computers to study Roman social history. His article was published as the first volume in the series *Studia Historica* from the young University of Oulu (founded in 1958) in northern Finland.[11]

The following year, Viljo Rasila was the first to publish a history book, a monograph where he applied computer-aided statistical methods to explore key themes in recent Finnish social history during the 1918 war. His main computational method, factor analysis, had been developed in the field of psychology. The book, *Kansalaissodan sosiaalinen tausta* (*Social background of the civil war*), appeared in 1968.

Heikki Waris, a professor and social historian at the University of Helsinki, reviewed the study for the *Historiallinen Aikakauskirja* and thanked Rasila especially for introducing new methods for historians to use.[12] In the same issue of the journal, however, Pertti Järvinen from the computing centre at Tampere University discussed Rasila's book and heavily criticised his choice of a statistical method. In his book's preface, Rasila acknowledged the computing centre and its 'mathematicians' who had helped him, but, importantly, Pertti Järvinen had not been involved in Rasila's project. Instead, Järvinen had taken an independent interest in this innovative approach to history and likely became the first computing professional to share his ideas in this journal.[13] All in all, Rasila's study accompanied many firsts simultaneously.

Issues of multidisciplinary soon impacted Pertti Huttunen. Based on an analysis by a colleague, it seems Huttunen's dissertation manuscript on Roman social history faced harsh criticism from a classical philologist in Helsinki, which led Huttunen to move his dissertation project to the University of Oulu.[14] For sure, such difficulties and change did not support finishing the study, but, importantly, they were not directly associated with the new, computerised method applied by Huttunen. He never returned to work in Helsinki, but forged a career in researching and lecturing (for instance, about the history of technology) in Oulu and in other universities.

Pertti Huttunen defended his doctoral dissertation and book *The social strata in the imperial city of Rome* in 1974. Arguably, Huttunen wrote the first Finnish doctoral dissertation in history to use computerised methods, although that same year (1974), Reino Kero also defended his doctoral dissertation of general history at the University of Turku, and he too had used a computerised method in his study on migration.[15]

Regarding the feedback surrounding his 1968 book, Viljo Rasila recalled in my interview with him that the method was widely noticed, but at that point in time it raised mostly confusion:

> The reception of the mathematical analysis was controversial. Researchers of economic and social history, Eino Jutikkala among them, welcomed it as opening new opportunities, but the school of historians following [Professor Pentti] Renvall and doing textual analysis ('*renvallilainen tekstianalyysiin nojaava koulukunta*') shunned it and doubted its usefulness.[16]

This ambiguity is relatively easy to understand when one considers the technological and data-processing options available at the time. Starting from mainframe computers and the programs available on them, computer technology for a long time worked mainly for quantitative research and did not really fit qualitative research designs. First and foremost, there was virtually no data to be processed in digital text formats. At this time, computers and the promise they represented undoubtedly encouraged historians (as well as social scientists before them) to carry out quantitative research, which grew more popular in universities during the 1970s. In certain history departments, this period left a relatively strong tradition of quantitative history research that has been more or less carried on ever since.

Nevertheless, it is important to note that historians had applied quantitative and computational methods in their research even before computers were available. In Finland, the breakthrough of these approaches occurred in the early 1960s, if not somewhat earlier.[17] In an interesting simultaneity to historians first learning about the use of computers, the first independent department of economic history in Finland, at the University of Helsinki, was established in 1966. Unlike the '"old" Finnish economic history' which was later seen as rather descriptive, the new economic history became characterised by 'systematic application of quantitative methods'.[18] From this perspective, embracing computers was not a beginning nor a revolution, but part of an evolutionary development in the scholarship of history. It was a step further, which later perhaps seems to us a bigger change than it actually was. However, this longer intellectual background of quantitative history, going back at least until the last decades of the 19th century, has been studied elsewhere.[19]

How did historians compare with social scientists in computer use? For instance, Kullervo Rainio, later Professor of Social Psychology at the University of Helsinki, visited Finland's first operational computer, an IBM 650, at a state-owned bank soon after the machine's inauguration in 1958. At that time, he took part in a visit arranged for the Suomen Psykologinen Seura (Psychological Association of Finland), and in 1960 he could learn using another computer in Helsinki with his complex mathematical calculations needed for simulating group behaviour in a computer program.[20]

In general, we can safely say that social science researchers started using computers well before historians.[21] In Tampere University, which until 1966 carried the name Yhteiskunnallinen korkeakoulu (College of Social Sciences), Viljo Rasila had for years been in the company of mostly social scientists and had become familiar with their statistical methods. This environment partly explains his early interest in and initiative to test and use a computer for scholarly work in history.

One could also surmise that Rasila was in a position to fully cooperate with social scientists at Tampere University, but that was not the case. When I interviewed him, he told me that there was a major political difference between himself (he was more conservative) and his colleagues who, for instance, in the department of sociology, were politically quite left-wing. Despite the shared interest in using computers, this political dissimilarity caused them to maintain a working distance from each other.[22]

In this respect, Rasila was rather typical. For a long while in the 1970s too, I suspect, this was a more general pattern: when compared with social science departments, history departments were much more conservative, including politically. This points out, intriguingly, that many contextual, historical factors could have an effect on and limit the circulation and exchange of scientific and scholarly tools such as the use of computer programs.

Tellingly of this technological milieu and the options available, it was predominantly a few researchers in social and general history who first started making use of computers. In the 1960s and the 1970s, the group of active history researchers totalled a few hundred, so they all knew each other and knew what others were doing,[23] even if those using computers remained a tiny minority. Further, Viljo Rasila penned a textbook entitled *Tilastolliset menetelmät historiantutkimuksessa* (*Statistical methods in history research*, 1973, 2nd edition 1977), including examples of computer-assisted operations, and that book became widely known among the profession, and especially among history students.

In summation, during roughly the first decade of computer use by historians, they used IBM and other mainframe computers for statistics, saving collected data, evidence, storing and processing it, forming tables, and then carried out various kinds of calculations and statistical analysis.

Research Projects: The 1970s

The early 1970s saw a new phase in historians' use of computers when the technology was incorporated into research projects. Such projects were considered fashionable, and the reorganised Academy of Finland granted funds for up-to-date research projects in the field of history too. In 1971, for instance, Vilho Niitemaa, Professor of General History at the University of Turku, presented a newly funded project focusing on people who have emigrated from Finland to distant countries (known as *kaukosiirtolaiset* in Finnish). The project included what Niitemaa labelled the 'ADP department', or individuals working on data collecting and compiling statistics with automatic data-processing tools. To store data, they used punched cards. The first doctoral dissertation to emerge from this project was written by Reino Kero, who, as mentioned above, defended his thesis in 1974.[24]

Conducting research in organised projects had become more common in the sciences in postwar decades. In the leading history journal, *Historiallinen Aikakauskirja*, several Finnish researchers wrote about current historical research projects in Sweden from the late 1960s onwards, and these reports included a few mentions of ADP systems which were either being tested or were already in use to store and handle information.[25]

Thus, historians continued to use computers for organising data and for statistical purposes in the 1970s, but, for them, making use of the 'computer' (as technology) had also become a tool for winning research funding. Using computers signalled taking part in advancing research with the latest ideas and technology, and being at the forefront of development.

Viljo Rasila's expertise in computers played a major role in encouraging a collaborative research project called *Muuttoliikeprojekti* (Migration Project), which focused on migration within Finland between 1850 and 1910, with a particular focus on industrialisation. That project was led by Professor of Finnish History, Pentti Virrankoski, from 1977. Virrankoski also directed one sub-project at the University of Turku while Rasila, now an appointed professor, led another research team at Tampere University, and Yrjö Kaukiainen a third team at the University of Helsinki. In this project, the workload for collecting data manually grew much larger than was anticipated. Still, the difficulties with the ADP programs and processing the data proved to be even more significant. Because of these surprises, the larger project ran out of funding in the early 1980s. Most of the human-collected and manually input data was never computerised.[26]

However, the sub-project team at Tampere constructed their database differently from that of the Turku team, and consequently the Tampere team and Rasila himself were able to use and process their materials with a computer, and publish research results. Importantly, the larger project had formed ties with the Swedish project already building a demographic database in the late 1970s, and they exchanged experiences in international seminars.[27] Surprisingly, there are hopes that this Tampere database could be used anew in the early 2020s, once again inspired by the Swedish example.[28]

In principle, such databases can have a very long lifespan. Nevertheless, the opposite seems to have been the rule, so that many Finnish projects collecting and processing data in history research have produced a very ephemeral legacy. Their datasets were left in archives with data formats that basically died out within a rather short period of time.

The international discussion concerning historians' use of computers was increasing from the late 1960s onwards. In that exchange, Finnish historians rarely contributed publications, although Viljo Rasila, at least, published two articles in international journals such as in the 1970 volume of *Economy and History*. Importantly, however, during the 1970s and continuing well into the 1980s, Finnish scholars had relatively dynamic transnational communications, especially with their Estonian colleagues from the Soviet Union who had pioneered using computers in history research. Juhan Kahk was one of several such Estonian colleagues who published studies (using both the Finnish and the English languages) also in Finnish history series.[29]

Microcomputers for Text Processing: The New Typewriter (Plus)

The impact of the computer on historians' practice was not only as a calculator, but even more so as a word processor. Typewriters were already being advertised for historians in *Historiallinen Aikakauskirja* in 1916. It took time, however, before they began to be widely used by historians. And relatively soon afterwards, the latest products of the IT industry emerged: smaller computers that could be used as an advanced typewriter. The spread of personal computers (PCs) or microcomputers opened up new possibilities for historians in the early 1980s.[30]

In Finland, Jussi T. Lappalainen was the first person to write to historians about the possibility of using a computer to write texts. He had heard of such a novelty from his son Vesa, who studied mathematics. Lappalainen explained that he first thought of writing archival notes on a computer in place of using the long-used edge-notched cards (or edge-punched cards, *neulakortti*). Father and son then co-wrote a short article entitled 'Historical research without papers', which was published in *Historiallinen Aikakauskirja* in 1983. At the time, Jussi Lappalainen, who had previously worked at the University of Jyväskylä, was as Associate Professor of Finnish History at the University of Turku.[31] When the first, still quite expensive, microcomputer landed in the history department's office in Turku, his colleagues were afraid of using it. Lappalainen, however, was convinced about the device's potential and wrote another article entitled 'Making text on the screen', after which his colleagues began to telephone him to glean some clarification. As a former publishing editor, Lappalainen also persuaded the popular Finnish novelist Kalle Päätalo to migrate to using a computer for his work. The learning phase involved some text vanishing from the computer's memory (or from the writing software) and this made the angry author revert to the typewriter for a while.[32] Despite the new technology, then, the (anticipated) main use of these new machines was familiar; it was typing. Computers replaced typewriters, and most of the historians started using computers as not-yet-so-advanced typewriters. Yet, social science historians soon discovered ways in which the PC could do more.

In 1985, a new historical research project at the University of Helsinki started using a microcomputer to save and study materials. Project members examined the Finnish famine of the late 1860s (*1860-luvun suuret nälkävuodet*) based on the latest developments in social science history. In that project, they utilised either quantitative or qualitative methods (or both) on a variety of materials. For both types of method, they developed new best practices using software for building databases and for word processing, including one project-member, Kari Pitkänen, writing a concise guide book for fellow historians entitled *Historiantutkija ja mikrotietokone* (*The historian and the microcomputer*, 1987).[33]

Many preferred to wait and see, however. Several historians have confessed that they themselves hesitated and postponed adopting the novel PCs in the mid-1980s, but by the beginning of the 1990s, nearly all had started to at least write with microcomputers.[34] A significant factor in this transition was the increased user-friendliness of PCs in the form of graphical user interfaces (in place of the command line interface). At the same time, PCs became cheaper and consequently more common. Soon after, the media started to excite people about a new information network: the internet. Considering the changes recently introduced by microcomputers, it is unsurprising that for many (older) historians the new online world of information networks remained for most of the 1990s quite distant.

Compared to older mainframe technology, microcomputers opened up a whole new spectrum of uses for historians to choose. Typing or text processing was by far the most widely adopted of these new uses and thus in many ways the most important one. But, in addition, on a PC one could also keep records and notes, and later draw maps and graphs, and take time to learn other new uses. Again, much of the development was gradual.[35]

Meanwhile, many other people were using microcomputers too. These included genealogists, who launched their own journal *Sukutietotekniikka* (*Computer technology for family research*) in 1984, and who worked together to insert data in digital formats, and later digitised parish registers and made them available online (HisKi). In some universities, linguists developed corpus linguistics and even historical linguistics. In the early 1980s, the Helsinki Corpus of English Texts was initiated. This ground-breaking digital text collection was completed and publicly distributed in 1991.[36] Quite a few historians became aware of these endeavours, but they remained distant to historical research.

Overseas, groups of historians established for themselves organisations such as the Association for History and Computing (AHC), which was proposed at a conference at the University of London in 1986. The AHC was dedicated to the use of computers in historical research and in 'promoting the use of computers in all types of historical study, both for teaching and research'.[37] Unlike their colleagues in many other countries, Finnish historians did not form a national association for history and computing, and to the best of our knowledge, they consequently took part to a very limited extent in this international discussion.

With every major change, quite a few historians at first postponed adopting the new technology. Who were these non-users of the (new) technology? Until well into the 1980s, they were those historians who were relying on textual analysis—basically, the majority of people in most history departments. They could use card files to make archival notes and to store their data, and other such manual or mechanical tools, and they used typewriters or perhaps had the department's typist transcribe their writings.

Gradually, for instance, cultural historians also switched their typewriters to PCs. Perhaps it took them a few more years, but it did happen, and soon, in the 1990s, it was only the most senior historians who did not change to writing on a computer, but hung on to the typewriter.

At the same time, Finnish researchers committed to the new cultural history avoided numbers and statistics, and in general quantitative methods. For instance, their colleagues in Italy and Germany more often used numbers and calculations to study microhistory. This avoidance can be regarded as a counter-reaction towards the general emphasis on quantitative methods such as statistical approaches in the 1970s. Instead, cultural historians studied textual evidence in the light of the then recent linguistic turn. Their emphasis was on using qualitative methods, especially 'close reading' of texts, as well as discussing and exploring narratives. Over time in the late 20th century, close reading became a leading (often the main or even only) method for legions of historians and other people studying texts, so much so that the literary historian and Professor Franco Moretti termed his new and different computer-assisted method 'distant reading'. Inspired by the Annales School of historians, he coined the term in 2000.[38] It has subsequently gained popularity as a response and complement to the dominance of close reading.

Enter the Internet: Anticipating a Digital Revolution?

In the early 1990s, the younger generation of historians discovered the internet, or networks of computers, that had been first built in the United States in the 1960s for military purposes and only came into wider, academic use by scientists during the 1980s. Furthermore, some historians soon took part in creating a new, virtual dimension to the world. In Finland, they first tested Gopher-based internet pages (before the html language) which were in use by 1994. At that time, the World Wide Web, or the Web, after being created at CERN, had begun its successful expansion as the information medium over the internet.

One of the early Finnish projects was the Electronic Centre for History Research in Finland. It first opened in late 1995.[39] The following year, it joined forces with other related projects, and these were transformed into a new national cooperation. Named as the Agricola network, this was a joint effort among historians in the universities, libraries and archives, and it was officially launched in 1996.[40]

The new Agricola site brought together people working with or interested in history, created new avenues of communication and enabled them to discuss their relevant issues in a very popular email list, H-verkko, nationally. They aimed to inform others and share news, as well as publish online. Importantly, one key component for the network builders consisted of educating historians and keeping them abreast of the internet's latest relevant developments. This included thinking ahead and writing about the possible futures of history research in the digital era: an anticipated digital revolution and what that might entail.[41] Further in connection to the Agricola network, a group of historians started to study IT history, especially in Finland, thus improving the shared understanding of living in a society in which computer technology was gradually applied everywhere.[42] Out of the Agricola network's publishing activities grew *Ennen ja nyt* (*Then & Now*), in existence since May 2001, which was the first national, refereed online journal in history.[43]

To summarise, historians were now using computers and their networks for searching and gathering information, including data about archives, and they sometimes even accessed the actual sources that someone had downloaded to their pages. This could easily be achieved transnationally, and for quite some time it seemed national borders were becoming less and less important. The burgeoning virtual world and its sites first complemented and then slowly began to replace former foundations of historians' work such as library indexes, travel to archives and archive guides, followed by books, phone books, etc. In scholarly communications, electronic mail or email correspondence instead of postal letters proved triumphant in the 'internet age'.[44]

For the first time, historians were also becoming familiar with sources that were 'born digital', such as email letters and digital art, and discussed the future of electronic sources. Two extreme questions surrounded whether everything would be saved electronically (a burden for historians) or whether the new electronic sources (such as early www-pages) would be deleted or otherwise lost within a relatively short time, leaving future historians without important materials from the 1990s.[45] Thinking about it now, the latter seems closer to what has actually happened. Furthermore, the digital revolution that took place proved to be slower than expected and transformed into a digital evolution that eventually invaded every aspect of life during the 2000s and onwards.

In the 50-year period examined here, the contextual changes for historians have been significant, ranging from the expanding universities to the evolution of the Finnish society at large. The historical profession in Finland in the early 1960s consisted of perhaps fewer than 100 people active in conducting research. The number of history professors in Finland was 17 in 1960, and it grew to 32 in 1970 to approximately 46 in 2000 and to 10 more in 2015, while the number of research units (larger university departments) rose from five to eight in the same time period. However, the number of university-educated history researchers (PhD) and lower-level positions grew much more extensively, particularly from the late 1990s onwards. In addition to universities, there were historians carrying out research elsewhere, especially in a few major institutions such as archives and the National Library.[46]

Starting in the 1990s, the Finland-based multinational corporation Nokia, selling new mobile phones, led the country's high-tech investments and image, and Finland became a leader in many IT developments. This probably encouraged also technologically open-minded historians to explore the new possibilities that the novelties might offer. Meanwhile, especially since 2000, the profession has both specialised further and internationalised heavily, and historians have in general perhaps become less and less knowledgeable of their domestic colleagues compared with experts abroad. Historians in the universities have also confronted an ever heavier competition for (external) research funding, which has contributed to their willingness to adopt new methods and ideas.

Digitising Sources and Offering Them Online

In many ways, digitisation of historical sources had its roots in microfilming similar materials. The state (national) archive in Finland started a project to microfilm documents in the late 1940s. It was the new general manager of the archive, Yrjö Nurmio, who led ground-breaking efforts to film important sources abroad, first in Sweden and West Germany, and thus made these archival collections that were considered relevant for Finnish historians easily available to researchers in Finland, on microfilm readers. Later in the 1950s and 1960s, Finns could also microfilm Soviet materials.[47]

During a longer period of time, a large collection of historical newspapers was microfilmed in Finland. Foreign newspaper collections could be purchased for use in Finnish libraries and universities. Microfilming and their use had then continued for about three decades when automatic data processing (ADP) started to become another option to store and access primary sources. While the history of microfilming might sound ancient and wholly irrelevant for historical researchers in the 2020s, this legacy is in fact a pertinent background to the digital newspaper collection.

The National Library at Helsinki had already established the Centre for Microfilming and Conservation in 1990, located in the small town of Mikkeli in Eastern Finland. They aimed to create a comprehensive microfilm collection of Finnish newspapers and journals. Meanwhile, the internet made its first breakthrough as a new and exciting channel to distribute information in digital formats in the early and mid-1990s.

Digitisation of cultural heritage began in Finland after the mid-1990s, with the Mikkeli centre playing a central role. From the perspective of newspaper collections, an essential turning point was the launching of the Nordic project Tiden in 1998. In the Finnish case, the digital collection of newspapers is for the most part based on microfilms, which means that both the quality of the microfilm and the quality of the original newspaper have an important impact on the accuracy of optical character recognition (OCR), which varies from decade to decade. After a busy few years, the National library was able to open the Historical Finnish newspaper archive online in 2001.[48]

The first collection of digitised newspapers already covered several decades of the 19th-century press. Historians could now carry out some of their historical research using digitised original materials, over the internet, via their own computers in their own offices.

Since its inauguration in 2001, this major online press archive has been constantly expanded and its user interface, such as search options, improved. These significant investments have made the National Library's DIGI Collection of newspapers and periodicals published in Finland arguably the most used historical digital source material in 2018.[49] In fact this collection is so complete especially regarding the 19th-century newspapers that in many cases they are enough for answering the researcher's question/s. This has made some researchers critical and asking if not the research questions where chosen so that one is able to limit his/her study into consulting only the digital materials, relying on keyword searches, and applying the rather conventional qualitative methods.

Evolving Digital Humanities and Emerging 'Digital History'

Gradually, in the 2000s and the early 2010s, an increasing number of historians became aware of and familiar with the massive amount of digital texts from primary sources that were processed by memory institutions such as libraries and archives around the world into digital formats and made available online. In retrospect, suddenly, there was an abundance of material suitable for qualitative and quantitative analysis online. Anyone could perform simple yet comprehensive keyword searches in these vast collections. It was (and is) easy to forget that such searches might be anything but perfect (due to the low quality of OCR results) because the accuracy of the search process was very difficult to assess.

Most researchers rapidly realised that one could only perform 'close reading' on a tiny fraction of those online sources because even just skimming them all went beyond anyone's capabilities time-wise. This gradually led progressive historians to think about obtaining and/or creating more adequate, computer-assisted methods and the means to get the most out of this wealth of digital sources. Among these, one can count the above-mentioned literary historian Franco Moretti.

Meanwhile, computerised methods and software with a longer development history such as GIS came to be used by a few historians in Finland in the 2000s. They used GIS to place and study historical information on maps of various kinds. Compared to GIS, textual analysis with computational tools and the newly emerging 'big data' was still very much being invented and developed during the early 2000s. Nevertheless, researchers of AI had made important progress in cooperation with linguistics since the 1980s, and a research field called natural language processing (NLP) was advancing. Based on complex statistical mathematics and algorithms, this work promised new tools for analysing texts too. The first peer-reviewed journal article where the rather recent method of 'topic modelling' was applied for historical materials was published in 2006.[50]

In Finland, too, the early 2000s witnessed inventions in software turned into new digital tools that historians could use. For instance, in the late 1990s, a group of medievalists and the National Archives had built an electronic version of Finland's medieval sources (*medeltidsurkunder*), producing an online database called Diplomatarium Fennicum.[51] In the mid-2000s, Tuomas Heikkilä joined forces with some IT specialists and together they started developing computational methods to group medieval texts. Their aim was to create a family tree, a stemma, based on the dis/similarity of those early scripts, in order to better study their origins as well as influences on each other.[52] Over the years, this new interdisciplinary cooperation has led to several international scholarly meetings called Studia Stemmatologica, as well as publications developing further stemmatological analyses.[53]

The availability of these digital materials combined with the introduction of new tools sparked many developments during the 2010s that are changing and will renew history research. Starting towards the middle of the decade, several national conferences and seminars have been organised to discuss such new research. The first two textbooks concerning historical research and digital methods were published in Swedish and Finnish, in 2014 and 2016, respectively.[54] In 2015, the major research funder for historians, the Academy of Finland, opened a call for projects to The Digital Humanities Academy Programme (2016–2019), which encouraged many to pay more attention to developments going on in this new research area. Some, but not quite all, of the outcomes of this wave of new research are presented in this book.

All this technological development and expectations for ever faster and wider analysis of the historians' 'big data' has also re-emphasised 'old' problems (stemming from the 1990s), such as the poor quality of OCR-processed digital texts. How can we overcome this obstacle to the use of these latest computational research methods? Challenges like this partly motivated some historians to plan the project Computational History and the Transformation of Public Discourse in Finland, 1640–1910, funded during 2016 to 2019, in which the low OCR accuracy in the digitised newspapers and periodicals was circumvented by basically using a method originally designed for bioinformatics—in this case, modified to recognise the reoccurrences of similar text passages systematically in several millions of pages of primary sources.[55]

These challenges are highlighting our need for developing novel ways of digital source criticism, but also for taking new, fresh perspectives on the digital evolution that surrounds us. An eye-opening example is offered by Johan Jarlbrink and Pelle Snickars, who studied the specific ways in which newspapers are transformed in the digitisation process, and concluded that in fact the massive digitisation has created large amounts of digital noise: 'that is millions of misinterpreted words generated by OCR, and millions of texts re-edited by the auto-segmentation tool', resulting in a new—and, moreover, unevenly distributed—layer being added to the shared cultural heritage.[56] This reinterpretation suggests and confirms, first, that we need to learn to live and come to terms with that digital noise and, second, that a totally new and so to speak born-digital (that is, generated by computer technology) demand for historians' tools in computer technology will be to reduce that digital noise.

Meanwhile, this emerging 'digital history' research has also been explored. In one inquiry, Finnish historians raised doubts about this new concept and/or identifying themselves with it. In other words, many responders expressed uncertainty about whether or not they were digital historians and/or digital enough, meaning that, as of 2016, few historians saw themselves as digital historians.[57] Among the critical issues that were identified through the inquiry were the importance of creating better, up-to-date information channels of digital history resources and events, providing relevant education, skills and teaching by historians, and the need to help historians and IT specialists to meet and collaborate better and more systematically than before.

One can hypothesise that two camps of historians were formed in the late 20th century, distinguished by their use of computer technology. On the one hand, everybody was more or less taking advantage of text processing (working with text files and mainly writing), PCs in general and the internet, in various ways. On the other hand, there were those sub-fields that (had) also continued with quantitative methods, such as statistics, for a long time. But many historians concentrated mainly on text processing. It is important to note that the new methods of digital humanities, based among other things on developing NLP (technology), were more eagerly adopted, and embraced even, by those researchers who focused on processing texts. To be more precise, it was a fraction of those historians who embraced the latest methods and also appropriated the term 'digital history', while the social and economic historians adhered for a longer period to their seasoned ways in quantitative methods.

Further, these new ideas and the digital humanities scholarship have in Finland, as elsewhere, been brought together in new laboratories for humanistic research. By far the largest effort nationally in this field, the Helsinki Centre for Digital Humanities, or HELDIG, was established at the University of Helsinki in 2016. By 2020, HELDIG has evolved into a vibrant centre of teaching and research in digital humanities, including digital history. The centre's multidisciplinary research groups, led by Eero Hyvönen and Mikko Tolonen among others, have concentrated on semantic web and building linked open data portals, such as the Sampo series, intended also as historians' research tools, and on using large but overlooked collections of library metadata to quantitatively examine the evolution of book publishing and the press over hundreds of years, respectively. In addition, a group of Finnish historians has been actively involved in the association Digital Humanities in the Nordic Countries and its DHN conference series held annually since 2016. In 2018, HELDIG was one of the key organisers of the third DHN conference, this time arranged in Helsinki. The overarching theme of the conference was Open Science, which challenges current and future historians in yet other ways. Historians and other scholars involved in the field of digital humanities may expect all of this to further advance their digital research capabilities in the future.[58]

Conclusion

To better understand where the present digital and computational history has come from and its place in the historical discipline, this chapter has studied the historians' use of computer technology, together with some associated technological influence in history research in the case of Finland. It is argued here that such an open and broad approach to these phenomena serves best to expose the complex and already quite extensive roots of the present-day digital history approaches.

Certainly, historical research has many layers of history with the digital, and this relationship continues to be formed in the mutual shaping of the research field, including its people and ways of doing things, technology and the society at large. Perhaps we can even say that the field of digital history today has not one but many histories, and its history remains open to a variety of interpretations.

On the one hand, it is difficult to exaggerate the changes that computer technology has brought to the work of historians (too) during the recent decades. Combined with other changes, the technological advances have positively enabled and enlarged historians' study options in unforeseen ways and scale, while they have also guided and reformed the research designs (see Table 2.1). On the other hand, it has been a long and circuitous route from computers being used for processing statistical data in the late 1960s (Viljo Rasila) and thereafter being used mostly by historians undertaking quantitative research, up until several technological advances and also disruptions (microcomputers, the internet and the World Wide Web, and related software), to the present day, where historians are able to perform their whole research process digitally, from planning to gathering materials, carrying out the analysis, including statistics (if any), writing their interpretation and then publishing the results online.

Nevertheless, it is evident that the use of IT was heavier in some sub-fields than in others, for many reasons. Those reasons range from theoretical underpinnings to copyright law, which has slowed both digitising and distributing certain primary sources from the 20th century.

From early on, divisions were created by different approaches to understanding history and consequently how the research was done. For a long time, starting from mainframe computers and the programs available on these, computer technology worked better for quantitative than qualitative research. That, in turn, might be one reason why the new 'digital history' was, albeit decades later, more eagerly welcomed by (some of the) historians analysing texts. This type of source had been the focus of their qualitative work for decades, and by the 2010s they needed new tools to handle the massive amounts of textual sources that organisations such as major libraries around the world had digitised and made available online during the last 15 to 20 years.

What remained the same during the 50 years in between was that the interpretations were made by the human mind of the historian. Unless perhaps those interpretations also changed while the technological environment and tools for making them were transformed? This is quite conceivable, which reminds us that we still know very little about the impact that computerisation has had on history as a field of study and its products from historical narratives to its theories of change and continuity. It is also time for the students of historiography and even philosophers of history to take a serious, deep look into the

Table 2.1: Milestones of computer use by Finnish historians.

1967	Two articles on using computers for scholarship: Viljo Rasila in *Historiallinen Aikakauskirja*; Pertti Huttunen on Roman social history.
1968	First monograph to use computer-aided statistical methods: Viljo Rasila, *Kansalaissodan sosiaalinen tausta* (*Social background of the civil war*).
1974	First two history PhDs using computerised methods: Pertti Huttunen and Reino Kero.
1970s	Computers in research projects: focused particularly on migration and mobility.
1983	First article (Lappalainen and Lappalainen) about PCs for historians' use.
1990	Centre for Microfilming and Conservation established in Mikkeli.
1996	The Electronic Centre for History Research in Finland (SHEK) for internet use and digitising sources begins (in the Mikkeli centre and elsewhere).
2001	Historical newspapers opened for research online and *Ennen ja Nyt* journal established online.
2014–2016	First two textbooks about digital history published in Finland.

Source: Author.

practical aspects of 'doing history',[59] where computer technology has become so central.

Whether embracing the new tools or shunning them, we should, however, remember what Melvin Kranzberg (a leading historian of technology) famously formulated as his first law. In our case, Kranzberg's rule, quoted as the epigraph to this chapter, means that we should take historians' thoughts and feelings about technology seriously. At times, they probably saw the computer technology as good, bad or both. More importantly, it reminds us that the computer has never been 'just a tool', and this is why we should collectively think more about using these changing products of IT developers and their bearing on our work.

Notes

1. Kranzberg 1986: 545.
2. Thomas 2004; see also Kahk 1984.
3. Specifically, I have studied and observed the field of digital history from 2015 onwards in two research projects funded by the Kone Foundation.
4. See also Kaiserfeld 1998; Jarlbrink 2015; Haapala, Jalava & Larsson 2017.
5. See also Paju 2019. For the Anglo-American milestones, see Thomas 2004.
6. Karonen 2019: esp. 19.
7. Tirranen 1964: 225–234.

[8] Huttunen 1992: 21, 28. This book by Huttunen includes republished articles and the ones relevant here were originally written in the late 1960s.

[9] Historiallinen Yhdistys ry. 1966–1967. *Historiallinen Aikakauskirja* 1/1968, 89–90; Åberg 2010: passim.

[10] Rasila 1967: 145; Viljo Rasila, interview on 17 May 2016. The 'brick group' (*tiiliryhmä*) was a coordinated research effort focused on studying Roman brick stamps and led by Jaakko Suolahti, Professor of General History at the University of Helsinki. See Bruun 1992: 133–134.

[11] Huttunen 1967; Rasila 1967: 145. See also Rasila 1970.

[12] Waris 1969: 73–74.

[13] Järvinen 1969: 57–59; Rasila 1969a: 60–61; Pertti Järvinen, email letters, 26 October 2018.

[14] Bruun 1992: esp. 135–136.

[15] Huttunen 1974; Kero 1974.

[16] Viljo Rasila, email letter 21 March 2016.

[17] Tommila 1998: passim.

[18] Mauranen 1988.

[19] See Iggers 2012: 43–45 and passim; Hudson & Ishizu 2017: ch. 2.

[20] Paju 2008; Rainio 2013.

[21] See Heyck 2015.

[22] Viljo Rasila, interview on 17 May 2016.

[23] See, for instance, Strömberg 1998.

[24] Niitemaa 1971; Reino Kero, email letter 6 June 2016. ADP stood for automatic data processing.

[25] Lindberg & Sovio 1969: 134–142.

[26] Virrankoski 1982: 23–28, passim. On manual work behind the digital, see Jarlbrink, Chapter 7, this volume.

[27] Rasila 1982; Virrankoski 1982; Haapala 1986. See also Nygren, Foka & Buckland 2014.

[28] Tampere Research Group for History of population, environments and social structures.

[29] Rasila 1969b, 1970; Kahk 1973; Virrankoski 2013: passim. See also Kahk 1984; Paju 2019.

[30] See, e.g., *Historiallinen Aikakauskirja* 5/1916, 73; Kirschenbaum 2016.

[31] Neulakortit—jokamiehen reikäkorttijärjestelmä. (Kirjoittanut K.) *Tekniikan Maailma* 1/1955, 30; Lappalainen & Lappalainen 1983; Lappalainen, email letter 26 February 2016.

[32] Lappalainen 1985; Lappalainen, email letter 26 February 2016.

[33] Häkkinen et al. 1989.

[34] Virrankoski 2013: esp. 314. See also Paju 2016.

[35] Lappalainen, email letter 26 February 2016.

[36] Rissanen & Tyrkkö 2013.

[37] Denley & Hopkin 1987.

[38] See Hackler & Kirsten 2016: 6. See also Kiiskinen 2010; Salmi 2011.

[39] Onnela 1995.

[40] Kallio, Kari: Agricolasta Suomen historiaverkko Internetiin. *Digitoday*. Julkaistu 12.8.1996 15:41; Tapio Onnela, oral information 10 October 2018.
[41] See esp. Onnela 1998.
[42] See, for instance, Suominen 2000; Paju 2008.
[43] See Ennen ja Nyt 2001.
[44] See Paju 2016.
[45] Suominen & Sivula 2016: passim.
[46] Karonen 2019: esp. 19 and passim.
[47] Nurmio 1952; Nuorteva & Happonen 2016: passim. See also Jarlbrink 2015.
[48] Bremer-Laamanen 2006.
[49] See Kettunen, Pääkkonen & Koistinen 2016.
[50] Brauer & Fridlund 2013.
[51] See Diplomatarium Fennicum's history.
[52] Tuomas Heikkilä, interview on 15 August 2016. See Roos, Heikkilä & Myllymäki 2006.
[53] See Heikkilä & Roos 2016.
[54] Parland-von Essen & Nybergh 2014; Elo 2016. See also Guldi & Armitage 2015.
[55] See Vesanto et al. 2017.
[56] Jarlbrink & Snickars 2017.
[57] See Paju 2016.
[58] Hyvönen 2018; Matres, Oiva & Tolonen 2018; Tolonen et al. 2019. See also Mäkelä & Tolonen 2018.
[59] See also Paul 2011, who suggests the study of historians' 'doings'.

References

Interviews and correspondence (all by the author)

Pertti Järvinen, email letters, 26 October 2018.
Tuomas Heikkilä, interview, 15 August 2016.
Reino Kero, email letter, 6 June 2016.
Jussi T. Lappalainen, email letter, 26 February 2016.
Tapio Onnela, oral information, 10 October 2018.
Viljo Rasila, email letter, 21 March 2016; interview, 17 May 2016.

Journals

(Mostly from the National Library of Finland: https://digi.kansalliskirjasto.fi/aikakausi/)
Digitoday 1996
Historiallinen Aikakauskirja 1916, 1968
Tekniikan maailma 1955

Literature

Brauer, R., & **Fridlund, M.** (2013). Historicizing topic models: a distant reading of topic modeling texts within historical studies. In L. V. Nikiforova & N. V. Nikiforova (Eds.), *Cultural research in the context of digital humanities: proceedings of international conference 3–5 October 2013* (pp. 152–163). St. Petersburg.

Bremer-Laamanen, M. (2006). Connecting to the past—newspaper digitisation in the Nordic countries. *Journal of Digital Asset Management, 2*(3–4), 168–171.

Bruun, C. (1992). Nyt Rooman historia! *Historiallinen Aikakauskirja 90*(2), 129–143.

Denley, P., & **Hopkin, D.** (Eds.) (1987). *History and computing.* Manchester: Manchester University Press.

Diplomatarium Fennicum. *Tietoa hankkeesta.* Retrieved 3 October, 2018 from http://df.narc.fi/info/project

Elo, K. (Ed.) (2016). *Digitaalinen humanismi ja historiatieteet.* Turku: Turun historiallinen yhdistys.

Ennen ja Nyt. (2001). *Arkistot kuukauden mukaan: toukokuu 2001.* Retrieved 22 February, 2019 from http://www.ennenjanyt.net/2001/05/.

Guldi, J., & **Armitage, D.** (2015). *The history manifesto.* Cambridge: Cambridge University Press. 1st edn. 2014. Retrieved from http://historymanifesto.cambridge.org/

Haapala, P. (1986). *Tehtaan valossa: teollistuminen ja työväestön muodostuminen Tampereella 1820–1920.* Tampere and Helsinki: Osuuskunta Vastapaino and Suomen historiallinen seura.

Haapala, P., Jalava, M., & **Larsson, S.** (Eds.) (2017). *Making Nordic historiography: connections, tensions and methodology, 1850–1970.* New York, NY: Berghahn Books.

Hackler, R., & **Kirsten, G.** (2016). Distant reading, computational criticism, and social critique: an interview with Franco Moretti. *Le foucaldien, 2*(1), 7. DOI: http://doi.org/10.16995/lefou.22

Heikkilä, T., & **Roos, T.** (2016). Thematic section on Studia Stemmatologica. *Digital Scholarship in the Humanities, 31*(3), 520–522. DOI: https://doi.org/10.1093/llc/fqw038

Heyck, H. (2015). *Age of system: understanding the development of modern social science.* Baltimore, MD: Johns Hopkins University Press.

Hudson, P., & **Ishizu, M.** (2017). *History by numbers: an introduction to quantitative approaches.* 2nd edn. London: Bloomsbury.

Huttunen, P. (1967). Tietokoneet Rooman sosiaalihistorian tutkimuksessa (The computer in the study of Roman social history). *Studia Historica: Acta Societatis Historicae Ouluensis* (pp. 29–64). Tomus I. Oulu: Oulun historiaseura.

Huttunen, P. (1974). *The social strata in the imperial city of Rome: A quantitative study of the social representation in the epitaphs published in the Corpus inscriptionum Latinarum, volumen VI.* Oulu: University of Oulu.

Huttunen, P. (1992). *Työ—tekniikka—historian muutos: kirjoituksia työn ja tekniikan historiasta.* Oulu: Oulun historiaseura.

Hyvönen, E. (2018). *Semanttinen web: linkitetyn avoimen datan käsikirja* (Semantic web: handbook of linked open data). Helsinki: Gaudeamus.

Häkkinen, A., Ikonen, V., Pitkänen, K., & Soikkanen, H. (1989). *1860-luvun suuret nälkävuodet: tutkimus eri väestöryhmien mielialoista ja toimintamalleista. Loppuraportti.* Helsinki: Helsingin yliopisto.

Iggers, G. G. (2012). *Historiography in the twentieth century: from scientific objectivity to the postmodern challenge.* 2nd edn. Middletown, CT: Wesleyan University Press.

Jarlbrink, J., & Snickars, P. (2017). Cultural heritage as digital noise: nineteenth century newspapers in the digital archive. *Journal of Documentation, 73*(6), 122–1243.

Jarlbrink, J. (2015). Historievetenskapens mediehantering. In M. Hyvönen, P. Snickars & P. Vesterlund (Eds.). *Massmedieproblem: mediestudiets formering* (pp. 225–247). Lund: Mediehistoriskt arkiv 30, Lunds universitet.

Järvinen, P. (1969). Voidaanko historiaa tutkia tietokoneella? *Historiallinen Aikakauskirja 67*(1), 57–59.

Kahk, J. (1973). New possibilities of using computerized historical analysis in the study of peasant households. In *Turun Historiallinen Arkisto 28* (pp. 375–389). Turku: Turun Historiallinen Yhdistys.

Kahk, J. (1984). Quantitative historical research in Estonia: a case study in Soviet historiography. *Social Science History, 8*(2), 193–200.

Kaiserfeld, T. (1998) Historikerna och tekniken: om betydelse av tekniska hjälpmedel för historieforskningen. In M. Hedin & U. Larsson (Eds.). *Teknikens landskap: en teknikhistorisk antologi tillägnad Svante Lindqvist* (pp. 365–377). Stockholm: Atlantis.

Karonen, P. (2019) Historiantutkimuksen ja yhteiskunnan yli puolitoistavuosisatainen vuoropuhelu: resurssit, rakenteet ja tulokset. In P. Karonen (Ed.), *Tiede ja yhteiskunta: Suomen Historiallinen Seura ja historiantutkimus 1800-luvulta 2010-luvulle* (pp. 13–44). Helsinki: Suomalaisen Kirjallisuuden Seura.

Kero, R. (1974). *Migration from Finland to North America in the years between the United States Civil War and the First World War.* Turku: Institute for Migration.

Kettunen, K., Pääkkonen, T., & Koistinen, M. (2016). Kansalliskirjaston digitoitu historiallinen lehtiaineisto 1771–1910: sanatason laatu, kokoelmien käyttö ja laadun parantaminen. *Informaatiotutkimus 35*(3), 3–14.

Kiiskinen, H. (2010). Talous, käytänne ja kvantitatiivinen analyysi kulttuurihistoriallisesti suuntautuneessa tutkimuksessa. In H. Rantala &

S. Ollitervo (Eds.), *Kulttuurihistoriallinen katse* (pp. 80–97). Turku: k&h, Turun yliopisto.

Kirschenbaum, M. G. (2016). *Track changes: a literary history of word processing*. Cambridge, MA: Harvard University Press.

Kranzberg, M. (1986). Technology and history: 'Kranzberg's Laws'. *Technology and Culture, 27*(3), 544–560. DOI: https://doi.org/10.2307/3105385

Lappalainen, J. T. (1985). Tekstintekoa näytöllä. *Historiallinen Aikakauskirja, 83*(4), 283–286.

Lappalainen, J. T., & **Lappalainen, V.** (1983). Historiantutkimusta ilman papereita. *Historiallinen Aikakauskirja, 81*(1), 75–78.

Lindberg. D., & **Sovio, P.** (1969). Katsaus Ruotsin tutkimusprojekteihin. *Historiallinen Aikakauskirja 67*(2), 134–142.

Matres, I., Oiva, M., & **Tolonen, M.** (2018). In between research cultures: the state of digital humanities in Finland. *Informaatiotutkimus, 37*(2), 37–61. DOI: https://doi.org/10.23978/inf.71160

Mauranen, T. (1988). Review of research in economic and social history in Finland in the 1970s and 1980s. *Scandinavian Economic History Review, 36*(3), 23–41. DOI: https://doi.org/10.1080/03585522.1988.10408125

Mäkelä, E., & **Tolonen, M.** (2018, 7–9 March) *DHN2018—an analysis of a digital humanities conference: Digital Humanities in the Nordic Countries 3rd Conference*. Proceedings of the Digital Humanities in the Nordic Countries 3rd Conference (pp. 1–9). Helsinki.

Niitemaa, V. (1971). Kaukosiirtolaishistorian tutkimusprojekti. *Historiallinen Aikakauskirja, 69*(2), 146–150.

Nuorteva, J., & **Happonen, P.** (2016). *Suomen Arkistolaitos 200 vuotta: Arkivverket i Finland 200 år*. Helsinki: Kansallisarkisto.

Nurmio, Y. (1952). Valtionarkiston toimesta ulkomailla suoritettavat mikrofilmaustyöt. *Historiallinen Aikakauskirja, 50*(4), 268–274.

Nygren, T., Foka, A., & **Buckland, P. I.** (2014). The status quo of digital humanities in Sweden: past, present and future of digital history. *H-Soz-Kult*. Retrieved from http://urn.kb.se/resolve?urn=urn:nbn:se:umu:diva-88730

Onnela, T. (1995). Email to H-verkko email list: 'Suomalaisen historiantutkimuksen elektroninen keskus' 14 November 1995. Retrieved 12 November, 2018 from http://historia.utu.fi/h-verkko/arkisto/0137.html

Onnela, T. (1998). Historiantutkimus internetin ja digitaalisen kumouksen aikakaudella. *Agricolan Tietosanomat* 5/1998. Retrieved 1 September, 2016 from http://agricola.utu.fi/julkaisut/tietosanomat-1998-2005/numero5-98/historiantutkimus.html

Paju, P. (2008). National projects and international users: Finland and early European computerization. *IEEE Annals of the History of Computing, 30*(4), 77–91.

Paju, P. (2016, 1 September). *Digitaalinen historiantutkimus: kyselytuloksia*. Report from the project Towards a Roadmap for Digital History in

Finland. Retrieved from https://digihistfinlandroadmapblog.wordpress.com/2016/09/01/raportti-kyselyvastauksista/

Paju, P. (2019, 6–8 March). International collaboration and Finland in the early years of computer-assisted history research: combining influences from Nordic and Soviet Baltic historians. In *Proceedings of the 4th Conference of the Association Digital Humanities in the Nordic Countries* (pp. 349–357). Copenhagen. CEUR Workshop Proceedings 2364.

Parland-von Essen, J., & **Nyberg, K.** (2014). *Historia i en digital värld*. Online book. Retrieved 10 September, 2018 from http://digihist.se/

Paul, H. (2011). Performing history: how historical scholarship is shaped by epistemic virtues. *History and Theory, 50*(1), 1=19. DOI: https://doi.org/10.1111/j.1468-2303.2011.00565.x

Rainio, K. (2013). Kuusitoista kilotavua—humanisti koodinmuuntimien ajassa. In *HY: Tietotekniikkapalvelut: 1960-luku*. Retrieved 28 June 2018 from http://www.helsinki.fi/atk/50v/1960-luku.html.

Rasila, V. (1967). Tietokone historiantutkimuksessa. *Historiallinen Aikakauskirja, 65*(2), 140–146.

Rasila, V. (1968). *Kansalaissodan sosiaalinen tausta*. Helsinki: Tammi.

Rasila, V. (1969a). Edellisen johdosta. *Historiallinen Aikakauskirja, 67*(1), 60–61.

Rasila, V. (1969b). The Finnish civil war and land lease problems. *Scandinavian Economic History Review, 17*(1), 115–135. DOI: https://doi.org/10.1080/03585522.1969.10407659

Rasila, V. (1970). The use of multivariable analysis in historical studies. *Economy and History, 13*(1), 24–53. DOI: https://doi.org/10.1080/00708852.1970.10418879

Rasila, V. (1982). Projektin hankkiman aineiston käyttömahdollisuudet. In *Muuttoliikkeiden ja sosiaalisen kehityksen väliset yhteydet Suomen teollistumisen alusta maan itsenäistymiseen* (pp. 42–60). Turku: Turun yliopiston historian laitos.

Rissanen, M., & **Tyrkkö, J.** (2013). The Helsinki corpus of English texts (HC). In A. Meurman-Solin & J. Tyrkkö (Eds.), *Principles and practices for the digital editing and annotation of diachronic data*. Studies in Variation, Contacts and Change in English 14. Helsinki: Varieng.

Roos, T., **Heikkilä, T.**, & **Myllymäki, P.** (2006). A compression-based method for stemmatic analysis. In ECAI 2006: Proceedings of the 17th European Conference on Artificial Intelligence.

Salmi, H. (2011). Traditions of cultural history in Finland, 1900–2000. In J. Rogge (Ed.), *Cultural history in Europe: institutions—themes—perspectives* (pp. 45–62). Bielefelt: transcript Verlag.

Strömberg, J. (1998). Avhandlingarna. In P. Tommila (Ed.), *Historiantutkijan muotokuva* (pp. 55–80). Helsinki: Suomen historiallinen seura.

Suominen, J. (2000). *Sähköaivo sinuiksi, tietokone tutuksi: tietotekniikan kulttuurihistoriaa*. Jyväskylä: Jyväskylän yliopisto.

Suominen, J., & Sivula, A. (2016). Digisyntyisten ilmiöiden historiantutkimus. In K. Elo (Ed.), *Digitaalinen humanismi ja historiatieteet* (pp. 96–130). Turku: Turun Historiallinen Yhdistys.

Tampere Research Group for History of population, environments and social structures. Retrieved 19 December, 2018 from https://research.uta.fi/hopes-en/database/

Thomas, W. G. III (2004). Computing and the historical imagination. In S. Schreibman, R. Siemens & J. Unsworth (Eds.), *A companion to digital humanities* (pp. 56–68). Malden, MA: Blackwell.

Tirranen, H. (1964). Katsauksia: biologisia historianselityksiä. *Historiallinen Aikakauskirja 62*(3), 225–234.

Tolonen, M., Lahti, L., Roivainen, H., & Marjanen, J. (2019). A quantitative approach to book-printing in Sweden and Finland, 1640–1828. *Historical methods: a journal of quantitative and interdisciplinary history, 52*(1), 57–78. DOI: https://doi.org/10.1080/01615440.2018.1526657

Tommila, P. (Ed.) (1998). *Miten meistä tuli historian tohtoreita.* Helsinki: Suomen historiallinen seura.

Waris, H. (1969). Kansalaissodan taustatekijät. *Historiallinen Aikakauskirja, 67*(1), 73–74.

Vesanto, A., Nivala, A., Rantala, H., Salakoski, T., Salmi, H., & Ginter, F. (2017, 23-24 May). Applying BLAST to text reuse detection in Finnish newspapers and journals, 1771-1910. In Proceedings of the 21st Nordic Conference of Computational Linguistics. Gothenburg, Sweden (pp. 54–58). Linköping Electronic Conference Proceedings. Retrieved from http://www.ep.liu.se/ecp/133/010/ecp17133010.pdf

Virrankoski, P. (1982). Projektin historia. In *Muuttoliikkeiden ja sosiaalisen kehityksen väliset yhteydet suomen teollistumisen alusta maan itsenäistymiseen* (pp. 7–29). Turku: Turun yliopiston historian laitos.

Virrankoski, P. (2013). *Historian professori ja laulajapoika: kulttuurin kuvia suuren muutoksen ajalta.* Turku: Memnon-kirjat.

Åberg, V. (2010). *Lisää muistia! 50 vuotta tietotekniikkaa Helsingin yliopistossa.* Helsinki: Helsingin yliopiston tietotekniikkakeskus.

CHAPTER 3

Towards Big Data

Digitising Economic and Business History

Jari Eloranta, Pasi Nevalainen and Jari Ojala

Prologue

An ambitious project was initiated in 2002 and concluded by 2007 by Finnish economic and business historians to analyse digitised news agency data in order to create a model to predict the behaviour of business enterprises. This project, entitled MetaSignal (later MetaAlert), was a joint venture between historians, journalism researchers, engineering scholars and economists working at the University of Jyväskylä and the Tampere University of Technology. The aim was nothing less ambitious than to create an artificial intelligence (AI) that could learn from the past to predict the future.

The AI was intended to compile automatically, categorise and analyse available online information to find so-called weak signals from a massive flow of information. To 'teach' the AI, the project used a massive news agency database, including roughly 20 million business newsfeeds from the early 1970s to the early 2000s. For the first time in Finnish historical research, the project also used digitised full-text *New York Times* newspaper data from the 1850s onwards, together with databases containing information about listed companies and stock market prices over an extended period of time.

How to cite this book chapter:
Eloranta, J., Nevalainen, P., & Ojala, J. (2020). Towards big data: Digitising economic and business history. In M. Fridlund, M. Oiva, & P. Paju (Eds.), *Digital histories: Emergent approaches within the new digital history* (pp. 45–67). Helsinki: Helsinki University Press. https://doi.org/10.33134/HUP-5-3

Needless to say, this bold initiative failed as the project did not have sufficient human resources or computational power circa 15 years ago to reach its goals. Nevertheless, as for the outcomes, the project did identify publications and networks that were valuable at the time and at least interesting even from today's perspective. One must bear in mind that the internet was still a newcomer at the turn of the millennium; thus, there were still many uncertainties as to which direction it would develop and which would be the most usable tools to find information on various topics. Moreover, the databases on emerging markets of the internet were also at a developing stage, and so was the price of information: the price of annual use of the databases used in the project roughly doubled every year.

By analysing the data available from open sources at the time and comparing it to the data purchased from the databases in the market, the project found, for example, that the very origins of the contemporary newsfeeds could be traced to few, well-established and old news agency firms or media companies.[1] It was not until the emergence of the digital camera, smartphones and social media when the supremacy of these companies began to collapse, at least to a certain extent.

The project members did not necessarily even notice at the time how fast the environment around them was changing. The project participants travelled to Stanford to learn about the latest trends in Silicon Valley and report their findings to the steering group. Therefore, it was the historians and the other humanists who were the first to inform the others in the meetings with the funding agency Tekes (Finnish Institute of Technology and Innovation, nowadays known as Business Finland) about interesting emerging companies in the United States, like Facebook.[2]

. . .

The MetaSignal project was just an outcome of a long tradition of compiling and using massive databases, distant reading methods and, most importantly, sophisticated methods among economic and business historians to analyse numerical and textual data. The use of a massive database to predict future trends in the MetaSignal project was not, obviously, a ground-breaking idea. On the contrary, computerised methods have been used in social sciences in this respect at least from the early 1960s, when the first attempts were made at the RAND laboratories.[3]

Economic and business historians have been the forerunners in the digital history data gathering and analysis for decades. This chapter attempts to discuss the major developments internationally and, in some specific cases, in Finland in the fields of digital economic and business history, concentrating on some of our own projects, as well as research outcomes by economic and business historians at the University of Jyväskylä and within our networks. We are not claiming that our projects are unique or ahead of their time in the field of economic and business history—on the contrary. However, we feel that these projects are indeed illustrative cases (such as the aforementioned MetaSignal) about the possibilities and challenges facing historians in the digital era.

After a section introducing the use of digitised data in economic and business history, we will briefly discuss the methodological challenges in the use of these methods, followed by sections concentrating on event data analysis and challenges involved in using various databases (with some examples). Thereafter, we focus our narrative on the use of digital sources and methods in business history. In the concluding discussion, we will address the challenges and opportunities offered by digitised sources, followed by some exposition of the remaining challenges.

Big Data in Economic and Business History

Big data is at the heart of economic history research, and has already been so for decades.[4] *Big structures, large processes, huge comparisons*, by Charles Tilly, a famous historical sociologist, was a book published in the mid-1980s that highlighted some of the early efforts in such scholarship. Tilly's classic studies urged researchers to study the macro-level societal structures systematically, to better understand large processes of change.[5] Tilly was also one of the forerunners of 'social science history', pushing sociological understanding to advance historical research. Economic historians were also part of this process and, to a certain extent, the first ones to explore and exploit the possibilities of social scientific methods and data in historical research.

Since the time of publication of Tilly's book, the datasets compiled and used by economic historians have become larger and more varied: numeric data is nowadays more often 'born digital'; and besides numbers, even economic historians are today more often using high-resolution digital images and digitised texts. The quantity of available data has increased dramatically, whereas the costs of storage have decreased—even though there is now a new challenge for academia arising from the costs of the best datasets and digitised library collections.[6] As Guttman and colleagues (2018: 269) note: 'A key characteristic of modern "big data" is that the volume of stored data exceeds human analytic capacity and pushes against the boundaries of currently-available computing power. For that reason, the magnitude of "big" is continually growing.'

By its principles, economic history research does not differ substantively from other types of historical research: economic historians compile data from original (archival) sources to provide answers to questions posed by scholars. What differs, though, is that the questions asked are often based on testable theoretical frameworks originating from social sciences and usually require a massive amount of data that, in turn, cannot be analysed without sorting the data into a database format, as well as by using some sort of quantitative methods. However, economic historians were forced to compile these types of datasets themselves for decades, whereas today there is a large amount of readymade data available, starting with various text corpuses (for example, digitised newspapers), statistical data provided by different national and international authorities (such as census records) and databases compiled by researchers, authorities and private enthusiasts in different fields, including genealogical associations. The latter type of 'citizen participation' or 'citizen science' to compile data will most likely increase in the future, as well as different kinds of official, linked register data. Nevertheless, even today, researchers studying especially the ancient and early modern eras are forced to mainly compile the datasets by themselves, whereas those concentrating on the more contemporary periods and topics have to face the challenges associated with the already existing datasets.

Using digitised sources is at the very core of international economic history. Computerised methods were embedded into the economic history research during the 'Cliometric Revolution' in the 1960s and 1970s, when the so-called 'historical economics' tradition emerged first in the United States, then also later in Europe. The first researchers in this tradition were mostly trained as economists—such as Alfred Conrad and John Meyer, and then Robert Fogel and Douglass C. North—using their theories, models and econometric methods to study and understand controversial topics in history, like the productivity and profitability of slavery. Obviously, mainstream historians were not totally convinced about their studies and methods, especially as some of the advocates of the 'new economic history' took historians head on vis-à-vis many big topics.[7] By the turn of the millennium, this battle had settled down, as more historians have adopted cliometric methods to be a part of their toolkit and as 'social science history' has become more common. Simultaneously, economists are taking history research more seriously. Nevertheless, the major journals in economic history today are more oriented towards economics than they were back in the 1950s.[8]

The most obvious outcomes of the 'new economic history' have been the historical growth studies in different countries, compiled together in the Maddison Project database maintained at the Groningen University.[9] Historical national account series and other long-run societal and economic time series form a basis for all comparative macroeconomic studies of history. These include data on population, prices, wages, structure of the economy (size of agriculture, industry and services), foreign and domestic trade, urbanisation, central (and local) government expenditures and, finally, GDP (per capita) that is based on all the other data series listed above. Historical national accounts have made comprehensive comparisons over long periods of time more credible between a growing number of countries. These datasets have been game changers in the field and have occupied a substantial role in the debates over long-run economic growth. Angus Maddison (2001) published his initial global growth figures spanning 2,000 years at the turn of the millennium, but he had already started putting these numbers out in various publications from the 1980s onwards. Obviously, his early figures were rather tentative, and the GDP per capita estimates in general for many developing states were too low. Recent efforts, for example, by Stephen Broadberry[10] and others, have exposed some of the flaws in these figures and extended our knowledge of not just European and Western development patterns, but also economic performance in Asia and Africa. These figures are now changing the debate over global trade and the so-called Great Divergence; that is, when and how China fell behind the West in the last 500 years.[11] In recent studies, the focus has shifted to account for new areas of interest, such as well-being and inequality.[12] Consequently, the existing Finnish historical national accounts from 1860 onwards were compiled by Riitta Hjerppe and the growth studies research group in the 1970s and 1980s, comprising 13 volumes in total, and they are still the benchmark in the study of Finnish economic history.[13]

Business historians, in turn, have been more focused on actors and related activities in the economy, whether by private persons, entrepreneurs, business enterprises or other groups. These actors represent the 'visible hand' of the aggregate economic system. Research on these actors, in turn, helps us to understand the evolution of economic structures. By looking at the American 19th-century railway companies, Alfred Chandler Jr. (1977) created the basic framework for the business strategy research. The methods used by modern business historians are more often qualitative, and the quantitative methods used are typically more descriptive than statistical ones.[14] Nevertheless, big data and methods used to analyse digitised databases have become more important also for business historians. This is simply due to the fact that either the data produced by entrepreneurs and enterprises over time are in most cases in numerical form and/or the volume of data is massive.[15] Even the early modern businessmen such as 13th-century *Commenda* traders in Genoa or late-18th-century Finnish businessmen produced a massive amount of letters and ledgers; some of those have lately been converted into a digitised format. The recent historical business data is already of digital origin. The shift to increasingly digitised material has enabled researchers to utilise larger quantities of material in qualitative research in future studies, including new ways to collect and analyse the material, including the use of AI in data mining and analysis.

Use of Quantitative and Qualitative Methods to Tackle Digital Sources

The use and analysis of quantitative data has been a hallmark of economic history research, especially since the turn towards more quantitative economic history, as we have already discussed. The aim of this more economics-influenced research has often been to attempt to find causal relationships between different phenomena; namely, to measure what were the factors explaining changes in phenomena proxied by various time series, cross-sectional or panel data. For example, during the past decades, there have been many attempts to compile data on, better measure and understand the dynamics of pre-industrial economies; for instance, to clarify the role of women, children and families in the pre- and early-industrialising societies.[16] Alongside the time series (or panels) of economic development, much attention has been placed on the study of equal or unequal distribution arising from this development.[17]

From the 1950s onwards, econometric tools such as regression analysis have emerged as a typical way of estimating the relationships between economic variables. Regression analysis is today a common tool both in economics and social sciences, and also in economic history. Thus, in order to understand what has been written in the field during the past decades, one has to be familiar with at least the basics of this method; or, rather, the set of regression and other econometric techniques for modelling and analysing several variables. More commonly, regression analysis estimates the conditional expectation of the dependent variable vis-à-vis a set of independent variables; for example, what was the importance of education, investments or policy indicators for the economic growth or, as we have done, the effect of new technologies for wages of different skill levels of employees.[18]

Certain aspects of regression analysis have also been criticised, such as the over-reliance on measures of statistical significance.[19] Historians are particularly worried how such methods are suited to the analysis of time series as the observable and unobservable factors might change over time, and also the sources of data are similarly subject to change. Some of the research has become perhaps even overly technical by nature, thus losing its relevance for broader historical narratives.[20] Finally, causal relationships are hard to pinpoint, especially from more qualitative data,[21] and in econometrics the very idea that causality could be ascertained from regression analysis has become quite contested.

Another way to analyse causal relationships is by using counterfactual modelling: namely, to analyse a scenario of 'what if' the phenomena had not have occurred or a different historical trajectory had taken place. Economic history also has a long tradition of counterfactual analysis, starting from the early writings of Nobel-prize-winning economic historian Robert Fogel. Those models have, however, been criticised time and again by historians.[22]

Event Data Analysis

Although the methods used by economic historians could and should be criticised for certain shortcomings, they are nevertheless something that other historians might wish to emulate when using digitised, 'big data' sources. These methods can also be used when analysing qualitative, textual datasets, by introducing 'binary thinking' to the analysis; that is, coding the textual data to enable quantitative analysis. We have used, for example, 'event data analysis' to code actions and activities found in historical data, like the 'strategic actions' of companies. The basis for event data analysis can be found in historical events that are arranged according their sequences. The coding of events (for example, strategic actions) enables comparing different actors, such as companies or business groups.[23]

While reducing texts to ones and zeroes might lead to over-simplifications, the use of more open methods, such as fuzzy set Qualitative Comparative Analysis (fs/QCA), has proved to be suitable for historical inquiries, as the set-theoretic relations frequently reveal more plausible causal relations than simple correlations.[24] Moreover, these types of methods can also be used to extrapolate larger datasets from smaller samples, in which typically statistical analysis has been near impossible. Often, the dichotomy between small-N qualitative case studies and large-N statistical studies has been overstated.[25] Essentially, they follow the same underlying logic of research. The best way to avoid the pitfalls of each is to engage in both or combine the strengths of each approach. These types of methods have been further developed by some Finnish business history and management scholars in particular.[26]

In international comparisons, comparable data, contexts and how the data helps make broader points about processes all play a role. For Finnish historians, though, even the question of the relevance of comparisons might sometimes alter the way in which we think about the sources and data. One of our own examples is from some years ago when we were using a large-N database which comprised information on Finnish and Swedish sailors. Thus, an obvious perspective for us was to compare these two countries in our analyses. For readers outside Scandinavia, however, this did not make much sense: the reviewers and editors of journals saw Sweden and Finland rather as complementary than interesting comparative cases in terms of our research question, and the paper was rejected time and again, before we fully realised this challenge and changed the paper accordingly.[27]

This type of categorisation is something we have tried to develop further also in our bibliometric work focusing on analysing trends in business history scholarships. As categories of the contents of journal articles in the ready-made databases (such as WoS or Scopus) are always subjective, we introduced certain measures to make such categorisations more objective in our study. Obviously, these are again methods used previously in other fields, but ones that can also be adapted to the study of economic and business history debates. For example, we engaged several researchers to do categorisations of previously published business history articles simultaneously, and then either used 'consensus' or average categorisations, or results of 'voting'. In the latter case, the 'votes' (zeros or ones by each individual doing the categorisation) for each category were summed up, and thereafter these sums of votes were calculated as a percentage of the maximum possible number of votes. These percentages were then taken to be the share of each category and as basis for further statistical analysis, namely to study why certain business history articles received the most citations.[28] The next obvious step is to introduce these bibliometric techniques to book-format publications, which would help us gauge the trends in a publication format that historians prefer, again broadening the analysis of interdisciplinary transference.

Making Big Data Work: Databases and Their Challenges

As we have shown here, economic and business historians have been engaged in creating their own databases for a long time by using a variety of primary sources.[29] The data collected from the original primary source material has typically been stored as digital images, Word and Excel files on the researchers' own computers, and perhaps distributed via email or cloud services, when sharing was needed, for example, to make a common writing project easier. That is the case even today in many instances. Regardless, currently there is a growing number of ready-made databases that have to a certain extent eased the work of economic and business historians, yet at the same time they have provided new types of challenges. First of all, the availability of these databases has motivated researchers to study topics for which the data is (easily) available, and to find connections between those variables for which we have information. To study Finnish economic and business history, it might be challenging to use some of the international datasets, as information on Finland might be lacking, or is otherwise irrelevant or even incorrect. Some of the most important international databases, however, do have some data for Finland as well, like the Maddison Project database described above; Clio-Infra (http://www.clio-infra.eu/), EH-net databases (http://eh.net/databases/), Global Price and Income History (http://gpih.ucdavis.edu/) and Swedish historical monetary statistics 1668–2008 (http://www.riksbank.se/research/historicalstatistics).

The challenge is, however, that in many of these datasets the data on Finland is to a certain degree confusing and even misleading. This, in turn, relates to the fact that the data has been compiled from national statistical sources or from previous research. In the Finnish case, we simply still lack some of the basic research; thus, the datasets are using the existing figures for Finland. The Maddison database, for example, uses the growth figures for Finnish GDP (per capita), for certain benchmark years, for the last 2,000 years by using inter- and extrapolation methods. Nonetheless, Finnish growth studies have produced more exact figures so far only from the 1860s onwards. Currently, though, there is project at the University of Jyväskylä to fill the gap from the 1500s to mid-1850s in order to have more reliable, internationally comparable time series for Finland as well.[30] This will, hopefully, make Finland more appealing as a unit to be used in international comparisons: currently, Finland is lacking from a number of international studies simply due to the fact that comparable data does not exist yet.

Some of the international databases have been especially valuable also for Finnish economic and business historians. Beside those noted above, two specific datasets recently used by Finnish scholars are worth noting: the Soundtoll Registers Online (STRO) compilation (soundtoll.nl) and the Swedish Seamen's House enrolment database.

The STRO compilation is a good example of how digitised, large databases can be constructed with reasonable costs and in a limited amount of time.[31] The STRO database is based on the archival data created in the Danish Elsinore in the Sound Toll that was established in the late 15th century and lasted until 1857. The STRO database includes roughly all the ships and their cargoes that passed the Danish Sound from 1634 to 1856, comprising 1.4 million ships. Of these ships, roughly 2.4%, that is 35,000 ships, came from or headed towards Finland. In order to understand Finnish international trade and shipping, the STRO is especially important as the Danish Sound was the only route for Finnish export and import trade to markets beyond the Baltic for centuries. The Baltic trade as a whole, in turn, was of utmost importance in understanding the early modern and modern growth of Europe, as this trade was, as Milja van Tielhof puts it, 'the mother of all trades'.[32] The Danish Sound data used in previous research[33] was mainly based on the Sound Toll Tables compilation by Nina Ellinger Bang and Knud Korst in the 1920s and 1930s.[34] Their data, though, covered only the period up until the early 1780s, and later Hans Christian Johansen extended the period up until the mid-1790s.[35] Thus, from the Finnish perspective, the STRO is fascinating as it covers the era from the late 18th century until the mid-19th century, which was in many respects an emerging era for Finnish export trade and shipping.

Nevertheless, although the STRO data is highly valuable for research in general and for Finnish history research in particular, it also entails many challenges that can at the moment only be partly solved in the online dataset. The names of places and commodities are currently being made uniform, as well as the different units used (weights, sizes, etc.), and, moreover, there are a number of mistakes in the dataset that might have been present already when the entries of the original customs data were made or later during the data-entry process of the database. At the moment, there is an extensive project in Leipzig being overseen by Dr. Werner Scheltjens to modify the data further; this version, STRO 2.0, will be launched in the coming years. Finnish economic historians are also collaborating closely with this work in order to have even better data to use to study Finnish long-term trade patterns.[36]

Another important database used by Finnish economic historians is the Swedish Seamen's House enrolment dataset. This database was compiled at the turn of the millennium by the Swedish National Archives in collaboration with the Swedish Genealogical Association. The database includes roughly 650,000 enrolment cases and 26 million data points from nine Swedish coastal towns and one Finnish town (Kokkola). Researchers at the University of Jyväskylä gained full access to the database more than 10 years ago, only to find out that there were many challenges with the data. Indeed, the database is a good, or bad, example of the challenges inherent in these types of databases.

First, the researchers did not have full access to the data in the beginning, which made quantitative analysis impossible. Many similar genealogical databases have been designed to help users find detailed information on, for example, their ancestors—not to perform statistical analyses. Second, the data did not need to be exact in terms of values and figures to serve genealogical inquiries and, therefore, in the datasheets sometimes numeric and textual data became mixed. This all meant that it took almost a decade for the researchers first to clean up the data, enrich it with additional information, and then standardise the monetary and other units (especially tonnage measures of ships) before it could really be used. This led to the third challenge that, again, is unfortunately rather common in many research projects using ready-made digitised databases. Namely, the database used in the research is to some degree different from the one that is available online at the Swedish National Archives website, and the researchers cannot, in accordance with the signed contract, publish the data they are using. Thus, hopefully in the future, the Swedish National Archives will publish the modified dataset separately on their website; this would be helpful for the research community at large, as this database is certainly highly valuable and the results have already been published in some of the most notable publishing forums.[37] There is already an initial agreement between the project researchers and the archive to publish the data in one form or another.

Digitising Business History

The magnitude of 'big' is also continually growing in the field of business history.[38] In practice, qualitative researchers can utilise much larger volumes and types of data than before and, on the other hand, different tools of analysis. The major development trend of recent decades is the diversification of the research field. Although the mainstream debate is still focused on businesses, entrepreneurs and entrepreneurship, the perspectives of research have widened over the last decades to cover a broad range of business-related themes. For example, the importance of interest groups, entrepreneurship of women and minorities, developing economies and environmental issues as part of business practices have emerged as major topics of discussion.[39] Even though most of the research is still being carried out in corporate archives, relying largely on textual material such as minutes and memos, it is because of the broadening of the scope of inquiry that the source material is quite sparse.

Finland's strength in business history research has traditionally been a comprehensive and open public archival service, which has guaranteed access to first-class material. One of the most important of these institutions is the National Archives (*Kansallisarkisto*), which has provided access to, among other things, abundant government documents, but also many archive collections of individuals and some private organisations. In Finland, the state has a strong position in society, and state documents, for example, contain not only information on legislation and administration, but also a huge variety of useful reports produced by various government organisations. The availability of sources has been supported by legislation under which a public authority document is in principle public.[40] Moreover, this also covers state-owned enterprises, depending on their legal form of action. Such archives also cover very interesting research sites that are difficult to access in many other countries. The archives of the state-owned telecom company (PTL Tele/Sonera) are available to researchers until the year 1994, when the company changed its legal form from a public authority into a limited liability company. An even more important archive for Finnish business historical research is the Central Archives for Finnish Business Records (*Elinkeinoelämän Keskusarkisto*), where the archives of many Finnish companies are currently located and easily accessible to scholars. Often, such archives require a licence to use, which typically does not form an obstacle to academic research. For example, a large number of private telecoms documents are available up until the 2010s.

Despite the quality of the archive service, access to archival material and its quality are still key issues. For a private company, handing over the archive to the archival establishment is voluntary. The quality and usability vary on a case-by-case basis. At worst, even the material of important companies has been virtually lost. For example, when a large company, whose older archive sources are conveniently located in the National Archives, was asked about its late-1990s archives, it became clear that the company had outsourced the management of these archives to a private archive management company, which in turn had transferred the material to its own repositories. Worst of all, there was not even a list available for that material. On the other hand, the private archive management company does not provide any 'extra services' without an extra charge. Hence, to even find out whether the archives are relevant for scientific use would require a laborious and costly preliminary inquiry. On the other hand, some companies have already digitised their archives. However, even if the material is in digital format, there is no guarantee that it will be accompanied by a proper search engine and metadata, or that the archive would be properly organised and/or that the researcher would have full access to the database.

Business history has a long tradition of using digital images and optical character recognition (OCR) techniques, similar to economic history. In this way, scholars themselves have digitised a considerable amount of material. These have already greatly accelerated the utilisation of broader amounts of information. These are mostly private, rather limited databases. When talking about the possibilities of these images and personal collections, it should be borne in mind that these are not usually complete sets. A business history scholar, rarely paid for their efforts in this regard, usually has to photograph only the 'necessary' documents. For this reason, these private collections usually serve specific research questions. It is clear that large-scale digitisation of the material should be done by archives or large, well-funded projects in a professional and systematic way, leading to a publication of the data in a commonly used form. Unfortunately, the digitisation projects of aforementioned key Finnish institutions are still only in their infancy. Digitisation has, first and foremost, captured the oldest material. On the other hand, new machine reading technologies are promising and will surely improve the usability of data in the future. Up until this point, very positive developments have taken place vis-à-vis search engines, making it easier for the researcher to find material from traditional archives.

Discussion of the business history method has touched upon the usability of the history research method in social sciences (such as organisational research), and how business historians can contribute to these discussions. Qualitative history research that takes into account temporal processes, contexts and coincidences has also been seen to be instrumental in building and modifying theoretical understanding.[41]

However, defining the method of historical research has become a problem: instead of a clearly defined method and source series, qualitative history research often takes advantage of different perspectives and sets of sources that may change as the research process evolves. The problem arises because historians are not accustomed to describing these research processes with the precision that is customary in social sciences, which in turn has begun to take replicability seriously. This debate has highlighted the need for business historians to pay more attention to describing their methods.[42] This requirement can also be viewed against the development of digital analytical methods. Since the idea of such methods is to automate the work, this requires event data coding in different ways, which in turn requires precision as well as continuous justification of choices. In this way, methodological precision and connection to theoretical models will be a more central part of the historian's daily routine.

Digitisation of business history sources and methods allows not only the use of qualitative data in larger quantities, but also the more intensive research collaboration. A particularly interesting example of using digital methods in business history research pertains to the 'Digital History of Telco and Exchanges in Finland and Sweden' consortium.[43] The project includes researchers, social scientists and historians from Aalto University and several Swedish universities, including the Stockholm School of Economics. Moreover, one of the authors of this chapter has participated in this collaboration. At the heart of this 'DigHist' project is a database, which includes the digital business archives of four business enterprises. Two telecommunications companies and two exchanges from Sweden and Finland have been selected for the project. These archives have been digitised for their most relevant parts. The coded digitised material is shared between the members of the consortium. For example, the database contains key sections of the Finnish state-owned telecom company's (PTL Tele/Sonera) archives (95 digitised archive boxes). Some of these have been digitised from the collections of the Finnish National Archives, but the others have been digitised from the material held by the current company Telia. Consequently, in one project, we were able to perform searches on all of the 764 Executive Team meetings (including attachments) that took place between 1981 and 1998. The software used also allows for the indexing of material and linking different documents to each other. Materials related to an interesting event can be assembled into a set of materials that make it easy to view relevant documents together. The sheer amount of data and the search functions make it possible to efficiently compile information on the desired topics.

At best, this type of working method enables quantitative exploitation of qualitative material and analysis. In addition, by working closely together, the project scholars have been able to develop a unique research design centred around collaboration across institutions and disciplines. Data availability, a common desktop and teamwork enable a highly effective and accurate research process combining different areas of expertise. Practical experience has shown that such a method also poses challenges. Finding information about a huge amount of data requires good knowledge of the case and the materials. To know what kind of potentially interesting things have happened in the company being researched (namely, the terms used in the company at different times), it is important that someone in the research group is knowledgeable about the subject and sources of the case. Again, easy and partially mechanical availability of the material may blind the scholar. Too narrow a focus on certain source series and 'relevant' documents may obscure the importance of the historical process and context, leaving the strengths of historical research untapped. In any case, such a way of working has proved to be a promising way of combining digital tools and theoretical knowledge with methods of historical research.[44]

Discussion and Further Challenges

Digitisation is part of the development of technology and society, and hence something that naturally enhances economic and business history research. Its direct impact is related to the available material, the amount and usability of which are greatly improved as digitisation proceeds further. In many cases, such as in business archives, digitisation could potentially proceed much faster, but such efforts have been hampered by the lack of funding and expertise. Although digitising research materials and methods does not bring anything other than more efficient tools for managing the research process, at its best it can also be used as a tool for speeding up and facilitating the development of methodology and science, as well as international collaborations.

For some, digitisation itself changes human and social sciences. At the heart of such 'Google of archives' thinking are massive increases in the amount of data and improvements in search functions. According to Berry and Fagerjord (2017), up until now, digitisation in human sciences can almost completely be understood as a mechanism for sorting availability and dissemination of material in large quantities. The discussion has dealt with technical issues that are considered to be part of the archive's or library's work. In fact, even the tools are not new in principle. As we have discussed here, databases and quantitative methods have been used for a long time, and even before PCs became available. Economic history has been a forerunner in this and the lessons learned by economic and business historians—both successes and failures—could and should, we argue, be used also more broadly among other historians. As Berry and Fagerjord conclude, the actual contribution of digitisation has to 'move beyond the purely instrumental and mechanical automation of processing of humanities materials'.[45]

Excessive and straightforward trust in digitisation is methodologically problematic. Using, for example, keywords, the desired documents can be found quickly from a large cache of data, yet a poor choice of keywords can lead the scholar to miss key contributions. Moreover, context and other areas are easily missed. The same applies to quantitative research, in which the researcher still needs to understand what dimensions and weights meant at different times and contexts. In that case, the researcher may unknowingly twist the history of an event in a way to reinforce his or her own hypotheses.[46] In reality, the need for someone to know the empirical material thoroughly does not disappear with the new digital collections and large-N methods. This is also an important starting point in all historical studies using, for example, regressions analysis: you need to know the units you are analysing before you analyse them, and what information you might still be missing from your analysis.

Furthermore, the sheer amount of information is a methodological problem, because the researcher needs to separate the necessary pieces from a massive amount of data. The committee which explored options for developing Finnish state-owned businesses published a 154-page report in 1985. However, the same committee delivered into the National Archives material that takes up about two shelf metres. Most of these consisted of unorganised documents, which contained numerous versions of the same memoirs, meeting invitations and drafts.[47] If this material were to be digitised and searched for, in practice, the same document would appear among the results tens of times, but only a few documents would increase our knowledge of the subject itself. We had a similar challenge with the MetaSignal project: using the large database containing news agency newsfeeds actually delivered the same information in the worst cases dozens of times. On the one hand, we could use this information to show the 'hype' around various topics, but on the other, it hindered the possibilities of performing proper quantitative analysis.

The creation and use of large digital collections require collaboration between several state and private actors. In the Finnish case, a specific role is played by the Finnish National Archives, which is responsible for the official documents created by the different state authorities. The Central Archives for Finnish Business Records (*Elka*), in turn, is the most important institution vis-à-vis private business archives and collections. The official collections (and to a certain extent also private archives) can be divided into roughly three groups, each entailing some specific challenges in today's digital world.

The first group consist of the 'old' paper archives, the total volume of which today is roughly 220 shelf-kilometres at the Finnish National Archives. Only a small fraction of this 'old' archival data has been or will ever be digitised; today, there are already 85 million digitised pictures available at the National Archives.

The goal is to digitise 20 per cent from this old material; mainly archives from the 1920s onwards. Nevertheless, the bulk of this material will also remain in paper format in the future.

Second, a large amount of paper format official documents resides with different state authorities that have been created since the 1970s, during the era of bureaucratisation, which are to be moved to National Archives in the coming years. The volume of these documents is around 135 shelf-kilometres. As it would not be sensible to build new warehouses to house such archives, the material will presumably be digitised *en masse* and the originals will be destroyed.[i] On the whole, this will mean that future historians who are looking for official documentation from 1970 onwards have to contend with *only* digitised archives. To a certain degree, the same is occurring in the private sector as well.

The third challenge relates to the so-called born-digital documents. The new service acquire for born-digital material is to be launched in year 2021; moreover a pilot project for private archives was under construction in 2020. Whatever the archival solution will be, both regarding public and private documents, the format will be digital. Thus, future historians will definitely need versatile skills to be able to use the digitised data and archives effectively.

In general, historical sciences have been the pioneers in the utilisation of information technology since the 1970s. Since then, digitisation has inevitably progressed, but as we have noticed, often slowly and sporadically. However, the advancement of digitisation has embodied undeniable advantages. Economic history at large has been forging ahead of other fields of history in using big data, digitised sources and quantitative methods. By using the rhetoric embedded in the theoretical debates of the discipline itself, economic history might eventually lose its comparative advantage as other, larger fields of history are catching up in using these data and methods, which in itself would be a good turn for debates about big issues in history, such as trade, slavery, development, environment, conflicts and so on.

There is a plethora of other challenges ahead for the field of history too, as well as economic and business history in particular. First, what materials should be digitised and when? This reflects the priorities among the scholars and the institutions that produce and maintain such records. Often, those priorities are not the same, which can create friction among the stakeholders. It also concerns resources and technologies available to facilitate such processes. Second, who has access and to what? While many archival collections are open access, some are not. And most published articles and books are not open access, which limits their use among scholars who are not institutionally linked and especially those who are located outside Western academic institutions. The same, of course, applies to the first concern about what materials are digitised; namely, for example, are business and economic records from the developing world less accessible those from the West? Third, new methods are emerging to analyse both the data itself as well as research trends, including bibliometric and AI methods. These methods can offer great insights, but they can also be used to direct funds towards the most 'popular' types of research at the expense of, at least in terms of perception, more marginal topics. This can foster groupthink and could be detrimental to smaller, interdisciplinary fields like economic and business history. Finally, there are great challenges among the various fields of history to remaster quantitative techniques to be able to make use of the new 'big data', given that the so-called cultural turn from the 1980s until the early 2000s had no real interest in quantitative analysis and that the 'Cliometric Revolution' often took economic historians to departments of economics. Now, there is a greater demand to bring back quantitative historians, who have the requisite skill set to work with these types of data and methods. However, to achieve that, humanities will have to compete with other fields, with higher wages and better resources, so this process will likely take some time.

. . .

As stated at the outset of this chapter, our MetaSignal project failed 15 years ago. Would it be possible to create such an AI with historical data to predict future today? A number of similar software solutions have already been created, using various kinds of data sources. However, with similar sources and algorithms that we were using, it is highly unlikely that the project would succeed even with today's computational power. Moreover, although digital methods in humanities and social sciences have developed significantly over the past 15 years, the use of these methods is still lacking behind the digitisation of sources. Nevertheless, it would certainly be beneficial to have historians on board to develop similar kinds of projects also in the future. AI methods are certainly already in use to deal with large datasets and analytical projects, and eventually they will become the cornerstones of historical analysis more broadly, although historians will have to exercise careful control over these efforts and remember the points of caution we have reflected on in this chapter.

Notes

1 Ojala 2005: 19.
2 The early project outcomes are summarised in Ojala & Uskali 2005.
3 See esp. Andersson 2012: 1411–1430.
4 See, e.g., Calafat & Monnet 2017; Ojala 2017: 446–456.
5 Tilly 1984. Tilly's research focused heavily on finding structural patterns in history in the long term, as evidenced in his classic study of European urbanisation and warfare (Tilly 1990).
6 Gutmann et al. 2018: 270, 280.
7 McCloskey 1978. See also Conrad & Meyer (1958). The debate about slavery came to a head over the book by Fogel & Engerman 1974, which was criticised by many, including Gutman 2003 and Sutch 1975. See

also Kolchin 1992 on critique of the follow-up book. For a review of the Cliometric Revolution and its achievements, see, e.g., Goldin 1995; Greif 1997; and Carlos 2010.

8 Whaples 1991; Eloranta, Ojala & Valtonen 2010.

9 See the Maddison Project database, version 2018, https://www.rug.nl/ggdc/historicaldevelopment/maddison/. On this database and its use, see Bolt & van Zanden 2014; Bolt et al. 2018.

10 Broadberry & Gupta 2006; Broadberry, Custodis & Gupta 2014; Broadberry et al. 2015.

11 See, e.g., Pomeranz 2009; de Vries 2010.

12 See esp. van Zanden, et al. 2014.

13 Hjerppe 1989.

14 Eloranta, Ojala & Valtonen 2010; Ojala et al. 2017.

15 For a broader discussion of data and methods in business history, see, e.g., Decker et al. 2015.

16 de Vries 2008; Humphries & Weisdorf 2015.

17 See, e.g., Hoffman et al. 2002; Milanovic, Lindert & Williamson 2010; Piketty 2015.

18 See esp. Allen 2001; van Zanden 2009; Ojala, Pehkonen & Eloranta 2016.

19 Ziliak & McCloskey 2016.

20 See esp. Sala-i-Martin 1997; Reckendrees 2017: 3.

21 Mahoney 2000; Ketokivi & Mantere 2010.

22 See, e.g., Atack 2018.

23 See esp. Lamberg & Ojala 2006: 22–25; Lamberg, Laurila & Nokelainen 2006: 307–312.

24 For an introduction to this method, see Fiss 2011: 393–420.

25 See, e.g., Mahoney & Goertz 2006; Jordan et al. 2011.

26 See esp. Pajunen 2008: 652–669; Järvinen et al. 2009: 545–574.

27 The final published article is Ojala, Pehkonen & Eloranta 2016.

28 On the models, see, e.g., Ojala & Tenold 2013: 17–35; Ojala et al. 2017: 305–333.

29 In the English case, we can go as far back as the 17th century; see Broadberry et al. 2013 for further discussion.

30 See jyu.fi/growth.

31 About the project, see: Gøbel 2010: 305–324; Veluwenkamp & Scheltjens 2018.

32 van Tielhof 2002.

33 See, e.g., Åström 1962; Åström 1963; Åström 1988.

34 Bang & Korst 1930.

35 Johansen 1983.

36 See, e.g., Eloranta, Moreira & Karvonen 2015; Moreira et al. 2015; Ojala & Räihä 2017; Ojala et al. 2018.

37 See esp. Ojala, Pehkonen & Eloranta 2016.

38 Cf. Gutmann et al. 2018.

[39] See, e.g., Amatori & Jones 2003; Scranton & Fridenson 2013.
[40] The Freedom of Information Act (621/1999).
[41] Kipping & Üsdiken 2014; Üsdiken & Kipping 2014; Wadhwani & Bucheli 2014; Decker 2017.
[42] See, e.g., Yates 2014; Decker, Kipping & Wadhwani 2015; de Jong, Higgins & van Driel 2015; Stutz 2019.
[43] See https://blogs.aalto.fi/digihist/.
[44] One of the papers resulting from this project (Cheung, Aalto & Nevalainen 2019) was selected as one of the best research method papers at the Academy of International Business conference in 2019.
[45] Berry & Fagerjord 2017: 14.
[46] See, e.g., the discussion of the problems involved with a study conducted by Timothy Leunig and Hans-Joachim Voth on smallpox deaths, concerning both the sources they used and the methods involved. See Vervaeke & Devos 2018.
[47] See the Committee Report 1985:2 (*Valtion liikelaitoskomitean mietintö*); committee archives in the Finnish National Archives.

References

Allen, R. C. (2001). The great divergence in European wages and prices from the Middle Ages to the First World War. *Explorations in Economic History, 38*(4), 411–447.

Amatori, F., & **Jones, G.** (2003). Introduction. In F. Amatori & G. Jones (Eds.), *Business history around the world*. Cambridge: Cambridge University Press.

Andersson, J. (2012). The great future debate and the struggle for the world. *The American Historical Review, 117*(5), 1411–1430.

Atack, J. (2018). Railroads. *Handbook of Cliometrics*, 1–29.

Bang, N. E., & **Korst, K. E. P.** (1930). *Tabeller over skibsfart og varetransport gennem Øresund 1661–1783, og gennem Storebælt 1701–1748: udarbejdede efter de bevarede regnskaber over Øresundstolden og Bælttolden; udgivne paa bekostning af en international indsamling*. Copenhagen: Gyldendalske Boghandel.

Berry, D. M., & **Fagerjord, A.** (2017). *Digital humanities*. Cambridge: Polity Press.

Bolt, J., & **van Zanden, J. L.** (2014). The Maddison Project: collaborative research on historical national accounts. *Economic History Review, 67*(3), 627–651.

Bolt, J., **Inklaar, R.**, **de Jong, H.**, & **van Zanden, J. L.** (2018). Rebasing 'Maddison': new income comparisons and the shape of long-run economic development. Maddison Project Working Paper, No. 10. Retrieved from http://www.ggdc.net/maddison

Broadberry, S., & **Gupta, B.** (2006). The early modern great divergence: wages, prices and economic development in Europe and Asia, 1500–1800. *Economic History Review, 59*(1), 2–31.

Broadberry, S., Campbell, B. M., & van Leeuwen, B. (2013). When did Britain industrialise? The sectoral distribution of the labour force and labour productivity in Britain, 1381–1851. *Explorations in Economic History, 50*(1), 16–27.

Broadberry, S., Campbell, B. M., Klein, A., Overton, M., & van Leeuwen, B. (2015). *British economic growth 1270–1870.* Cambridge: Cambridge University Press.

Broadberry, S., Custodis, J., & Gupta, B. (2015). India and the great divergence: an Anglo-Indian comparison of GDP per capita, 1600–1871. *Explorations in Economic History, 56*, 58–75.

Calafat, G., & Monnet, É. (2017). The return of economic history? Books & Ideas.net. Retrieved from http://www.booksandideas.net/IMG/pdf/2017-30-01-economic-history.pdf

Carlos, A. M. (2010). Reflection on reflections: review essay on reflections on the cliometric revolution: conversations with economic historians. *Cliometrica, 4*(1), 97–111.

Chandler Jr., A. D. (1977). *The visible hand: the managerial revolution in American business.* Cambridge, MA: Harvard University Press.

Cheung, Z., Aalto, E., & Nevalainen, P. (2019). *Changing criteria for internal legitimacy and the internationalization process of a state-owned enterprise.* Paper presented at AIB conference, Copenhagen.

Conrad, A. H., & Meyer, J. R. (1958). The economics of slavery in the ante bellum South. *Journal of Political Economy, 66*(2), 95–130.

de Jong, A., Higgins, D. M., & van Driel, H. (2015). Towards a new business history? *Business History, 57*(1), 5–29.

De Vries, J. (2008). *The industrious revolution: consumer behavior and the household economy, 1650 to the present.* Cambridge: Cambridge University Press.

De Vries, P. (2010). The California School and beyond: how to study the Great Divergence? *History Compass, 8*(7), 730–751.

Decker, S. (2017). Paradigms lost: history and organization studies. *Management and Organizational History, 11*(4), 364–379.

Decker, S., Kipping, M., & Wadhwani, R. D. (2015). New business histories! Plurality in business history research methods. *Business History, 57*(1), 30–40.

Eloranta, J., Moreira, M. C., & Karvonen, L. (2015). Between conflicts and commerce: the impact of institutions and wars of Swedish–Portuguese trade, 1686–1815. *Journal of European Economic History, 44*, 9–50.

Eloranta, J., Ojala, J., & Valtonen, H. (2010). Quantitative methods in business history: an impossible equation? *Management & Organizational History, 5*(1), 79–107.

Fiss, P. C. (2011). Building better causal theories: a fuzzy set approach to typologies in organization research. *Academy of Management Journal, 54*(2), 393–420.

Fogel, R., & Engerman, S. (1974). *Time on the cross.* Boston, MA: Little, Brown & Co.

Gøbel, E. (2010). The sound toll registers online project, 1497–1857. *International Journal of Maritime History, 22*(2), 305–324.
Goldin, C. (1995). Cliometrics and the Nobel. *Journal of Economic Perspectives, 9*(2), 191–208.
Greif, A. (1997). Cliometrics after 40 years. *American Economic Review, 87*(2), 400–403.
Gutman, H. G. (2003). *Slavery and the numbers game: a critique of time on the cross,* Vol. 82. Champaign, IL: University of Illinois Press.
Gutmann, M. P., Klancher Merchant, E., & Roberts, E. (2018). 'Big data' in economic history. *Journal of Economic History, 78*(1), 268–299.
Hjerppe, R. (1989). *The Finnish economy 1860–1985: growth and structural change.* Helsinki: Bank of Finland.
Hoffman, P. T., Jacks, D. S., Levin, P. A., & Lindert, P. H. (2002). Real inequality in Europe since 1500. *Journal of Economic History, 62*(2), 322–355.
Humphries, J., & Weisdorf, J. (2015). The wages of women in England, 1260–1850. *Journal of Economic History, 75*(2), 405–447.
Järvinen, J., Lamberg, J. A., Murmann, J. P., & Ojala, J. (2009). Alternative paths to competitive advantage: a fuzzy-set analysis of the origins of large firms. *Industry and innovation, 16*(6), 545–574.
Johansen, H. C. (1983). *Shipping and trade between the Baltic area and Western Europe 1784–1795.* Odense: Odense University Press.
Jordan, E., Gross, M. E., Javernick-Will, A. N., & Garvin, M. J. (2011). Use and misuse of qualitative comparative analysis. *Construction Management and Economics, 29,* 1159–1173.
Ketokivi, M., & Mantere, S. (2010). Two strategies for inductive reasoning in organizational research. *Academy of Management Review, 35*(2), 315–333.
Kipping, M., & Üsdiken, B. (2014). History in organization and management theory: more than meets the eye. *Academy of Management Annals, 8*(1), 535–588.
Kolchin, P. (1992). More time on the cross? An evaluation of Robert William Fogel's without consent or contract. *Journal of Southern History, 58*(3), 491–502.
Lamberg, J.-A., & Ojala, J. (2006). Evolution of competitive strategies in global forestry industries: introduction. In J.-A. Lamberg, J. Näsi, J. Ojala & P. Sajasalo (Eds.), *The evolution of competitive strategies in global forestry industries: comparative perspectives.* World forests Vol. IV (pp. 22–25). Dordrecht: Springer.
Lamberg, J.-A., Laurila, J., & Nokelainen, T. (2006). Competitive activities of forestry industry firms: a coding manual for event history analysis. In J.-A. Lamberg, J. Näsi, J. Ojala & P. Sajasalo (Eds.), *The evolution of competitive strategies in global forestry industries: comparative perspectives.* World forests Vol. IV (pp. 307–312). Dordrecht: Springer.
Mahoney, J., & Goertz, G. (2006). A tale of two cultures: contrasting quantitative and qualitative research. *Political analysis, 14*(3), 227–249.

Mahoney, J. (2000). Strategies of causal inference in small-N analysis. *Sociological methods & research, 28*(4), 387–424.

McCloskey, D. N. (1978). The achievements of the cliometric school. *Journal of Economic History, 38*(1), 13–28.

Milanovic, B., Lindert, P. H., & Williamson, J. G. (2010). Pre-industrial inequality. *Economic Journal, 121*(551), 255–272.

Moreira, C., Eloranta, J., Ojala, J., & Karvonen, L. (2015). Early modern trade flows between smaller states: the Portuguese–Swedish trade in the eighteenth century as an example. *Revue de l'OFCE, 140*, 87–109.

Ojala, J., Karvonen, L., Moreira, M. C., & Eloranta, J. (2018). Trade between Sweden and Portugal in the eighteenth century: assessing the reliability of STRO compared to Swedish and Portuguese sources. In J. W. Veluwenkamp & W. Scheltjens (Eds.), *Early modern shipping and trade: novel approaches using sound toll registers online* (pp. 151–173). Leiden and Boston, MA: Brill.

Ojala, J., & Räihä, A. (2017). Navigation acts and the integration of North Baltic shipping in the early nineteenth century. International Journal of Maritime History, 29(1), 26–43.

Ojala, J., & Tenold, S. (2013). What is maritime history? A content and contributor analysis of the *International Journal of Maritime History*, 1989–2012. *International Journal of Maritime History, 25*(2), 17–35.

Ojala, J., & Uskali, T. (2005). *Mediajättien aika: uusia heikkoja signaaleja etsimässä*. Helsinki: Inforviestintä.

Ojala, J. (2005), Mediaimperiumien heikot signaalit. In J. Ojala & T. Uskali (Eds.), *Mediajättien aika: uusia heikkoja signaaleja etsimässä*. Helsinki: Inforviestintä.

Ojala, J. (2017). Taloushistorian paluu ja liiketoimintahistorian nousu. *Historiallinen Aikakauskirja, 115*(4), 446–456.

Ojala, J., Eloranta, J., Ojala, A., & Valtonen, H. (2017). Let the best story win—evaluation of the most cited business history articles. *Management & Organizational History, 12*(4), 305–333.

Ojala, J., Pehkonen, J., & Eloranta, J. (2016). Deskilling and decline in skill premiums during the age of sail: Swedish and Finnish seamen, 1751–1913. *Explorations in Economic History, 61*(July), 85–94.

Pajunen, K. (2008). Institutions and inflows of foreign direct investment: a fuzzy-set analysis. *Journal of International Business Studies, 39*(4), 652–669.

Piketty, T. (2015). About capital in the twenty-first century. *American Economic Review, 105*(5), 48–53.

Pomeranz, K. (2009). *The great divergence: China, Europe, and the making of the modern world economy*. Princeton, NJ: Princeton University Press.

Reckendrees, A. (2017). Economic history in times of transition. *Scandinavian Economic History Review, 65*(1), 1–5.

Sala-i-Martin, X. X. (1997). *I just ran four million regressions* (No. w6252). Cambridge, MA: National Bureau of Economic Research.

Scranton, P., & **Fridenson, P.** (2013). *Reimaging business history*. Baltimore, MD: Johns Hopkins University Press.

Sutch, R. (1975). The treatment received by American slaves: a critical review of the evidence presented in Time on the Cross. *Explorations in Economic History, 12*(4), 335–438.

Stutz, C. (2019). History and organizational theorizing blended: Insights from exploring the corporate social responsibility field (Doctoral dissertation). Jyväskylä: Department of history and ethnology, University of Jyväskylä. Retrieved from http://urn.fi/URN:ISBN:978-951-39-7981-2

Tilly, C. (1984). *Big structures, large processes, huge comparisons*. New York, NY: Russell Sage Foundation.

Tilly, C. (1990). *Coercion, capital, and European states, AD 990–1990*. Cambridge, MA: Basil Blackwell.

Üsdiken, B., & **Kipping, M.** (2014). History and organization studies: a long-term view. In M. Bucheli & R. D. Wadhwani (Eds.), *Organizations in time* (pp. 33–55). Oxford: Oxford University Press.

Van Tielhof, M. (2002). *The 'mother of all trades': the Baltic grain trade in Amsterdam from the late sixteenth to the early nineteenth century*. Leiden: Brill.

Van Zanden, J. L. (2009). The skill premium and the 'Great Divergence'. *European Review of Economic History, 13*(1), 121–153.

Van Zanden, J. L., **Baten, J.**, **Mira d'Ercole, M.**, **Rijpma, A.**, **Smith, C.**, & **Timmer, M.** (Eds.) (2014). *How was life? Global well-being since 1820*. Paris: OECD Publishing.

Veluwenkamp, J. W., & **Scheltjens, W.** (Eds.) (2018). *Early modern shipping and trade: novel approach using sound toll registers online*. Leiden: Brill.

Vervaeke, A., & **Devos, I.** (2018). Much ado about nothing? Reconsidering the smallpox effect: height in the nineteenth-century town of Thielt, Belgium. *Tijdschrift voor Sociale en Economische Geschiedenis, 14*(4), 56–83.

Wadhwani, R. D., & **Bucheli, M.** (2014). The future of the past in management and organization studies. In M. Bucheli & R. D. Wadhwani (Eds.), *Organizations in time* (pp. 3–30). Oxford: Oxford University Press.

Whaples, R. (1991). A quantitative history of the *Journal of Economic History* and the cliometric revolution. *Journal of Economic History, 51*(2), 289–301.

Yates, J. (2014). Understanding historical methods in organization studies. In M. Bucheli & R. D. Wadhwani (Eds.), *Organizations in time* (pp. 265–283). Oxford: Oxford University Press.

Ziliak, S. T., & **McCloskey, D. N.** (2016). Lady Justice versus cult of statistical significance. In G. E. DeMartino & D. N. McCloskey (Eds.), *The Oxford Handbook of Professional Economic Ethics* (pp. 352–365). New York, NY: Oxford University Press.

Åström, S. E. (1962). *From Stockholm to St. Petersburg*. Helsinki: Suomen Historiallinen Seura.

Åström, S. E. (1963). *From cloth to iron: the Anglo-Baltic trade in the late seventeenth century*. Helsinki: Societas Scientiarum Fennica.

Åström, S. E. (1988). *From tar to timber: studies in Northeast European forest exploitation and foreign trade, 1660–1860*. Helsinki: Societas Scientiarum Fennica.

CHAPTER 4

Digital History 1.5

A Middle Way between Normal and Paradigmatic Digital Historical Research

Mats Fridlund

History is one of the oldest and most conservative humanist disciplines, which begs the question how it could react to the current third 'generation' or 'wave' of digital history and its new potential to transform the practice of historians' research. History as a discipline is according to some digital historians at a crossroads, 'in a transitory moment'[1] and 'standing on the edge of a conceptual precipice'. The 'understanding and practice of traditional history' has been said to be 'facing a fundamental "paradigm shift"' and 'straddling a line between revolution and continuity' and that the resolution of 'this tension is going to be a central part of historians' tasks over the coming years'.[2] Some historians claim that 'digital history has become the buzz-word for avant-garde historical scholarship in the digital age',[3] while others worry about external interests and pressures from funders, governments and industrial stakeholders and the possibilities of reallocation of resources and 'fear for the hermeneutic character of the humanities, and a reduction of humanities research to data crunching or to a view that proclaims the search for underlying patterns and structures in human history and culture to be its essence'.[4] The overall concern is that history will be transformed into a new primarily quantitatively focused discipline

How to cite this book chapter:
Fridlund, M. (2020). Digital history 1.5: A middle way between normal and paradigmatic digital historical research. In M. Fridlund, M. Oiva, & P. Paju (Eds.), *Digital histories: Emergent approaches within the new digital history* (pp. 69–87). Helsinki: Helsinki University Press. https://doi.org/10.33134/HUP-5-4

where traditional 'analogue history' focused on narrative and close and deep reading of primary sources will be marginalised.

This chapter want to take these hopes and fears of a paradigm shift in history seriously and I will use my training as a historian and theorist of modern science and technology to analyse and conceptualise what such a paradigmatic change of historical science might mean. To do this, I will discuss what I have elsewhere identified to be the main methodological strands of computational digital history and in this use research from history and philosophy of science on revolutionary and paradigmatic change within science, and especially Thomas Kuhn's historical and philosophical research on scientific revolutions.[5] In doing this, I have made the choice to, rather than provide an empirical case study of the practices of current digital historians, combine a description of some of the current practices within historical research with a larger conceptualisation of what I and other digital historians have identified as some of the central methodological elements of the new digital history.

The reason for this is that I consider it to be crucial for current and future digital historians to analyse and think reflectively about their new emergent historical practices. We need empirical descriptions of current historical practice, but we need critical reflections and conceptualisations even more. As a conceptually minded historian, it is crucial for me to have conceptual tools that helps us better see and better understand. In this, I am inspired by Joseph Schumpeter's statement on the foundation of historical analysis:

> Analytic effort starts when we have conceived our vision of the set of phenomena that caught our interest, no matter whether this set lies in virgin soil or in land that had been cultivated before. The first task is to verbalize the vision or to conceptualize it in such a way that its elements take their places, with names attached to them that facilitate recognition and manipulation, in a more or less orderly schema or picture.[6]

Thus, the central task of this chapter is to attempt to conceptualise and attach names to some of the central elements of the new emerging digital history practices so that we can start our analytic efforts to better understand the new emerging digital history.

Paradigmatic Change in Sciences, History of Science and Historical Sciences

There are especially two main areas of Thomas Kuhn's research on scientific revolutions that are of relevance to understanding the current changes within digital history. The first is Kuhn's research on what he described as 'the second Scientific Revolution' of the 19th century and on the historical impact of quantification of earlier qualitative research fields. Quantification, Kuhn argued, was central for understanding the historical development of scientific research and, in 1961, in an article published just before *Structure of scientific revolutions* and at the same time as the historical sciences were entering their first quantitative 'Cliometric Revolution', Kuhn investigated 'the effects of introducing quantitative methods into sciences that had previously proceeded without major assistance from them'.[7] Kuhn starts his article describing how the Social Science Research Building at the University of Chicago on its facade

> bears Lord Kelvin's famous dictum: 'If you cannot measure, your knowledge is meager and unsatisfactory.' Would that statement be there if it had been written, not by a physicist, but by a sociologist, political scientist, or economist? Or again, would terms like 'meter reading' and 'yardstick' recur so frequently in contemporary discussions of epistemology and scientific method were it not for the prestige of modern physical science and the fact that measurement so obviously bulks large in its research?[8]

In his article Kuhn studies how the physical sciences achieved this exemplary and aspirational character for other sciences to follow, something which still is very much with us in the current debate on digital humanities and digital history. The reason for physics' status as the contemporary model science, Kuhn posited, could be understood as coming from that

> physicists, as a group, have displayed since about 1840 a greater ability to concentrate their attention on a few key areas of research than have their colleagues in less completely quantified fields. In the same period, if I am right, physicists would prove to have been more successful than most other scientists in decreasing the length of controversies about scientific theories and in increasing the strength of the consensus that emerged from such controversies. In short, I believe that the nineteenth-century mathematization of physical science produced vastly refined professional criteria for problem selection and that it simultaneously very much increased the effectiveness of professional verification procedures.[9]

And the reason for this in its turn came from how the physical sciences "came to make use of quantitative techniques at all'.[10] Perhaps surprisingly to some, then and now, the physical sciences had not always been based on measurements and mathematics. Some parts of physics, what Kuhn described as the 'traditional sciences' in the form of astronomy, optics and mechanics, had developed considerably quantitatively before the first scientific revolution, while the relatively new 'Baconian sciences', 'the study of heat, of electricity, of magnetism, and of chemistry', had not been a systematic field of inquiry previously, but 'owed their status *as sciences* to the seventeenth century's characteristic insistence upon experimentation and upon the compilation of natural histories, including histories of the crafts'.[11] Their quantification and a wider and more thorough mathematisation of physics overall took place during the first half of the 19th century and was accompanied by a number of new instruments, conceptualisations, theories and institutionalisations, which was part of what Kuhn described as a second scientific revolution of the sciences. The larger question in focus of this chapter is whether the historical sciences is currently in such a Kuhnian moment.

The second relevant area of Kuhn's research is his more widely known general theory of scientific change that was first presented in *Structure of scientific revolutions* (1962) and that he continued to revise and refine for the remainder of his career. Kuhn's theory uses the history of scientific development especially during the first scientific revolution from the 15th to the 17th centuries to design a theory that outlines how a traditional or 'normal science' through a scientific revolution transforms into a new science, a radically different paradigm of knowledge practice. In this perspective, the response of a scientific community to 'crisis' in the form of a major epistemological disruption usually follows either of two main paths, what can be described as the reintegration and domestication of the new disruption as part of the existing framework of traditional 'normal' science, or the revolutionary transformation of the traditional science into a new science.

Kuhn's theory of scientific revolutions has been important in not just helping historians of science conceptualise changes within the natural sciences, but also in helping historians in general to better understand change within their respective domains. It is difficult to exactly translate Kuhn's terminology to other areas and as I. Bernard Cohen points out, there are many problems with using Kuhn, such as that 'historians and philosophers of science do not agree on what constitutes or defines a revolution in science; they do not have an objective test for the occurrence of such a revolution', and that 'there are certain kinds of revolutions in science that do not exactly fit Kuhn's schema'.[12] Nevertheless, despite these obstacles, several historians have used Kuhn's conceptualisations to understand change also within historical disciplines. As David Hollinger has pointed out, 'Kuhn's terms have been employed explicitly by historians of art, religion, political organization, social thought, and American foreign policy'.[13] Those historians also include Thomas Kuhn himself, as is clear from his remark on an upcoming academic discussion of Martin Bernal's 'Black Athena' theory of ancient history, when he stated that it 'was being held far too soon and that disciplines did not usually respond so quickly to fundamental challenges'.[14]

Aware of these problems, I use Kuhnian terminologies as ideal types (in a Weberian sense) to help me conceptualise the recent past, present and future developments within digital historical practice and to outline two major responses to the challenges of the new computational digital history, as well as sketch a possible methodological middle way navigating between the two. This is an extension of previous research of mine where I, as a part of an empirical digital history study, identified and outlined what I saw as the major methodological strands within current digital history research. Following Kuhn, I have described the two main ideal type responses towards the new disruptive digital methodologies as them either being domesticated and naturalised as part of traditional history, what Kuhn would describe as 'normal science', which I have termed *digital history 1.0*, or taking the second more revolutionary route in the form of a paradigmatic *digital history 2.0*, radically transforming and disciplining the practice of historical research.[15] However, as an alternative to these two main routes of conservation or revolution, I also outline a potential third 'middle way' between the 'normal' practice of historical science and a potentially 'paradigmatic' digital history. The overarching question is whether the new digital historians will want to transform, and succeed in transforming, the historical discipline overall, to break off and form a new historical discipline, or whether they prefer to remain part of history's 'disciplinary mosaic'.[16]

Our Invisible Digital History

The digital has already changed historians' practice so that today 'all historians are already digital' whether or not they 'self-identify as digital historians',[17] although perhaps in ways invisible to or at least not reflected upon by most historians. History is already changed through historians' everyday use of digital tools and materials, something which can roughly be divided into the production, communication, presentation and administration of historical research.[18] The following description might to some appear trivial, banal or mundane, but that should not diminish its importance; on the contrary, this ordinariness makes it even more important for understanding the wider impact of the digital on the historians' craft.

The first and most important influence of digitisation is on historians' production. Like other office workers, the overwhelming majority of historians have since the 1980s been relying on digital computers as their foremost research tool. Most importantly, computers are used for writing and note-taking and since at least the 1990s also for organising and storing primary and secondary digital source materials, often in such portable digital document formats as photographed, scanned or born-digital images of archival documents, texts, photographs, artifacts, journal articles and books. The existence on most historians' computers of hundreds or thousands of files with names ending in suffixes such as .doc, .pdf, .xls and .jpg provides ample material evidence of the impact on historians' practice from reading, watching, manipulating and writing of digital materials.

Digitisation's second major impact is on how we historians communicate with institutions and individuals that provide access to source materials for our research, such as archives and libraries, as well as with other historians and non-historical researchers within our research fields. Since the 1990s, emails, mobile and smart phones, text messaging and social media has afforded historians ever faster and wider communication possibilities. Third, the digital has impacted the historians' practice through making possible their research results to be communicated through new digital forms of representations. This is through presentations at academic conferences, seminars and talks, primarily through much easier and efficient use of digital images, figures and graphs, as well as the increased use of digital presentation software programs such as PowerPoint, Keynote and Prezi as well as online presentations and meeting using digital applications such as Skype and Zoom. In addition, preliminary and finished research is routinely presented in the form of digital documents to colleagues, conferences and publishers, as conference and seminar papers, manuscripts, preprints and offprints of articles, chapters and books. The final way in which historians' research practice has been impacted is with regard to its practical organisation and administration, through the various ways in which the digital tools and formats described above, together with the internet, have changed the possibilities for conducting research more effectively and (mostly if not always) with less costs in time and money. This includes all the ways in which we use the internet and especially search engines, such as Google, Bing and Baidu, to gather practical information about locations, access and opening hours for archives, libraries and museums, as well as conducting practical matters such as booking travel and buying books, source materials and artifacts through services such as Amazon, eBay and Alibaba, and registering and paying online for conferences or memberships in professional organisations.

This normal everyday digital impact on the historian's craft is most often invisible. The hidden digital tools and computational algorithms built into these various applications enabling our research are probably not much reflected upon by most historians, but these concealed tools have enhanced traditional history by making it faster, easier and cheaper in money as well as in time and energy. However, there are also other domesticated forms of digital methods and tools that in more conscious, reflective and visible ways have influenced historians' practice, something which I describe as digital history 1.0.

Domesticated Normal Science: Digital History 1.0

By conceptualising various aspects of historians' practice as 'digital history 1.0', I mean to accentuate that already today many historians, in addition to the invisible application of digital tools discussed above, have intentionally although often without much apparent thought appropriated digital methodologies as a part of their standard historical research practice. Digital history 1.0 includes how historians have integrated the use of digitally enhanced tools and materials as a part of their normal research practice, such as digital databases and resources such as Google, Wikipedia and JSTOR for digitally augmenting their historical research.[19] Such historians might, however, not see themselves as doing 'digital' history, but just 'history', as these digital applications have often been domesticated and seamlessly incorporated into 'normal history'. This digital ignorance or blindness is a returning complaint of digital historians, with statements such that 'the average historian is at most a passive user of digitised sources in which he/she mostly sees a substitute for the material original' and 'carrying out fairly traditional research as if the [digital] resource was not there (but hopefully citing it nevertheless)'.[20]

In the vocabulary of the historian and philosopher of science Thomas Kuhn these historians have augmented their 'normal science'—'history'—of historical research with the use of various forms of digital sources, tools and methods. By normal science, Kuhn means the established and dominant scientific tradition of conducting research existing within a scientific discipline which 'often suppresses fundamental novelties because they are necessarily subversive of its basic commitments'.[21] The ignorant attitude among normal historians referred to above can be seen as exemplifying this. Another example is when one digital historian complains about traditional historians' blindness to how the digital has changed the historians' practice, how most historians today 'combine traditional/analogue and new/digital practices, at least in the information gathering stage of their research'. However, 'reflection is often missing. On more than one occasion I have heard historians proclaim to be non-digital, as if this were something of which to be proud, while evidently making use of digital resources in their research.'[22] Yet another digital historian describes 'a degree of condescension and suspicion towards digital resources from many mainstream historians'.[23] These examples could easily be multiplied.

And still, digital history 1.0 has already visibly changed historians' practice: first, by increasing the number of citations and the diversity of primary sources used, as well as a disproportionate use of citations to online sources.[24] One example is from Canada, the first country to have two of its major newspapers the *Toronto Star* and the *Globe and Mail* digitised in 2002. Research on history doctoral dissertations uploaded to the ProQuest database between 1997 and 2010 showed a 991% increase in citations to the *Toronto Star* after it had been digitised, 'as opposed to minor increases and even decreases for other newspapers'.[25] Connected to this, digitisation has also changed how historians think of their *archives*. Traditionally, for most historians, an emblem of becoming a 'real' historian and marking something of a rite of passage is to carry out research in a physical archive located in a particular (often remote) place where you sit and go through dusty and perhaps previously unread pages of primary sources in the form of paper documents such as letters, minutes, reports, etc. In the digital age, these traditional archives are often supplemented or surpassed by online document archives that you can access from your office chair at your home institution. But even when the historians do visit physical archives, their practice has been changed by the digital in that 'analytical work is displaced from the archives'. This is also due to new digital tools, as the

> use of digitized finding aids, digitized collections, and digital cameras [that] have altered the way that historians interact with primary sources.

> While the centrality of archives to the research process remains, the nature of interactions with archival materials has changed dramatically over time; for many researchers, activities in the archives have become more photographic and less analytical.[26]

By changing the possibilities of access to distanced primary materials, the new digital resources have transformed history.

One striking example of how the digital history practices can be transformative while almost methodologically invisible comes from the research by historians Sönke Neitzel and Harald Welzer on the politics and world view of German Second World War soldiers that was based on a previously unused source material in British and American archives in the form of several hundred thousand pages of transcripts of interrogations with German POWs. This groundbreaking in-depth research on this 'mind-boggling amount of material' was only made possible through the use of digital methodologies and was described in the following way in their monograph *Soldaten*: 'We were able to digitize all of the British documents and most of the American material and sort through it with the help of content-recognition software.'[27] This is all that is said. No further words on their digital research methodology such as what software, search methods or keywords that were used. The choices made and opportunities created by the digital tools have been made almost totally invisible.

It appears that Toni Weller is correct in stating that 'for most historians, the challenges of the digital age are not ones that are seen to directly concern their research' and that the suggestion by an author commenting on the tenure, promotion and review process 'that "learning to use a database, scan materials, and query that database all consume time that could be used to write" is probably a reasonably accurate reflection of the way the majority of historians perceive digital scholarship'.[28] However, there are those historians where the digital is a primary methodological focus in their research practice and who are practising a more radical form of 'digital history 2.0'.

Revolutionary Paradigmatic Science: Digital History 2.0

Some digital historians appear to see digitisation's 'profound transformation' of history as inevitable, in that they state that as 'datasets expand into the realm of the big, computational analysis ceases to be "nice to have" and becomes a simple requirement'.[29] This new paradigmatic digital history practice 'offers a stark contrast to what has become standard historical practice'.[30] The current revolutionary enthusiasm is in some ways reminiscent of digital history's first wave in the 1970s when 'it looked like history might move wholesale into quantitative histories, with the widespread application of math and statistics to the understanding of the past' and resonate with the past 'hyperbole that saw computational history as making more substantial "truth" claims, or the invocation of a "scientific method" of history'.[31] The question is whether also the current putative computational revolution will live up to the high hopes and hypes or if it also will wane to become just another small specialised sub-discipline of the historical discipline or that it perhaps will abandon history and emigrate, like many of the first generation of digital historians who left the humanities for the social sciences and its new, more quantitatively inclined sub-disciplines, such as social and economic history.

The question is whether this new potentially revolutionary historical paradigm can be described, in Thomas Kuhn's words, as the outcome of a scientific revolution 'from which a new tradition of normal science can emerge'.[32] Kuhn described 'what all scientific revolutions are about' in that they

> produced a consequent shift in the problems available for scientific scrutiny and in the standards by which the profession determined what should count as an admissible problem or as a legitimate problem-solution. And each transformed the scientific imagination in ways that we shall ultimately need to describe as a transformation of the world within which scientific work was done.[33]

After a paradigm shift, it is not just what is valued as good research that has shifted, but the discipline's core elements are transformed and the field is reconstructed 'from new fundamentals, a reconstruction that changes some of the field's most elementary theoretical generalizations as well as many of its paradigm methods and applications'.[34] What is accomplished in this is the transformation of the 'disciplinary matrix'—what is considered as the relevant and central methods, significant data, instruments, theory, methods, concepts and working practices. Below, some of the major elements of the possible disciplinary matrix of digital history 2.0 will be outlined.

Digital history 2.0 is taken to represent research practices with a potential to form a new digital historical paradigm primarily focused on new quantitative and computational methods to undertake text analysis and manipulations and visualisations of historical data. Its research systematically use various digital applications and quantitative methodologies for big-data text and data mining, calculations and visualisations, such as topic modelling, network analysis and text and data scraping. Most of these methods necessitate investments in acquiring expertise in or collaborators skilled in coding and database methodologies.

Like with paradigm change within the sciences, the new digital history practice transforms the existing practice by introducing new focus and altering what is valued, making some of the existing ideals and standards less relevant or obsolete in favour of new values and concepts salient to the particular characteristics of the new history. One such new key aspect of the digital history 2.0 can be described as *compression*, which characterises methods that allow the historian 'to begin with the complex and winnow it down until a narrative emerges from the cacophony of evidence'.[35] This is in contrast to 'normal history' where historians, 'like good detectives, test their merit through *expansion*: the ability to extract complex knowledge from the smallest crumbs of evidence, that history has left behind. By tracing the trail of these breadcrumbs, a historian might weave together a narrative of the past.'[36] Some historians even question whether the digital turn will so much change history's foundational concepts to 'render the word "narrative" too confining for describing what historians produce' and to make *historiographies* into a 'more encompassing term'.[37]

Normal historians prefer to describe the empirical foundations of their conclusions in terms of documents, sources and at times even 'facts', while the new digital historians often prefer to talk about 'data'. Jim Mussell describes perhaps *the* core aspect of the new digital history just in that it 'requires a change in focus from document to data'.[38] Data as information, in forms that are able to be processed by computers, is central to the new digital history, qualitatively as well as quantitatively. Its qualitative effect is the view favouring 'data' to signify what counts as the preferred and proper basis for constructing a historical argument. The quantitative impact lies in that the new digital texts provide copious and often very easily accessible source materials for historians. In 2008, a senior digital historian stated with special reference to the recently started digitisation efforts by Google Books, online digital image collections and the creation of digital newspaper archives that it was 'now quite clear that historians will have to grapple with abundance, not scarcity' and that 'nearly every day we are confronted with a new digital historical resource of almost unimaginable size'.[39] In that sense, history could be seen as having entered the era of *big data* or perhaps better 'biggish data'.[40] How much data it takes to makes it 'big' has been described as 'in the eye of the beholder', in that if 'there are more data than you could conceivably read yourself in a reasonable amount of time, or that require computational intervention to make sense of them, it's big enough!'[41] One example of such big data for historians are the online Old Bailey records (*www.oldbaileyonline.org*), which consist of almost 200,000 criminal trials between 1674 and 1913 and 127 million words.[42]

The rise of online archival research and the loss of the manual physical handling of original primary sources is one example of how the material practice of the historian is changing in the digital era. Another example of a radically new social dimension consists of *multidisciplinary teamwork*. This might be one of the most challenging aspects of the new history to many traditional historians. Although many examples exist of co-authored works in history, it is still far from the norm, and when it does occur it is rarely with collaborators from outside historical disciplines. Another changing practice is a shift to totally new activities in that 'less than 5% of the time spent on a project will be time spent analyzing and visualizing data', with the majority 'spent on collecting, cleaning, and interpreting'.[43] Another aspect of the changing historical practice is new digital forms of *publications* as the traditional paper forms of historical publications are not seen as 'suited to the fast-changing discourses of the digital age—demonstrated by the fact that most pure digital history texts tend to be in the form of websites, blogs and online articles and journals rather than the traditional historical outlet of the monograph'.[44] Such new digital forms of publications also make possible new dynamic and interactive forms of presentations with inclusion of digital sound and video files, as well as scalable images, maps and network graphs.

To conclude this discussion of the changing practice of the new digital history practice, I will quote the two computer scientists behind the Culturomics project who also helped to develop the Google Ngram Viewer and when criticised for not having included any historians in their project explained it thus:

> Even when we found historians who shared our enthusiasm, there were still great barriers to working together. For instance, [a meeting was convened with] about a dozen interested history students and faculty. The historians who came to the meeting were intelligent, kind, and encouraging. But they didn't seem to have a good sense of how to wield quantitative data to answer questions, didn't have relevant computational skills, and didn't seem to have the time to dedicate to a big multi-author collaboration. It's not their fault: these things don't appear to be taught or encouraged in history departments right now.[45]

In short, history had failed in being willing to work like computer science.

Semi-Automatic History: Digital History 1.5

Some digital historians propose a less radical transformation than that promised by digital history 2.0, where 'historians do not need to learn new technologies or computer codes; they do not need to become computer scientists'. They disagree with those advocating a revolutionary transformation of the historical practice and argue that a part of 'the problem thus far has been too much emphasis on historians becoming something they are not; to the detriment of the fundamental skills and expertise that is the craft of the historian'.[46] The real challenge lies, such historians argue, 'in persuading the vast majority of historians of the benefit of even relatively simple information technology, not in developing specialist historical tools and methods that would only ever be of relevance to a minority of historians'.[47] Some like Gerben Zaagsma want to go somewhat further and consider that the 'real challenge is to be consciously hybrid and to integrate "traditional" and "digital" approaches in a new practice of doing history'.[48] 'Digital history 1.5' aligns itself with such views and can be described as an acknowledged and reflective digital history 'without the programming' that consist of the use of semi-automatic historical methodologies in between normalised 'digital history 1.0' and paradigmatic 'digital history 2.0' research methods.[49]

Digital history 1.5 is a hybrid or mixed methodology in that it is a combination of quantitative and qualitative historical research methodologies, and semi-automatic as it combines a large amount of manual evaluation with the systematic use of automatic analysis vested in pre-programmed offline and online calculation and visualisation applications and tools using digital text and databases, such as Google Books, Early English Books Online (EEBO) and digitised historical newspaper archives. That this digital history is without programming is of course not absolutely true in that it does use digital applications based on a lot of computer code and many mathematical algorithms, but this coding and programming is invisible as it is pre-packaged in the various applications and tools: it is 'black-boxed' to the historian user.[50]

What differentiates digital history 1.5 from digital history 1.0 is that it consists of a systematic use of digital tools and sources where the digital methodology is the central method enabling the investigation. Furthermore, it incorporates a conscious reflexivity about the digital sources, resources and methods used in the investigation and is being reflective about its respective strengths and weaknesses. At the same time, it is not 'digital history 2.0' in that in its investigation it is using pre-programmed applications and resources without any additional coding of software, advanced programming of applications or tuning of digital techniques and methodologies. Some specific digital history 1.5 methodologies are semi-automatic text extraction and presentation, which combine quantitative computer-enabled 'distant reading' of big data digital text corpora and qualitative 'close reading' of extracted individual texts.[51] This takes the use of semi-automatically extracted and processed databases where the individual texts can be newspaper and journal articles that could be collected using various online search interfaces such as those that exist at various online newspaper and journal archives.

To conclude this treatment of the hybrid practice of digital history 1.5, two of its central methodological elements will be conceptualised. This is inspired by Ted Underwood's article 'Theorizing research practices we forgot to theorize twenty years ago', which argues the need for digital humanists to 'think more rigorously and deliberately about existing practices'.[52] The first central element is its key technology, as well as a central engine of the potential digital history revolution, in the form of the *search engine*. One problem with talking about 'search' for digital historians is that it is, as Underwood states, 'a deceptively modest name for a complex technology that has come to play an evidentiary role in scholarship'.[53] By 'search' is meant the algorithmic mining of large electronic databases that since the 1990s has been used by humanists. Furthermore, the term 'search' only points to its use as a finding tool and leaves out its wider methodological implications and—echoing digital historians' criticism of traditional historians' negligence of their digital tools as discussed above—that the 'scholarly consequences of search practices are difficult to assess, since scholars tend to suppress description of their own discovery process in published work'.[54] Therefore, as a way of contributing to digital history's conceptual development and to make the existing digital history methodologies more explicit and reflective, I have elsewhere described and named an already existing quali-quantitative digital history methodology. I thus proposed the term *readsearch* for the methodology of using online keyword searches as being 'a new hybrid concept denoting a quali-quantitative methodology combining targeted close manual and machine distant reading through the use of search engines on large digital text corpora'.[55]

Furthermore, I have attempted to further explicate the various forms of readsearch methodologies and problematise the use of search for research. Taking inspiration from Underwood, who explains that 'a full-text search is often a Boolean fishing expedition for a set of documents that may or may not exist',[56] and in line with this I differentiate between different readsearch methodologies by categorising them into three main forms: *spearfishing*, *angle* and *trawl readsearch*. 'Spearfishing readsearch' designates a form of search consisting of browsing through a large text corpora close to what can be described as 'online microfilm browsing', in that the search interface is using various keywords or dates to focus the search, but at the same time allow the reader to immerse him- or herself in the text until he or she comes across any relevant findings. When using 'angle readsearch', the researcher searches for texts referring to one specific unique event, person or place and thus like an angler adapts the angles (the search terms) to tailor them for best catching a particular fish (an event or entity). Finally, in the use of 'trawl readsearch', the search is used to find many hits of a general term, word or phenomena and this is the form of readsearch where the distant machine reading plays the largest part. Like when fishing using a trawl, this is a combination of machine and manual reading. After a large fishing trawler makes a catch in its trawl, it hoists it up and empties the catch onto the vessel and then manually goes through the catch to sort out and 'throw back' the unwanted catch: fish of the wrong species or too small to matter, as well as garbage caught up in the trawl. Similarly, the texts found through a search's machine reading is in a trawl readsearch examined manually to sort out the valuable and searched-for texts. This is a methodology especially used when tracing the change of a concept or a term over time. Some readers might find these methodological neologisms as too idiosyncratic to be meaningful and whether digital historians in the future will follow in adapting the specific readsearch terminologies is of less importance. What is crucial for them to follow, however, is in reflecting on their digital epistemology, what their use of digital methods does to the historical knowledge being produced and to explicitly conceptualise and theorise their practice as historians using digital tools and resources.

The second main element of digital history 1.5 connects to historian Andreas Fickers' claims that as a response to the salience of the new digital sources, the discipline of history needs 'a new digital historicism'. This historicism should be 'characterized by collaboration between archivists, computer scientists, historians and the public, with the aim of developing tools for a new digital source criticism'.[57] Along with many digital historians, I would add to this the need for a *digital resource criticism* that extends historians' critical faculties to the digital resources they use, such as the search engines, algorithms, programs and applications. Overall, a digital historian 'requires a more advanced understanding of the affordances of the digital in order to perform more advanced research'.[58] Historians, like most users of digital technologies, use technology 'without reflection, without understanding how it *actually* works' and thus need to develop a new digital reflexivity. Like historians are trained to consider and look for the contextual and authorial biases of our historical sources we need to think about 'the worldviews built into our tools',[59] as too often we tend to forget 'that our digital helpers are full of "theory" and "judgement" already. As with any methodology, they rely on sets of assumptions, models, and strategies. Theory is already at work on the most basic level when it comes to defining units of analysis, algorithms, and visualization procedures.'[60] In doing this, the traditional skills of historians

> are still necessary, but the focus on practice—on doing things with data—extends their application, forcing a recognition of the constructed nature of evidence and its relation to the absent past. Necessarily speculative, the historian must bring his or her expertise to bear on these digital environments and evaluate the plausibility of what they both embody and imply.[61]

When we historians start 'to think digitally', we can gain a better understanding of the underlying mechanisms, algorithms, programmed omissions and choices of our digital tools and allow the historian 'to be a better critic, a better consumer of digital data, a better user',[62] and thus a better historian.

Conclusions: Business as Usual or Going Fully Digital?

This chapter has in many ways gone against historians' normal practice. Instead of trying to see the patterns and causes of past events after the dust has settled it has tried to discern the contours of emerging phenomena and to conjecture about possible future outcomes. This it has done to try to better understand which way or ways history will take in our ever increasing digital age. Will it be the old-trodden one or a new and radically different path? This has been a necessarily speculative exposition of three routes for digital historians that could be summarised as unreflective normalisation, paradigmatic transformation and reflective appropriation. In this, it has tried to point to the third middle way as a wider route for historians who are neither satisfied with just continuing with their historical 'business as usual' by staying agnostic about its already existing digital methodological dimensions nor prepared to join the specialised minority of historians who will go 'fully digital' by learning to code or enter into collaborations with computer and information scientists. In this, I align myself with previous digital historians, such as Toni Weller, who have argued that 'part of the "them and us" problem thus far has been too much emphasis on historians becoming something they are not; to the detriment of the fundamental skills and expertise that is the craft of the historian.'[63]

To conclude, let us return to Thomas Kuhn and take some solace from his statements 'that there can be small revolutions as well as large ones, that some revolutions affect only the members of a professional subspecialty'[64] and on rare occasions 'two paradigms can coexist peacefully'.[65] Furthermore, history teaches us that revolutions, scientific as well as political, always come at a cost and bring losses as well as benefits, such as in

> the transition from an earlier to a later theory, there is very often a loss as well as a gain of explanatory power. Newton's theory of planetary and projectile motion was fought vehemently for more than a generation because, unlike its main competitors, it demanded the [conceptual] introduction of an inexplicable force that acted directly upon bodies at a distance. Cartesian theory, for example, had attempted to explain gravity [mechanically] in terms of the direct collisions between elementary particles. To accept Newton meant to abandon the possibility of any such explanation.[66]

However, although the new ways of understanding the world were triumphant, 'the price of victory was the abandonment of an old and partly achieved goal. For eighteenth-century Newtonians it gradually became "unscientific" to ask for the cause of gravity.'[67] The task ahead for us historians is to make sure that, whoever will succeed in shaping the apparently inevitable further digitisation of the historical discipline, into a domesticated or revolutionary historical practice or something in between, that history's rewards outweigh its losses.

Notes

1 Graham et al. 2015: 35.
2 Weller 2013b: 1; Graham et al. 2015: 35. William Cronon in 2012 as President of the American Historical Association said that he 'increasingly believe[s] that the digital revolution is yielding transformations so profound that their nearest parallel is to Gutenberg's invention of moveable type' (see Cronon 2012).
3 Weller 2013a: 195.
4 Zaagsma 2013: 24; Weller 2013a: 195.
5 Fridlund 2017; Fridlund & La Mela 2019.
6 Schumpeter 1954: 42.
7 Kuhn 1961: 162.
8 Ibid.: 161.
9 Ibid.: 190.
10 Ibid.: 185.

[11] Ibid.: 186, emphasis in the original.
[12] Cohen 1987: 24, 31.
[13] Hollinger 1989: 108.
[14] Bernal 1991: xix.
[15] My distinction between digital history 1.0 and 2.0 is similar to but more general than that of Jim Mussell, who primarily discusses changing digital history practice in relation to the digitisation of source materials. See Mussell 2013: 80–91.
[16] Graham et al. 2015: 4.
[17] Ibid.: xvii.
[18] This description focuses on the historian as a researcher and does not include changes to the historian's practice as a teacher, administrator or public historian.
[19] Besides using 'invisible' domesticated digital tools such as word processing, email, search engines and electronic articles, pictures and documents in their normal professional research practice.
[20] Zaagsma 2013: 18; Mussell 2013: 90.
[21] Kuhn 1970: 5.
[22] Zaagsma 2013: 17.
[23] Weller 2013b: 4.
[24] Bilansky 2017: 517.
[25] Graham et al. 2015: 48.
[26] Rutner & Schonfeld 2014: 8.
[27] Neitzel & Welzer 2012: ix–x.
[28] Weller 2013b: 3.
[29] Graham et al. 2015: 4.
[30] Ibid.: 1.
[31] Ibid.: 23.
[32] Kuhn 1970: 84.
[33] Ibid.: 6–7.
[34] Ibid.: 85.
[35] Graham et al. 2015: 2.
[36] Ibid.: 1, emphasis added.
[37] Ibid.: 32.
[38] Mussell 2013: 81.
[39] Daniel J. Cohen in Cohen et al. 2008: 455. Cohen was echoing and answering the question posed in 2003 by his digital history predecessor Roy Rosenzweig in an article entitled 'Scarcity or abundance?'.
[40] Graham et al. 2015: 264.
[41] Ibid.: 3.
[42] Hitchcock et al. 2012.
[43] Graham et al. 2015: 235.
[44] Weller 2013b: 4.
[45] Aiden & Michel 2011.

[46] Weller 2013b: 1.
[47] Anderson 2008.
[48] Zaagsma 2013: 17.
[49] My designation of digital history 1.5 and 2.0 is close to what Zaagsma describes as 'plain IT' and 'enhanced IT' respectively (see Zaagsma 2013: 12).
[50] Fridlund 2017; Fridlund & La Mela 2019: 12.
[51] Moretti 2000; Moretti 2005; Moretti 2013.
[52] Underwood 2014: 64.
[53] Ibid.
[54] Ibid.: 65.
[55] Fridlund & La Mela 2019: 13. This is similar to 'critical search' as described by Jo Guldi (see Guldi 2018).
[56] Underwood 2014: 64.
[57] Fickers 2012: 26.
[58] Mussell 2013: 91.
[59] Graham et al. 2015: 54.
[60] Rieder & Röhle 2012: 70.
[61] Mussell 2013: 91.
[62] Graham et al. 2015: 267.
[63] Weller 2013a: 195.
[64] Kuhn 1970: 49.
[65] Ibid.: xi.
[66] Kuhn 1961: 184.
[67] Ibid.

References

Aiden, E. L., & Michel, J.-B. (2011). Thoughts/clarifications on Grafton's 'Loneliness and Freedom'. *Culturomics*. Retrieved from http://www.culturomics.org/Resources/faq/thoughts-clarifications-on-grafton-s-loneliness-and-freedom

Anderson, I. (2008). History and computing. Blog *Making history: the changing face of the profession in Britain*. Retrieved from http://www.history.ac.uk/makinghistory/resources/articles/ history_and_computing.html

Bernal, M. (1991). *Black Athena: Afroasiatic roots of classical civilization*, Vol. II: *The archaeological and documentary evidence*. New Brunswick, NJ: Rutgers University Press.

Bilansky, A. (2017). Search, reading, and the rise of database. *Digital Scholarship in the Humanities, 32*, 511–527.

Cohen, I. B. (1987). Scientific revolutions, revolutions in science, and a probabilistic revolution 1800–1930. In L. Krüger, L. J. Daston, & M. Heidelberger (Eds.), *The probabilistic revolution*, Vol. 1: *Ideas in History*. Cambridge, MA: MIT Press.

Cohen, D. J., Frisch, M., Gallagher, P., Mintz, S., Sword, K., Murrell Taylor, A. M., Thomas, III, W. G., & Turkel. W. J. (2008). Interchange: the promise of digital history. *Journal of American History, 95*, 452–491.

Cronon, W. (2012, 1 January). The public practice of history in and for a digital age. *Perspectives in History Online*. Retrieved from http://www.historians.org/publications-and-directories/perspectives-on-history/january-2012/the-public-practice-of-history-in-and-for-a-digital-age

Fickers, A. (2012). Towards a new digital historicism? Doing history in the age of abundance. *VIEW: Journal of European Television History and Culture, 1*, 19–26.

Fridlund, M. (2017, 18 May). *Digital History 1.5: Historical research between domesticated and paradigmatic digital methods*. Video fil]. Umeå: Hum Lab, Umeå University. Retrieved from https://web.archive.org/web/20200510185709/http://stream.humlab.umu.se/?streamName=digital_history_1_5

Fridlund, M., & La Mela, M. (2019). Between technological nostalgia and engineering imperialism: digital history readings of China in the Finnish technoindustrial public sphere 1880–1912. *Tekniikan Waiheita, 35*(1), 7–40.

Graham, S., Milligan, I., & Weingart, S. (2015). *Exploring big historical data: the historian's macroscope*. London: Imperial College Press.

Guldi, J. (2018). Critical search: a procedure for guided reading in large-scale textual corpora. *Journal of Cultural Analytics*. DOI: https://doi.org/10.22148/16.030

Hitchcock, T., Shoemaker R., Emsley, C., Howard, S., McLaughlin J., et al. (2012, 24 March). *The Old Bailey proceedings online, 1674–1913*. Version 7.0. Retrieved from http://www.oldbaileyonline.org

Hollinger, D. A. (1989). *In the American province: studies in the history and historiography of ideas*. Baltimore, MD: Johns Hopkins University Press.

Kuhn, T. S. (1961). The function of measurement in modern physical science. *Isis, 52*, 161–193.

Kuhn, T. S. (1970). *The structure of scientific revolutions*. 2nd edn. Chicago, IL and London: University of Chicago Press.

Moretti, F. (2000). Conjectures on world literature. *New Left Review* n.s. *1*(1), 54–68.

Moretti, F. (2005). *Graphs, maps, trees: abstract models for a literary history*. London: Verso.

Moretti, F. (2013). *Distant reading*. London and New York, NY: Verso Books.

Mussell, J. (2013). Doing and making: history as digital practice. In T. Weller (Ed.), *History in the digital age* (pp. 79–94). London and New York, NY: Routledge.

Neitzel, S., & Welzer, H. (2012). *Soldaten: on fighting, killing, and dying: the secret World War II tapes of German POWs*. New York, NY: Simon & Schuster.

Rieder, B., & Röhle, T. (2012). Digital methods: five challenges. In D. M. Berry (Ed.), *Understanding digital humanities* (pp. 67–85). Houndmills: Palgrave Macmillan.

Rutner, J., & Schonfeld, R. C. (2014). *Supporting the changing research practices of historians*. New York, NY: Ithaka S+R.

Schumpeter, J. A. (1954). *History of economic analysis*. Oxford: Oxford University Press.

Underwood, T. (2014). Theorizing research practices we forgot to theorize twenty years ago. *Representations, 127*, 64–72.

Weller, T. (2013a). Conclusion: a changing field. In T. Weller (Ed.), *History in the digital age* (pp. 195–205). London and New York, NY: Routledge.

Weller, T. (2013b). Introduction: history in the digital age. In T. Weller (Ed.), *History in the digital age* (pp. 1–19). London and New York, NY: Routledge.

Zaagsma, G. (2013). On digital history. *BMGN—Low Countries Historical Review, 128*(4), 3–29.

CHAPTER 5

Building Historical Knowledge Byte by Byte

Infrastructures and Data Management in Modern Scholarship

Jessica Parland-von Essen

Introduction

Historians are very good at source criticism, but in the digital era this requires good provenance data. Historians should also step up to the demand for transparency and open scholarship that comes with digital humanities. Research and knowledge has to be well documented and reliable. This means we need good data management, but also better and more integrated services and infrastructures.

Despite often exceptionally rich descriptive metadata in the cultural heritage sector, research life cycle data management is not easy and finding sources might be difficult due to questions of metadata formats or granularity of publication. The humanists' workflow and practices regarding use of sources is often hybrid and only partly digital.[1] In this chapter, I will analyse different digital data types and infrastructures from the point of view of a historian and discuss the needs of historical research and knowledge creation. Questions about data

How to cite this book chapter:
Parland-von Essen, J. (2020). Building historical knowledge byte by byte: Infrastructures and data management in modern scholarship. In M. Fridlund, M. Oiva, & P. Paju (Eds.), *Digital histories: Emergent approaches within the new digital history* (pp. 89–102). Helsinki: Helsinki University Press. https://doi.org/10.33134/HUP-5-5

management and information structures are important to solve, so that it is possible to formulate service needs and user stories for historical research data services. I will propose a model for planning research data management and data publication for historians. The chapter focuses on the Finnish research sector, but includes relevant international infrastructures and initiatives.

The Concept of FAIR Data

FAIR data was minted as a concept in an expert meeting among science data experts, and resulted in a seminal article on research data management published in 2016.[2] The concept, which was a more than needed completion to the Open Science, Open Access and Open Data rhetoric, won immediate approbation within the European Union and other data-aware stakeholders. It was obvious that open data or access was not by far enough to solve the issues with science reproducibility, let alone the efficiency goals of the Digital Single Market. Data cannot always be open and there were other, more technical hurdles, too. Data needed to better managed, and the money invested in research should not be wasted by sloppy planning. To make the most of our data, it has to be organised and taken well care of. Only then can we combine datasets and build digital knowledge by linking publications and data in sustainable and trustworthy ways.

In short, the FAIR principles state that data should be Findable, Accessible, Interoperable and Re-usable. It turns out that these fine words in practice result in very technical definitions. When going into details, we soon exceed the level most scholars in the humanities should have to be bothered with. We should simply have workflows and services that support these principles, but for that to happen, all stakeholders have to raise their awareness and understand what is necessary to accomplish regarding services and infrastructures.

Let's take a short look at the principles and how they could be translated into a relevant form for our purposes. F stands for *Findable*. What this actually means is machine-readable. The amount of data today is so immense that it is important that computers cannot only sort out data, but also act upon it and find what is really relevant. This means, for instance, not only that digitising text so that it is only in image form is not sufficient, but also that the content of text needs to be organised in more specific, semantic ways: it requires structured metadata and keywords, as well as common and persistent identifiers for concepts like persons or place names. Furthermore, the metadata has to be available for and utilised by different kinds of indexing and search tools.

A means *Accessible*. This, in practice, today means data that can be downloaded over the web, or at least the internet. Both machines and humans should be able to understand the information the data represents or contains, and it should not be transferred or changed in non-transparent or undocumented ways. I, as in *Interoperable*, is a tough one. It means you should be able to combine datasets and copy metadata smoothly, without losing any information.

This means you should comply with existing standards and formats. As research data management in many ways is in its infancy and the information systems are still largely insufficient or impractical, this is difficult. It is necessary to balance the needs of the research and serve the actual research use, which must be prioritised. Unfortunately, many researchers are inclined to think that their data is far more different and unique than it actually is or needs to be. Usually, it is possible to find *some* aspect of the data that somehow relates to something else, be it source, structure or some semantics of the content. As people tend to understand how much effort they have put into their own work and development, it is too easy to underestimate the value of other people's work. The *not invented here* syndrome[3] can easily trump real creative openings and slow down research. Particularly in the life sciences, there have been many important insights and tools developed (bioinformatics might be the oldest domain-specific field within research data management). We should copy as much and as fast as we can from other, successful domains.

R, which is *Re-usable* data, means that it has a functioning licence or rights statement, but also that it has been thoroughly documented so that another researcher, or the composer of the dataset in 10 years for that matter, can take a dataset and use it again. Often, researchers spend up to 80% of their time creating or cleaning their data.[4] Therefore, careless documentation can be considered an inexcusable waste of resources and time.

The utmost goal, besides efficiency, is of course trustworthy, high quality research. The digital environment has the unfortunate quality of being simultaneously dynamic and unreliable. Links, even in scientific publications, tend to break.[5] This phenomenon is called link rot. Similarly, the content behind the link might change in a devious, unnoticeable way, which is called content drift. To address this problem, one of the main building blocks of FAIR data are *persistent identifiers*. Above, I mentioned identifiers for different kinds of concepts, which makes it easy to trace and link information. Researchers might have their own identifiers in the form of an ORCID, which is personal, unique and resists changes in name form or affiliation, and makes it possible to differentiate people with the same or similar names. Correspondingly, the datasets and articles should have their own identifiers, a URN or a DOI, which makes citing clear and unambiguous. The point is then the persistence; namely, the sustainability of this identifier. This means that we need platforms and services that provide and manage them on a long-term basis. This has a direct connection to the importance of infrastructure, which I will address later in this text.

To a historian, it is obvious that one has to address problems of sustainability in the long-term perspective, as well as that the sources need to be well documented. Are there other means for evaluating the trustworthiness or suitability of the data for our needs? Or to ensure that the data are authentic and have maintained their integrity? We need to know who said what, where and when. *Simultaneously, we also need to accept that our own research outputs should meet these requirements.*

The example of citations, the ultimate goals and tests for the data, demonstrates well the problem of sustainability. We should ask ourselves how can I cite (link to) my (digital) source in a persistent and unambiguous way and how can someone else cite the data I have created? There are recommendations for this, but they are not obviously sufficient or easy to implement. The national Finnish guideline for citing research data offers principles for citing a dataset, but how to cite more dynamic resources and what to do[6] when the resource does not provide identifiers or possibilities to download or save (partial) snapshots? Or even if the researchers manage to download the needed data, where do they archive it conveniently? The questions of data management during research are inescapable for all these practical, technical reasons. However, data management is even more complex for historians, because of questions about personal data regulation, ethical issues and copyright.

The Historian's Data Life Cycle

In Finland, the government and major research funders have promptly adopted the Open Science ideology, and research data was included in the policies at an early state.[7] There has been quite extensive work done on a national level regarding services, formats and recommendations. In parallel, there has been an effort for interoperability and digital preservation within the cultural heritage sector. This has produced services like the search portal Finna.fi and the national preservation services.[8] These and their future development are of course both important from a historian's point of view. Still, the situation for research data is quite different, since research data does not come with a clear legislation, accountability and centuries-old tradition of long-term or even short-term management. Responsibilities are often unclear when it comes to both rights and costs. In the humanities, researchers are used to expecting free or subsidised services when it comes to sources and information management. On the other hand, the research outputs are clearly considered to be the property of the researcher, at least concerning copyright. The work within humanities is considered creative and personal and thus often falls under intellectual property rights legislation.

The problem is, of course, that ownership is not a simple concept when it comes to digital resources. There are many kinds of rights and responsibilities entailed in 'owning': who has the right to access, copy, use, give access, agree on use, alter or destroy a dataset? Who has the responsibility to keep the platforms running, create metadata, plan for migrations, manage access for the next decades and curate the metadata or data if errors are found? It sometimes seems that some believe that the researcher herself should have all the rights with no responsibilities, even after the research has ended. This obviously does not work. There has to be an agreement and a balance in responsibilities and rights management. The researcher might have to give up some of the control

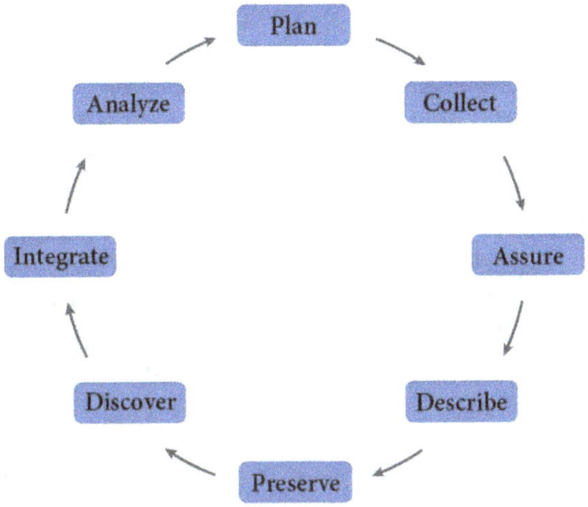

Figure 5.1: The DataONE data life cycle. Source: Author.

of her data in return for someone taking care of it. This calls for trust from both parties and concordance on common interest and explicit agreements. This is usually not a problem, but problems tend to arise from insufficient research data management planning. The agreeing would best be done in advance, preferably not by dictates from one party or the other, but by joint interests which should be easy to identify. Since the historian rarely makes up the data, but refines existing digital or non-digital data, there are usually concerns that need to be taken into account already when the data is created. Therefore, the data management life cycle always starts with planning.

There are different interpretations of the research data life cycle, but generally they tend to be variations of models that reflect the traditional way of understanding how the research process works in theory (see Figure 5.1). The idea is that there is always a project and one or several funders. Although often presented as a circular, never-ending process, one premise seems to be linear progression of the research process, as well as of science and knowledge building. This is, as any historian or other researcher knows, obviously a construct that nicely resonates with the way in which scientific publication traditionally works, with outputs that are corresponding, constructed narrations about the research process. The reality is much more chaotic and unorganised, which any data librarian will also willingly admit. The traditional publishing comprises snapshots, reports frozen in time, documenting what has been done, for dissemination and future reference. Still, these knowledge bytes are cumbersome, ambiguous and digitally discrete from the sources.

Thus, the single 'byte' of new knowledge has actually been quite open for future interpretation, often difficult to spot and point to. Even though the novelty might be a new interpretation or insight, there might also be included other new information or 'factoids', all of which become buried within an extensive narration impenetrable for computers. Much of the information now being digital, there might be an opportunity to critically assess how we communicate our knowledge and are open to transformation within scientific publishing. Often, digitisation has meant diversification as well as convergence.[9] When we now bring data into the world of publication, there are immense possibilities for opening the whole process, enhancing documentation and sharing knowledge in new ways.

The historian has to decide upon how many of the sources can or should be linked to, in other words how many should be digitised, if the sources aren't digital and how digitisation should be achieved. Or perhaps the links are all external, linking to existing trustworthy digital sources? Data collection and creation is more complex in digital humanities than in traditional humanities research, since questions of documenting provenance and deciding on data and metadata formats will affect the research in profound ways. There are some cases where established standards exist, like TEI (xml format by the Text Encoding Initiative) for encoding text. But TEI in itself will not solve problems of interoperability on a deeper semantic level. It would, for instance, always be advisable to use good external references as identifiers for all concepts whenever possible. Also, the plan for publication might set limits to what the researchers should do, since the platform they choose might have some bearing on the formats, metadata and granularity of the publication. If the researchers use other people's digital resources (OPEDAS or Other People's Existing Data and Services, as named by a leading FAIR data expert Barend Mons[10]), they obviously need to find out extensive information about them, not only the technical and historical provenance, but also about how the data is structured and coded. Often, a historian uses OPEDAS created not by researchers, but by heritage institutions. As the use context changes, the data provider institutions generally do not have readymade generic solutions for managing and publishing research data, especially when it is produced by outsiders.

One of the unfortunate traits of the traditional data life cycle model is that publication turns up as a distinct step in a specific and late stage of the process. This hides the fact that the most efficient and impactful way of doing research might be doing it transparently *all the way*. Since this both forces the researcher to implement some type of data management and opens up for collaboration and spotting quality issues at early stages, this can accelerate the work and enhance the quality of the research. After publishing raw versions of data, unforeseen help can turn up, when colleagues become aware of what the researcher is doing. Close collaborations have not always been an option in historical research, which carries the heavy burden of romantic lonely genius syndrome, but luckily times are changing. Stealing other people's ideas and data is not the first thing most researchers think of. Rather, by publishing raw data, the researchers can get their work registered at an early stage, instead of waiting for the final peer review. Better collaborating and coordinating than working in silence.

Version control is the next crucial aspect of the data cycle. If you ask an archivist, they would probably want to save every version of everything. Even worse, this might mean not just saving the information you need to recreate the needed version of a dataset, but saving complete copies of each version, independent of all redundancy that would create. Version control is generally not that well developed in traditional archives. However, every version that is published needs metadata and, preferably, a persistent identifier. But this does not mean that the researchers have to save everything, every single byte. The researchers simply have to be sure that the dataset can be presented in an exactly identical form when asked for at a later point in time. In case somebody made a citation or important conclusion based on it, it should be possible to reconstruct what has happened. It is very important to be clear about it, if this is something the researchers do *not* commit to, when they publish data.

Managing research data is not the same thing as archiving it, and handling digital data requires a somewhat different approach. Here, storage and data management are relevant components building trustworthiness of the documentation. Citation is one of the main functions of persistent identifiers in research. The researchers should be mindful creating them though, since every persistent identifier is a commitment to manage the dataset or at least its metadata forever. It will cost somebody a substantial amount of effort and work. And even if the dataset is deleted, a tombstone page should be maintained. Here, the well-managed research infrastructures and data services come into the picture as essential supporters of research.

Generally, one could consider there to be three different types of datasets that are relevant for historians (see Figure 5.2). First, there is the master data produced and often published by government institutions, like the cultural heritage data. Unfortunately, it is not always well versioned or documented (red in Figure 5.2). It could be data of any kind for any use, but it might be relevant for a historical research question due to a long time series or for some other reason. Second, there are generic research datasets, which are produced by researchers for scientific use (green). Here, you find datasets like corpuses or some of the surveys published by the Finnish data archive. Much data of this kind can also be found, for instance, with the National Institute of Health or other domain-specific research institutes or government bodies. These datasets are validated and often cumulative. The third type of research data is a research output, created to underpin a specific study or article (blue). These data need to be saved, albeit the interest for reuse might be minute, for the simple reasons of reproducibility of the research and merit for the creator.

The historian often finds her digital sources within the first or second category of data. But as she proceeds with her work, the question of publishing second- or third-type data becomes increasingly pressing. Now, there is no single clear path to publishing this kind of data, which is often a derivate of cultural heritage data. Additionally, researchers within the humanities many times deal with sensitive data or data under copyright, which makes storing

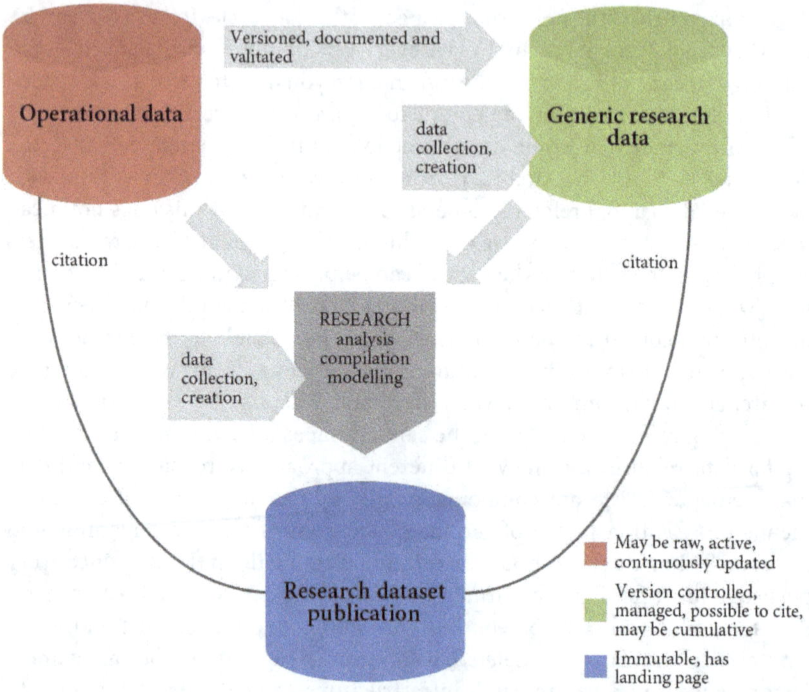

Figure 5.2: Main types of data used by historians and how those are interrelated. Source: Author.

and publishing even more difficult. I will discuss the options later in this chapter when discussing research infrastructures.

There is often more to a digital humanities research outcome than just a dataset and a result explained in a narrative form. It needs to be pointed out that the historian often handles a double narration: one of the research process and then another, which is the actual new knowledge. This is the normal situation when carrying out qualitative research or being unable to present or refer to the actual tools and methods used. However, when using computers and computational methods, the process and outcomes like dynamic databases or visualisations could and should also be included in the outputs, in addition to information about the sources or actual data. For this, the existing solutions are few and the methodology is very thin. Preservation of databases has developed somewhat, but documentation and preservation of dynamic user interfaces and other kinds of complex code is still in its cradle. It is well known that they need an extensive amount of curation to be kept usable for more than some years. This means that they are both risky and costly to preserve. Still, some effort to save these is better than just abandoning digital projects at the end of project funding. The problem is usually to find the party willing to take the responsibility. Therefore, this is also one thing that best would be solved at the point of planning the research.

Source Criticism and Research Assessment

Assessing digital sources requires a substantial amount of metadata. I need to discuss this theme more closely to explain why and how data management planning and infrastructures are relevant not only for creating FAIR data, but also for carrying out high quality research in history in a digital environment.

A digital document does not have an 'original' copy. Instead, it is recreated every time the source is rendered from a digital file consisting of zeroes and ones. Everything is just copy, while the analogue versions, which are the ones we can perceive with our senses on the screen or in our ears, are generated by software and hardware that have a decisive effect on what they actually apprehend. The calibration of the screen or the sampling frequency of an audio file might affect how one interprets what is represented or real. In cases where a physical original exists, one can always check it, but if the source is born-digital, this becomes impossible. Therefore, there is a need for technical metadata.

The best way to evaluate the trustworthiness of a digital source, as is commonplace for the historian, is to check its provenance. In practice, the researchers need to assess the organisation or person who has delivered the source. Can they show documentation about the technical and administrative life cycle of the source? Do they comply with the Open Archival Information System (OAIS) standard or do they have other certificates for digital preservation?[11] Do they use and manage persistent identifiers that are globally unique and persistent? Can they present extensive metadata, including checksums? The checksums are important digital seals for calculating the integrity of files, but they do not work across file formats, which is why the researchers need to have a good trail of documentation and management of persistent identifiers. The formats might have changed during the life cycle of the data. What else has happened in terms of migrations, curation, cleaning and enhancing the data? Is everything convincingly documented?

There are several kinds of metadata. To be able to represent a digital source in a similar or corresponding way we need technical and structural metadata that helps one choose the right tools and understand possible offset. We also need administrative metadata that informs about the rights and responsibilities attached to the data. Furthermore, we need descriptive metadata, which helps with finding and organising the data, as well as with the usual historical source criticism around what, who, when, why and other contextual information. This is the part of information that is most threatened in research data, due to reasons of personal data. Data archives often prefer anonymised data, which means crucial historical information is permanently lost from the historian's point of view. This is also the reason why the current research data archives do not provide sufficient services for many historians. The organisations that do this best are institutions like the Swedish and Finnish literary societies, which have a profound understanding of the importance of the personal and unique as part of the greater whole and of the research processes within cultural studies and history.

It is important to understand the ephemeral nature of digital information, not only when it comes to the historian's own sources, but also concerning working with data. If research is to be possible to repeat, the digital operations undertaken should be well documented. Code should be documented and saved and versions of the dataset have to be managed. Not everything has to be saved, but one should consider versioning and documentation when significant changes are made.[12] Conversions, cleaning and mapping need to be accounted for, since they may affect the outcome of the research. And as technologies become obsolete over time, all types of metadata are necessary. Otherwise preservation will not be possible.[13] This part of the data management should be planned together with data librarians and professional data stewards.

Infrastructure and Services

Reliable and good quality research craves good citations and linking. The historian's digital sources can be found in cultural heritage institutions or in many other places that sometimes, but not always, offer possibilities to create FAIR data by pointing to the sources in exact and sustainable ways. Often, the researcher needs to clean and organise the data, which in turn creates a new dataset.

According to the European Commission, research infrastructures (RIs) are facilities, resources and services used by the science community to conduct research and foster innovation. The Finnish Academy is lengthier in its definition:[14]

> Research infrastructures refer to a reserve of instruments, equipment, information networks, databases, materials and services enabling research at various stages. Research infrastructures may be based at a single location (single-sited), scattered across several sites (distributed), or provided via a virtual platform (virtual). They can also form mutually complementary wholes and networks. Europe hosts several large-scale research infrastructures that are open to collaborative use across national boundaries.

The Open Science and Research Initiative report addressed RIs.[15] This report distinguished between services, data and equipment. This classification has also been implemented in the national Research Infrastructure catalogue, which provides persistent identifiers for these (https://research.fi/).[16] Many infrastructures provide two or three of these types of resources. The national strategy for RIs[17] demonstrates that we have advanced infrastructures for linguistics, register research and social sciences. The national consortium for supplying digital publications for the research libraries within all domains is also, for some reason, considered a humanities and social sciences infrastructure.

The cultural heritage sector is left out, except for the shared search portal Finna, which serves the public as well as the research community at large when it comes to traditional research publications (namely, articles and monographs). This means the search portal aggregates some relevant research data for historians, like individual photographs or archival collections, research dataset metadata from the Data archive (a patchwork with very few internal links and of highly varied granularity) and research literature from all fields. The European cultural heritage portal Europeana does the same, except leaving out the literature and focusing on the traditional but digitised sources.

The main problem is, besides missing sufficient persistent identifier management, the lacking information structures. The digital objects vary in size from single photographs to archival collections and corpuses with almost non-existing descriptive metadata from a historian's point of view. Saying this, I do not want to belittle the enormous and important work that has been done to bring all this metadata together. It has been an extremely valuable effort, with thorough implications for the cultural heritage sector in Finland, which has taken huge steps towards openness and digitisation. However, for research we still require better representations of the sources and their internal relations. Important digital sources are omitted, including databases provided by the institutions themselves, not to mention historical research databases elsewhere, whose producers often face great difficulties getting hold of sustainable funding or sufficient data management for their digital research outputs. The cataloguing of these resources, documentation and linking datasets derived from cultural heritage data in general is today left to the researcher, who generally has few possibilities to maintain these after the funding ends. Today, the historian most often has to be content with publishing discrete research datasets as simple files, which have weak and only human-readable links to other digital resources. Also, the reuse value is less than it probably would have to be, due to this approach and meager machine-readable semantics.

Both the Language Bank of Finland and the data archive have juridical mandates to store this kind of data, but the researcher has an extensive responsibility too. The slightest flaw in consents or rights questions easily becomes an insurmountable hurdle for archiving or sharing the data. There are also reasons to question whether this kind of publishing is the one and only, or whether there could be more suitable platforms or structures than the currently available solutions.

Digital media are not only unstable and diverse, but they are also often more disposed for interactivity and a dynamic communication that happens in dialogue, even co-creation with the readers/users.[18] In fact, it might be a mistake not to consider this kind of publishing and knowledge creation in a research domain that is so relevant and open to popularisation and popular culture. Different kinds of map and wiki applications can be used for sharing historical knowledge. Wikis are especially suitable due to their very transparent and clear version management. They also enable very good structuring and linking of data.[19] In fact, the wiki technology combined with careful data management would offer an almost out-of-the-box solution for FAIR data.

The historian needs to carefully plan her data management. Questions of personal data, consent and copyright need to be addressed at an early stage before even starting the research. This does not mean that one has to decide on every detail or stick to the plan whatever happens. In fact, the opposite is often true: the plans have to be modified or redone, when new issues arise. The research process in digital humanities is often iterative, oscillating between qualitative and quantitative methods, and research questions sometimes have to be adjusted or revised.

From the very beginning, it is important to plan for managing data files, backups and versions. Also consider the types of data that will be included and analyse the need for documentation needed for citations and reproducibility. It is not necessarily a good idea to get a resolvable persistent identifier for every single data object. Instead, one should be pragmatic and consider the dataset as a part of the surrounding information universe and try to create meaningful, machine-readable and sustainable relations to that universe. Do not produce new data objects where you can reliably point to external ones. Also, one should be mindful about the granularity: Which are meaningful entities to make findable and for which to create metadata?

When it comes to infrastructures, we have to operate with what we have got, but historians could also give valuable input in creating a meaningful larger network of digital historical knowledge by engaging even more in questions of common or interoperable infrastructures. There are large infrastructure initiatives like DARIAH-EU, CLARIN-ERIC, Europeana and the European Open Science Cloud (EOSC), but there is still not a suitable solution that would serve historians well in publishing and linking their research outputs. It is essential that historians discuss these questions with other stakeholders, the cultural heritage institutions, the scientific libraries and their own research institutions and funders to find sustainable solutions and drive infrastructure development in directions that serve knowledge creation, not only as separate projects, but as a linked network of information.

Notes

1 Antonijevic & Stern Cahoy 2018.
2 FORCE11; Wilkinson et al. 2016.
3 Not invented here 2018.
4 Data science report 2016.
5 Klein et al. 2014; Jones et al. 2016.
6 Finnish Committee for Research Data 2018; Research Data Alliance 2015.
7 Parland-von Essen 2017; see also openscience.fi.
8 See Finna.fi, kdk.fi and digitalpreservation.fi.

[9] Anderson 2007; Manovich 2013.
[10] See Mons 2018.
[11] See, e.g., the DCP online guide on OAIS: Lavoie 2014 and the standard **ISO 16363:2012**.
[12] Language Bank of Finland.
[13] PREMIS preservation metadata.
[14] Academy of Finland 2018b.
[15] Avoimuuden politiikat tutkimusinfrastruktuureissa: Selvitys 2015.
[16] RIs, https://research.fi/.
[17] Academy of Finland 2018a.
[18] Salgado 2009; Nygren 2013; Marttila 2018; Viinikkala et al. 2016.
[19] See, e.g., Wikisources, Wikimedia, Wikidata and Tieteen termipankki. See also Wikidocumentaries and Wikimaps.

References

Academy of Finland (2018a). *Finland's strategy and roadmap for research infrastructures 2014–2020.* Interim report. Retrieved from http://www.aka.fi/globalassets/tiedostot/aka_infra_tiekartta_raportti_en_030518.pdf

Academy of Finland (2018b). *Research infrastructures.* Retrieved from http://www.aka.fi/en/research-and-science-policy/research-infrastructures/

Anderson, C. (2007). *The long tail.* Random House, London.

Antonijevic, S., & **Stern Cahoy, E.** (2018). Researcher as bricoleur: contextualizing humanists' digital workflows. *Digital Humanities Quarterly, 12*(3). Retrieved from http://www.digitalhumanities.org/dhq/vol/12/3/000399/000399.html

Avoimuuden politiikat tutkimusinfrastruktuureissa: Selvitys. (2015). *Avoin tiede ja tutkimus -hanke, Avoimuuden politiikat -työryhmä.* Retrieved from http://urn.fi/URN:NBN:fi-fe2016122731714

Data science report. (2016). *Crowdflower.* Retrieved from http://visit.crowdflower.com/r/416-ZBE-142/images/

European Commission. *About research infrastructures. What are research infrastructures?* Retrieved from https://ec.europa.eu/research/infrastructures/index.cfm?pg=about

Finnish Committee for Research Data. (2018). *Tracing data: data citation roadmap for Finland.* Retrieved from http://urn.fi/URN:NBN:fi-fe201804106446

FORCE11. *The FAIR data principles.* Retrieved 29 September 2018 from http://www.force11.org/group/fairgroup/fairprinciples

ISO. 16363:2012: *space data and information transfer systems. Audit and certification of trustworthy digital repositories.* Retrieved from http://www.iso.org/standard/56510.html

Jones, S., Van de Sompel, H., Shankar, H., Klein, M., Tobin, R., & **Grover, C.** (2016). Scholarly context adrift: three out of four URI references lead to changed content. *PLoS One, 12*(1), e0171057. DOI: https://doi.org/10.1371/journal.pone.0167475

Klein, M., Van de Sompel, H., Sanderson, R., Shankar, H., Balakireva, L., Zhou, K., & Tobin, R. (2014). Scholarly context not found: one in five articles suffers from reference rot. *PloS One, 9*(12), e115253. DOI: https://doi.org/10.1371/journal.pone.0115253

Language Bank of Finland. *Life cycle and metadata model of language resources.* Retrieved from https://www.kielipankki.fi/support/life-cycle-and-metadata-model-of-language-resources/

Lavoie, B. (2014). *The Open Archival Information System (OAIS) reference model: introductory guide*, 2nd edn. DPC Technology Watch Report 14-02. DOI: https://doi.org/doi.org/10.7207/twr14-02

Manovich, L. (2013). *Software takes command.* New York, NY: Bloomsbury Academic.

Marttila, S. (2018): *Infrastructuring for cultural commons.* Espoo: Aalto University Series, doctoral dissertations.

Mons, B. (2018). *Data stewardship for open science: implementing FAIR principles.* New York, NY: Chapman and Hall/CRC.

Nygren, T. (2013). Digitala material och verktyg: möjligheter och problem utifrån exemplet spatial history. *Historisk Tidskrift, 133*(3), 474–482.

Parland-von Essen, J. (2017). Från open access till open science. Framväxten av öppen forskning och vetenskap. *NORDICOM-INFORMATION, 39*(1), 97–103. Retrieved from http://nordicom.gu.se/sites/default/files/kapitel-pdf/von_essen_97-103.pd

PREMIS preservation metadata. Retrieved from http://www.loc.gov/standards/premis/

Research Data Alliance. (2015). *Data citation of evolving data.* Recommendations of the Working Group on Data Citation. Retrieved from https://rd-alliance.org/system/files/documents/RDA-DC-Recommendations_151020.pdf

Salgado. M. (2009). *Designing for an open museum: an exploration of content creation and sharing through interactive pieces.* Taideteollisen korkeakoulun julkaisusarja A 98.

Viinikkala, L., Yli-Seppälä, L., Heimo O. I., Helle, S., Härkänen, L., Jokela, S., Järvenpää, L., Korkalainen, T., Latvala, J., Pääkylä, J., Seppälä, K., Mäkilä, T., & Lehtonen, T. (2016). *Reformation representation. Mixed reality narratives in communicating tangible and intangible heritage.* DIHA & NODEM Special Session at 22nd International Conference on Virtual Systems and Multimedia VSMM, Kuala Lumpur.

Wikipedia. (2018). *Not invented here.* Retrieved from https://en.wikipedia.org/wiki/Not_invented_here

Wilkinson, M., Dumontier, M., Aalsbersberg, J. J., Hoekstra, H. E., & Boyer, D. M. (2016). The FAIR guiding principles for scientific data management and stewardship. *Scientific Data, 3*, 160018. DOI: https://doi.org/10.1038/sdata.2016.1

CHAPTER 6

Big Data, Bad Metadata

A Methodological Note on the Importance of Good Metadata in the Age of Digital History

Kimmo Elo

Introduction

During the past decade, digital humanities has emerged as a new paradigm seeking to gather scholars interested in applying computational methods on their research materials. This development has been supported by the almost exponential growth of either born-digital or digitised materials currently available for researchers. Further, the availability of computational research tools is much better today than, say, five or 10 years ago.

New terminology like big data, data mining and text mining well illustrate the massive growth of digital data available for research purposes. At the same time, the digital research agenda is filled with huge expectations regarding exploratory research, the growth of scientific and societal knowledge or new forms of data analysis. Some scholars have rather strong expectations about how digital humanities should change our whole understanding of knowledge and how knowledge is presented.[1]

This chapter supports the general understanding of digital humanities as an important, computational field of research for the Humanities and social

How to cite this book chapter:
Elo, K. (2020). Big data, bad metadata: A methodological note on the importance of good metadata in the age of digital history. In M. Fridlund, M. Oiva, & P. Paju (Eds.), *Digital histories: Emergent approaches within the new digital history* (pp. 103–111). Helsinki: Helsinki University Press. https://doi.org/10.33134/HUP-5-6

sciences in general, and for historical research in particular. The chapter stems from the deep conviction of a scholar rooted in the intersection of computational, historical and social scientific research that exploring digitised historical sources could help us to gain new insights and improve our understanding of the past.

At the same time, however, this chapter is motivated by my worry that, as regards historical research, thus far much attention has been paid to the creation of digital research material, but too little has been to paid to the creation of research data. To clarify my point, with *research material*, I refer to original, primary sources like documents, letters, photographs, etc. With *research data*, I refer to corpora consisting of both the original material and additional, descriptive information derived from the original material. To put it bluntly, we are almost over-flooded by the former, but there still is no shared or common strategy about how to cope with the latter. The importance of the latter is, however, reflected by the fact that many universities are developing research data management practices.[2]

The main thesis of this chapter is that more attention should be paid and more resources should be invested in metadata creation. The next section introduces the very concept of metadata and tackles the question of why metadata matters. The second section presents arguments about why metadata should be considered as an important part of digitising projects. The chapter is rounded up with concluding remarks related to the future work in digital history.

What Is Metadata and Why Do We Need It?

Due to the limited space available for this chapter, I refrain from a literature review and just point out some of the most important aspects related to metadata and discussed (mostly) by librarians or archivists. Metadata is widely understood and defined as 'data about data' and, thus, is expected to provide information about the content of the material it is linked with. In other words, metadata should summarise the most important content. According to *The metadata handbook*, metadata should be constructed in a way which 'fully supports findability and discovery'.[3]

According to Allen Benson, metadata is a descriptive model, a summary report to present the main content according to a formalised structure consisting of information-bearing entities.[4] Richard Pearce-Moses defines metadata creation as the 'process of creating a finding aid or other access tools that allow individuals to browse a surrogate of the collection to facilitate access and that improve security by creating a record of the collection and by minimizing the amount of handling of the original materials'.[5] Hence, metadata is an ontological model providing a structure for information arrangement. At the same time, metadata creation is a descriptive process aiming at filling in the ontological model with material-related, descriptive information.

I am quite convinced that the ontological side is not the core problem. Several well-developed models exists as to how metadata should be structured or what descriptive elements are available in order to guarantee a standardised, formalised metadata.[6] Further, as regards born-digital materials specialists have been discussing from the late 1990s onwards how this development affects ontological requirements for the metadata.[7]

Hence, the real problem is the metadata creation process, especially when this process must be started from scratch and/or with only limited previous knowledge about the full content of the material to be modelled and summarised into metadata. Although the metadata should fulfil a relatively straightforward task (namely, support findability and discovery), at least three main pitfalls should be taken seriously.

First, what or who determines the elements included in the metadata structure? The answer to this question widely determines the content described and formalised in the metadata. At the same time, however, it has a strong impact on both findability and discovery, since metadata queries are limited to the fields used in the model. A more complicated issue relates to hierarchies or sub-categories typical for historical sources (for example, 'building'–'house' or 'building'–'church'). Two examples should clarify the point. Let us first consider a novel. A standard metadata includes the author(s), the title, the publisher, the year of publication, the genre and a few keywords used to summarise the main content. In most cases, these elements suit well the needs of a reader looking for certain novels. But how about a researcher looking, for example, for novels with a certain type of protagonist or a certain person/figure? Or, second, a photograph collection. Once again, many elements to be included in the metadata are quite straightforward and obvious (timestamp, photographer, title), but how about persons, places or abstract elements like gestures, memes or visual effects? The answers depend on the supposed group of end-users and, thus, make the material unusable or unfindable for certain groups.

Second, what or who determines the terminology (for example, keywords, descriptions) used to describe content? Once we have determined what content should be summarised in the metadata, we need to determine how different content-related aspects are described. Once again, standardised dictionaries, keyword indices, etc. exist, so there is rarely a need to reinvent the wheel by creating a new vocabulary. The challenge is to maintain coherence; that is, to ensure that the same (or similar) content is described in the same terms. To use a simple example, if there are bunches of photographs all having different kinds of buildings in them, all of these photographs should be found if one searches for 'building'. But should the end-user be able to find buildings of the type 'church' as well? Once again, findability should guide the process of metadata creation.

And, third, who creates and maintains the metadata? Prior to the digital era, collection management and metadata creation have been almost solely in the hands of librarians and archivists, especially when it came to the creation and maintenance of large document collections.[8] Today, many collections are created, maintained and made available by private organisations, institutions and companies. This is partly due to the limited resources of public institutions like state archives or libraries, but also thanks to the reduced costs of digitisation, the increase of easy-to-use solutions for data management and hosting, and to the growth of data-sharing platforms like cloud-based services. The other side of the coin is that a majority of these platforms is rather weak and underdeveloped in metadata creation and maintenance, especially as regards the content description. One solution enjoying growing popularity is 'crowdsourcing', a process where 'ordinary people' help the maintainers to create descriptive metadata. There are many examples ranging from 'tagging' over 'person identification' to 'linked data creation', all of them producing interesting and promising results, but also highlighting many problems mostly related to the heterogeneous quality of the resulting metadata and difficulties in ensuring the correctness of input.[9]

Why Digital History Should Take Metadata Seriously

A quick survey in recent literature around digital history reveals that questions related to metadata creation have rarely been debated among digital historians. Instead, historians seem to be educated to use metadata when searching for sources, not to question the metadata itself. In other words, we are used to relying on metadata created by archivists or librarians.[10] This was a good practice in the times when collections were mainly and dominantly housed by libraries and archives.

The digital era has already changed this division of labour, and there is no evidence whatsoever that this would change in the future. Quite the contrary, billions of gigabytes of born-digital textual and visual materials are produced and made available without any, or with only weak and incomplete, metadata. However, without a proper metadata, materials 'are simply a meaningless collection of files, values and characters'.[11] And as Edelstein and colleagues point out: 'Historians increasingly find themselves utilizing digital databases as the idea of the searchable document and the virtual archive reorganize how libraries, research institutes, teams of scholars, and even individual researchers present and share interesting sources.'[12]

Quite much effort, money and time have been invested in the digitising of historical textual materials like manuscripts, documents, letters, etc. As a result, historians have access to a vast number of digitised text and can view and query digitised indexed document collections and editions online. One of the most prominent examples is the 'Republic of Letters' project, focusing on historical networks of correspondence between scholars from all around the world.[13] Another similar project is the 'Letters of 1916 Digital Edition' project, one of the first crowdsourced humanities projects, as well as histoGraph, which also uses crowdsourcing for metadata creation.[14]

In their evaluation of the 'Letters of 1916' project, the authors note that '[t]he meaning of the term "metadata" was unclear for most participants'.[15] This seems to be linked to a wider aspect, namely that '[m]uch attention in the past fifteen years has been directed toward text digitization',[16] forcing 'scholars to access historical sources in a new way: through specific words'.[17] As a result, most digitised collections available online are 'focused on searching, not browsing'.[18] Hence, findability might be good (thanks to the power of full text search in digitised text documents), whereas discovery might be poor.

Modern text mining methods can be of help when historians are dealing with digitised textual corpora. Further, computational methods like (semi-) automated document classification or indexing can make the metadata creation process easier and more effective. However, the current tendency to make old documents available as PDF collections worsens the situation. The positive thing in using the so-called layered PDF format is that end-users can see the original document, but also use search and copying functionalities through the text layer. The negative side is that in most cases the text layer is an exact, character-based reconstruction of the page (mostly based on the corrected results from the optical character recognition (OCR) process), not a raw text laid out and paginated according to the original design. As a result, hyphened words, to give an example, on two lines are not understood as one, but as two separate words (of which the first ends with a hyphen!). My reader can imagine what kinds of limitations result from this kind of practice for document discovery, even if the research interface offers expanded search capabilities like regular expressions. This is because most search engines are based on pattern matching, whereas, for example, irregularly split words do not have a distinct pattern.

Another growing challenge is that sources relevant for historians and social scientists include not only textual collections, but also visual or audio materials like photographs, music, films and so on. Although the question of metadata creation is relevant for all digitised collections, the real challenge relates to non-textual materials. Since the share of information delivered in non-textual, mostly visual forms is steadily growing, the problem of findability and discovery of such materials is of increasing relevance also for historians. There exists already vast collections of such materials, but at the same time our tools to directly query visual or audio materials are very limited, yet slowly improving.[19] For example, many digitised historical photographs include non-recognised persons or places, but the problem is also relevant for today. According to de Figueirêdo and Feitosa '[a]pproximately 350 million photos are added to Facebook each day[, but most of them] are not annotated'.[20] The problem here is not just about forgetting, but also about findability and discovery. Non-annotated photographs cannot be queried, and they do not appear in search results, even if their content was relevant for the query. How are we expected to find, for example, photographs with 'Konrad Adeanuer' on them if we lack both techniques to identify (that is, to name) persons behind recognised faces and metadata containing information about persons shown on the photographs?

Many recent articles point out that digitised collections and online resources affect the way in which scholars discover and access historical sources. Instead of selecting research material from the sources by close reading, research material is increasingly selected by using search engines or by applying methods of computer-aided, distant reading. Two biasing consequences seem worth being noted. First, the use of search engines and other online resources might influence and steer scholars to favour materials available online and, consciously or unconsciously, to change their research questions to suit digitally available materials. Second, scholars might not be aware of missing or incomplete metadata possibly affecting and limiting research results. This second aspect is especially relevant for non-textual material collection, but has at least some relevance also in regard to textual data offered as simple, non-indexed PDF document collections. Another problem is that many collections do not provide any information about the completeness (or better: incompleteness) of their data.

Discussion

This chapter has tackled the question of the relevance of metadata for historical research. Metadata is understood as 'data about data', an ontological model summarising the main content of the data. The very idea of metadata is to make the source material findable and discoverable. In the current digital era characterised by the exponential growth of digitised materials and the availability of vast online resources, both goal-settings gain in importance also for historical research.

Based on the arguments presented above, I conclude that metadata is extremely relevant also for historians. On the one hand, historians increasingly use and explore online resources like historical document collections or photograph corpora. Most of these online portals offer search engines or other possibilities to query the collections. Instead of selecting material by the process of reading the material document by document, material selection is increasingly based on search results. Since there is no reason to believe that this will change in the future, historians should be interested in ensuring that all relevant aspects are searchable, findable and discoverable.

On the other hand, the whole collection management is in flux, as digitised collections are made available by a wide variety of actors. If there exist no standards for quality management of data collection, how can findability and discovery be guaranteed? Once again, the ontological side is not the problem. The problem is the process of creating annotations and metadata.

A third aspect should be added to the two points above. Historical digitisation projects often deal with materials of which only trained historians possess knowledge. With all respect to librarians and archivists, we cannot expect them to have an in-depth knowledge of historical persons, events or eras. Despite this, these two groups are still in charge when national, governmental and official collections are digitised and annotated with metadata.

Although there is no easy patent solution regarding how to ensure metadata quality for historical collections, historians should be encouraged to engage in digitisation projects in their own fields of expertise. As Reilly point out, libraries, but also archives, 'must ensure that they maximize the visibility of their collections—not just to the general public but to those in the education system'.[21] In this respect, historians should engage as mediators between the research community and libraries and archives.

Historians value original documents and are trained to source criticism and to work in archives. At the same time, they are quite reliable on what is involved in the quality of collection management and hosting in archives, and many archivists and librarians enjoy a high respect for their expertise. A good archivist can fill the gaps in a researcher's inquiry and, thus, find relevant and reliable sources.

The shift from this human-to-human interface towards a human-to-computer interface replaces the 'silent knowledge' of an archivist with algorithms run by the computer. The search process itself might be more effective and quicker, but the other side of the coin is that the user has only limited possibilities to explain her intentions. As pointed out above, a scholar is forced to figure out correct terms and words for his query, but still he cannot be sure whether he receives all (or even the most) relevant materials.

To round up my argument: it is by far not sufficient to digitise original sources if we cannot ensure findability and discovery. Digitised original sources must be processed into research data consisting of the original content plus descriptive metadata summarising the essential content of the material. Metadata creation should not be disparaged, nor should it be seen as a quick, dirty task to be completed as soon as and as inexpensively as possible. Research data is the most valuable content of a vast material collection, since it enables both findability and discovery. If scholars cannot rely on getting reliable results when committing searches in online collections, the digital leap manifested by proponents of digital humanities might end with a belly flop.

Notes

1 See, e.g., Burdick et al. 2012.
2 See, e.g., https://www.helsinki.fi/en/research/research-environment/research-data-management.
3 Register & McIlroy 2015.
4 Benson 2009: 161–162.
5 Pearce-Moses 2005: 112–113.
6 Benson 2009; Gonzales 2014; Valentino 2017.
7 Langdon 2016.
8 Edelstein 2017: 401.
9 See, e.g., Stvilia 2009; Reilly 2012; Stvilia 2012; Turin 2015; Valentino 2017; Wusteman 2017.

[10] Edelstein 2017: 401.
[11] See https://www.fsd.uta.fi/aineistonhallinta/en/data-description-and-metadata.html.
[12] Edelstein 2017: 401.
[13] Stanford University 2013.
[14] Letters 1916–1923 Consortium 2016; University of Luxembourg 2018.
[15] Wusteman 2017: 133.
[16] Edelstein 2017: 417.
[17] Huistra 2016: 220.
[18] Ibid.: 222.
[19] See, e.g., Huang, Ma & Gong 2014; Ries & Lienhart 2014; Ko & Lee 2015; Vinyals et al. 2015; Li, Wang & Zhang 2016; Osadchy, Karen & Raviv 2016; Wang, Wang & Liu 2016; Zhong, Liu & Hua 2016; Li et al. 2017.
[20] de Figueirêdo & Feitosa 2015: 203.
[21] Reilly 2012: 39.

References

Benson, A. C. (2009). The archival photograph and its meaning: formalisms for modelling images. *Journal of Archival Organization, 7*(4), 148–187.

Burdick, A., Drucker, J., Lunenfeld, P., Presner, T., & **Schnapp, J.** (2012). *Digital_Humanities*. Cambridge, MA: MIT Press.

de Figueirêdo, X., & **Feitosa, H.** (2015). Semi-automatic photograph tagging by combining context with content-based information. *Expert Systems with Applications, 42*(1), 203–211.

Edelstein, D. (2017). Historical research in a digital age: reflections from the mapping the republic of letters project. *American Historical Review, 122*(2), 400–424.

Gonzales, B. (2014). The conversion of MARC metadata for online visual resource collections: a case study of tactics, challenges and results. *Library Philosophy and Practice (e-journal)*, 1–64.

Huang, M., Ma, Y., & **Gong, Q.** (2014). Image recognition using modified zernike moments. *Sensors & Transducers, 166*(3), 219–223.

Huistra, H. (2016). Phrasing history: selecting sources in digital repositories. *Historical Methods: A Journal of Quantitative and Interdisciplinary History, 49*(4), 220–229.

Ko, C.-N., & **Lee, C.-M.** (2015). Image recognition using adaptive fuzzy neural network based on lifting scheme of wavelet. *Artificial Life and Robotics, 20*(4), 353–358.

Langdon, J. (2016). Describing the digital: the archival cataloguing of born-digital personal papers. *Archives and Records, 37*(1), 37–52.

Letters 1916–1923 Consortium. (2016). *Letters of 1916 digital edition*. Retrieved from http://letters1916.maynoothuniversity.ie/

Li, K., Wang, F., & Zhang, L. (2016). A new algorithm for image recognition and classification based on improved bag of features algorithm. *Optik—International Journal for Light and Electron Optics, 127*(11), 4736–4740.

Li, W., Chen, L., Xu, D., & Gool, L.V. (2017). Visual recognition in RGB images and videos by learning from rgb-d data. *IEEE Transactions on Pattern Analysis and Machine Intelligence, PP*(99), 1–1.

Osadchy, M., Keren, D., & Raviv, D. (2016). Recognition using hybrid classifiers. *IEEE Transactions on Pattern Analysis and Machine Intelligence, 38*(4), 759–771.

Pearce-Moses, R. (2005). *A glossary of archival and records terminology.* Chicago, IL: Society of American Archivists.

Register, R., & McIlroy, T. (2015). *The metadata handbook.* Retrieved from http://themetadatahandbook.com/wp-content/uploads/2015/01/Metadata-Handbook-Preview-Revised.pdf

Reilly, S. K. (2012). Collaboration to build a meaningful connection between library content and the researcher. *New Review of Information Networking, 17*(1), 34–42.

Ries, C. X., & Lienhart, R. (2014). A survey on visual adult image recognition. *Multimedia Tools and Applications, 69*(3), 661–688. Copyright: Springer Science+Business Media, New York, 2014; last updated 30 August 2014.

Stanford University (2013). *The republic of letters.* Retrieved from http://republicofletters.stanford.edu/

Stvilia, B. (2009). User-generated collection-level metadata in an online photo-sharing system. *Library and Information Science Research, 31*(1), 54–65.

Stvilia, B. (2012). Establishing the value of socially-created metadata to image indexing. *Library and Information Science Research, 34*(2), 99–109.

Turin, M. (2015). Devil in the digital: ambivalent results in an object-based teaching course. *Museum Anthropology, 38*(2), 123–132.

University of Luxembourg (2018). *histoGraph.* Retrieved from http://histograph.eu/

Valentino, M. (2017). Linked data metadata for digital clothing collections. *Journal of Web Librarianship, 11*(3–4), 231–240.

Vinyals, O., Toshev, A., Bengio, S., & Erhan, D. (2015, June). Show and tell: a neural image caption generator. In Computer Vision and Pattern Recognition conference (pp. 3156–3164).

Wang, Y., Wang, X., & Liu, W. (2016). Unsupervised local deep feature for image recognition. *Information Sciences, 351*, 67–75.

Wusteman, J. (2017). Usability testing of the letters of 1916 digital edition. *Library Hi Tech, 35*(1), 120–143.

Zhong, S.-H., Liu, Y., & Hua, K. A. (2016). Field effect deep networks for image recognition with incomplete data. *ACM Trans. Multimedia Comput. Commun. Appl., 12*(4), 52:1–52:22.

CHAPTER 7

All the Work that Makes It Work

Digital Methods and Manual Labour

Johan Jarlbrink

Automation is a temptation and a promise, and perhaps a threat. Old jobs disappear as robots and software do what human workers used to. Is this also the case with research within the humanities? Computers can process datasets of texts so large that it would take several lifetimes for scholars just to read it. Computers are excellent in finding patterns that are hard to recognise for human eyes and brains. What should researchers do when computers are much better in doing what scholars used to?

In this chapter, I will argue that digital research is far from automatised.[1] A human being is still needed to make sense of results, of course. I will focus on something else, not on the creative ways in which scholars interpret data outputs, but on the dull tasks that make data outputs possible. Most datasets need cleaning, editing and error checking. The outcome of automatic processes needs to be examined by someone who goes through the results; sometimes it needs to be corrected manually. Such procedures are often left out completely or only mentioned in brief when digital methods are discussed. Yet, they have a significant impact on results and need to be taken seriously.

I will mainly focus on various forms of text analysis, based on my own experiences and what colleagues have told me, as well as cases described in the

How to cite this book chapter:

Jarlbrink, J. (2020). All the work that makes it work: Digital methods and manual labour. In M. Fridlund, M. Oiva, & P. Paju (Eds.), *Digital histories: Emergent approaches within the new digital history* (pp. 113–126). Helsinki: Helsinki University Press. https://doi.org/10.33134/HUP-5-7

literature. The cases are meant to shed light on an often neglected part of digital methodologies, but the mundane aspects of data cleaning and curation are also significant beyond the field of digital humanities. Such procedures can be understood as 'a crucial part of the materiality of how scholarly and scientific work is done'.[2] The manual work needed to feed, improve and evaluate digital processing belongs to a long history of little tools and (supposedly) insignificant back-end operations that have made different kinds of research output possible. Digital scholarship, as traditional archival research and experimental work in laboratories, involves material and conceptual actors as well as human ones.[3]

In the first section, I will give a short background and explain why I think manual digital work matters. Three empirical sections will exemplify various kinds of manual operations. First, I describe human-assisted computational analysis in the humanities in the 1950s, 1960s and 1970s. Second, I present my own experiences from a project based on 19th-century newspapers. Third, I tell the story of how a colleague of mine used digital Named Entity Recognition (NER) in combination with pen and paper.

Invisible Work

Glimpses of the manual work that makes digitisation and computational analysis possible are sometimes given by accident. Google Books preserves a large part of our printed cultural heritage in a digital form, but also some of the hands that were needed to operate the scanners and handle the printed volumes. Just as the secretaries of the early 20th century, who left traces of themselves in the typewritten texts only as a result of errors, accidents make Google employees become visible in the digital database. Index fingers covered in condom-like pink gloves are included in many of the images now available online. They serve as a reminder of the people and work that feed the digital infrastructures.[4] Part of the workforce digitising printed materials is less visible. Much of the post-processing needed to produce useful digital surrogates is being outsourced to companies hiring low-wage workers in Cambodia and India.[5]

This kind of hidden work makes digitisation seem more straightforward and automatised than it is. The same goes for various forms of computer-assisted analysis. Tamraparni Dasu and Theodore Johnson has stated that:

> In our experience, the tasks of exploratory data mining and data cleaning constitute 80% of the effort that determines 80% of the value of the ultimate data mining results. Data mining books … provide a great amount of detail about the analytical process and advanced data mining techniques. However they assume that the data has already been gathered, cleaned, explored, and understood.[6]

Much of the cleaning can be done with software. Even an easy-to-use program such as Microsoft Excel allows you to search and replace, filter, merge, separate and delete different kinds of data. More advanced or custom-made tools allow you to fine-tune the process. Still, such procedures need to be monitored in order to ensure the quality of the outcome. Sometimes software fail, and sometimes they need assistance from human pattern recognition. With a limited dataset, it can be more efficient to correct and edit by hand instead of spending time finding and running a software that will require additional and manual error checking anyway.

Algorithms solve problems according to specified rules. That is why they may be of limited use if a dataset is noisy and patterns are irregular. 'Signals are always surrounded by noise, even to the extent that we cannot always decipher which is which.'[7] Hadley Wickham explains (alluding to Leo Tolstoy) that 'tidy datasets are all alike but every messy dataset is messy in its own way'.[8] A dataset can be corrupt in numerous ways, but there is only one way in which it is flawless. The multiple possibilities of errors, and the irregularity of their occurrence, can make it difficult to specify the rules on how to solve problems algorithmically. In some cases, the fastest way may be to do some of the work manually.

As Dasu and Johnson point out, cleaning has a significant impact on results. Yet, detailed discussions on cleaning and error-checking processes are rare in introductions and chapters on methodology. Introductions usually describe digital tools, not manual or semi-manual tasks.[9] The role of digital tools and models is often discussed in terms of black boxes, with an input and an output and an obscure software in the middle. Such black boxes must be opened up in order to make research processes transparent.[10] Manual and semi-manual procedures can be said to represent another black box, however, perhaps even more opaque. They can be difficult to describe in a transparent way since they rely on human pattern recognition, a sensitivity to individual cases and the ability to make informed distinctions between information and noise.

A History of Manual Labour

As Markus Krajewski has pointed out in his media history of service, before digital servers there were human servants: human calculators, research assistants and secretaries.[11] The birth of automatised data processing did not do away with them. When Vannevar Bush speculated on the future research potentials of computers in 1945, he described a machine that 'will take instructions and data from a roomful of girls armed with simple keyboard punches, and will deliver sheets of computed results every few minutes'.[12] Father Robert Busa is often referred to as the first scholar to use the capabilities of computers within the humanities. However, his project also involved 'a roomful of girls'. His interest started in the 1940s when he studied the preposition 'in' in the works of Thomas Aquinas. This research would clearly benefit from the technologies developed to speed up data processing in business and administration. Busa partnered with IBM and during the following decades they constructed an index of the full vocabulary in the works of Aquinas, published in 1974 as *Index Thomisticus*. In words that echo in recent publications on distant reading, Busa stated that: 'What had first appeared as merely intuition, can today be presented as an acquired fact: the punched card machines carry out all the material part of the work of (making a concordance).'[13]

The process was far from automatic though. The mainframe computers available at the time required 'a constant procession of human servants'.[14] In 1964, Busa had a team of 60 people assisting him with editing, programming and machine operations. Around 35 staff members were required for key-punching texts, verifying, listing, sight-checking and punch-card processing (the data was later transferred to magnetic tapes). In 1951, he estimated that it would take four years to complete the index. The reason why the project was not finished until the mid-1970s was mainly the laborious work of pre-editing and proofreading. 'Busa calculated that the thirty years of work he and others had spent on it amounted to roughly one million man hours.'[15] The foundational project of what would become digital humanities was truly a manifestation of the manual work needed to process data with computers.

The labour-intensive process did not discourage other scholars from using computers in their research (perhaps because those who introduced new methods seldom emphasised the importance of manual tasks). When the *Index Thomisticus* was completed in 1974, Busa was no longer alone. Linguists were among the early adopters, as well as some historians. Swedish historians were introduced to the idea that 'Clio faces automation' in an article by Carl Göran Andræ from 1966. Andræ explained that modern computers provided solutions to problems related to massive source materials. With data coded onto punch cards, or optical and machine-readable paper forms, it was possible to sort large amounts of data mechanically or electronically. In many cases, the systems were used as search engines, but they could also perform statistical calculations. The examples he gave included databases of coded newspaper articles, correlations between election results and census data, and the geographical distribution of unions and memberships in popular movements. Andræ concluded, as Busa before him, that: 'The mechanical work can now be left to computers.'[16]

Details on the actual research process are rare in publications by the first generation of computer-using Swedish historians.[17] Assistants, secretaries and machine operators may have been essential parts of the research process, but they were rarely acknowledged in the end results. Some clues can be found, however, and the impression they give is quite different from Andræ's optimistic view. The most laborious tasks concerned coding, in this case referring to the transfer of data from source documents to machine-readable formats (punch cards or optical markings on paper forms). A Swedish pioneer, the press historian Stig Hadenius, explained in 1967 that it took 'not more than 16 people' to extract the data needed for a pilot study on political news between 1896 and 1908.[18] A large project on Sweden during the Second World War had a group of researchers investigating newspaper debates during the war. In order to render the newspaper material searchable, they coded 165,000 articles to create an index based on punch cards. The research team manually coded 138 variables for every article.[19] In the 1970s, a series of dissertations from Lund University used similar methods to process newspaper articles on various topics during the postwar era. Gunnel Rikardsson, who wrote about *The Middle East conflict in the Swedish press* (1978), did not elaborate on the manual tasks, but explained that six people had been involved in the process and that the 'coding work was experienced as exacting, mainly due to the high degree of concentration needed'. When the newspaper data was finally coded, however, the computer took over the workload: 'Manual processing had not been possible.'[20]

In his article from 1966, Andræ speculated on future research possibilities. Governmental agencies were already using computers to store and process data. Thus, for future historians who wanted to analyse the data, computer skills would be an absolute necessity. Most of the sources that historians worked with in the 1960s and 1970s were not 'born digital' though. The technologies (such as Optical Character Recognition, OCR) transferring analogue data to digital media showed promising results, but the majority of the research projects relied on manual labour. Millions of hours were spent on manual coding, punching and proofreading. The name of the research centre founded by Busa in the early 1960s was *Centro per L'Automazione dell'Analisi Letteraria*. Yet, and contrary to the automation emphasised in the name, photographs from the centre show what was often left unnoticed when research output was presented: rows of human operators, most of them young women.[21]

Struggling with Noisy Newspapers

The manual tasks needed today are of a different kind. The digitisation of sources is part of many research projects, but with scanners and software for OCR the digitisation of printed texts can be more or less automatised. Even handwritten texts can to some degree be digitised with the help of OCR technology. A significant difference, though, is that archives and libraries do much of this work for us. This is especially true for newspapers and books, parliamentary records and collections of audio-visual media, paintings and maps, and other museum artifacts. As long as the copyright allows for it, texts and images are made available online. In most cases, we do not need (and cannot afford) 35 assistants transferring data from one medium to another. Full-text search, topic modelling and tools for text analysis often make it unnecessary to code individual texts manually.

And yet, not all datasets are ready for processing out of the box; many of them can be very messy. As Carl Lagoze has pointed out, traditional archives and libraries used to guarantee the integrity of their records, at least in principle.

Control and curation were meant to facilitate the provenance and stability of data. The digitisation of collections and archival records has meant a fracturing of this control zone.[22] When millions and millions of pages are transferred (or translated) into digital formats, no one can guarantee the integrity of the data anymore. For large datasets of non-canonical texts in particular, libraries have spent less resources on curation, leaving researchers with much of the cleaning and preparation. Newspaper databases are notorious in this respect. Frequent OCR errors are well known, problems related to text segmentation less so, but both kinds of errors make it difficult to process the texts without manual interventions.

In one of my projects, I wanted to analyse discursive patterns in newspaper reports about the electrical telegraph in mid-19th-century Sweden.[23] From the National Library of Sweden, I was able to download a complete dataset covering one major newspaper from 1830 to 1862, about 10,000 pages. A systems developer helped me to penetrate the data (the first person who was asked refused to work with a dataset this noisy). Our first goal was to find every article containing the words 'electrical' and 'telegraph' ('elektrisk' and 'telegraf' in Swedish). Since we expected a high frequency of OCR errors, we used a Levenshtein distance to identify corrupted versions of our keywords, allowing three characters to be added, replaced or missing. In this way, we got 489 different hits for 'electrical' and 4,017 for telegraph. This was all done with a few simple commands, and the result came quickly.[24]

Not all of the hits had anything to do with the electrical telegraph though, and in order to filter out the false positives I had to go through the lists manually. That 'dialektisk' and 'apoplektisk' referred to something else was easy to figure out, but what about 'pelektriska' and 'elepris'? What about 'tograf', 'tfiesraf' and 'ttlefrnf'? Such combinations of characters can only be interpreted in the context of their appearances in the newspaper. In order to single out the proper keywords, I had to search the database and read the texts. It turned out that many of the incomprehensible words generated by the OCR actually referred to the electrical telegraph. My corpus would have been much smaller if I had not spent some time on this semi-manual step.

With an edited list of keywords, it was possible to locate every 'textblock' in the XML-files where 'electrical' and 'telegraph' co-occurred. A textblock is a unit of text identified as a coherent text by the text segmentation tool used in the digitisation process. However, nineteenth-century newspapers are difficult to process for the tool. The small print, the lack of headlines and the packed columns give few graphical clues on where one text finishes and another one starts. Human eyes can see it quite easily, while digital tools make several mistakes. Many libraries send the auto-segmented newspaper pages to private firms with outsourced divisions in Eastern Europe, Cambodia and India. The job of the staff is to correct the segmentation where it has failed.[25] The National Library of Sweden have skipped this crucial step in the process, however. I had to do the job myself.

We soon discovered that the textblocks generated by the tool had little to do with the texts as they were printed in the paper. Short news items from the same column were regularly merged into one single textblock, and longer texts chopped up into shorter pieces. The only way to single out the texts I wanted was to read through the whole corpus of identified textblocks and delete the unrelated parts. I also deleted text lines and combinations too difficult to decipher, such as '1PlApfos2kOS2viKfSbmNAl' and 'rilet4R12bin1dPRRmo-8botoFrfutmfsOMMFgpgFvf'. I did not read the texts as carefully as I would have done if close reading was my main research method. But still, I had to read them.

With a somewhat clean dataset we could finally start to explore what the texts had to say about the electrical telegraph. We used a fairly simple and transparent method to identify semantic patterns. We looked at words co-occurring in a sliding window, and used the network analysis tool Gephi to find clusters of frequently co-occurring words. We still had some problems with noise though. Our method identified co-occurring words no matter the quality of the OCR, but for the final analysis we wanted to merge corrupted versions with the uncorrupted (for example, 'oeanen' and 'oceanen' (the ocean), 'Mo«se' and 'Morse'). Once again, we used a Levenshtein distance to pick out the most likely candidates to be merged, but I went through the lists to confirm the results manually.

In the end, we came up with some new and fascinating results. Many of the ideas we frequently associate with the electrical telegraph were more or less absent in the newspaper reports. Very few mentioned anything about the utopian potential of the new medium, it was not seen as an immaterial way of communicating and the idea that it 'freed communication from the constraints of geography' must be contextualised.[26] A bureaucratic discourse on regulation was much more prominent than a utopian on liberation, many of the articles described the material components of the new network instead of immaterial flows of electrical signals, and the geographical prerequisites (such as ocean floors and mountains) that determined where cables could be laid out were described in detail. I recognised much of this already when I read the texts in order to delete the noise, but I believe the quantitative analysis made the conclusions more convincing.

Scholars writing about computational text analysis usually emphasise the need to combine distant and close reading.[27] You need to switch between different perspectives to get an understanding of general patterns, as well as individual cases. In my own research, I already had to read the texts more or less closely in order to clean and prepare the corpus. When I reviewed the lists and graphs of frequently co-occurring words, I had an in-depth knowledge about the dataset on which they were based, making it easier to interpret the output. The time I spent reading and editing turned out to be well invested, but the process was very different from what I had imagined when I started the project.

Recognising Named Entities

What media technology we consider to be the first one ever invented depends on our definition of media. One common definition emphasises that a medium is a technology for the storage and/or transfer of information.[28] In that case, the tally stick might be the oldest media technology in human history. A tally stick keeps track of things you want to count (days, people, objects, etc.) and makes it possible to save the counts for later and to transport them from one place to another. The oldest one found, a bone from a baboon with carved markings, is at least 40,000 years old. 'Although our ancestors could not have known it, their invention of the notched stick has turned out to be amongst the most permanent of human discoveries.'[29] That my colleague Erik is using their invention to keep track of an imprecise digital tool in 2018 would definitely be beyond their imagination. Erik counts on paper though, not a bone from a baboon.

Tools for NER make it possible to identify and extract names of persons (even mythological creatures), organisations and places in digitised texts, as well as expressions of time (1857, 'next week'), monetary values and so on. The extracted data can be used for geographical visualisations, for network analysis, in timelines and as building blocks in other kinds of text analysis. HFST-SweNER, a language-processing technology developed to extract named entities from Swedish texts, is based on a dictionary as well as rules for identifying entities not in the dictionary, but likely candidates based on their contexts.[30] Tests have shown that it works fairly well for a curated corpus of texts from the 1990s, but will it work for 19th-century newspaper texts?

Erik Edoff is a media historian interested in geography. In one of his projects, he tries to figure out how new communication technologies in the 19th century reorganised the notion of space.[31] Was the world getting smaller when telegraphs, railroads, canals and steamships made it possible to communicate across space in a shorter time or in no time at all? Did far-away places come closer as a result of a time-space compression? One way to examine this (but certainly not the only one) is to identify and count place names in newspapers before and after the introduction of the new technologies (Erik selected papers from 1850 and 1890). Were names of distant locations printed more frequently when news travelled faster? The first results generated with NER indicated that places in the local region were in fact getting relatively more attention when new connections made communication faster, compared to places outside of the region. These were exciting results, since they seemed to show that the impact of the new technologies was different from what is usually believed. The question then became whether these numbers could be trusted. Did the tool find all the place names printed in the papers? If not, was it biased towards local Swedish place names?

In order to calculate the precision and recall, Erik chose a few newspaper issues for every title and year in the corpus. He read through the NER-tagged text files manually, and kept track of valid hits and false negatives in two

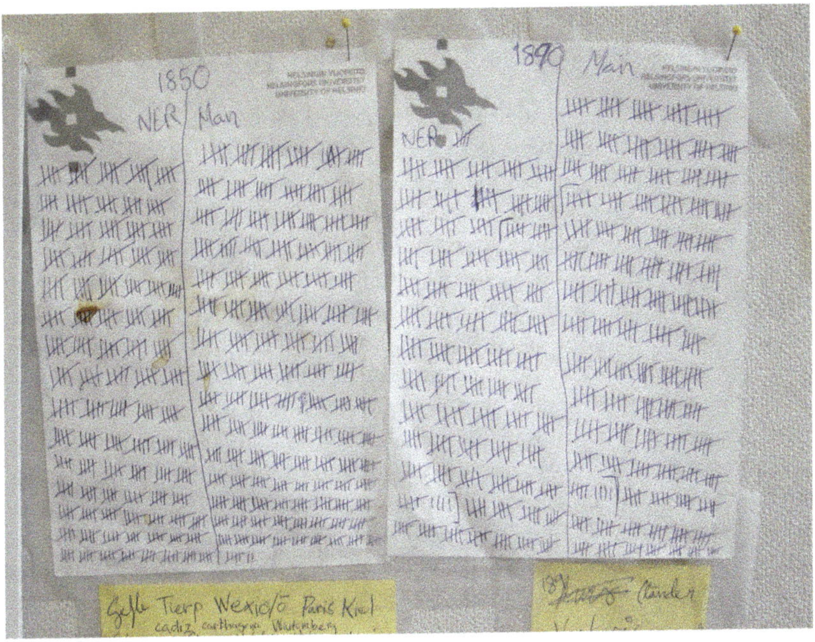

Figure 7.1: How many named entities (locations) did NER find, and how many more did Erik find? New locations not tagged by the tool were recorded on post-it notes. Source: Author.

columns on a couple of paper sheets. The method of counting was basically the same as the one used by our distant ancestors making notches on a bone: one mark for every word counted (see Figure 7.1). The brackets enclosing some of the counts separate place names mentioned in advertisements and lists, such as weather reports, stock market prices, etc. Those entities were more difficult to identify for the digital tool. There are other and perhaps more sophisticated ways to count occurrences of place names. But pen and paper are often efficient tools for minor tasks. No downloading or installing is required, and no special training. The interface makes the paper easy to use, and it is highly flexible.

The manual control revealed that the tool had left several place names untagged. For some reason, it did not recognise locations such as Paris, Kiel or Swinemünde, nor the Swedish towns Gävle (in the 19th century: Gefle), Växjö (Wexiö) and many minor towns and villages. One explanation might be the old spelling, but in some cases (when the spelling changed between 1850 and 1890), the tool recognised the old spelling, but missed the new. And the spelling does not explain the case of Paris. One geo-administrative category was left untagged almost completely: the parish. Today, it is hardly used outside of the Swedish church, but in the 19th century it was one of the most common ways in which Swedish locations were identified. Apart from these place names, Erik found several locations untagged because of OCR errors. All of the entities identified manually were fed back into the system in order to make the final hit list more complete.

It turned out that the trend indicated by the first results was even more prominent once the false negatives were included. The relative frequency of places in far-away countries did not increase with the introduction of new communication technologies. Rather, locations close to the towns where the newspapers were published got more attention in 1890 compared to 1850. Erik's close reading of the sample issues provided him with some possible explanations. New places were put on the map thanks to new communication technologies: railway intersections, telegraph stations, bridges where steamships picked up passengers and goods, locks connecting canals and lakes. The places most frequently mentioned were those in the region, such as neighbouring towns and villages connected by railway, harbours close to home and regional centres nearby where telegrams were sent. New communications brought neighbours together. What was already close came even closer, while distant places were as far away as they were before. The repetitive task of recording place names on paper paid off in an interesting and convincing analysis. NER was a helpful tool, but it needed human assistance.

Troubleshooting Black Boxes

Digital models and tools will continue to improve. In the future there will, hopefully, be no need to carry out many of the manual tasks described in this text. OCR is getting more accurate every year; for some languages, NER seems to work fine already. On the other hand, as digital research practices are becoming more widespread, researchers will try to use the methods for new kinds of materials and in new areas—even areas where they will not run as smoothly. If we limited our research to clean datasets, very little would be accomplished. Many of the manual tasks carried out by research assistants and undergraduates in the 1960s are automatised today. New tools can achieve things unthinkable 50 years ago, but not always without human interventions. New problems seem to arise as old ones are taken care of.

The long history of information management can be seen as a series of new solutions generating old problems. In a fascinating article about the paper technologies used by Carl Linneus, in his big data-project on the natural system, Staffan Müller-Wille and Isabelle Charmantier note a 'curious dynamic' in the attempts to master information overload. 'The many technologies that were designed to contain information actually fuelled its further production, partly by providing platforms for more efficient data accumulation, partly by bringing to the fore new structural relations and patterns within the material collected.'[32] The result of technologies, developed to create order, overview and searchability, is often a new information overload. The digital media of today have other capabilities than Linneus' paper slips and lists, but their operations are not as precise and clean as we might think. Rotten data, spam and noise thrives in a digital habitat (an interesting research topic in itself).[33] As shown by libraries' digitisation efforts, new technologies are far from perfect and human assistance is sometimes needed to keep them on track.

To edit, clean and validate large datasets manually or semi-manually may seem highly ineffective. In many cases, however, these procedures can be quite effective. Reading, counting, deleting and merging texts and other kinds of data in a manual or semi-manual fashion is a way to bridge distant and close reading. Insights from such encounters with data can be fruitful in the final analysis. It might also be a way to dig deeper into the inner workings of the digital tool on which the researcher is relying, to figure out how a specific dataset was processed and why the output turned out as it did. Troubleshooting is a good way to start if we want to examine what is inside the black boxes.

Notes

1 The research presented here is part of the project 'Digital Models: Techno-historical collections, digital humanities & narratives of industrialisation', funded by the Royal Swedish Academy of Letters, History and Antiquities.
2 Star 2002: 109.
3 On the role of marginal (and yet central) figures, actions and technologies in the history of science, see Becker & Clark 2001 and Krajewski 2018.
4 Thylstrup 2018: 42–43. See also Price & Thurschwell 2005.
5 Fyfe 2016.
6 Dasu & Johnson 2003: ix.
7 Parikka 2012: 111.
8 Wickham 2014: 2.
9 See, e.g., Jockers 2013; Graham, Milligan & Weingart 2016; Rockwell & Sinclair 2016.
10 Rieder & Röhle 2012.
11 Krajewski 2018.
12 Bush 1945: 104.
13 Robert Busa quoted in Burton 1981: 1.
14 Krajewski 2018: 308.
15 Burton 1981: 3.
16 Andræ 1966: 96.
17 Jarlbrink 2015.
18 Hadenius 1968: 68.
19 The coding manual is now available online. See Åmark 2013.
20 Rikardsson 1978: 59–60.
21 Jones 2018.
22 Lagoze 2014.

[23] Jarlbrink 2018.
[24] The newspaper noise is further explored in Jarlbrink & Snickars 2017.
[25] Fyfe 2016: 565.
[26] Carey 2008: 157.
[27] Jockers 2013: 26; Blevins 2014: 126; Hitchcock & Turkel 2016: 953.
[28] Mitchell 2017.
[29] Ifrah 2000: 64.
[30] Kokkinakis et al. 2014.
[31] Edoff, forthcoming.
[32] Müller-Wille & Charmantier 2012: 4.
[33] See Parikka & Sampson 2009; Eriksson 2016.

References

Andræ, C. G. (1966). Clio inför automationen. *Historisk Tidskrift, 86*(1), 47–79.

Becker, P., & **Clark, W.** (Eds.) (2001). *Little tools of knowledge: historical essays on academic and bureaucratic practices.* Ann Arbor, MI: University of Michigan Press.

Blevins, C. (2014). Space, nation, and the triumph of region: a view of the world from Houston. *Journal of American History, 101*(1), 122–147.

Burton, D. M. (1981). Automated concordances and word indexes: the fifties. *Computers and the Humanities, 15*(1), 1–14.

Bush, V. (1945). As we may think. *The Atlantic Monthly*, July, 101–108.

Carey, J. W. (2008). *Communication as culture: essays on media and society.* London and New York, NY: Routledge.

Dasu, T., & **Johnson, T.** (2003). *Exploratory data mining and data cleaning.* Hoboken: John Wiley.

Edoff, E. (forthcoming). Revolutions in communication? Digital methods and nineteenth century Swedish press.

Eriksson, M. (2016). Close reading big data: the echo nest and the production of (rotten) music metadata. *First Monday, 21*(7). DOI: https://doi.org/10.5210/fm.v21i7.6303

Fyfe, P. (2016). An archaeology of Victorian newspapers. *Victorian Periodicals Review, 49*(4), 546–577.

Graham, S., Milligan, I., & **Weingart, S.** (2016). *Exploring big historical data: the historian's macroscope.* London: Imperial College Press.

Hadenius, S. (1968). En kvantitativ innehållsanalys av dagspressen: teknik och användning i modern historisk forskning. In *Opinion och opinions bildning som historiska forskningsobjekt: Föredrag vid Nordiska fackkonferensen för historisk metodlära på Hässelby slott 4–6 maj 1967.* Oslo: Universitetsforlag.

Hitchcock, T., & **Turkel, W. J.** (2016). The *Old Bailey proceedings, 1674–1913*: text mining for evidence of court behavior. *Law and History Review, 34*(4), 929–955.

Ifrah, G. (2000). *The universal history of numbers: from prehistory to the invention of the computer*. New York, NY: John Wiley.

Jarlbrink, J. (2015). Historievetenskapens mediehantering. In M. Hyvönen, P. Snickars & P. Vesterlund (Eds.), *Massmedieproblem: mediestudiets formering*. Lund: Lunds universitet.

Jarlbrink, J. (2018). Telegrafen från distans: ett digitalt metodexperiment. *Scandia, 84*(1), 9–35.

Jarlbrink, J., & **Snickars, P.** (2017). Cultural heritage as digital noise: nineteenth century newspapers in the digital archive. *Journal of Documentation, 77*(6), 1228–1243.

Jockers, M. (2013). *Macroanalysis: digital methods & literary history*. Urbana, Chicago and Springfield, IL: University of Illinois Press.

Jones, S. (2018). Reverse engineering the first humanities computing center. *Digital Humanities Quarterly, 12*(2).

Kokkinakis, D., Niemi, J., Hardwick, S., Lindén, K., & **Borin, L.** (2014). HFST-SweNER: a new NER resource for Swedish. In N. Calzolari, K. Choukri, T. Declerck, H. Loftsson, B. Maegaard, J. Mariani, A. Moreno, J. Odijk, S. Piperidis (Eds.), *Proceedings of the Ninth International Conference on Language Resources and Evaluation (LREC'14)*. No. 391. Reykjavik, Iceland: European Language Resources Association.

Krajewski, M. (2018). *The server: a media history from the present to the Baroque*. New Haven, CT: Yale University Press.

Lagoze, C. (2014). Big data, data integrity, and the fracturing of the control zone. *Big Data & Society, 1*(2), 1–11. DOI: https://doi.org/10.1177/2053951714558281

Mitchell, W. J. T. (2017). Counting media: some rules of thumb. *Media Theory, 1*(1), 12–16.

Müller-Wille, S.. & **Charmantier, I.** (2012). Natural history and information overload: the case of Linnaeus. *Studies in History and Philosophy of Biological and Biomedical Sciences, 43*(1), 4–15. DOI: https://doi.org/10.1016/j.shpsc.2011.10.021

Parikka, J. (2012). *What is media archaeology?* Cambridge and Malden, MA: Polity Press.

Parikka, J., & **Sampson, T. D.** (Eds.) (2009). *The spam book: on viruses, porn, and other anomalies from the dark side of digital culture*. Cresskill, NJ: Hampton Press.

Price, L., & **Thurschwell, P.** (2005). Invisible hands. In L. Price & P. Thurschwell (Eds.), *Literary secretaries/secretarial culture*. Aldershot and Burlington, VT: Routledge.

Rieder, B., & **Röhle, T.** (2012). Digital methods: five challenges. In D. M. Berry (Ed.), *Understanding digital humanities*. Houndmills: Palgrave Macmillan.

Rikardsson, G. (1978). *The Middle East conflict in the Swedish press: a content analysis of editorials in three daily newspapers 1948–1973*. Stockholm: Esselte studium.

Rockwell, G., & Sinclair, S. (2016). *Hermeneutica: computer-assisted interpretation in the humanities*. London and Cambridge, MA: MIT Press.

Star, S. L. (2002). Infrastructure and ethnographic practice: working on the fringes. *Scandinavian Journal of Information Systems, 14*(2), 107–122.

Thylstrup, N. B. (2018). *The politics of mass digitization*. London and Cambridge, MA: MIT Press.

Wickham, H. (2014). Tidy data. *Journal of Statistical Software, 59*(10), 1–23. DOI: https://doi.org/10.18637/jss.v059.i10

Åmark, K. (2013). *Sverige under andra världskriget: pressregister 1938–1945*. Stockholms universitet, Historiska institutionen: Svensk nationell data tjänst (SND). Retrieved from snd.gu.se/catalogue/file/3386

PART III

Distant Reading, Public Discussions and Movements in the Past

CHAPTER 8

The Resettlement and Subsequent Assimilation of Evacuees from Finnish Karelia during and after the Second World War

Mirkka Danielsbacka, Lauri Aho, Robert Lynch, Jenni Pettay, Virpi Lummaa and John Loehr

Introduction

The consequences of forced migrations are felt globally and are faced by millions of people each year. A critical question is how these refugees adjust to their new environments and eventually integrate into the host population. A number of factors can influence the ultimate assimilation of migrant populations and these are frequently related to the characteristics of the migrants (for example, demographic variables and socio-economic background), flight (for example, cause of flight), host country or region (for example, natural resources) and the resettlement policies of host populations. One way to measure the successful settlement and assimilation of displaced populations is to look at the number of times an individual relocates after their initial arrival in a host country and to analyse which factors affect these moves. In general, the more individuals move, the less likely they are to integrate.[1] In this

How to cite this book chapter:
Danielsbacka, M., Aho, L., Lynch, R., Pettay, J., Lummaa, V., & Loehr, J. (2020). The resettlement and subsequent assimilation of evacuees from Finnish Karelia during and after the Second World War. In M. Fridlund, M. Oiva, & P. Paju (Eds.), *Digital histories: Emergent approaches within the new digital history* (pp. 129–147). Helsinki: Helsinki University Press. https://doi.org/10.33134/HUP-5-8

chapter, we investigate the evacuation of Karelia—a unique forced migration event that took place in Finland during the Second World War—and the socio-demographic and environmental factors associated with the relocation and settlement of Karelian evacuees during and after the war.

Our methodological approach builds on the socio-economic tradition of conducting digital history in which we use quantitative data and methods to analyse and interpret a question of historical importance (the assimilation of Karelian evacuees). Therefore, it might be more accurate to define the methodological approach used here as quantitative history, rather than 'new digital history', even though it can certainly be argued that all quantitative history is essentially digital history. In line with many of the new digital history projects, our data has been digitised and compiled with the help of new digital tools (see 'Material and Methods', below) and we have an interdisciplinary research team of biologists, computer scientists, sociologists and historians with considerable experience working on these and similar datasets. However, analysing these newly extracted data has been executed with rather common statistical methods (for example, regression models) that are in line with the quantitative tradition of social and economic history.

During the Second Word War, an estimated 40 million Europeans fled their homes in what is widely considered to be the worst refugee crisis in modern history.[2] Finland faced this problem after it ceded Karelia to the Soviet Union in the aftermath of the Winter War (1939–1940) and once again after the Continuation War (1941–1944). Almost all Karelians were evacuated to the remaining parts of Finland. It has been said that Karelians have had the 'sad privilege of being the only refugee group in the world to have been displaced three times within a short period of four years—1940–1944'.[3] Two of these displacements were forced and resulted from the Soviet occupation of Karelia in the Winter War and at the end of the Continuation War, but one, during the Continuation War, was a voluntary migration back to recaptured Karelia.

Previous historical and cultural studies of Karelians have concentrated on describing the Karelian evacuees and their assimilation in Finnish society,[4] Karelians' memories of the evacuations and the land they lost in Karelia,[5] and the resettlement policy of the Finnish government.[6] In addition, previous sociological and epidemiological studies of Karelian evacuees have mainly focused on the long-term effects of forced migrations on mortality,[7] income[8] or socio-economic status[9] by comparing displaced Karelians with the rest of the Finnish population. These studies have frequently been conducted with the same 10% sample data (n = 411,629) from the 1950 population census, which was the first full census implemented in Finland. Karelians can be extracted from these data because there is information on the place of residence from the year 1939 which is prior to the initial evacuation. A constraint of this dataset, however, is that it is limited to variables available in the years 1939, 1950 and in follow-up datasets from 1970s onwards. Studies conducted with these data have found that after the Second World War Karelian men had higher socio-economic standing and higher income than their non-displaced counterparts.[10] Sarvimäki and colleagues suggest that one reason for this is that Karelians were more likely to move from their initial placement areas to other regions in Finland in search of better employment opportunities than non-displaced Finns. This suggests at least one explanation for the finding that younger male Karelians reached a higher socio-economic position when compared to non-displaced Finnish males. In addition, displaced people transitioned faster from agrarian to modern occupations than non-displaced Finns, which could have also affected their improved socio-economic standing.[11] On the other hand, a study by Haukka and colleagues found that displaced Karelians had higher overall mortality and ischemic heart disease mortality than the rest of the Finnish population. It is interesting to note, however, that when compared to international research on the long-term effects of forced migration, Karelians had lower suicide rates.[12]

Previous studies have not used micro-level data to explore whether Karelian evacuees differed in their migration histories as a function of their background characteristics. Background characteristics of Karelians as well as environmental factors of a host country may associate with likelihood of migration; furthermore, migration history could reflect the assimilation of Karelians. More specifically we explore: Who moved back to Karelia when they had the opportunity? And who remained in western Finland? Which environmental factors affected the likelihood of return? How much, on average, did Karelians move after the second evacuation (that is, how easily did they settle after the Second World War)? What were the characteristics of the evacuees who moved most frequently and what factors predict faster assimilation?

Karelian Evacuees

Two separate wars were fought with the Soviet Union on the eastern border of Finland. The Winter War started on 30 November 1939, when the Soviet Union attacked Finland, and lasted until 13 March 1940. During this first war, Finland lost 11% of its land territory, including its second biggest city, Vyborg. The Soviet occupation of Karelia forced approximately 407,000 people to flee their homes and to be placed elsewhere in western Finland.

Before 1950, Finland was predominantly an agrarian country, and agricultural occupations were even more common in Karelia than in other parts of the country. Approximately 230,000 evacuees (57%) earned their living from agriculture. Not all of them were farmers, however, and some were agricultural workers who did not own the farm they worked on. These farms were, on average, smaller than farms in other parts of Finland.[13]

The initial placement of the evacuees was poorly planned and organised due to the sudden start to the Winter War and rapid advance of the Soviet troops. Migrants were initially housed in public buildings that were used as shelters and only later were transferred to private residences. In the summer of 1940, an

Emergency Settlement Act and compensation law were passed. With the settlement law, farmers could obtain new land to farm and, with the compensation law, the state would pay for the lost property.[14]

Land for evacuees was acquired from the state, the Church and municipalities, but it was also frequently seized from private owners. Although Finnish authorities attempted to carry out land acquisitions with voluntary purchases, many farmers were forced to sell their land. The purpose of the Emergency Settlement Act was not to ensure that Karelian farmers would be fully compensated for the land they had lost, but rather was to make sure that those Karelians who made their living from agriculture could continue to do so.[15]

Between the Winter and Continuation Wars, evacuees who made their living from agriculture, especially those who had their own farms in Karelia, had the hardest time adjusting because the Emergency Settlement Act forced them to wait before they received land. This may have caused additional friction between evacuees and the host population because of the hard labour shortage with which evacuees were expected to help.[16] But it was the placement of Karelian evacuees among Swedish-speaking Finns that aroused the most criticism. This was because placing Finnish-speaking Karelians in bilingual municipalities could have endangered the delicate relationship between Swedish- and Finnish-speaking populations. The language question came to the fore once again after the Continuation War, when Karelians had to be settled permanently in the remaining parts of Finland.[17]

Because carrying out the Emergency Settlement Act was slow, only about 13,000 new small farms were actually founded and only 6,000 of these contracts were finalised by the summer of 1941, even though many more applications were received. With the onset of the Continuation War in the summer of 1941, Finnish troops reconquered the Russian occupied regions, which gave Karelians the opportunity to return to Karelia. Evacuees who had received emergency settlement farms were then allowed to cancel their contracts; more than half of them did so by March 1943 and returned to Karelia. Nevertheless, a few hundred households kept their emergency settlement farms and gave up their claims on their land in Karelia.[18] Approximately 70% of the original evacuees (280,000) who had initially settled elsewhere in Finland voluntarily moved back to their previous home in Karelia, while the remaining 30% decided to remain in their new location. The number of evacuees who returned was higher in some locations of origin (for example, over 80% for Sortavala) and lower in others (for example, 40% to 60% for Viipuri). Farmers were more likely to return (~75%), and although returning to locations near the front line was not allowed, some disobeyed and returned anyway. A long period of trench warfare kept the front line quite stable from January 1942 until summer 1944 when the final Soviet offensive began.[19]

The Continuation War ended in the autumn of 1944 and the border was redrawn back to where it had been in 1940 and everyone who had returned to Karelia between the wars was evacuated once again.[20] This time, the evacuation and placement of evacuees were much more systematic than they had been after the Winter War. In May 1945, the Parliament approved the Land Acquisition Act (*Maanhankintalaki*), which guided the settlement policy.[21] According to the Act, groups that were entitled to receive land were evacuees who had made their living from agriculture, disabled soldiers, war widows, war orphans, soldiers who had served on the frontline or had a family and several other smaller groups. Evacuees submitted almost 48,500 applications for land; 92% of these were accepted and evacuees were placed in certain initial placement areas. In the summer of 1945, they started to move to other places, partly because they were ordered to and partly due to their own initiative. The official placement plan only applied to the agricultural population, which meant that townspeople and industrial workers were free to choose where they wanted to settle. Resettlement of the agricultural population was based on the idea that people from the same villages would be able to stay in the same areas and that their placements would correspond to the climatic, economic and religious circumstances of the area from which they were evacuated. The official placement plan was only applied in its strictest form to farmers, and among them those who were entitled to farm. This constituted about 35% of all evacuees. Although they were in the minority, the final resettlement plan resulted in most of the farmers having to move again. As a result, in the years immediately following the war, movements may have been more prevalent among farmers than other evacuees.[22]

Material and Methods

Here we use the recently digitised Migration Karelia (MiKARELIA) database, which contains over 160,000 adult Karelians and a wide range of data on births, marriages, occupations and movements of these forced migrants. The original source material for the database comes from a register compiled in the book series *Siirtokarjalaisten tie* (Anon. 1970; the title directly translates to: *Karelian migrants' road*), which systematically recorded the experiences of evacuees.

Interviews took place between 1968 and 1970 and were performed by approximately 300 trained interviewers. Each entry lists the full name (maiden name if applicable), profession, birth date, birth place and all movements (towns or cities of residence) from birth until the date of the interview, as well as their spouse's names, professions, birth dates, birth places and years of marriage for those who married. Children's names, birth years and birth places are also listed. These basic demographic data are presented in a standardised format for each entry. There is a variety of other data as well, including, for example, whether men had served in the army during the war and whether women had participated in the Lotta Svärd organisation (an all-female paramilitary organisation).

The resulting registers contain a vast amount of data on the Karelian migrants, but in book format, they are poorly suited to quantitative analysis. Therefore, a project was initiated to digitise these data, which ultimately resulted in the generation of the MiKARELIA database. Data entries were scanned at 300 dpi using a Canon c5250i copier and saved in pdf format. ABBYY Fine Reader 12 (ABBYY production LLC 2013) was used to scan pdf documents for optical character recognition (OCR) and the output saved in html format. An open source software program[23] was written to convert Fine Reader produced html files to a simpler xml format containing the data entries. The program reads and extracts the source text to produce a JSON file containing all extracted data. These data can then be used to populate a structured database.[24]

Obviously, the MiKARELIA database represents only those Karelians who were alive in 1968 to 1970 when the interviews were conducted. However, Loehr and colleagues have estimated that these data include records on approximately 75% of the Karelian migrants who were alive at this time. Therefore, MiKARELIA can be considered to be a population-based database and not just a statistical sample of Karelians.[25] The MiKARELIA database is being further improved and replenished by combining it with other datasets (for example, the Karelia database 'Karjala-tietokanta', which contains digital demographic information from about 70 parish registers of the ceded Karelia from the end of the 17th century until the start of Second World War).

One key advantage of the MiKARELIA database, for example, as compared to the Statistics Finland 10% sample data from the 1950 population census, is that while in the sample data individual level variables (for example, migration of Karelians) are only available for the year 1950 and from 1970 onwards,[26] in MiKARELIA there are individual level data on evacuees during the Second World War (for example, whether they served during the war and whether they returned back to Karelia during the Continuation War). Therefore, the MiKARELIA database offers excellent opportunities to explore with considerable detail the migrations of Karelians during and after the Second World War in addition to a variety of socio-demographic and environmental factors that were associated with their decisions to migrate.

To determine whether Karelian evacuees differed in their migration histories as a function of their background characteristics, the current study involved analysing the already existing MiKARELIA database and combining it with a database on the location of all the cities and towns involved in the evacuations, and their population sizes. Populations of towns located in Finland and Karelia were obtained from the Statistical Yearbooks of Finland 1939.[27] In addition, for each place, we obtained coordinates to locate them on the map and calculate the effect of several geographical dimensions on the probability of returning home during the war (1941–1944). To do this, information was gathered from multiple sources on the internet and maps. Most of the coordinates could be found directly from the history books of the *Suomen sukututkimusseura* (the Finnish Genealogy Society), while the rest were searched from Google Maps—a map utility served by Google Incorporation (Google Maps, Finnish Genealogy Society).

Sample selection

Although interviewees provided some information on other members of their family (for example, spouses and children), in our analyses we focused solely on individuals who were interviewed and on which we had the most complete and systematically recorded information. Thus, the statistical unit for this research is the family, rather than each family member separately, given that families were presumed to have moved together. In addition, children (individuals who were born after 1925) were excluded from these analyses. These individuals would have been 15 years old or younger in 1941 when the first opportunity to return to Karelia was possible. The birth location, rather than the location in Karelia at the moment of the evacuation, was used because the location of the evacuees immediately prior to the evacuation was only recorded for a small subset of individuals, whereas birth place was available for more than 90% of the total sample. Finally, only those who were born in Karelia were chosen. These selection criteria left us with a sample of 59,477 Karelian evacuees. Each population size parameter (birth population, population of first destination in Finland and population of return destination in Karelia, which was used in the maps) was log transformed for reasons of statistical inference (that is, the effects of population size are not expected to be merely additive) and to aid fitting the models.

Variables

As a dependent variable, we use a binary variable: whether an individual returned to Karelia or not (0 = no, 1 = yes). In our sample, 52% returned, which is a somewhat lower number than the overall proportion of evacuees who returned, which was reported to be approximately 70%. This may be because we are both missing the oldest Karelians who might have been more likely to return than the younger ones (and had died by the time of the interviews in 1968 to 1970), and also missing those who were children (less than 15 years old) during the war. Our other dependent variable is the total number of moves after 1945 and up until 1970. In our sample, Karelians had on average 1.02 (SE 0.005) moves, which varied between 0 and 19. The majority, however, moved at least once (54%).

As independent variables we use: sex, age, occupation in 1970 (farmer or non-farmer; we are expecting that farmer was the most 'stable' occupation, that is, one can assume that they were already farmers in Karelia), whether he or she had children in 1940, longitude and latitude of birth location, longitude and latitude of first destination in Finland and population size in birth location and first destination in Finland (see Table 8.1 for descriptive statistics).

We used generalised linear logistic and Poisson regression models to analyse these data. In the case of returning to Karelia during the Continuation

Table 8.1: Descriptive statistics for those who returned Karelia and those who did not (%/mean, (SE)).

	Returned Karelia 1941–1944	
	Yes	**No**
Sex (%)		
Women	53.1	46.9
Men	52.2	47.8
Age (mean)	30.7 (0.06)	28.9 (0.06)
Farmer (%)		
Yes	73.5	26.5
No	42.9	57.1
Have children (%)		
Yes	60.6	39.4
No	48.5	51.5
Birth destination longitude (mean)	29.8 (0.01)	29.7 (0.01)
Birth destination latitude (mean)	61.0 (0.004)	60.9 (0.005)
Destination longitude (mean)	24.8 (0.02)	25.3 (0.02)
Destination latitude (mean)	61.9 (0.01)	61.6 (0.01)
Destination population size (mean)	18280.1 (351.6)	43327.9 (743.5)
Birth population size (mean)	12559.33 (116.9)	17915.5 (212.3)

Note: Demographic variables n = 49,780; environmental variables n = 29,622. Source: Authors.

War, we explain our binary dependent variable (returned to Karelia = 1, did not return = 0) using a logistic regression and the coefficients of the predictors are interpreted as odds ratios. An odds ratio above 1 indicates a greater likelihood of the event compared to the reference category, and an odds ratio below 1 indicated a smaller likelihood when all other covariates entered into the model are held constant. To model the number of moves after the Continuation War, we used both a logistic regression (no moves = 0, at least one move =1) and a Poisson regression which fits these count data (namely, the number of moves) better than a normal distribution. Poisson regression coefficients can be interpreted in a similar manner as linear regression coefficients such that negative coefficients indicate a negative relationship and positive coefficients indicate a positive association with the outcome variable when all other covariates are held constant.

Results

The evacuees in the MiKARELIA database we used here were from areas west and north of Lake Ladoga, which are the regions Finland lost to the Soviet Union. The distribution of evacuees' homes at the time of evacuation are illustrated in Map 8.1. Geographically, the top destination as well as the rest of the distribution are generally widely spread across southern Finland (see Map 8.2). The distribution of returning evacuees to Karelia during the Continuation War is similar to the baseline in 1939, with a few exceptions in southern Karelia. The number of people who returned is, of course, fewer than the number who left from those same places (see Maps 8.1 and 8.3).

Return to Karelia during the Continuation War

Evacuees were spread across an area spanning 60 to 70 degrees latitude, with most people concentrated in the south, especially in areas below 64 degrees latitude (see Map 8.2). Map 8.2 shows the percentage who returned from each evacuation destination in western Finland. Here, it is evident that the degree to which the return rate depends on location is complex. However, return rates below 50% are more common at lower latitudes and a higher percentage of people returned to northern parts of Karelia. Evacuees were spread quite evenly across an area of Finland spanning 19 to 31 degrees longitude. At more western longitudes, the proportion of those who returned to Karelia is greater.

Overall, Karelians placed in northern and western Finland were more likely to return. Evacuees were spread across towns and cities of varying populations, but those evacuated to the areas in the largest category (population size greater than 20,000), fewer than 60% returned. No other relationships between population size and return rate were obviously evident (Map 8.2).

Results shown in Table 8.2 are from a two-stage stepwise logistic regression model in which the dependent variable is whether or not a person returned to Karelia, and the independent variables are added to the model in two stages: first, all socio-demographic variables and, second, all environmental variables. Results from Model 1 show that men were less likely to return than women. In subsequent sensitivity analyses, this difference disappeared, however, once the fact that many men were serving in the army was taken into account (results of sensitivity analyses are not shown in Table 8.2). In addition, results suggest that age was not a significant predictor of returning to Karelia. Being a farmer was, however, and the predicted probabilities (calculated from odds ratios) of returning for farmers was 73% as compared to non-farmers, which was 43%. (Note: In Model 2, which also takes into account environmental factors, the probabilities were 76% and 53% for farmers and non-farmers respectively.) Therefore, the adjusted probabilities did not differ much from the unadjusted distribution (see Table 8.1). Having children was also positively associated with returning to Karelia.

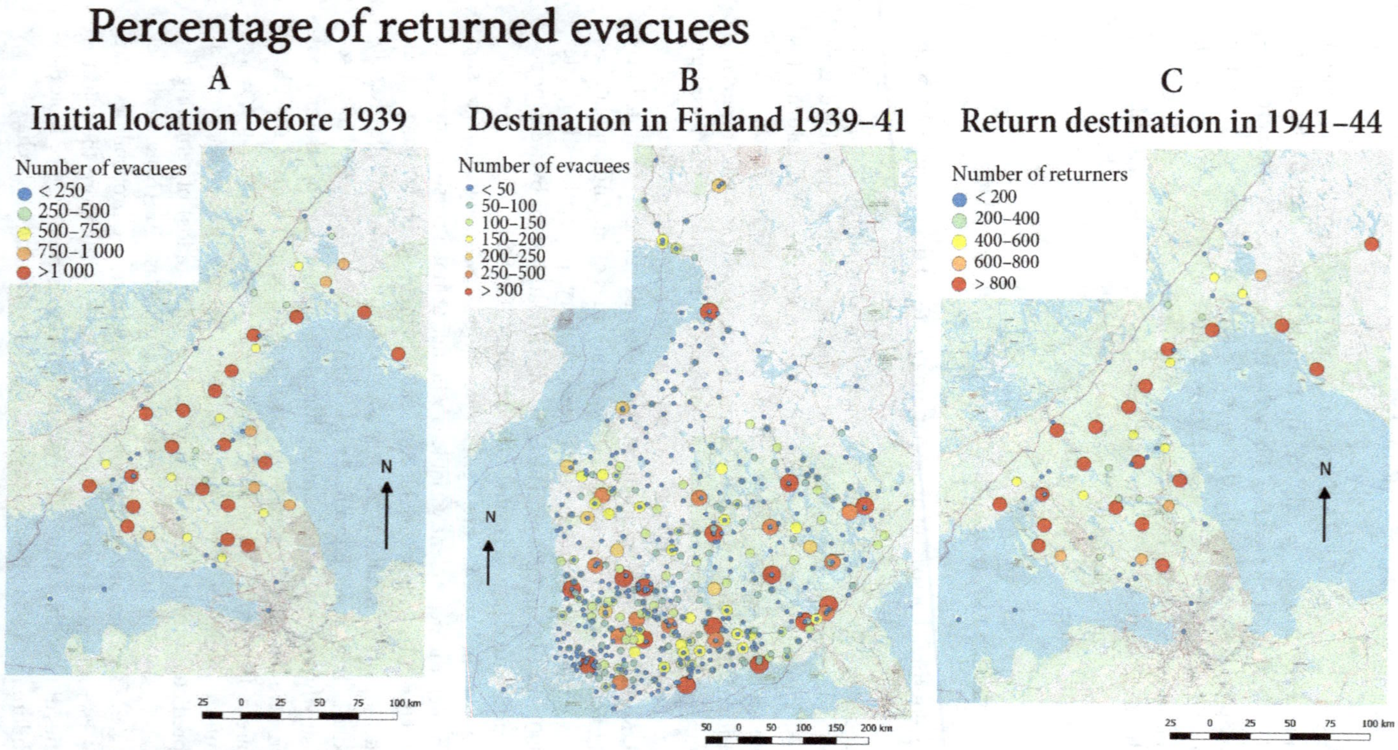

Map 8.1: Dispersal patterns of Karelian evacuees 1939–1944. First (A) the locations where Karelians were evacuated from. Secondly (B) the distribution of displaced evacuees in Western Finland. Finally (C) the locations of the retruning Karelians to homeland during Continuation War. Source: Authors.

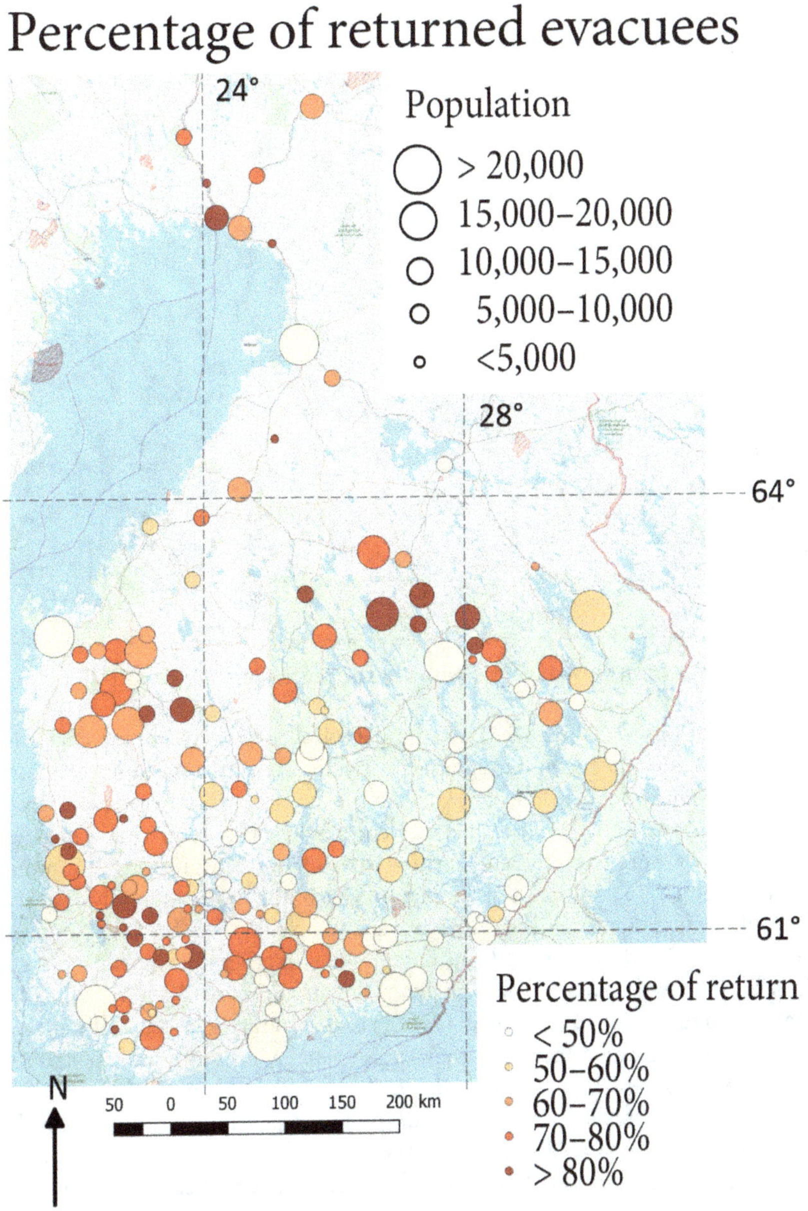

Map 8.2: The proportion of evacuees who returned to Karelia from towns in western Finland during the Continuation War. Source: Authors.

Table 8.2: Association between socio-demographic and environmental factors with the likelihood of returning to Karelia during Continuation War.

	Model 1					Model 2				
				95% CI					95% CI	
	OR	SE	p	lower	upper	OR	SE	p	lower	upper
Sex										
Women (ref.)										
Men	0.83	0.02	0.000	0.80	0.86	0.84	0.02	0.000	0.80	0.88
Age	1.00	0.001	0.091	1.00	1.00	1.01	0.002	0.000	1.01	1.01
Farmer										
No (ref.)										
Yes	3.64	0.08	0.000	3.49	3.79	2.78	0.08	0.000	2.61	2.95
Have children (%)										
No (ref.)										
Yes	1.38	0.03	0.000	1.32	1.44	1.19	0.04	0.000	1.12	1.27
Birth destination longitude						0.78	0.02	0.000	0.75	0.81
Birth destination latitude						2.31	0.08	0.000	2.15	2.48
Destination in Finland longitude						0.89	0.01	0.000	0.88	0.90
Destination in Finaland latitude						1.04	0.01	0.002	1.01	1.06
Destination population size						0.74	0.01	0.000	0.73	0.76
Birth population size						0.98	0.02	0.126	0.95	1.01
n	49,780					29,622				
McFadden's Adj r2	0.067					0.102				

Note: Results from two-stage stepwise logistic regression. Source: Authors.

Results of Model 2 (Table 8.2) take into account several environmental variables, in addition to socio-demographic variables. Results from this regression model support the conclusions drawn from the maps shown above: people from more western and northern birthplaces were more likely to return and evacuees who went to more westerly and northerly destinations in Finland were more likely to return. In addition, the population size of the destination town or city in Finland was significantly and negatively associated with the likelihood of returning to Karelia during the Continuation War. In other words, people placed in less populated areas were less likely to remain and more likely to return to Karelia. Taking these environmental factors into account did not alter the effects of socio-demographic factors, although age was significantly and positively associated with returning, meaning that older people were more likely to return.

Map 8.3 indicates that evacuees from the larger populations have relatively fewer people returning, although the association was not statistically significant in the regression model. In addition, places located nearer to the front line, especially in the Karelian Isthmus, had relatively fewer people returning.

Migration after the Continuation War

Our second dependent variable considered the number of moves after the Continuation War. First, we investigated those Karelians who had moved at least once after their first placement (Table 8.3). Here, men were more likely than

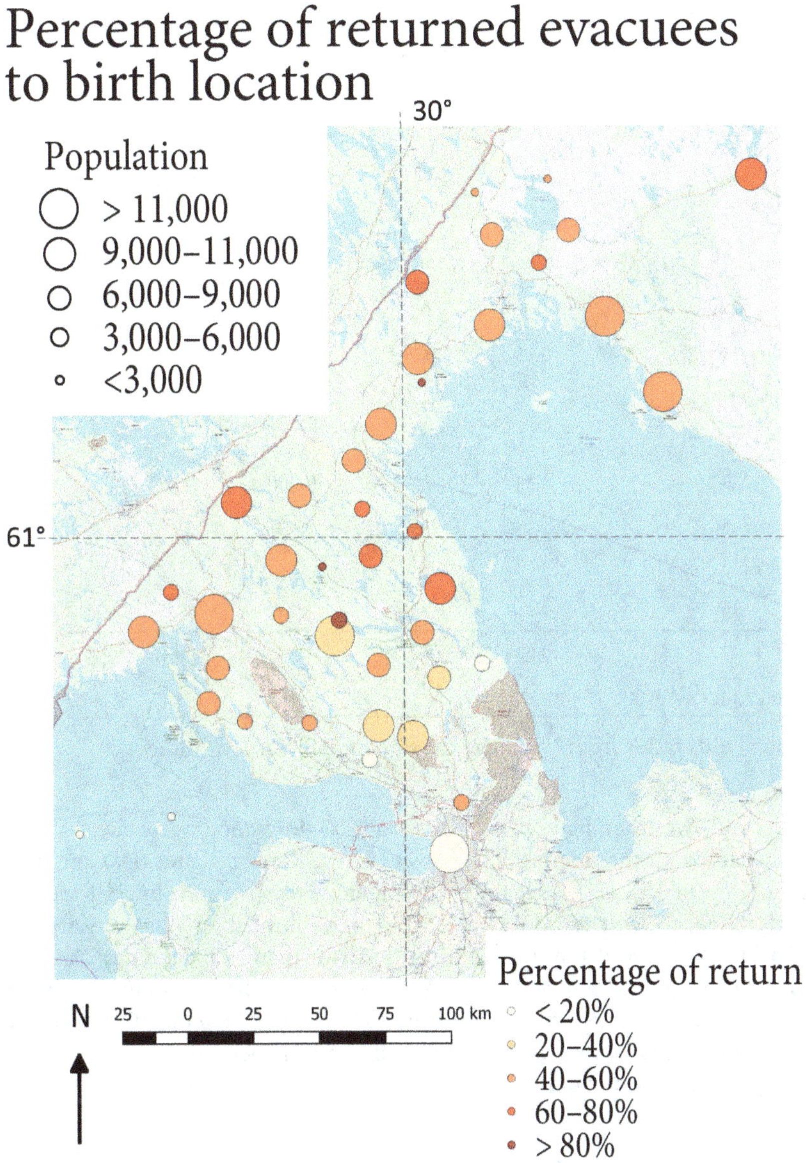

Map 8.3: Proportion of evacuees who returned to their natal locations in Karelia. Source: Authors.

women to move at least once. Also, the younger these individuals were, the more likely they were to move multiple times. Being a farmer was also positively associated with the likelihood of moving at least once. In addition, those who had returned to Karelia during the Continuation War were more likely to move at least once after the war than those who did not return.

Table 8.3: Socio-demographic factors and whether or not individuals returned to Karelia associated with the likelihood of Karelians to move at least once after Continuation War

				95% CI	
	OR	**SE**	**p**	**lower**	**upper**
Sex					
Women (ref.)					
Men	1.26	0.02	0.000	1.22	1.31
Age	0.99	0.001	0.000	0.98	0.99
Farmer					
No (ref.)					
Yes	1.11	0.02	0.000	1.06	1.16
Returned Karelia					
No (ref.)					
Yes	2.22	0.04	0.000	2.14	2.31
n	49,241				
McFadden's Adj R2	0.034				

Note: Odds ratios from logistic regression model. Source: Authors.

Second, we examined whether the same socio-demographic factors were associated with the frequency of moves among Karelians after the Continuation War (Table 8.4). As was the case with any moves, men, younger Karelians and those who returned to Karelia during the Continuation War were all more likely to move more after the Continuation War than women, older Karelians and those who did not return to Karelia when they had a chance. However, farmers were less likely than non-farmers to move more after the Continuation War. This was the only factor that was differently associated with moves when compared to the previous model (Model 1).

Discussion and Conclusions

Our primary aim in this chapter was to study how the migration histories of Karelian evacuees during and after the Second World War were influenced by a variety of social, environmental and demographic characteristics. Which evacuees were more likely to move back to Karelia when they had the opportunity? Which environmental factors influenced an individual's decision to return or remain? How many times, on average, did the Karelians move after the second evacuation and who moved the most and who settled the fastest?

Table 8.4: Socio-demographic factors and whether or not one returned to Karelia after the Winter War is associated with the frequency of moves among Karelians after the Continuation War.

	coeff.	SE	p	95% CI lower	upper
Sex					
Women (ref.)					
Men	0.10	0.01	0.000	0.09	0.12
Age	–0.02	0.0005	0.000	–0.02	–0.02
Farmer					
No (ref.)					
Yes	–0.16	0.01	0.000	–0.18	–0.14
Returned Karelia					
No (ref.)					
Yes	0.40	0.01	0.000	0.38	0.41
n	49,241				
McFadden's Adj. R2	0.022				

Note: Coefficients from Poisson regression model. Source: Authors.

We used the new MiKARELIA database which has unique individual level information on moves of Karelians during and after the Second World War. Our results are mainly in line with previous studies,[28] although very few of these have concentrated on factors related to returning to Karelia during the war. We found that both socio-demographic and environmental factors were associated with returning to Karelia during the Continuation War.

In detail, we found no sex differences in the likelihood of returning once we took into account the fact that many men were serving in the army during the Continuation War. Previous studies[29] have shown and this study confirms that farmers were more likely to return than non-farmers. In addition, once environmental factors are taken into account, the models show that older individuals were more likely to return than younger ones. This suggests that those Karelians who were in a more stable phase of life and who were probably more attached to their home districts (for example, had family and land and were older) were more likely to return to Karelia. Environmental factors also made a difference. People placed in more westerly and northerly destinations in Finland were more likely to return,[30] while at the same time Karelians who were from more western and northern birthplaces were also more likely to return. In addition, evacuees who were placed in smaller towns were also more likely to return. Importantly, these environmental factors, which had been documented previously in other studies, were still significant predictors of returning to Karelia even when socio-demographic variables were controlled for. A major advantage of this study is that we can take several characteristics into account at once and draw the conclusion that, for instance, occupation (namely, being a farmer) did not alone explain the variation in returning to Karelia.

While analysing the number of moves after the Continuation War, we discovered that nearly half of the Karelians actually settled permanently in their first location (46%). Those who had moved at least once were also more likely to be farmers. This was probably the result of the resettlement policies and the Land Acquisition Act,[31] which required farmers to wait to acquire their own land. However, after this initial displacement, the farmers were less likely than others to move, which suggests that they probably settled the fastest. Finally, younger people, men and those who did return to Karelia during the war were more likely to move at least once after the war ended and these evacuees also moved more overall. The positive association between evacuees who returned to Karelia and subsequent movements after the war ended is particularly interesting because it seems to contradict our findings on the characteristics of those who returned and those who moved more after the war. In other words, although farmers were more likely to return to Karelia when an opportunity came and individuals who returned were more likely to move after the war ended, those who moved more after the war were also less likely to be farmers. This indicates that there may be yet-to-be-determined factors influencing the relationship between returning to Karelia and geographic mobility after the war and suggests that these relationships need to be investigated further.

The main strengths of this chapter are that we were able to utilise individual level data on a large number of Karelians to study their migration during and after the Second World War. A key advantage of this kind of database and the methods used in this chapter are that we were able to simultaneously take into account several factors that are associated with the frequency of migration.

The main limitations of this study are data related. For example, we do not have data on the oldest Karelians and currently we only have occupations for people in these data from when they were interviewed in 1970. These issues are related to the fact that the original data were collected in 1968 to 1970. However, a crucial advantage of having digitised these data is that we can in the future continuously update and supplement these data with other source material and merge them with other large quantitative databases available for the Finnish population.

Future studies could investigate more closely the migration profiles of different sub-groups of Karelians. For instance, what happened to those farmers who did not return to Karelia during the Continuation War or to those evacuees who settled in their first location after the Continuation War? By examining more closely the movements of different groups of Karelians, we may also explore how the early settlement of evacuees is linked to the long-term outcomes associated with forced migration.[32]

Notes

[1] Kuhlman 1991.
[2] Lowe 2012.
[3] Kliot 2007: 57–78.
[4] See, e.g., Waris et al. 1952; Paukkunen 1989; Kananen 2010.
[5] See, e.g., Raninen-Siiskonen 1999; Armstrong 2004; Fingerroos 2010; Savolainen 2015.
[6] See, e.g., Waris et al. 1952; Hietanen 1982; Laitinen 1995a.
[7] Haukka et al. 2017.
[8] Sarvimäki et al. 2009; Sarvimäki et al. 2018.
[9] Sjöblom 2016.
[10] Sarvimäki et al. 2009; Sjöblom 2016.
[11] Sarvimäki et al. 2009.
[12] Haukka et al. 2017.
[13] Hietanen 1982: 67, 105.
[14] Waris et al. 1952: 52, 327.
[15] Ibid.: 104–111; Hietanen 1982.
[16] Hietanen 1982: 114–115.
[17] Kulha 1969: 80–82.
[18] Waris et al. 1952: 110; Hietanen 1982: 226–230; Laitinen 1995b: 52–138.
[19] Waris et al. 1952: 53–56, 328.
[20] Simonen 1965.
[21] Waris et al. 1952; Sarvimäki et al. 2009.
[22] Laitinen 1995b: 52–138; Waris et al. 1952: 65–74, 112–127.
[23] Salmi & Loehr 2017.
[24] Loehr et al. 2017. See also Lynch, Lummaa & Loehr 2019a; Lynch et al. 2019b who have used the same data.
[25] Loehr et al. 2017.
[26] See more on Statistics Finland data: Sarvimäki et al. 2009; Sjöblom 2016; Haukka et al. 2017; Sarvimäki et al. 2018.
[27] Statistics Finland 1940.
[28] See, e.g., Hietanen 1982; Lynch et al. 2019; Waris et al. 1952.
[29] See, e.g., Hietanen 1982: 114–115; Lynch et al. 2019.
[30] Waris et al. 1952.
[31] Ibid.: 65–74, 112–127; Laitinen 1995b: 52–138.
[32] Cf. Sarvimäki et al. 2009; Haukka et al. 2017.

References

Armstrong, K. (2004). Remembering Karelia: a family's story of displacement during and after the Finnish wars. New York, NY: Berghahn Books.

Fingerroos, O. (2010). *Karjala utopiana*. Jyväskylä: Jyväskylän yliopisto.

Haukka, J., Suvisaari, J., Sarvimäki, M., & Martikainen, P. (2017). The impact of forced migration on mortality: a cohort study of 242,075 Finns from 1939–2010. *Epidemiology, 28*(4), 587–593.

Hietanen, S. (1982). *Siirtoväen pika-asutuslaki 1940: Asutuspoliittinen tausta ja sisältö sekä toimeenpano.* Historiallisia tutkimuksia 117, Helsinki: Suomen historiallinen seura.

Kananen, H. (2010). *Kontrolloitu sopeutuminen: Ortodoksinen siirtoväki sotien jälkeisessä Ylä-Savossa (1946–1959).* Jyväskylä: Jyväskylän yliopisto.

Kliot, N. (2007). Resettlement of refugees in Finland and Cyprus: a comparative analysis and possible lessons for Israel, In A. M. Kacowicz & P. Lutomski (Eds.), *Population resettlement in international conflicts: a comparative study* (pp. 57–78). Plymouth: Lexington Books.

Kuhlman, T. (1991). The economic integration of refugees in developing countries: a research model. *Journal of Refugee Studies, 4*(1), 1–20.

Kulha, K. (1969). *Karjalaiset Kanta-Suomeen: Karjalaisen siirtoväen asuttamisesta käyty julkinen keskustelu vuosina 1944–1948.* Jyväskylä: Gummerus.

Laitinen, E. (Ed.) (1995a). *Rintamalta raiviolle: Sodan jälkeinen asutustoiminta 50 vuotta.* Jyväskylä: Atena Kustannus Oy.

Laitinen, E. (1995b). Vuoden 1945 maanhankintalain synty, sisältö ja toteutus. In E. Laitinen (Ed.), *Rintamalta raiviolle: Sodan jälkeinen asutustoiminta 50 vuotta* (pp. 52–138). Jyväskylä: Atena Kustannus Oy.

Loehr, J., Lynch, R., Mappes, J., Salmi, T., Pettay, J., & Lummaa, V. (2017). Newly digitized database reveals the lives and families of forced migrants from Finnish Karelia. *Finnish Yearbook of Population Research, 52*, 56–69.

Lowe, K. (2012). *Savage continent: Europe in the aftermath of World War II.* London: Viking.

Lynch, R., Lummaa, V., & Loehr, J. (2019). Self sacrifice and kin psychology in war: threats to family predict decisions to volunteer for a women's paramilitary organization. *Evolution and Human Behavior, 40*(6), 543–550 DOI: https://doi.org/10.1016/j.evolhumbehav.2019.06.001

Lynch, R., Lummaa, V., Panchanathan, K., Middleton, K. M., Rotkirch, A., Danielsbacka, M., O'Brien, D., & Loehr, J. (2019). Integration involves a trade-off between fertility and status for World War II evacuees. *Nature Human Behaviour, 3*, 337–345. DOI: https://doi.org/10.1038/s41562-019-0542-5

Paukkunen, L. (1989). *Siirtokarjalaiset nyky-Suomessa: Jyväskylän yliopiston yhteiskuntapolitiikan laitoksen tutkimuksia.* Jyväskylä: Jyväskylän yliopisto.

Raninen-Siiskonen, T. (1999). *Vieraana omalla maalla: Tutkimus karjalaisen siirtoväen muistelukerronnasta.* PhD thesis, University of Joensuu.

Salmi, T., & Loehr, J. (2017). Kaira-core [computer software]. Lammi Biological Station. Retrieved from https://github.com/Learning-from-our-past/Kaira-core

Sarvimäki, M., Uusitalo, R., & Jäntti, M. (2009). *Long-term effects of forced migration.* IZA Discussion Paper No. 4003. Retrieved from https://ssrn.com/abstract=1351167

Sarvimäki, M., Uusitalo, R., & Jäntti, M. (2018). *Habit formation and the misallocation of labor: evidence from forced migrations*. Department of Economics, Aalto University, Working Paper. Retrieved from http://hse-econ.fi/sarvimaki/

Savolainen, U. (2015). *Muisteltu ja kirjoitettu evakkomatka: Tutkimus evakkolapsuuden muistelukerronnan poetiikasta*. Joensuu: Suomen Kansantietouden Tutkijain Seura.

Sjöblom, E. (2016). *Karjalan evakoiden elämänurat: Sopeutuminen elämään pakkomuuton jälkeen*. Master's thesis of Sociology. University of Helsinki.

Simonen, S. (1965). *Paluu Karjalaan: Palautetun alueen historiaa 1941–1944*. Helsinki: Otava.

Statistics Finland. (1940). *Statistical yearbook of Finland 1939*. Helsinki: Tilastollinen päätoimisto.

Waris, H., Jyrkilä, V., Raitasuo, K., & Siipi, J. (1952). *Siirtoväen sopeutuminen. Tutkimus karjalaisen siirtoväen sosiaalisesta sopeutumisesta*. Helsinki: Otava.

CHAPTER 9

Towards Digital Histories of Women's Suffrage Movements

A Feminist Historian's Journey to the World of Digital Humanities

Heidi Kurvinen

Introduction

During the past decade, the amount of digitised material has exploded,[1] but they are not available to all researchers in an equal manner. The entrance to the field of digital humanities requires cultural and technological capital which excludes or marginalises researchers who do not have the skills to conduct digital analyses by themselves or do not have access to the organisational support. According to Matthew K. Gold, it is research-intensive universities containing sufficient financial and human resources that have been able to embrace the digital turn.[2] Again, this ability to focus on digital research and hire personnel to carry out the analysis has formed a 'circle of good' stabilising their status within the field. Other universities, not to mention individual researchers, have been less fortunate, but simultaneously digital analysis tools increase the expectations that we as scholars are expected to accomplish.[3]

Gender is one of the factors that seems to affect the ability of researchers to take part in the digital turn. Farida Umrani and Rehana Ghadially discuss the

How to cite this book chapter:

Kurvinen, H. (2020). Towards digital histories of women's suffrage movements: A feminist historian's journey to the world of digital humanities. In M. Fridlund, M. Oiva, & P. Paju (Eds.), *Digital histories: Emergent approaches within the new digital history* (pp. 149–163). Helsinki: Helsinki University Press. https://doi.org/10.33134/HUP-5-9

aspect of empowerment that is connected to the access of computers for women by using the division between 'information rich' and 'information poor' people.[4] Even though their approach is connected to third-world countries and the use of computers in general, I find the division useful also in the context of digital humanities. Similarly, researchers within humanities and social sciences are nowadays divided into those who have skills and access to digital research methods and those who don't. Based on stereotypical gender role expectations (such as viewing technology as masculine coded) with which most generations of current historians have been raised, men have often better opportunities to explore the field even if the starting point is the same with their female colleagues. The reason for this, as Miriam Posner has pointed out, is that middle-class white men are more likely to have been encouraged to explore with computers at a young age than women or other marginalised groups.[5] At the same time, most present-day researchers are regardless of gender already to some extent participating in the digital turn as the mixing of traditional and new (digital) research practices have become a self-evident part of our present-day work as scholars, in the form of digital voice recorders, digital cameras and the use and analyses of digital texts and images.[6]

In this chapter, I will discuss what is needed when a historical scholar with limited digital skills wants to take a step towards learning how to conduct digital analyses, towards becoming a digital historian. As a feminist historian, I will combine this approach with a discussion of the relation of feminist research and digital humanities. In line with practice in feminist research, I will be using a self-reflexive approach and asking how the increase in the understanding of digital methods influences our research questions in feminist history. Do digital humanities tools transform our work as feminist historians? How can digital analyses develop the field of gender history in general and the history of feminism in particular? Can a scholar who has limited technological skills engage with an informed and critical discussion with digitised materials?

Even though the main points of my chapter apply to all historical research, a focus on gender analysis is worth making as gender seems to have remained a rather limited category of analysis among digital historians. And although not all gender historians identify their work as feminist, there is a strong connection between the two,[7] which makes the discussion of the relation between feminism and digital analysis a valid starting point for this chapter. The intention is not, however, to claim that there is a clear difference between feminist history and historical research in general, but to participate in the discussion of the meanings of feminist approaches to digital humanities and ponder why in particular feminist historians should be part of these discussions.

Feminism and Digital Humanities

At first, the combination of feminist research and digital analysis may seem as strange bedfellows, but for the past decade feminist digital humanities research has been conducted in various fields in the Anglo-American world, in particular, and scholars have engaged in critical discussion of the relation between feminism and digital humanities. Some scholars have problematised this relation by deconstructing the gender-neutrality of digital analysis tools in order to find ways to overcome the divide between male producers and female users of computational tools.[8] Others have asked how the use of a large amount of data fits with feminist research that relies on gender-sensitive reading.[9] Scholars have also found similarities between feminist research and digital humanities approaches, such as collaborative research. According to Janine Solberg, feminist research and digital humanities may even form a fruitful pair since the idea of an ethical (feminist) researcher encourages the scholar to be open for multiple viewpoints and to position oneself as a researcher and conduct the research in a transparent manner (features that are also valued in digital humanities).[10]

Discussion on a feminist approach to digital humanities has mainly focused on pondering how gender, race and other marginalising factors can be taken into account when compiling datasets and digital archives. In addition, the responsibility of feminist scholars to unsettle digital humanities' 'retro-humanist' practices that maintain a canonical understanding of what is relevant to digitise have been pointed out.[11] However, less has been written about the actual methodological practice of conducting a feminist digital humanities project. Nevertheless, there are some exceptions. In her insightful article on the US suffragette Frances Maule, Solberg, for example, points out how the new technology made it possible for her to find information about Maule, whose life was relatively unknown when she discovered her. At the same time, new information that she was able to find thanks to digitised material changed the interpretations of Maule's texts used by Solberg in her work.[12] Thus, digitised data can help us to find sporadic information of our research subject and combine these pieces of information more easily than previously. Mass digitisation may also widen our opportunities to find traces of people who have been marginalised in the past or purely forgotten, which is consistent with the core ideas of feminist research.

In spite of the existing literature on feminism and digital humanities, feminist digital history seems to be an under-discussed area of study. For instance, scholars of feminist historiography of rhetoric, Jessica Enoch and Jean Bessette, argue that feminists have used digitally born materials to study women's lives, but historians have rarely pondered how digital methods could widen their scope of study.[13] A few exceptions have appeared in feminist literary history, in particular, but the field is still narrow. This seems problematic because the digital turn has already started a revolution in history which will potentially profoundly change our scholarship and require us to learn new tools, as Alexis Lothian and Amanda Phillips have formulated.[14] Also due to this, gender-sensitive historians should start to pay attention to the challenges and opportunities that the digital turn will cause in our field.

The argument follows Solberg as well as Enoch and Bessette, who have demanded more discipline-specific discussions on the role of digital analysis tools and digital research materials.[15] According to my understanding, a focus on gender history is particularly important because, as an already marginalised sub-field of a traditionally masculine discipline, it may not otherwise be able to answer the demands of financers that have started to highlight the importance of digital methods. In addition, gender sensitivity is needed to guarantee that digitisation of archival sources and other material such as print media or books do not focus solely on canonical pieces or notable people of history. Even though gender has been written into history increasingly since the 1960s, digitised collections often maintain gender bias when men's history tends to be viewed as more important. Furthermore, a move towards more digitally aware research may require that gender historians, alongside gender scholars in other fields, start to discuss how women's and other minority groups' abilities to conduct digital humanities research could be supported. However, the intention of this chapter is not to strengthen the essentialist notion of women as less capable than men of conducting digital analysis, but by using my own research field as a starting point to instead problematise what is needed to support scholars such as myself who do not have the basic digital skills, making it difficult to start on their own.

Taking the First Steps in the World of Digital Humanities

In Finland, the first computer started to operate in 1958 and a relatively rapid computerisation has taken place in the country since the 1960s. This has also had its effect on research. Historian Viljo Rasila was already writing about computer-assisted research in 1967 and used these kinds of methods in his work.[16] However, when I began my studies at university as a fresh undergraduate student in 1999, I did not own a computer, and neither did many other students at this time. Computer-assisted methods did not belong to the curriculum and in spite of the accelerating computerisation of the Western world, for many they remained primarily a tool for writing and for using publishing or photo programs. This applied also to my relationship with computers, which explains why I never learned to understand properly how computers work as operational systems. For me, computers remained tools that I used to write and I knew only as much of them as was needed to complete that task.

As a scholar who began her postgraduate studies in the mid-2000s, I was even able to conduct my PhD studies without ever hearing the words 'digital humanities'. I first became familiar with the field as late as in 2015 when editing an article on that matter for a Finnish peer-reviewed journal as part of my duties as a sub-editor. I became instantly intrigued; but for a person with limited IT skills; it felt overwhelming to even try to figure out how I could use the approach in research. As for many, I assume, the first push towards this took place after a year while I was writing a research proposal for a major financing body and tried to figure out how I could elevate the state of art so that my project would be successful in receiving funding. I started to read digital humanities literature and tried to understand what all this could mean for my project.

By reading the texts, I started to realise that digital humanities projects were often collaborative initiatives (that is, not everyone needs to know how to code). However, at that time, I was working as a visiting scholar at a Swedish university with a Finnish research grant, which meant I found it difficult to start looking for collaborative partners. How could I even start to look for them, I was asking myself. In short, I lacked the institutional support as well as technical skills that would have helped me to explore the field on my own.

For a year, every now and then, I read articles on digital humanities, some of which made more sense to me than others. I was, for instance, exhilarated to find out that distant reading could be combined with close reading, the latter of which is the method I am most familiar with. However, the basic question remained the same: How could I start to understand the process of the analysis? Simultaneously, I changed universities and my new colleagues helped me to find pages that offered guidance for different analysis tools, such as The Programming Historian, but it still felt difficult to start learning on my own. Luckily, in the spring of 2018, I was selected for the practical course on digital humanities organised by the project 'From Roadmap to a Road Show' led by Mats Fridlund. It turned out to be the first step towards understanding what digital humanities could actually mean for my historical research. As my project, I selected a small-scale case study of the use of the word '*naisasialiike*' (women's suffrage movement) in the biggest national newspaper *Päivälehti* (1889–1904) / *Helsingin Sanomat* (1904–) at the turn of the 19th and 20th centuries.

Learning by One's Mistakes

Janine Solberg has argued that digital environments can be used as safe spaces to test our research ideas.[17] In her work, Solberg did not rely on big data, but used digitised material to trace pieces of information of her research subject. However, her argument also seems suitable for a scholar who combines a big data approach with close reading of a relatively small pool of data, as is the case in this chapter.

Previously, I had used the National Library of Finland's digital newspaper archive from time to time to look for information. However, I had only used the search option, without trying to familiarise myself with the platform. Due to this, I had the habit of writing down the texts that interested me and it was only when preparing the data for the course that I realised that an OCR view of the text would make it easier to gather the data. However, from the literature, I had learned that not all letters would necessarily appear the same in the OCR text as they were in the original.[18] This was painfully clear concerning the material from *Päivälehti*, in which the articles were published by using fraktur, an old German font type. For instance, the machine was unable to recognise the letter 'w' as such, but it was often written with 'm' or with a combination of two letters such as 'n' and 'i'. Also similar kinds of errors took place with other letters such as 's', which had different kinds of typographical variations in the original text. Furthermore, wider spacing of words which was used to highlight certain words in the newspaper texts, such as surnames, caused trouble for the machine. More importantly, the machine was unable to recognise the newspaper columns which ran in an uneven manner at that time. This meant that the OCR view did not include texts in the order they were mentioned, and I had to copy the paragraphs manually. This included removing paragraphs that were not part of the article I was interested in and ascertaining that all the paragraphs of my article had been copied to the file. Due to these problems, the OCR view made it only slightly easier to prepare the material than my original manner of writing everything manually. While the newest articles might had had only a couple of errors, older texts were often impossible to understand based on the OCR. This meant that I had already read through some of the texts while correcting the OCR, making me familiar with the material. The same kinds of problems have also been noticed by other scholars who have problematised the idea of digital analysis as a rapid way to conduct research with newspaper material.[19]

My first experience with any kind of a data analysis software took place in May 2018, when I participated in the earlier-mentioned digital history course. Based on my project abstract, in which I had suggested that I would use a statistical natural language processing tool called MALLET for carrying out topic modelling analysis of the data, I had been assigned to a MALLET group led by the digital historian Mila Oiva. In addition, Juho Savela was providing technical support. My first challenge on the course was to learn to understand what can be made when using the command prompt of my computer. After that, I learned some basic commands for MALLET which helped me to start playing around with the material. Thus, the course gave me a basic understanding of how the command prompt functions worked and what I as a researcher could do with the material by using MALLET. However, the process of writing this chapter has been a test in which I have used MALLET and my own computer as a safe space for learning more by using the 'learn by your mistakes' method. Gradually, this has deepened my understanding of the process, even though there are still many things I do not understand.

One of the major revelations during the process has been that combining digitised material with technologically assisted analysis needs suitable research questions. According to Solberg, digital tools change our ways of discovering, accessing and making sense of the past. To be more specific, digital environments can reorientate us 'both physically and conceptually' if we choose to be active technology users instead of remaining as passive users of them.[20] Similarly, Jacqueline Wernimont has defined the division of male creators and female users of digital tools as one of the critical questions that feminist digital humanities needs to address.[21] Furthermore, other feminist scholars have engaged in critical discussion of what is enough to make the field more diverse and whether the ability to code is a necessity for all digital humanities scholars.[22] In my case, the move towards a more active user of digital tools meant that my original research questions changed during the process. I realised that MALLET would not be the best option to trace the transnational influences of feminist ideas as I had originally thought. Instead, it offered a window towards the variety of topics connected to which the word *naisasialiike* was used. In the following, I will outline the process of carrying out the analysis as well as ponder whether digital analysis of a relatively small pool of newspaper articles can bring new information concerning the early feminist movement in Finland.

The Importance of Search Words

In the project plan, I outlined the research period to cover the years between 1889 and 1929. I used *Päivälehti*'s first publishing year as a starting point for the search period because the first women's organisation *Finsk Kvinnoförening —Suomen Naisyhdistys* had been established five years earlier in 1884.[23] The period ends in 1929, when the New Marriage Law was approved in Finland, forming one kind of an end point for the early feminist movement.[24] When outlining the period like this, I assumed that it would consist of a reasonable amount of data that I could use in my analysis. Surprisingly, the number of texts using the word *naisasialiike* proved to be relatively low. The search brought 51 results, one of which was a list of literature for Christmas presents. Because the list contained only one item that was relevant for the theme, I did not take it into account. Other hits were mentions as part of larger articles dealing with various women's organisations and their gatherings or books that dealt with women's issues. Additionally, the pool of data consisted of few notifications for meetings organised by the Women's Feminist Union (*Naisasialiitto Unioni*), among others.

The search also brought to light other astonishing revelations. At first, the word *naisasialiike* seems not to have belonged to the newspaper's vocabulary at all, since the first hit was from the year 1896 (12 years after the first women's organisation had been established). Before 1900, the word *naisasialiike* had been used only five times and continued to be used quite rarely until the 1920s: between 1900 and 1920, it appeared 12 times. Thus, it seems that the word made its breakthrough in the 1920s, even though it was still used only occasionally. This is slightly surprising because the 1920s was a relatively quiet period in the Finnish women's movement compared to earlier decades.

One explanation for the concentration of the use of *naisasialiike* may be that, during the 1920s, it was used as a retrospective term to look back on the history of the women's movement. However, throughout the studied period, it appears also as an umbrella term that was used to refer to women's emancipatory demands of its own time. In other words, *naisasialiike* seems to have become a label that was used both by the women's movement activists and their opponents, and it was accepted by the newspaper's editorial office. Thus, the question remains: Why did the most active years of early feminism as a movement in Finland not cause wider coverage in the pages of *Päivälehti / Helsingin Sanomat*? The question is particularly interesting because the word *naisasialiike* is the one that is commonly used in the research to refer to the early feminist movement in Finland. Due to this, it could have been assumed that the word had appeared in public discussion at the turn of the century.

When looking for answers to the above-mentioned question, it is worth taking into account that the results would have been different if I had used different search words. For instance, Hieke Huistra and Bram Mellink have reminded us that a digital humanities scholar needs to choose the right search words to receive reliable results.[25] However, the problem is that a topic can be described with a variety of words that appear at different times, the meaning of which may change in different contexts and throughout the studied period. In *Päivälehti / Helsingin Sanomat*, the words '*feminismi*' (feminism) and '*feministi*' (a feminist) received 11 hits respectively between 1889 and 1929, but the usage of them took place mostly before the 1920s. The word '*naisliike*' (women's movement), which refers to all kinds of women's organising (both feminist and non-feminist), received 255 hits, which suggests that issues relating to women's status in society were not yet directly connected to feminist organising at the turn of the 19th and 20th centuries. The most comprehensive word was '*naisasia*', which received 897 hits. It was used for the first time in 1890, after which it appeared continuously throughout the research period, suggesting that women's issue as a theme was part of the public discussion of its time, but it was not connected to a specific movement per se. An analysis of the usage of the word *naisasia* would, therefore, give us a more comprehensive understanding of the early feminism in Finland, but the cleaning of the material would also require a considerable amount of work, which was not possible in the scope of this chapter. Furthermore, such big data would have made it difficult to use this process as an opportunity to reflect on the relation between feminist research and digital humanities. Comparison of the usage of various words dealing with women's issues nevertheless reveals the development of terminologies which has been shown to be one of the strongest sides of big data analysis. However, as Alex Mold and Virginia Berridge remind us, these kinds of results also need to be contextualised and triangulated with other sources/traditional research methods in order to receive a more accurate understanding of the results provided by the digital analysis.[26]

As pointed out earlier, a close reading of research material is one of the corner stones of feminist research, and digitised computer reading of big data seems to be in contradiction to this. One solution to overcome this conflict is to combine computer-assisted analysis with close reading of the material or parts of it, as Johan Jarlbrink, Pelle Snickars and Christian Colliander have suggested, among others.[27] Based on my small-scale project, a combination of distant and close reading is not only necessary to validate the results, but the combination also gives new perspectives on the material—one example of which is the connection between national and transnational discussion in Finnish feminism.

Previous scholars who have worked with archival material or used media texts in a more traditional manner have extensively shown how the so-called first-wave feminism was committed to national issues in Finland even though the early feminists, at the same time, had wide transnational networks. For instance, Alexandra Gripenberg saw women's emancipation as necessary for human progress and therefore it had to be strived for universally. Simultaneously, her work towards women's emancipation was tied with nationalism.[28] Both sides of early feminism also appear in my data, which I recognised while cleaning the material for the analysis. However, the digital analysis also revealed different nuances in the dynamics between national and transnational aspects of early Finnish feminism, as will be shown in the last section of this chapter.

How the Analysis Was Made

The project was started by preparing the dataset of 50 texts for the analysis, after which I conducted topic modelling with 10, 15 and 20 topics. At first, the topics produced by MALLET seemed like a foreign language to me and the fact that every round of analysis could bring different kinds of word lists was puzzling. Even though I was mechanically able to make the right commands, the ability to start the analysis required a new way of interpreting the lists produced by the computer. This I could not have done without the guidance of Mila Oiva, who patiently used her own research as an example to walk me through the process of shifting my way of thinking. Learning a new way of interpreting the word lists was not the only challenge: I also had some problems with stop-words. Some of them kept popping up in the topics even though I had added them to the list. However, the final round of topic modelling offered satisfactory clean topics even if they still contained some of the listed stop-words, such as the foreign words '*del*', '*und*' and '*des*', as well as abbreviations such as 'klo'. Because the pool of data was small, I chose to make the analysis based on 10 topics, which brought the clearest image of the data (see Table 9.1).

Three out of 10 topics pointed out to transnational exchange of ideas with words that referred to foreign countries in general or by name and to nationalities or countries in plural. However, there were differences between these three topics. While the first one clearly referred to international connections in media in forms of news reports, the second one attached internationalism to the past of the women's movement and the third topic connected international connections and women's movement congresses, pointing to the transnational nature of the women's movement. Other topics were clearly national by nature, but nationalism became a marker for only one of them which included the word '*isänmaan*' (nation's), for instance.

Otherwise, the topics emphasised meetings of various women's organisations and particular individuals such as Maikki Friberg. Four of the topics include words referring to men. Two of them seem to point to the negotiation

Table 9.1: Topic modelling with 10 topics.

Topic	Keywords	Themes
0	kongressin ihmiset del ulkomailla suomalaiset teki sisältää ranskan lehdet pitäen prete otettiin tavoin kansainliiton merkitsee helsingissä tahi monessa aihetta italialaista	kansainvälisyys, kongressit, uutisointi *internationality, congresses, news coverage*
1	suomen osaston naisliiton lucina tohtori puhui helsingin naisten ohjelma maikki friberg liiton olga lausui opettaja esitti hagmanin kuulla alkoi unionin	naisasiajärjestöt, kokoukset, raportointi *women's organisations, meetings, reporting*
2	puhuja tehdä elämän naisen lapset suurta mies elämä piti yleinen miehet tehtävä määrässä äiti olosuhteet elää nuori sai alustaja tehty	kokoukset, nainen, roolit, mies, lapsi *meetings, a woman, roles, a man, a child*
3	naisten naiset saa saada työtä naisia miesten kodin osaa yhteiskunnan osa naisille pois lopuksi maan saanut ulkopuolella muutamia olemassa nähden	nainen, roolit, julkinen elämä *a woman, roles, public life*
4	owat nainen naisen naisasialiikkeen maissa naisasialiike oliwat syntynyt toiminnan joukko wuotta naisyhdistyksen asema eiwät työn maassa osasto omasta toimintaa kehityksen	kansainvälisyys, ylirajaisuus, historia *internationality, transnational, history*
5	naisten suomen kotitalouden liiton hyväksi klo alalla esitelmä seurasi suomessa nykyjään kokous saksan liitto ohjelmassa kaikissa saapunut kansallisliiton suomi esitelmän	kokoukset, kansainvälisyys, naisasiajärjestöt *meetings, internationality, women's organisations*
6	mies professori miehen nim nainen naista naisen voinut esittää perheessä mielestä arvoa ensinkään prof suhteessa tunnettu pitää olevien määrin käy	mies, arvio, naisen rooli *a man, review, a woman's role*
7	ibsenin tuli ibsen lapsia väkijuomien tyttöjen naimisiin perintönä isä ammatin runouden paloviinan lapsen jokaisen ominaisuudet vanha valtiopäivillä saivat selville vieläpä	Ibsen, raittius, mies, naisen rooli, äitiys *Ibsen, temperance, a man, a woman's role, motherhood*
8	suomen kansan lasten laki maamme oikeus eduskunnassa rouva äänioikeus pitäisi asioissa itselleen lain yleisesti miehen kansamme toimintaan isänmaan j.n.e tietä	naisten asema, äitiys, kansallisuusaate *women's status, motherhood, nationalism*
9	warten dagmar von die hywin sai wiime saawat warsin rahaston walittiin prior naisasia hywäksi woi des anne tiedekunnassa und erityinen	naisasia, keskeiset henkilöt *women's issue, main persons*

Source: Author.

between women's and men's roles, while others bring men's point of view to the women's question to the centre. This can be explained with the variety of writers and their relation to the women's movement. Texts that appeared in the regular column of the Women's Feminist Union were most probably written by women's movement activists themselves, as were some other texts published in the paper. However, other texts presented opinions of prominent men. Motherhood is part of three topics, whereas temperance appears to be part of only one topic. The emphasis on women's maternal roles seems accurate because, during the early 20th century, bourgeois women argued on behalf of a social motherhood locating motherhood as women's most important task in the society. According to Sulkunen and others, this bipartisan citizenship was supported by a majority of Finnish women by the 1920s.[29] On the contrary, the marginal role of temperance within the topics is slightly surprising.

What do the above-mentioned outlines tell us about the data? First, as an unexperienced user of MALLET, as pointed out earlier, I began the process by staring at the list of keywords offered by the software without really knowing how I could interpret them. Due to this, I used the scattered ideas I had gained of the texts while carrying out the above-presented classification, even though I had not read all the texts with a similar intensity. Thus, a combination of digital analysis and a close reading of the material helped me to pinpoint the topics that might have otherwise remained unnoticed.[30] Second, the strength of the digital analysis is in its manner of presenting the data in a different form, which highlights certain patterns. In this case, it is evident that the discussion on the women's movement was conducted as part of the Finnish public sphere and nationally topical issues. Simultaneously, foreign countries served as a standard reference point and the women's movement appeared as a transnational phenomenon even though it was connected to national discussions. Third, the public discussion offered room also for men to define their stance towards the women's issue. Fourth, rather surprisingly, certain milestones in the development of women's status were not connected to the women's movement in the public debate. For instance, themes such as women's suffrage (1906) and the New Marriage Law (1929) did not raise discussion in which the word *naisasialiike* had been used.

Thus, it is evident that digitised material has the potential to show us surprising results, features that we don't expect to find from the material, as Mold and Berridge have pointed out.[31] However, to be able to understand these results more profoundly, they need to be contextualised both thematically and journalistically. That is to say that computer-assisted analysis also needs a human to contextualise the results (an example of which are media texts that should not be seen as a number of separate articles, but instead as part of the publication context of their time).[32] For instance, the length of articles had great variation at the turn of the 19th and 20th centuries. *Päivälehti / Helsingin Sanomat* published short news and reports as well as extensively long congress reports, which were often several pages in length. Potentially, this affects the results as I assume has been the case with the discussion on temperance. Based on the topic modelling, temperance had a relatively minor role in the public discussion, but based on close reading of the data it was a recurring theme within the material. However, it was not discussed as part of the longer articles, but only mentioned briefly in other texts. Elsewhere, I have also argued the need to bear editorial practices in mind while historians use media texts to make interpretations of past phenomena. This is particularly important while using digitised materials that easily shadow the journalistic processes behind the texts by taking them out of the context.[33] In my opinion, contextualising may also form the bridge that brings digital humanities and feminist history closer together, moving them from being strange bedfellows to being a functional pair.

Conclusion

In this self-reflexive chapter, I have discussed my own road to digital humanities, a journey which has actually only just begun. I believe that my reflections correlate with those of many of my fellow historians and other humanists who have started their scholarly work before the increasing digitisation of the society and are now trying to figure out how the digital methods can be used. What did I learn when conducting my small-scale case study?

Based on my experience, I agree with Solberg, who has argued that digital environments create 'new ways of interacting with' the material.[34] I would like to add that, at least for scholars with limited digital skills, they offer an opportunity to conduct the research in a more self-aware manner, when every step of the process needs more thought than a traditional research day working with paper archives, for instance. For a feminist scholar, digital humanities may also serve as a channel for emancipation if the scholar chooses to actively participate in the process of analysis instead of relying on the results produced by IT support. However, to be able to do this, we need the support from our universities to focus on this kind of a large-scale project that also requires time for learning new skills.

My experience clearly demonstrates that conducting a basic digital analysis is possible even for a beginner if she receives sufficient support to carry it out. Additionally, the practice is the best way to increase one's understanding of digital analysis. When the understanding increases, the research questions become more accurate at the same time. Within the limits of this small-scale project, the results were not mind-blowing, but they merely strengthened the results of other scholars focusing on the intertwined relation between national and transnational in the history of early feminism. However, the data also reveals new and previously unresearched questions, such as the use and development of vocabulary relating to women's issues in Finland. Furthermore, results of big data analysis expose new ways of perceiving the material which may revolutionise gender history by revealing gender in places that previous research has been unable to grasp. By also challenging feminist scholars to take a step back and examine the material from a distance, digital humanities has the potential to change our understanding of gendered patterns in the past.

These questions require more sophisticated digital analysis than has been possible in this chapter, but it is an inspiring direction towards which I hope to be able to move, alongside other feminist historians in the future. One way to do this is to develop grassroots digitisation projects in which gender, race and other marginalising factors could be taken into account when selecting the objects of digitisation. These kinds of projects have the possibility of developing the field by producing more localised and situated data collections that challenge the history we are writing and offer a broader participation in digital history work also for those with basic technological skills.[35]

Notes

1 Huistra & Mellink 2016: 221.
2 Gold 2012. See also Earhart & Taylor 2016.
3 Solberg 2012: 67.
4 Umrani & Ghadially 2003: 359–360.
5 Posner 2012.
6 Solberg 2012: 69.
7 See, e.g., Kurvinen & Timosaari 2016.
8 Wernimont 2013.
9 See, e.g., Rhody 2016.
10 Solberg 2012, 66. See also, e.g., McKee & Porter 2010: 155–156.
11 See, e.g., Risam 2015.
12 Solberg 2012: 59–60, 70.
13 Enoch & Bessette 2013.
14 Lothian & Phillips 2013.
15 Solberg 2012; Enoch & Bessette 2013.
16 Rasila 1967: 140–146; Paju 2008: 85–87; Paju 2016: 5.
17 Solberg 2012: 67.
18 See, e.g., Jarlbrink, Snickars & Colliander 2016: 29–30.
19 See, e.g., Mold & Berridge 2018: 7.
20 Solberg 2012: 54–55.
21 Wernimont 2013.
22 See, e.g., Bailey 2011; Posner 2012.
23 See, e.g., Jallinoja 1983.
24 Saarimäki 2018: 75.
25 Huistra & Mellink 2016: 222–223.
26 Mold & Berridge 2018: 7–11. See also Bergenmar & Leppänen 2017: 235.
27 Jarlbrink, Snickars & Colliander 2016.
28 Kinnunen 2016: 653.
29 Sulkunen 1989; see also Saarimäki 2018: 74.

[30] See also Jarlbrink, Snickars & Colliander 2016.
[31] Mold & Berridge 2018.
[32] Kurvinen 2018; Huistra & Mellink 2016: 221.
[33] Kurvinen 2018.
[34] Solberg 2012: 68.
[35] Earhart & Taylor 2016. See also Bergenmar & Leppänen 2017: 240, 242.

References

Bailey, M. Z. (2011). All the digital humanists are white, all the nerds are men, but some of us are brave. *Journal of Digital Humanities, 1*(1). Retrieved from http://journalofdigitalhumanities.org/1-1/all-the-digital-humanists-are-white-all-the-nerds-are-men-but-some-of-us-are-brave-by-moya-z-bailey/

Bergenmar, J., & **Leppänen, K.** (2017). Gender and vernaculars in digital humanities and world literature. *NORA—Nordic Journal of Feminist and Gender Research, 25*(4), 232–246.

Earhart, A. E., & **Taylor, T. L.** (2016). Pedagogies of race: digital humanities in the age of Ferguson. In M. K. Gold & L. F. Klein (Eds.), *Debates in the digital humanities*. Minneapolis, MN: University of Minnesota Press. Retrieved from https://dhdebates.gc.cuny.edu/read/untitled/section/58ca5d2e-da4b-41cf-abd2-d8f2a68d2914

Enoch, J., & **Bessette, J.** (2013). Meaningful engagements: feminist historiography and the digital humanities. *College Composition and Communication, 64*(4), 634–660.

Gold, M. K. (2012). *Whose revolution? Towards a more equitable digital humanities*. The Lapland Chronicles. Retrieved from http://blog.mkgold.net/2012/01/10/whose-revolution-toward-a-more-equitable-digital-humanities/

Huistra, H., & **Mellink, B.** (2016). Phrasing history: selecting sources in digital repositories. *Historical Methods: A Journal of Quantitative and Interdisciplinary History, 49*(4), 220–229. DOI: https://doi.org/10.1080/01615440.2016.1205964

Jallinoja, R. (1983). *Suomalaisen naisasialiikkeen taistelukaudet: Naisasialiike naisten elämäntilanteen muutoksen ja yhteiskunnallis-aatteellisen murroksen heijastajana*. Helsinki: WSOY.

Jarlbrink, J., **Snickars, P.**, & **Colliander, C.** (2016). Maskinläsning: Om massdigitalisering, digitala metoder och svensk dagspress. *Nordicom Information, 38*(3), 27–40.

Kinnunen, T. (2016). The national and international in making a feminist: the case of Alexandra Gripenberg. *Women's History Review, 25*(4), 652–670.

Kurvinen, H. (2018). Toimittajat ja toimitukselliset prosessit mediatekstien takana. *Historiallinen Aikakauskirja, 116*(3), 310–322.

Kurvinen, H., & **Timosaari, N.** (2016). Feministitutkijat historiatieteen haastajina. In J. Pulkkinen & K. Väyrynen (Eds.), *Historian teoria: Lingvistisestä käänteestä mahdollisuuksien historiaan* (pp. 209–236). Tampere: Vastapaino.

Lothian, A., & **Phillips, A.** (2013). Can digital humanities mean transformative critique? *E-media studies, 3*(1). DOI: https://doi.org/10.1349/PS1.1938-6060.A.425

McKee, H. A., & **Porter, J. E.** (2010). Rhetorica online: feminist research practices in cyberspace. In E. E. Schell & K. J. Rawson (Eds.), *Rhetorica in motion: feminist rhetorical methods and methodologies* (pp. 152–170). Pittsburgh, PA: University of Pittsburgh Press.

Mold, A., & **Berridge, V.** (2018). Using digitised medical journals in a cross European project on addiction history. *Media History*, pre-published. DOI: https://doi.org/10.1080/13688804.2018.1506698

Paju, P. (2008). National projects and international users: Finland and early European computerization. *IEEE Annals of the History of Computing, 30*(4), 77–91.

Paju, P. (2016). *Raportti digitaalisen historiantutkimuksen kyselyvastauksista.* Retrieved from https://digihistfinlandroadmapblog.files.wordpress.com/2016/09/digitaalinen-historiantutkimus-kyselytuloksia5.pdf

Posner, M. K. (2012). *Some things to think about before you exhort everyone to code.* Miriam Posner's Blog. Retrieved from http://miriamposner.com/blog/some-things-to-think-about-before-you-exhort-everyone-to-code/

Rasila, V. (1967). Tietokone historiantutkimuksessa. *Historiallinen Aikakauskirja, 65*(2), 140–146.

Rhody, L. M. (2016). Why I dig: feminist approaches to text analysis. In M. K. Gold & L. F. Klein (Eds.), *Debates in the digital humanities.* Minneapolis, MN: University of Minnesota Press. Retrieved from http://dhdebates.gc.cuny.edu/debates/text/97

Risam, R. (2015). Beyond the margins: intersectionality and the digital humanities. *DHQ: Digital Humanities Quarterly, 9*(2). Retrieved from http://www.digitalhumanities.org/dhq/vol/9/2/000208/000208.html

Saarimäki, P. (2018). Bourgeois women and the question of divorce in Finland in the late 19th and early 20th centuries. *Scandinavian Journal of History, 43*(1), 64–90. DOI: https://doi.org/10.1080/03468755.2017.1353192

Solberg, J. (2012). Googling the archive: digital tools and the practice of history. *Advances in the History of Rhetoric, 15*(1), 53–76. DOI: https://doi.org/10.1080/15362426.2012.657052

Sulkunen, I. (1989). Naisten järjestäytyminen ja kaksijakoinen kansalaisuus. In R. Alapuro, I. Liikanen, K. Smeds & H. Stenius (Eds.), *Kansa liikkeessä* (pp. 157–175). Helsinki: Kirjayhtymä Oy.

Umrani, F., & **Ghadially, R.** (2003). Empowering women through ICT education: facilitating computer adoption. *Gender, Technology and Development, 7*(3), 359–377.

Wernimont, J. (2013). Whence feminism? Assessing feminist interventions in digital literary archives. *Digital Humanities Quarterly, 7*(1). Retrieved from http://www.digitalhumanities.org/dhq/vol/7/1/000156/000156.html

CHAPTER 10

Of Great Men and Eurovision Songs

Studying the Finnish Audio-Visual Heritage through NER-based Analysis on Metadata[1]

Maiju Kannisto and Pekka Kauppinen

Introduction

Part of a nation's cultural heritage is produced and preserved through audio-visual archives. Whatever has made it into the archival collection has passed severe processes of selection, which secure for certain cultural products a place in the cultural memory of a society. This process is called canonisation.[2] In this chapter, we explore how the canon is built up in the national audio-visual archive in the digital age. We study this by asking which people and what events and periods are 'remembered' not by the members of a nation, but by a collective national memory resource, the online audio-visual archive of a national public service broadcaster. Like particular natural and historic sites considered as 'heritage', and thus referring to a cultural and historical resource for all generations, past radio and television is now protected through copyright and continued cultural recirculation and exploited as both private and public property.[3] Our study focuses on the Finnish public service broadcasting company

How to cite this book chapter:
Kannisto, M., & Kauppinen, P. (2020). Of great men and Eurovision songs: Studying the Finnish audio-visual heritage through NER-based analysis on metadata. In M. Fridlund, M. Oiva, & P. Paju (Eds.), *Digital histories: Emergent approaches within the new digital history* (pp. 165–180). Helsinki: Helsinki University Press. https://doi.org/10.33134/HUP-5-10

Yle (former Yleisradio, founded in 1926) and its online archive. The dataset used in our research consists of Yle's archival metadata, which we analyse as a historical source material using the method of Named Entity Recognition (NER) as it is implemented in the digital tool the Finnish rule-based named-entity recogniser (FiNER).

Yle's online archive, The Living Archive (*Elävä arkisto*), presents part of Finland's audio-visual history. The archive is an illuminating case study as it is a large editorial historical audio-visual service with open access metadata, as well as a high profile among Yle's media output. It was first launched in 2006 on the 80th birthday of the Yle Company and the Living Archive enabled Yle to celebrate its history, while at the same time providing the public with new ways of watching television programmes online. The core idea behind the Living Archive is that audio-visual clips are historical source materials—documents from and about the national past representing Finland's national audio-visual heritage. In this way, the archive contributes the nation-building process by formulating collective national identity, as suggested by Benedict Anderson in his theory of nations as imagined communities.[4] As media researcher Derek Kompare suggests, the audio-visual heritage serves as a base of legitimacy for audio-visual media and memory; namely, as something worthy of attention, preservation and tribute. It can be used as a cultural touchstone, instantly signifying particular times.[5]

The Living Archive continually publishes new material from Yle's archives for viewing and listening via the online service. What is published is based on topicality, new copyright licences, Yle's current programming strategies, audience wishes and new archival discoveries.[6] Archival material has accumulated from the first audio recordings at the beginning of the 20th century to the present: Yle selects and presents the audio-visual archive material for current users in constantly new ways by adding and framing the material in 'background articles', written by journalists and archivists. Media history researcher Mari Pajala has analysed the ways in which the Living Archive attempts to make the material 'alive' and meaningful in the present through its journalistic front page, background articles and the possibility for interaction. In this way, by tying in moments of archive television with current events and television programmes, the archive continually connects the present with the past.[7]

The aim of this chapter is to produce new knowledge on the canon built in the Living Archive. However, at the same time, metadata as a source material and name recognition as a tool in a historical study must be analysed because the canon is connected with the limits and possibilities offered by the digital material and tool. In this chapter, we first introduce the research material and our method, the metadata used and the NER-based analysis. This analysis, using the FiNER tool, enables the identification of particular historical individuals, events and years from the metadata material. Finally, we discuss the limits and possibilities of our research process and results.

Finding Voices and Images of the Finnish Past: Metadata and FiNER Analysis

So far, since 2006, tens of thousands of audio-visual clips have been published in the Living Archive, so a computer-assisted method is needed to make larger sense of such a vast source material. The historical researcher's role in delimiting and selecting relevant material for analysis is crucial to the success of the computer-assisted analysis results. In this chapter, the research data does not consist of the media clips of the media files stored in the Living Archive as such, but of the metadata of the media information of these media files. Yle made this metadata material available on 3 January 2018.[8] Of this metadata, we selected the columns describing the title of the media, the promotion title and the description of the content (in Finnish). These columns describe the content of media clips, but not in general the author information. We did not want to include the latter in this study as we preferred to focus on the constructed national heritage and the individuals presented therein—not the authors of the various media documents. This could, however, be a relevant topic for future historical research.

The use of metadata as data is problematic in some respects because the material is inconsistent and contains some double data and gaps, as well as, at times, false information. An essential part of the historical source criticism is thus to find out the classification and guidelines that have been used to create the metadata. In the Living Archive metadata, the media descriptions have been produced in three main ways. (1) Descriptions have been made by the authors of the original programmes in connection with their original production to serve as programme information for other media. (2) The reporter or administrator of the Living Archive has written a short description of the clip's content in its subject field. Since this description field has not been displayed to the end user, this field is not always completed, and thus about one-tenth of the fields are empty. (3) Due to technical failure in the migration of the archival clips in 2011 (the transfer from one technical platform to another), the media information on the clips' still images were incorrectly entered in the media clips' subject field.[9] Therefore, in place of the description of the audio-visual content, this field contains the content of the still image, together with the photographer's name. Only the content of some video clips published before 2011 may have been edited and supplemented after that year. In the analysis, we have been aware of the above-mentioned issues and taken them into account as much as possible (for example, we excluded the photographers from the analysis).

NER is a task in Information Extraction consisting in identifying and classifying some types of information elements, called Named Entities (NE). It is stated that NER analysis usually responds to the five typical questions in the journalism domain: what, where, when, who and why.[10] In our analysis, we utilised FiNER,[11] a rule-based NER tool loosely based on the Swedish NER

HFST-SweNER.[12] At the time of our study, FiNER had not yet been used extensively as a research tool and thererfore this chapter is also partly a methodological experimental study.[13] FiNER was created for the FIN-CLARIN consortium at the University of Helsinki, which is the Finnish part of the European CLARIN (Common Language Resources and Technology Infrastructure) collaboration for developing research infrastructure for language-related resources in humanities and social sciences.

FiNER utilises the Helsinki Finite-State Toolkit and its implementation of the pmatch (partial string matching) function,[14] which allows the compilation and implementation of pattern-matching rules as computationally efficient finite-state transducers (FSTs). FiNER's pattern-matching rules employ a number of strategies in finding and disambiguation names, including hints in string structure (such as uppercase letters, affixation, etc.), collocations, runtime adaptation and gazetteers (lists of names). The FiNER tool accepts any plain-text input, but works best on running text that adheres to Standard Finnish spelling and typographic conventions. We used a set of UNIX text-processing utilities to extract relevant segments from the tabular metadata for tagging, as well as to filter out any superfluous data that might slow down or interfere with the NER process.

In order to calculate total frequencies for names in the data, each matched word segment in the output first had to be lemmatised (that is, reverted to its uninflected form). Thus, we had FiNER output lemma forms and morphological analyses for each word and created a Python script that extracted matched sequences and used morphological information to lemmatise each of them. Once all names had been printed out in their lemmatised forms, their frequencies in the data could be calculated with relative ease.

As digital history researchers Kimmo Elo and Olli Kleemola have pointed out, it is essential for the researcher to understand how the computer-assisted analysis produces the results.[15] Thus, we looked at the frequency lists of different categories of FiNER analysis from the perspective of the possibilities and limits set by the technical characteristics of the tool, as well as possible errors. After having removed the names that occurred as a result of technical error, we put together TOP10 and TOP20 lists from the names that have received most mentions in different categories. Finally, in order to understand the results, it was important to check the background articles in the Living Archive and to contextualise them tentatively with Finnish cultural and political perspectives.

Great Men, Journalists and Musicians as Remembered Persons

People's names are generally better recognised than other name entity types.[16] FiNER recognised nearly 12,000 people in our research material; in the analysis, we focused on those who had received most mentions. When analysing the people, we found three main groups dominating the historical personage of the Living Archive: great men, journalists and musicians (see Table 10.1). Among

Table 10.1: Top 20 of the most frequently mentioned people in the metadata of the Living Archive listed by FiNER.

Number of mentions	Top 20 people	Their professions
353	Urho Kekkonen (includes 'Urho Kekkonen' and 'Kekkonen')	President of Finland
223	Arto Nyberg	journalist
125	Kirka	musician
111	Marjukka Havumäki	journalist
105	Vesa-Matti Loiri	musician, actor
90	Mauno Koivisto	President of Finland
89	Mikko Alatalo	musician, journalist, politician
89	Matti	
86	Bettina Sågbom	journalist
78	Matti Rönkä	journalist
78	Danny	musician
76	Päivi Istala	journalist
74	Göran Palm	journalist
73	Mannerheim	President of Finland
71	Paula Koivuniemi	musician
71	Jaakko Selin	journalist
69	Lasse Mårtenson	composer, musician
69	Antti	
68	Susanna Ström-Wilkinson	journalist
64	Juha Laaksonen	journalist

Note: Photographers are excluded. Source: Author.

the Top 20 of the most represented people, President Urho Kekkonen is the most frequently mentioned person. Kekkonen (1900–1986) was the longest-serving President of Finland (1956–1982) and a politician who achieved an almost unchallengeable political position during his long presidency. President Kekkonen's prevalent role in the archival clips is also emphasised by the fact that his trusted photographer Kalle Kultala received the second most mentions in the material, although this is due to an incorrect overwrite in the media information. Kekkonen is the protagonist in many articles, which include a number of video and audio clips from election campaigns, presidential visits and public speeches, as well as clips of him carrying out his hobbies. During his 25 years of presidency, Kekkonen gave 25 presidential New Year's speeches and hosted 22 Independence Day receptions, both of which are essentially national audio-visual broadcasts, repeated annually and among the most watched programmes on Finnish television.

President Kekkonen was connected to the Finnish Broadcasting Company Yleisradio in many ways. First, he had close personal relations with people working there. Second, his political career was concurrent with the development of broadcasting in the 1930s and 1940s. Finally, he often appealed to the people in his radio speeches during the growth in radio licences. It can be argued that his long reign was comparable to the monopoly of Yleisradio.[17] Media researchers Lotta Lounasmeri and Johanna Sumiala have argued that President Kekkonen used the new mass media skillfully. He managed to combine different roles by acting as a sovereign political leader in the mass media while, on the other hand, at other less formal occasions, performing as a man of the people by skiing, fishing and meeting people in the countryside.[18] Iconic images of the photogenic president were spread across the mass media, making these audio-visual presidential representations part of the nation's public memory. In this way, the Living Archive played an important but previously mainly neglected role in preserving and presenting a political part of the national audio-visual memory. Furthermore, President Kekkonen not only appears in the archival clips, but also as a character in documentaries, drama series and sketch shows, and as a reference point to which other politicians were reacting. This is not just a past but also a very active part of the national memory, as the cult of President Kekkonen still strongly survives as a nostalgia and longing for strong leadership.[19]

Among the Top 20 of the most mentioned people, there was also another President of Finland, Carl Gustaf Emil Mannerheim (1867–1951), who could be characterised as a great man in national history. Mannerheim, Marshal of Finland, was frequently mentioned, even though he appears in few contemporary audio-visual sources. However, he is retrospectively presented in the archive through later historical photographs, film clips, and radio speeches and documents. Furthermore, Mannerheim's character became a part of Finnish popular culture in the form of a controversial doll-animated short film in 2008 and through other films. According to historian Tuomas Tepora, the contradicting views have been an essential part of Mannerheim's mythical role in Finnish cultural memory.[20] His legacy also appears in the material when talking of The Mannerheim League for Child Welfare and the Knights of the Mannerheim Cross, awarded to Finnish soldiers.

Along with the great men, men in general dominate the media clips: 72 of the first 100 people are men. Of the 10 women mentioned, the top eight are Yle journalists; only singer Paula Koivuniemi and President Tarja Halonen are also cited. As is well known, in the Western historiographic tradition, women have rarely been treated as active actors until recent years and therefore they have not been given much space in national historiography. Although the tradition has been challenged for almost 50 years now, women are still underrepresented in most canonised historical narratives.[21] This is also the case in the

Living Archive, in spite of equality work being in operation for a long time now. This is also related to the history of the feminisation of Finnish professions. President Tarja Halonen was the first female Finnish President (2000–2012). This can also be observed among the journalism profession, another dominant group in the archive. At Yleisradio in 1972, only 35% of the journalists were women,[22] and the number of female journalists only increased significantly from the 1970s onwards.

In general, the journalists of Yle to a great extent appear in the material. The Top 20 listing includes eight Yle journalists (see Table 10.1). In the metadata, journalists are mentioned in many respects. News anchors are mentioned in connection with the archival news clips, while journalists working on the Living Archive are mentioned in connection with the background articles. Journalist Arto Nyberg is the second most frequently cited person in the archive. He has since 2004 hosted a popular talk show named after him, where many Finnish public figures and celebrities have visited and many clips therefrom are published in the Living Archive. In this audio-visual history, journalists are the key figures and agents behind the production of the media clips and thus appear frequently in the material more in this capacity as facilitators and producers, rather than as objects of newsworthy events. This important factor of the media production system needs to be taken into account.

In addition to journalists and presidents, many musicians are also mentioned in the audio-visual archive: six are included in the Top 20 listing. What unites these musicians is great popularity, which often comprises long careers stretching to several decades of hit songs. When compared to the most frequently mentioned bands listed by FiNER, the musicians are more focused on older pop singers and evergreen hits, while the bands category is more versatile and focuses on newer bands. The most frequently mentioned artists are those who have had visibility in Yle's music programmes, such as Eurovision Song Contests and festival recordings. For example, Mikko Alatalo's prominence in the archive emanates from his versatile TV work in Yle's music programmes in the 1970s and 1980s.

Eurovision Song Contests, Sports and Wars Unite the Nation

Music also plays an important role in FiNER's list of the most frequent events. In part, this is due to Yle's major role in recording music festivals and preserving them for the audio-visual heritage in the Living Archive. However, the largest national audio-visual event is not a national but a European event in the form of the Eurovision Song Contest. As an annual and long-lasting television event, the song contest has been an important event of popular culture. Historian Mari Pajala has argued that the Eurovision Song Contests have become a prominent part of Finnish national memory and history. The regular annual contests have particularly participated in Finnish nation-making by creating media discussions surrounding the meaning of nationality in the collective cultural memory. The Living Archive reviews both the successes and the failures of Eurovision. Finland has historically been very unsuccessful in the contests, but this finally changed in 2006 with the hard rock band Lordi's victory. The long tradition of negative experiences and the decades of disappointment were then forgotten as public festivals reupted in market squares all over Finland.[23] In addition to the international contest, the national Eurovision qualifiers are presented extensively in the archive, which gives many artists a place in the national audio-visual history.

Another popular category of events is major sports competitions, such as the European and World Championships in ice hockey and track and field. The broadcasting of these major sport events has been strategically significant to the Finnish Broadcasting Company since they attract large audiences and are therefore legitimising the company's role as a public service broadcaster.

The third category relates to war. Wars and political conflicts identified by FiNER are listed as events, together with music, sport, art and entertainment, which can, however, be analytically difficult for comparisons. Among the wars, the Finnish Winter and Continuation Wars are particularly well represented in the media material. These wars are significant episodes in Finnish history and form part of the national mythology formulated through national publicity, as well as, for example, through their appearance in schoolbooks.[24] Therefore, these two wars also form an important part of Finnish cultural memory.[25] The Living Archive preserves the remembrance of wars in connection with different anniversaries.

According to Pajala, many of the traditional moments of the television year are explicitly related to nationality: Eurovision Song Contests and sport events unite the national public in excitement at the presence of their own representatives, while the state's sovereignty is celebrated at the President's Independence Day Reception, and in the national war films.[26] These national audio-visual events are accumulated and added to the Living Archive annually.

Nationally Significant Periods as Recognised by Yle

Different periods from the 1960s to the 2010s are remembered relatively evenly in the Living Archive, even though most of the programmes have been preserved only in the last two decades (see Figure 10.1). However, it is important to note that in FiNER's analysis, the recognition of the decade numbers is a challenge: FiNER may not recognise these without using clues from the text contexts, and may instead interpret them as ordinary words rather than as markers for historical periods. This produces gaps in the time series. There are three peak years in the FiNER frequency list: 1976, 1995 and 2008. When tracing these years from the media material, we noticed that during these periods there were an extraordinary number of significant political and cultural events.

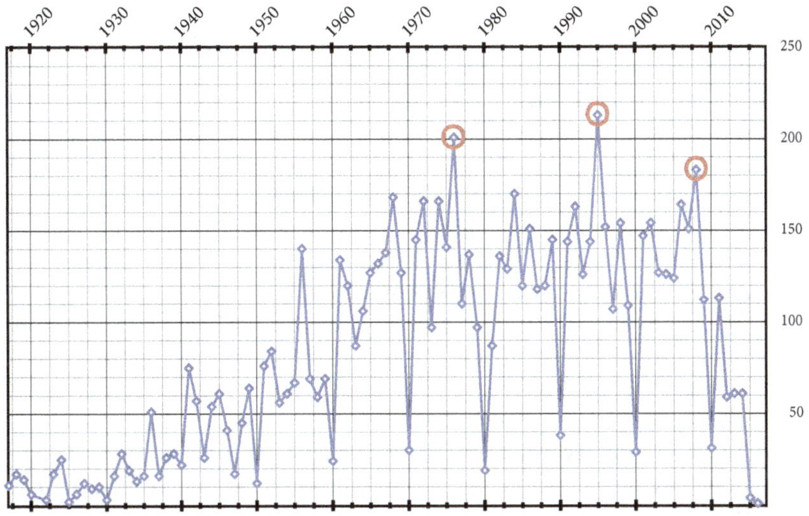

Figure 10.1: The occurrence frequencies of the years 1917–2017 in the time series identified by FiNER from Yle's metadata material. Note: The peak years 1976, 1995 and 2008 have been circled. Since the summer of 2015, all the programmes of the Living Archive have been published via the Areena platform, which causes a harsh decrease in the metadata material.[28] Source: Author.

We suggest that these events have become key experiences determining the past and are thus significant parts of the national memory.[27] These historical events are presented in the background articles and collectively remembered in the Living Archive.

Among the 1976 media clips, the long-distance runner Lasse Virén's wins in the 5,000- and 10,000-metre runs at the Montreal Olympics and the drama series *Myrskyluodon Maija (Maija of Myrskyluoto)*, shown on Yle's main channel, are both highlighted as key collective experiences. The latter television series was set in the Finnish archipelago during the 19th century and pictured the life of the protagonist Maija and her family in six episodes. Lasse Mårtenson, who was among the Top 10 in FiNER's list of the most represented people, composed the music for the series. The series has been characterised as unforgettable by many, in large part due to the music. In actual fact, the piano transcription of the theme music is the best-selling Finnish music publication of all time.[29] The Living Archive contains several background articles about both the music and new versions of the songs, such as the highlights of 15 versions of the theme music performed by various artists.[30] As evidenced by its many occurrences in our source material, the melancholic composition apparently succeeded in touching the collective Finnish psyche and therefore in becoming a prominent part of the national audio-visual heritage.

In 1995, two main events dominate the media material. The first was that Finland joined the European Union. This was the topic of a large number of media clips, such as news and current affairs programmes, as well as sketches, and there are many background articles belonging to the EU thematic. The second event was winning the Ice Hockey World Championship, which was and has continued to be a key national experience. Ice hockey is Finland's largest sport in terms of media visibility and every spring the Ice Hockey World Championships attract a large national audience. The televised winning final in 1995 was watched by 46% of all Finns. Cultural historian Hannu Salmi has connected the boom of ice hockey to changes within the Finnish media landscape. In the 1980s, when the national team began to enjoy success, ice hockey became more visibile and television rights became the subject of a struggle between public service and commercial media companies.[31] The victory in 1995 was the first World Championship win for any Finnish sports team and the nation was united in celebrating the victory together. In public, the victory was made into a question of national self-esteem.[32] Therefore, remembering the great victory also has an important role in the Living Archive.

During the third peak year of 2008, the key experiences are connected to the political elections, which received significant media attention. In Finland, the Finns Party (*perussuomalaiset*, formerly the True Finns Party) was the biggest winner in the municipal election and brought forward a strong criticism of the existing immigration policy in public discussion. Another notable political event that contributed to the 2008 peak was an event occurring outside Finland, when, in the United States, Barack Obama was elected President. However, most of the accumulated media clips during the year concerned the Kauhajoki school shooting, when a student shot and killed 11 people, including himself. After an earlier Finnish school shooting in Jokela the previous year, it was not possible to treat the Kauhajoki shooting as an individual incident, and journalists thus tried to find political and social explanations for the tragedy (for example, related to gun legislation).[33] The Living Archive documented this debate.

In addition to these events, many other 2008 media clips focused on the 30th anniversary of the Finnish rock festival *Provinssirock*. Even if many key experiences are connected with Finnish or world history, the audio-visual nature of the archive places a particular emphasis on audio-visual events. These events emphasise the particular role of Yle—for example, regarding television series, the Eurovision Song Contest, sports and footage of music festivals. Therefore, the national audio-visual heritage is Yle's particular heritage and its particular contribution to Finnish history; Yle owns a large proportion of the Finnish audio-visual heritage. Commercial media companies, like MTV founded in 1957, have no similar archives and there are no programmes left from the early decades of the independent Finland. During the early years of television, programmes reached large audiences, allowing programmes to create iconic images and become part of the national public memory.[34] However, in the

Living Archive, commercial television and radio are left aside, rendering it an important resource for the public service company Yle in the struggle among the various media to legitimise its cultural position.

Finally: The Limits and Possibilities of Interpretation

Digital archives are organic entities that grow and change their shape as new materials are added.[35] The strategy of Yle's Living Archive is to grow constantly, which produces a cyclical nature for the production of this national audio-visual heritage. Annually recurring events related to the audio-visual culture have generated the most archival material over the years. In this way, Yle has created a national audio-visual annual calendar to commemorate significant moments, like Independence Day. Another strategy of the Living Archive, tackling contemporary topical issues, in turn, binds the past to this present moment. The archive actively follows current topics and events. This strategy equals Derek Kompare's notion that the legitimation of television, as in the case of archive, was based not on the existing canon, as it had been with film, but on the idea of heritage. While the canon tends to be separated from everyday life and located in a refined, timeless sanctuary, a heritage is part of the lived, historical experience of a culture.[36] Both of Yle's strategies have succeeded in producing the most popular content in the archive, such as responses to topical issues and death notifications for public figures.[37]

It is important to note that the choices of which media clips are published in the Living Archive and their output are political choices that remain invisible to archive users.[38] As Pajala has pointed out, the archive has limited possibilities to publish anything not shown by public service television. As a result, former legislation and cultural norms continue to restrict today's debate on the subject of audio-visual archives.[39] In addition, the copyright agreements significantly shape the publication choices, as not all of Yle's archive material can be published. During the first years, the only materials published were Yle's own journalistic programmes and films redeemed from old film companies. Another restriction is that all released music has to be reported to copyright organisations, but since 2015, a separate agreement has made it possible to publish many old music programmes, such as the Finnish qualification competitions for the Eurovision Song Contest and the music programme *Hittimittari* from the 1980s. A drama agreement in 2016 has also enabled Yle to release drama series and films, with long publishing rights. However, this is not only about a question of choice, since not all of the old material is actually available. Only since 1984 has all self-produced TV material been archived. In addition, the old programmes may have very poor metadata, making them more difficult to locate.[40]

In addition to the choice of data, we also have to take into account FiNER's specific internal limitations, which are similar to those of other rule-based

NER systems: any shortcomings in rule formulation or gazetteers result in false positives and misclassification of matched names, which if no rule applies, can make a name go altogether unnoticed. Single-word names of organisations and events are particularly difficult to identify without context clues or structural hints. This is particularly true for short texts such as the metadata entries, where the reader is often assumed to be familiar with names and their referents. In the case of rule-based NER systems, any misses and tagging errors are human in nature as they arguably reflect the system developer's ability or inability to formulate exhaustive rules, as well as their oversights when building the gazetteers.

Metadata as a research material also raises wider ontological questions of historical knowledge: What can we really know about the audio-visual cultural heritage on the grounds of metadata and FiNER analysis? Digital history researcher Michael J. Kramer discusses the relationship between historians and digital archives and describes history as a meta-metadata.[41] There are so many layers of interpretation: metadata is not merely descriptive, but is also already an interpretation of an archivist. Another issue stems from the fact that the results of the FiNER analysis are the lists of frequencies of names. These frequencies are not directly related to media material: FiNER as a tool has its own limitations and rules on how it interprets and categorises the metadata that has been pre-processed by the researcher, something which also brings its own specific limitations. Finally, the historical researcher interprets the results of FiNER. We suggest that it is actually already a meta-meta-metadata of the target of study. In order to understand all these layers of interpretation, we need collaboration between archivists and historians to make visible the guidelines and ways of writing metadata. The most fruitful approach would be for them to cooperate in negotiating how metadata best serve both parties.

A historian also needs to be aware of the functional logic of the digital tool for being able to recognise the bumps on the road of interpretation.[42] Our NER-based analysis revealed an interesting emphasis on people, events and years in the audio-visual heritage constructed by the Living Archive. However, the FiNER analysis did not shed light on why and how these certain topics are represented in the archive. Instead, what the analysis did show is why audio-visual heritage is constructed in a certain way.

Metadata, like Yle's metadata, is often messy and requires a significant amount of selection and pre-processing. In addition, the metadata material, as well as the digital tool, has limitations, as described above.[43] The large volume of data can compensate for some of the technical limitations. However, it is important to acknowledge that, in the humanities, the shift from small smart data to big data is not just technological; in fact, it seems to be even more of a methodological shift. Methodologically, it means the shift from close reading to distant reading. In this paradigm, instead of reading a few selected texts, we can analyse an entire collection of relevant textual data.[44] However, the cultural contextualising and close reading of the themes pointed out by the results of NER-based analysis still play an important role in the analytical process. Only after the cultural contextualising and close reading do the word lists come alive, so they can animate the role of the audio-visual heritage in the construction of the Finnish imagined national community broadcast on radio and television.

Acknowledgements

We would like to thank the research project From Roadmap to Roadshow, funded by Kone Foundation, for organising the Digital History Finland workshop. Assistance provided by Yle's Living Archive was greatly appreciated. Thanks also to editors and anonymous reviewers for their suggestions and criticisms, all of which made this a better text.

Notes

1 An earlier, Finnish language version of this research entitled *Kekkonen, Euroviisut ja Helsinki—kansallinen audiovisuaalinen perintö NER-analyysin tunnistamana* was published in the journal *Ennen ja nyt* (2/2019). This edited version is published with the permission of the journal *Ennen ja nyt*.
2 Assmann 2008: 100.
3 Kompare 2005: 103.
4 Anderson 2007/1983.
5 Kompare 2005: 102–103.
6 Yli-Ojanperä 2018.
7 Pajala 2010: 134, 142.
8 Material is in the form of a CSV file, which is 18 megabytes in size and contains 34,816 entities.
9 Elina Yli-Ojanperä's interview 23 May 2018.
10 Marrero et al. 2013: 484.
11 In this chapter, we use a work version between two publications, which, however, is very similar to the version that has been published at the end of the year 2018. See http://urn.fi/urn:nbn:fi:lb-2018091301.
12 Kokkinakis et al. 2014.
13 However, see Kettunen et al. 2017.
14 Karttunen 2011.
15 Elo & Kleemola 2016: 154.
16 van Hooland et al. 2015: 13.
17 Puro 2016: 23–24.
18 Lounasmeri & Sumiala 2016: 3–4.
19 On the cult of President Kekkonen and his popular cultural image, see Kallioniemi, Kärki & Mähkä 2016.
20 Tepora 2015b: 8–11.
21 Halldórsdóttir, Kinnunen & Leskelä-Kärki 2016: 19.
22 Kurvinen 2013: 68.
23 Pajala 2006: 351–368.

[24] Torsti 2012: 135–155; Ahonen 2017: 10–11, 92–95.
[25] Tepora 2015a.
[26] Pajala 2006: 24; Pajala 2012.
[27] Cf. Sumiala-Seppänen 2007: 283; Torsti 2012: 63–73. On collective memory, see Benton 2010: 1, 5.
[28] Elina Yli-Ojanperä's interview 20 June 2019.
[29] Helsingius 2010.
[30] Yle Elävä arkisto (Living Archive) 2015.
[31] Salmi 2015: 13, 32–46.
[32] Kannisto 2015: 95–96.
[33] Raittila et al. 2009: 112.
[34] Pajala 2010: 135.
[35] Jarlbrink & Snickars 2017: 1240.
[36] Kompare 2005: 105.
[37] Yli-Ojanperä 2018.
[38] Cf. Jarlbrink & Snickars 2017: 1229.
[39] Pajala 2010: 140.
[40] Yli-Ojanperä 2018.
[41] Kramer 2014.
[42] See also Elo & Kleemola 2016: 154.
[43] See also Kannisto 2016.
[44] Schöch 2013.

References

Ahonen, S. (2017). *Suomalaisuuden monet myytit: Kansallinen katse historian kirjoissa*. Helsinki: Gaudeamus.

Anderson, B. (2007/1983). *Kuvitellut yhteisöt: Nationalismin alkuperän ja leviämisen tarkastelua*. Tampere: Vastapaino.

Assmann, A. (2008) Canon and archive. In A. Erll & A. Nünning (Eds.), *Cultural memory studies: an international and interdisciplinary handbook* (pp. 97–107). Berlin and New York, NY: Walter de Gruyter.

Benton, T. (2010). Introduction. In T. Benton (Ed.), *Understanding heritage and memory* (pp. 1–5). Manchester: Manchester University Press.

Elo, K., & **Kleemola, O.** (2016). SA-kuva-arkistoa louhimassa: Digitaaliset tutkimusmenetelmät valokuvatutkimuksen tukena. In K. Elo (Ed.), *Digitaalinen humanismi ja historiatieteet* (pp. 151–190). Historia mirabilis 12. Turku: Turun Historiallinen Yhdistys.

Halldórsdóttir, E. H., **Kinnunen, T.**, & **Leskelä-Kärki, M.** (2016). Doing biography. In E. H. Halldórsdóttir, T. Kinnunen, M. Leskelä-Kärki & B. Possing (Eds.), *Biography, gender and history: Nordic perspectives* (pp. 7–34). Turku: k&h, kulttuurihistoria, Turun yliopisto.

Helsingius, B. (2010). *Mårtenson, Lasse (1934–2016)*. National Biography of Finland. Studia Biographica 4. Helsinki: Suomalaisen Kirjallisuuden Seura. Retrieved from https://kansallisbiografia.fi/kansallisbiografia/henkilo/1095

Jarlbrink, J., & Snickars, P. (2017). Cultural heritage as digital noise: nineteenth century newspapers in the digital archive. *Journal of Documentation, 73*(6), 1228–1243. DOI: https://doi.org/10.1108/JD-09-2016-0106

Kallioniemi, K., Kärki, K., & Mähkä, R. (2016). Kekkonen ja rock'n'roll. In M. Kaartinen, H. Salmi & M. Tuominen (Eds.), *Maamme—itsenäisen Suomen kulttuurihistoria* (pp. 395–414). Helsinki: Suomalaisen Kirjallisuuden Seura.

Kannisto, M. (2015). Sankarit kultajuhlissa. In B. Heiskanen & H. Salmi (Eds.), *Kiekkokansa* (pp. 72–101). Helsinki: Teos.

Kannisto, M. (2016). Uusi, ehompi, paras? Digitaaliset tekstilouhinnan työkalut televisiotutkimuksessa. *Lähikuva, 29*(1), 62–70. DOI: https://doi.org/10.23994/lk.56578

Karttunen, L. (2011). Beyond morphology: pattern matching with FST. In C. Mahlow & M. Piotrowski (Eds.), *Systems and frameworks for computational morphology, volume 100 of communications in computer and information science* (pp. 1–13). Berlin and Heidelberg: Springer.

Kettunen, K., Mäkelä, E., Ruokolainen, T., Kuokkala, J., & Löfberg, L. (2017). Old content and modern tools: searching named entities in a Finnish OCRed historical newspaper collection 1771–1910. *Digital Humanities Quarterly, 11*(3). Retrieved from http://www.digitalhumanities.org/dhq/vol/11/3/000333/000333.html

Kokkinakis, D., Niemi, J., Hardwick, S., Lindén, K., & Borin, L. (2014). HFST-SweNER—a new NER resource for Swedish. In N. Calzolari, K. Choukri, T. Declerck, H. Loftsson, B., Maegaard, J. Mariani, A. Moreno, J. Odijk & S. Piperidis (Eds.), *Proceedings of the Ninth International Conference on Language Resources and Evaluation (LREC'14)*. Reykjavik, Iceland: European Language Resources Association.

Kompare, D. (2005). *Rerun nation: how repeats invented American television.* London and New York, NY: Routledge.

Kramer, M. J. (2014). Going meta on metadata. *Journal of Digital Humanities, 3*(2). Retrieved from http://journalofdigitalhumanities.org/3-2/going-meta-on-metadata/

Kurvinen, H. (2013). *'En mä oo mies enkä nainen. Mä oon toimittaja': Sukupuoli ja suomalainen toimittajakunta 1960- ja 1970-luvulla*. Acta Universitatis Ouluensis B Humaniora 113. Oulu: Oulun yliopisto.

Lounasmeri, L., & Sumiala, J. (2016). Promootiokulttuurin kuningas Kekkonen. *Lähikuva, 29*(2), 3–5. Retrieved from https://journal.fi/lahikuva/issue/view/3995

Marrero, M., Urbano, J., Sánchez-Cuadrado, S., Morato, J., & Gómez-Berbís, J. M. (2013). Named Entity Recognition: fallacies, challenges and opportunities. *Computer Standards & Interfaces 35*(5), 482–489. DOI: https://doi.org/10.1016/j.csi.2012.09.004

Pajala, M. (2006). *Erot järjestykseen! Eurovision laulukilpailu, kansallisuus ja televisiohistoria.* Nykykulttuurin tutkimuskeskuksen tutkimuksia 88. Jyväskylä: Jyväskylän yliopisto.

Pajala, M. (2010). Cultural memory and its limits on the Finnish public service broadcaster's online archive. *Critical Studies in Television, 5*(2), 133–145.

Pajala, M. (2012). Televisio kulttuurisen muistin mediana: Miten itsenäisyyspäivä alkoi merkitä sotamuistelua? In E. Railo & P. Oinonen (Eds.), *Media historiassa,* Historia mirabilis 9 (pp. 127–150). Turku: Turun historiallinen yhditys ry.

Puro, J.-P. (2016). Puhumalla hallitseminen: Vahvan johtajuuden ilmentyminen Kekkosen radiopuheissa vuosina 1937–1967. *Lähikuva, 29*(2), 22–42. Retrieved from https://journal.fi/lahikuva/issue/view/3995

Raittila, P., Haara, P., Kangasluoma, L., Koljonen, K., Kumpu, V., & Väliverronen, J. (2009). *Kauhajoen koulusurmat mediassa.* Tampereen yliopisto, tiedotusopin laitos: Journalismin tutkimusyksikkö. Retrieved from http://tampub.uta.fi/bitstream/handle/10024/65360/978-951-44-7654-9.pdf

Salmi, H. (2015). Kiekkokansa ryhmäkuvassa. In B. Heiskanen & H. Salmi (Eds.), *Kiekkokansa* (pp. 13–46). Helsinki: Teos.

Schöch, C. (2013). Big? Smart? Clean? Messy? Data in the humanities. *Journal of Digital Humanities, 2*(3). Retrieved from http://journalofdigitalhumanities.org/2-3/big-smart-clean-messy-data-in-the-humanities/

Sumiala-Seppänen, J. (2007). 'Joku raja ja loppu se on saatava tällaisille keskusteluille!' Jatkoaika ja kansallisten kertomusten konflikti 60-luvun suomalaisessa televisiossa. In J. Wiio (Ed.), *Television viisi vuosikymmentä: Suomalainen televisio ja sen ohjelmat 1950-luvulta digiaikaan* (pp. 280–291). Helsinki: Suomalaisen Kirjallisuuden Seura.

Tepora, T. (2015a). Mikä tekee 'sota-ajasta' muistettavan? Sota ja kollektiivinen muistaminen. *Ennen ja nyt, 2015*(2). Retrieved from http://www.ennenjanyt.net/2015/08/mika-tekee-sota-ajasta-muistettavan-sota-ja-kollektiivinen-muistaminen/

Tepora, T. (2015b). Sota, Tuntematon ja Mannerheim. *Futura, 34*(3), 5–11.

Torsti, P. (2012). *Suomalaiset ja historia.* Helsinki: Gaudeamus.

van Hooland, S., De Wilde, M., Verborgh, R., Steiner, T., & Van de Walle, R. (2015). Exploring entity recognition and disambiguation for cultural heritage collections. *Literary and Linguistic Computing, 30*(2), 262–279. DOI: https://doi.org/10.1093/llc/fqt067

Yle Elävä arkisto (2015). *Myrskyluodon Maija monella tavalla.* Retrieved from https://yle.fi/aihe/artikkeli/2015/07/30/myrskyluodon-maija-monella-tavalla

Yli-Ojanperä, E. (2018, helmikuu). *Yle Elävä arkisto.* Avoin digitaalinen kulttuuriperint—course, slides. Yle.

Yli-Ojanperä, E. Producer-in-chief, Yle Living Archive. Interviewed by Maiju Kannisto by email 23 May 2018 and 20 June 2019.

Data systems

FiNER: http://urn.fi/urn:nbn:fi:lb-2018091301
Tools for processing FiNER output: https://github.com/pkauppin/finer-utilities

CHAPTER 11

Tracing the Emergence of Nordic *Allemansrätten* through Digitised Parliamentary Sources

Matti La Mela

Introduction

Allemansrätten, a right of public access to nature, is an integral part of the identity and lifestyle of the people in the Nordic countries. This principle, which is commonly seen as an age-old tradition, allows everyone to access and use resources in the wild even without the landowner's consent. Despite its major role in contemporary Nordic societies, the roots and the development of this institution are little researched and not well known. This chapter contributes to the historical revision of *allemansrätten* by studying public uses of the concept in Finland in the 20th century. Such a broad study is possible using the recently digitised documents of the Finnish Parliament, which offer a unique view on how central societal concepts have been defined and used in public discussion. The chapter asks how and when *allemansrätten* actually emerged as a term, and to which discursive environments the concept was tied in the public debates of the 20th century.

How to cite this book chapter:
La Mela, M. (2020). Tracing the emergence of Nordic *allemansrätten* through digitised parliamentary sources. In M. Fridlund, M. Oiva, & P. Paju (Eds.), *Digital histories: Emergent approaches within the new digital history* (pp. 181–197). Helsinki: Helsinki University Press. https://doi.org/10.33134/HUP-5-11

The aim of the chapter is to challenge the common view of *allemansrätten* as an age-old and stable tradition, and to demonstrate how the concept is historically constructed and has been flexibly used as part of different political discourses. In particular, the chapter focuses on the principle of universality inherent to the modern *allemansrätten*. Even though it is acknowledged today that *allemansrätten* took its form only with the modern processes of urbanisation, growth of free time, and development of new ways of recreation in nature after the 1930s, many authors build continuity to pre-modern Nordic legal culture or access practices.[1] On the other hand, some critics have proposed that *allemansrätten* was actually an ideological move to socialise private land to the use of everybody.[2] Most recently, however, a mid-way has been sought, where the past and modern cultures of access to nature are discussed separately, to emphasise differences in the social contexts and to demonstrate the parliamentary political support given to *allemansrätten* in the 20th century.[3]

The chapter uses methods of text mining, and uses the Finnish parliamentary documents as its source. This digitised data has been created only very recently, and is discussed therefore rather thoroughly in the second section of the chapter. It is notable, however, that other digitised sources, for instance newspapers, have already been used for studying parliamentary debates.[4] The digitised newspapers are currently available only until 1929. The new digitised parliamentary documents, therefore, are not only an important dataset for studying policy and law-making, but also offer an important perspective over the broader public debate after 1929, which no other complete digital collection in Finland currently represents. The digitised parliamentary sources of other countries have been used in historical and social scientific research. These include straightforward debate analysis through keyword searches, but also the use of more complicated methods such as sentiment analysis.[5]

This chapter studies the history of the uses of *allemansrätten* in the parliamentary data in two steps. First, in the section entitled 'Allemansrätten Emerges', below, keyword searches and frequency analysis is used for discovering the general trajectory of the term in the complete dataset from 1907 until 2000. The parliamentary debates are understood as reflecting common language use of the time, and thus reflecting topics which were central for the contemporary public discussion. Second, in the section entitled 'Allemansrätten since the 1970s', below, the aim is to study differences in the discursive environments where *allemansrätten* was used. Key parliamentary debates are identified, and the parliamentary data is text-mined into two detailed debate corpora from the 1970s and 1990s. These two corpora are analysed with collocation analysis and topic modelling, and the results are contrasted with each other. The hypothesis of the chapter is that the term appears only after the Second World War, which has been preliminarily confirmed from sporadic sources.[6] However, in which discussions did this take place, and how was the modern and commonly acknowledged concept appropriated in the public discussion?

Digitised Parliamentary Talk of the 20th Century: Quantity and Quality

Parliamentary documents are a classic source in history. They are used to study the past national legislative work, but also offer a broader view on the political culture and political language, as well as major societal issues of the time.[7] Internationally, parliamentary sources have been digitised only in the past 10 years and are now available for research use.[8] In the Finnish case, the parliamentary documents of the latest decades have been available digitally for several years; however, the digitisation of the documents of the unicameral parliament from 1907 until 2000 were finished only recently: the online digital collection was inaugurated in September 2018.[9]

The digital collection includes the documents of the Finnish *Eduskunta*, unicameral Finnish Parliament, which convened for the first time in 1907, when the country still formed an autonomous Grand Duchy as part of the Russian Empire. The parliamentary reform leading to *Eduskunta* was radical at its time, as it expanded the suffrage to the whole of the male and female population and, first in the world, enabled women to stand for election. From a more concrete point of view, however, there was important institutional continuity, as the national and local representative rights had already been exercised since the 1860s. The national Diet or Assembly of Estates, which gathered the representatives of the four estates for legislative work, had convened in 1809 and after that regularly since 1863. As Pekonen has shown, foreign parliamentary practices were carefully studied in the 19th century and the basis for the parliamentary procedure was established, for example, regarding minute keeping.[10]

The digitised collection comprises the printed volumes that have been compiled during the parliamentary season (ranging usually from February to January).[11] The parliamentary sources contain both static documents, which were the basis of the parliamentary work or produced in the legislative process, and dynamic minute keeping, which recorded the speeches and the procedure of the sessions. It is important to note that even though the minutes were recorded in detail and directly, they have gone through minor editing in the transcription process at the Records Office (for example, regarding the use of dialects).[12]

The parliamentary documents follow until 1975 the publication practices established already in the 19th century, according to which the documents were grouped together per legislative case (minutes proceed chronologically). The materials of the season were published both in Finnish and in Swedish, of which the Finnish collection forms the complete collection, and Swedish texts include translations of the main documents and a summary of the minutes. The annual publications consist of two to four volumes of the Minutes of the parliamentary sessions (*Pöytäkirjat*), one volume of the Swedish summary (*Protokoll i sammandrag*), three to five volumes of the Documents in each language (*Asiakirjat, Handlingar*) and the Annexes (*Liitteet*, only in Finnish).[13] For the season 1975/II (which started in September), the Documents and Annexes began to be regrouped in Documents series (A–F in Finnish, A–D in Swedish) according to their type. Besides this, a separate Index (*Hakemisto, Register*) was published, which had been included prior to 1975/II in the last volume of the Minutes.[14] The index of the Minutes has been extracted during the digitisation into a separate file for the seasons 1948 to 1975/I.

The digitised material has been published online by the Finnish Parliament.[15] In the digitisation process, the separate volumes have been scanned, optical-character recognised (OCR) and stored as PDF/A files. The online interface allows keyword searching of the text content of the pdf files, which, however, has considerable challenges due to errors and typographical features included in the OCR output.[16] The separate pdf files (the different printed volumes) can be downloaded and used separately. This complete dataset consists of 92.4 GB of optically recognised pdfs, of which 61.6 GB are in Finnish and 30.8 GB are in Swedish. The pdf files have been named according to their publication types (described above) and publication year, but the dataset does not include any text or metadata files.

For this chapter, the text content of the pdfs was extracted with the pdftotxt tool included in the open source Xpdf.[17] The pdf format does not offer a good structure for the text, and the text output was cleaned for the analysis conducted here. In 'Allemansrätten Emerges' below, the raw documents could be used while they suited keyword searches and close reading of the search results. For the topic modelling carried out in 'Allemansrätten since the 1970s', below, two debate corpora were refined manually: only selected law cases were picked, and from these, only speeches by representatives were extracted and corrected into simple text.[18]

As the digitisation of the parliamentary documents has been carried out with printed material, the OCR quality of the material is generally very good. However, it varies a lot and needs cleaning to be used for detailed textual analysis. As there is currently no previous research or evaluation of the quality of the material, I conducted a very rough analysis of the word recognition rates concerning the complete material per decade. I used the LAS-tool,[19] which has a functionality for word recognition rate.[20] The recognition was conducted per file, and an average was calculated for document type per year.

As shown in Figure 11.1, the recognition rates are between 60% and around 95%, mainly being over 80%. In comparison to the digitised Finnish newspapers, the quality is very good, as a word accuracy of around 70% to 75% has been reported for the historical newspapers.[21] It is notable, however, that the quality varies to some degree in the parliamentary material, and is lowest for the documents published in the 1920s and 1930s. Furthermore, the LAS-tool uses only one language when detecting recognition rate in the complete file. The Minutes in particular have a lower detection rate for the earlier years, as Swedish was used more commonly by the MPs. Thus, the real recognition rate is slightly higher than shown in the graph, but the general trend surrounding the quality of the digitisation is clearly visible.

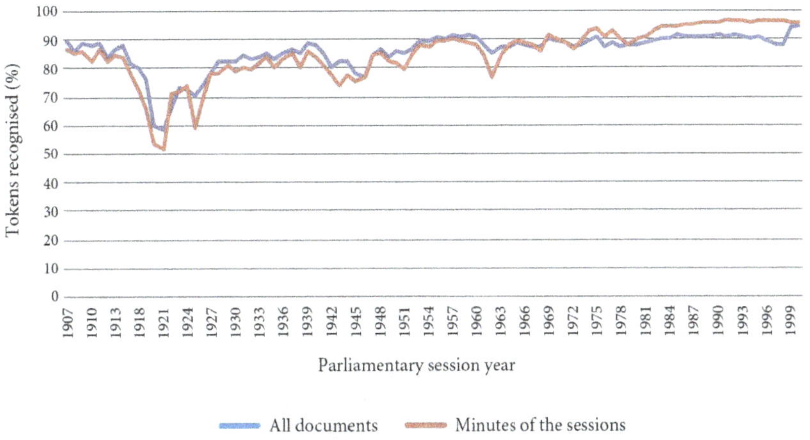

Figure 11.1: Tokens recognised on average per year in the Finnish-language, digitised parliamentary documents. Source: Author.

Allemansrätten Emerges: From Every Man to Fishing and to Modern Access Rights

In this section, I will explore the emergence of *allemansrätten* as a commonly known and shared concept in the Finnish public discussion of the 20th century. This history is not known, and offers an important perspective on the temporal tension inherent in *allemansrätten*. On the one hand, *allemansrätten* is commonly narrated as an age-old tradition or as deriving from the specific Nordic culture. For instance, in autumn 2018, the Finnish outdoor association *Suomen Latu* launched a public campaign broadly visible in the national media, which aims to add *allemansrätten* to UNESCO's list of intangible cultural heritage.[22] On the other hand, the scholarship has acknowledged, mainly in the Swedish case, that *allemansrätten* saw the light of day only after the 1930s, with the development of urbanisation and modern mass outdoor recreation.[23] As Kardell writes, since its first appearances in the 1930s, *allemansrätten* 'grew to become part of the Swedish nation's soul (*folksjälen*)'.[24]

How is the case with Finland, then? On a general level, it is known that also in Finland, the term *allemansrätten*, or *jokamiehenoikeus* in Finnish, becomes commonly used only after the Second World War.[25] The parliamentary data allows us to study the trajectory of the term during the whole century. It also fills an important gap, as the digitised national newspapers are available only until 1929. I will first trace the appearance of the term in the parliamentary data, and then focus on particular instances by studying, on a sentence level, in which ways *allemansrätten* could be used in public talk. In this mapping, I will use the complete dataset, and in the following section of the chapter, I will focus on more limited corpora to study the discursive environments in more detail.

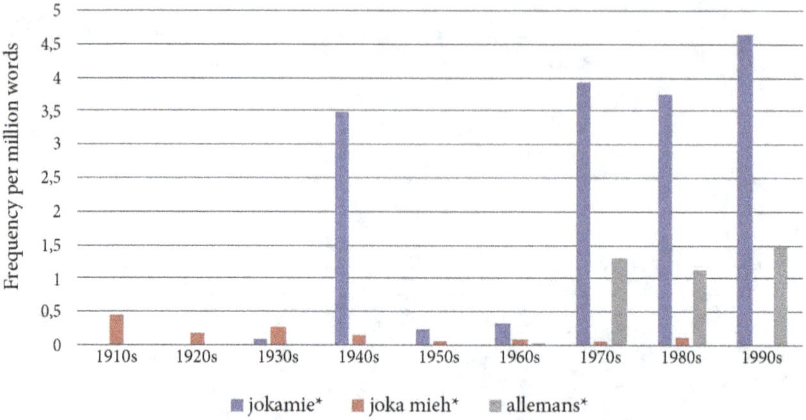

Figure 11.2: Frequencies of 'everyman*' ('*jokamie**', '*joka mieh**' in Finnish, and '*allemans**' in Swedish) per million words in the parliamentary documents per decade. Source: Author.

I used multiple keywords in the search in order to shed light on the differences between the uses in the two national languages, Finnish and Swedish, and to capture a broader variety of terms used.[26] As we can see from Figure 11.2, there are differences with regard to how much the terms were used. Before the 1940s, the Swedish term *allemansrätten* is not used at all, and the Finnish '*joka miehen*' (every man's) appears to some extent. In the 1940s, there is a curious peak in the use of the term in Finnish. Finally, only in the 1970s, the use of the written forms '*jokamiehen*' (everyman's) and '*allemans**' really boom and become common. The other word forms are used less frequently and disappear.

When we look at the actual uses of the terms in the parliamentary data, we can shape three periods. In the pre-Second World War era, the term 'everyman' referred to a common, ordinary person. During the Second World War, 'everyman' was used in the context of nature and outdoor activities with the introduction of the wartime 'everyman's right of fish'. Finally, only gradually since the 1960s, 'everyman' became employed in its main contemporary meaning as describing *allemansrätten*.

The Finnish '*joka mies*', everyman or every man, is obviously a term that has already appeared in the language for a longer amount of time. In this meaning, it refers to an ordinary person or generally everybody. It is important to note that this Finnish term translates into the Swedish '*var man*' (everyman), and does not bear similarity to the Swedish-language word root *alleman* pointing at *allmän* (common, general) and *allmänningar* (the commons). In general, then, the origins of the Finnish vocabulary are less bound to land ownership and social conflict.[27] Moreover, in the early century, the term was not yet used in the context of outdoor activities or access to nature. We find manuals, guidebooks and even magazines for the 'everyman' (for example, the 'Everyman's—and every woman's—weekly' first published in 1907, later called the 'Everyman's weekly').[28] In the parliamentary data of the early century, this is how '*joka mies*' (every man) was used. In the Minutes of 1935, national defence was supported by stating that the 'defence question is a question for every man'.[29]

Interestingly, the first major uses of 'everyman' as explicitly concerning public access to nature took place in the early 1940s in relation to fishing rights. During the wartimes, temporary fishing rights were enacted in Finland in 1941 to alleviate the shortage of food. At first, the rights concerned fishing in one's local waters, but these were extended in 1943 to allow for some years fishing for everyone in all parts of the country. The right concerned non-commercial fishing by the household, but allowed special permissions for professional fishers, who were immigrants away from their home lakes. The right became labelled as 'everyman's right to fish' or 'everyman's fishing' (*jokamiehen kalastusoikeus, jokamieskalastus* or, in Swedish, *var mans fiskerätt*).[30] In Parliament, there was also criticism raised against this right; however, its temporary and exceptional nature was acknowledged. In 1946, in the aftermath of the war, it was noted how among the 'everyman fishers' (*jokamieskalastaja*)[31] there were also many immigrants and locals who were in dire need of fish. It was noted by the social democrat MP Tuomas Bryggari how this right should not only be made an exception, but 'a general law, so that every citizen would have the right to fish'.[32]

The discussion about 'everyman's fishing' continued in the 1950s, but it was only in the 1960s that the 'everyman' was used to refer to the modern *allemansrätten*. However, we still find discussion about fishing and 'everyman' as everybody or a common person as in 'everyman's sports'. In the parliamentary data, the first uses of *allemansrätten* is in Finnish in 1964. In his question to the government, the left-wing MP Kalevi Kilpi (and others) asked about how the future outdoor legislation would react to the question of no trespassing signs. Kilpi added how according to 'custom there existed a so-called everyman's right to roam on another's land without the permission of the owner'.[33] This is the period when the term *allemansrätten* became very common in Sweden. The word appeared as part of land planning and urban nature use in the late 1930s, and in the early 1950s, the public in Sweden could read in the newspapers how *allemansrätten* did not really appear in Swedish law, but gave everyone the right to move freely in the woods since the early times. In Finland, sporadic appearances are found in these years, but the country seemed to follow its western neighbour only in the following decade.

In the 1970s, then, the term *allemansrätten* became very widely used in the parliamentary data. This peak is explained also by the particular moment, while the new outdoor legislation was discussed in the parliament in the early 1970s. However, this expansion in the use of *allemansrätten* is also due to the term becoming common in the Finnish language, perhaps even a rhetorical motif describing public access rights in general. The peak in the uses of *allemansrätten* does not decrease, but stays at the same level and even increases in the following decades. Moreover, the term *allemansrätten* becomes mainly associated with the area of public access rights to nature. Already at the time, the term was commonly used in public and scholarly discussion in Sweden. This is an indication that the interpretation and demarcation of the modern concept of *allemansrätten* in Finland was influenced by the Swedish discussions, which is also confirmed by the legal scholarly discussion on access rights to public and private spaces in Finland.[34]

Even though the digitised newspaper collections are incomplete, it is important to confirm the results with the newspaper material and use it as a parallel dataset to control possible quality problems related to the parliamentary data. I conducted similar keyword searches in the Finnish National Library newspaper dataset until 1929, and used the Sanoma Digital Archives, which host a handful of major Finnish newspapers with national coverage, such as *Helsingin Sanomat* and *Iltasanomat*. The results are very similar. From 1900 until 1929, there are no appearances of *allemansrätt** (or *alle mans rätt**), and I found uses of '*var man*' (everyman) similar to the Finnish-language use of 'everybody' and 'common person'. The Sanoma Archives' sources also demonstrate the peak in the 1940s with references to the 'everyman's right to fish'. The first uses of the modern term '*jokamiehenoikeus*' (*allemansrätten*) are found in the 1960s, and the term becomes common in the 1970s material. The first reference from 1962 is in a letter from a reader to the newspaper *Helsingin Sanomat* about the recent private road legislation and whether walking on private roads was permitted.[35]

It seems clear, then, that the term *allemansrätten* became commonly used only after the 1960s. How stable have the modern uses been? In the following section, I will explore more carefully the discursive environments where the modern term has been used by contrasting the parliamentary debates of the 1970s with those of the early 1990s—a moment of Finland's economic and political opening, for example, concerning the EC/EU membership.

Allemansrätten since the 1970s: Mapping the Shifts in Discursive Environments

Today, *allemansrätten* is a well-known concept which has extended outside its core meaning of public access rights to nature. *Allemansrätten* has been used in other areas than nature to designate the importance of public access rights—for example, how 'public libraries are an everyman's right'. Moreover, the concept has been branded as something uniting the Nordic countries, but also representing several key values of these societies, such as Nordic freedom, clean nature and equality.[36] What can we learn about the uses of the concept and its expansion beyond a mere 'right to roam' by looking at the parliamentary debates?

In this section, we investigate and contrast the uses of *allemansrätten* at two moments in time: in the early 1970s, when *allemansrätten* was becoming a commonly used concept, and in the early 1990s, when the term had become an irreplaceable part of discussion about public access rights to nature. This is achieved by studying the co-occurrence of *allemansrätten* with other terms in the two moments in time with collocation analysis and topic modelling. As the focus is on public discussion, the minutes of the parliament are used in this section. Moreover, the uses of the Finnish term *jokamiehen/oikeus* only are followed, as the majority of the parliamentary speech was in Finnish.

When looking at the debates of the 1970s, concordance searches[37] for the term reveal important concentrations of *allemansrätten* in 1973, 1974, 1976 and 1978. They help to identify the key legislative debates in which *allemansrätten* was used and became defined. In the early 1970s, the new Outdoor Recreation Act was discussed and enacted in Parliament. In 1974 and 1976, the debates regarded the expropriation law and, in 1978, the public use of nature was a topical part of the legislative work on the chemical treatment of forest vegetation.

In the 1990s, several concentrations of the use of the term are found with concordance searches. As expected, the clusters in the 1990s are more numerous and regard a broader variety of themes. In the 1970s, 170 concordance hits are found, which consist of over 90 hits about the Outdoor Recreation Act only and of two smaller concentrations of 10 to 20 hits. In the minutes of the 1990s, on the contrary, 401 hits are found, which are divided rather equally in smaller clusters appearing every year. Most annual hits (56) are found in the 1996 minutes. In the 1990s, *allemansrätten* appeared as part of debates on nature use and the natural environment, such as hunting and fishing laws and natural protection legislation. *Allemansrätten* was, however, taken into political debate also in relation to questions about Finland's international relations: the EC/EU membership and legislation concerning foreign ownership in Finland. *Allemansrätten*, therefore, was used in the 1990s more broadly than merely in the context of access rights in the natural environment.

If we move closer to the level of text, this broadening in the uses of the term becomes more visible. For the comparison, I formed two equal-size debate corpora (about 250,000 characters), which were about similar legislative topics. Similarity of the corpora was sought to minimise the effects created by the mere variance in the legislative topics discussed at the two moments in time. The 1970s debates were used as a starting point, and were contrasted with the legislative projects of the 1990s, which regarded environmental protection, fishing and recreational use of nature.[38] Furthermore, the corpus was cleaned for obtaining more accurate results for the analysis of co-occurrences: first, the words in the two corpora files were lemmatised with the LAS tool presented in 'Digitised Parliamentary Talk of the 20th Century', above. Second, the texts were trimmed by removing other characters than alphabet letters and deleting the names of the MPs and commonly repeated phrases, such as the greetings addressed to the speaker at the beginning of talks.

When looking at the collocates of '*jokamie**' (everyman*) (statistically the most commonly appearing terms with '*jokamie**'[39]), we find that *allemansrätten* retains a common core, but has been used to deliver rather diverse messages. The most frequent collocates shared by both corpora include 'right', 'citizen', 'nature', 'ice / lure fishing' and 'Finland', but also 'Nordic'. When we look at differences in collocation (collocates that are not found in the other corpus), the picture becomes nuanced. There are collocates which related mainly to the differences in law projects discussed (even though similar debates were selected for the comparison), such as 'recreational use' or 'chemical treatment product' in the 1970s.

There seem to be differences in relation to how internal or external the uses of *allemansrätten* have been. The collocates in the 1970s point to the discovery, stabilisation and internal debate about the concept. The most frequent collocates include, for instance, the terms 'age-old', 'property right' / 'property' and 'landowner', and among the statistically most common one finds 'historical', 'heritage' and 'socialise'. In the 1990s, the horizon seems to be broader, and *allemansrätten* appears rather as something that is being challenged by or being related to the outside world. In the 1990s, the statistically most common collocates include 'unique', 'outsider', 'trample' and 'spoil', and also terms related to space, such as 'international', 'Europe', 'European' and 'integration'. Even though the 1990s corpus does not include direct debates about EC membership, the discussions on *allemansrätten* seem to generate questions related to the opening of the borders. Similar fears about the overuse or the weakening of the access rights to nature due to EC membership were also raised in neighbouring Sweden in the early 1990s.

Finally, the differences in co-occurrences between the two corpora are studied by using topic modelling. Topic modelling is a method where separate topics ('patterns of tightly co-occurring terms') are detected in the text corpora through probability analysis.[40] Topic modelling has proved to be a powerful tool, especially when organising and classifying a large quantity of text documents.[41] In this section, we do not examine the different topics that are found in the corpus, but we study in detail the topics in which *allemansrätten* appears. The topic modelling was carried out using the MALLET tool.[42] MALLET includes automatic removal of stop words, and after testing several shares of topics, MALLET was run to find 80 topics in both corpora.[43] Besides building the topics, MALLET produces an output file, where the words in the corpus are annotated by their topic number. The results of '*jokamie**' (everyman*) appearing in different topics is presented in Figure 11.3.

As illustrated very clearly in the graph above, MALLET clustered *allemansrätten* mainly to two different topics. To a large extent, this results due to the functionalities of the method, as the data had been lemmatised and the written word forms used in the 1970s and 1990s were different: topic 49 includes the term '*jokamies*' (everyman), whereas topic 76 includes the term '*jokamiehenoikeus*' (*allemansrätten*), which, as we have seen, had become the common written form in the 1990s

In addition to this, we can discern again a different discursive environment for the two topics and the uses of *allemansrätten* in the 1970s and 1990s. Topic

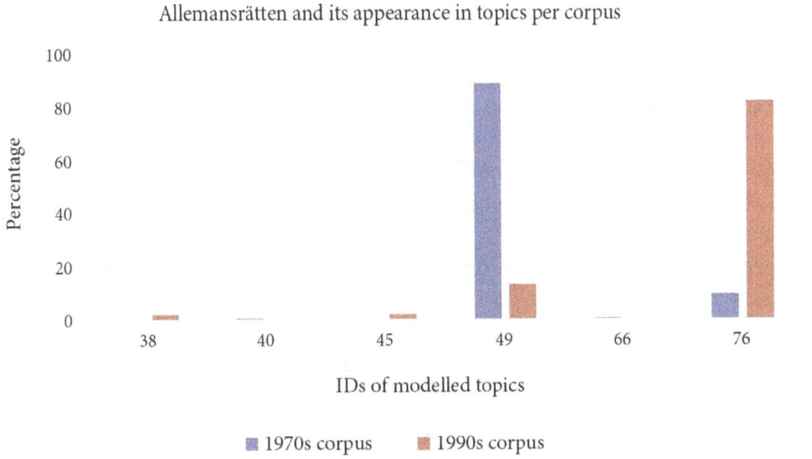

Figure 11.3: Topics in which the term '*jokamie**' (everyman*) was grouped in the topic modelling (per corpus). Source: Author.

49 is mainly about *allemansrätten*: the main keyword given in topic 49 is '*jokamies*' (everyman). This topic includes terms about political debate (political parties) on nature, nature use and access rights. Topic 76, on the other hand, does not have '*jokamiehenoikeus*' (*allemansrätten*) as the main keyword, but the first words of the topic are 'talk', 'damage', 'needs to' and 'pay', and then '*jokamiehenoikeus*'. Further down the list of topic terms we find 'damage', 'problem', 'forest fire', 'Finnish', 'companies' and 'integration'. No names of political groups are listed in topic 49, and its terms are more related to necessity and change, rather than political negotiation or argumentation.

It seems, then, that *allemansrätten* expands beyond its 'traditional' range of reference in the period. In the 1970s, *allemansrätten* appears as part of political debate in which the concept was contested, but the contestation limited itself to the question of access rights to nature. The discussion focused on *allemansrätten* itself and its roots. Based on a close reading of the corpus, we can highlight as an example the comment put by the agrarian party MP Mikko Kaarna in 1973: 'whatever is meant by this everyman's right, it seems that everybody aims to interpret it in his own way, some of us in a very broad sense'.[44] After this, Kaarna referred to the laws which already regulated outdoor access. In the 1990s, however, *allemansrätten* conveyed meanings in the political debate that were matters external to access to nature, and rather related to international relations and questions of national identity. For instance, in the debate on the law on natural protection, agrarian party MP Markku Koski emphasised 'how the right, that was very broad for the Finns, should be valued, namely *allemansrätten*, which does not exist in other European countries to the same extent as in Finland'.[45]

Conclusion

This digital history of *allemansrätten* in the recently digitised documents of the Finnish Parliament has allowed light to be shed on the trajectory of the Finnish *allemansrätten*. The methods used in this chapter (keywords search and collocation analysis) have been useful for identifying key debates and studying long-term changes in those debates related to *allemansrätten*. The chapter has shown how the vocabulary of 'everyman' was already being used extensively before the term *allemansrätten* came into use. The introduction of fishing rights in the early 1940s presents an important turning point, and depicts key tensions in access rights to nature. Universality in the fishing rights, which is at the core of today's *allemansrätten*, was criticised with references to the dishonest 'vagabond fishermen' and damages done to the honest locals.[46] In fact, even though voices were heard for making fishing permanently open for everyone, 'everyman's fishing' was soon limited to allow fishing in the areas where the 'everymen' resided. Importantly, economic reasons, including economic distress, were behind the decision to open the fishing rights. In a similar way, the discussions on wild berry picking in the late 19th century regarded the possibilities for the poor of the rural areas.[47] Only when strangers outside the local community arrived as 'everymen' to the woods and lakes did it become crucial to define the limits of access rights: the broadening (and creation) of the right was done for economic reasons, not based on a cultural tradition.

The Finnish vocabulary of '*allemansrätten*' slowly began to point to universal access rights to nature after the 1950s. In fact, at some point in the 1950s, two conceptual traditions became united. The modern institution of *allemansrätten* in Finland was modelled after the Swedish example, yet, the Swedish term was not translated into Finnish, but the Finnish expression of 'common man's' and 'normal' access to nature used for wartime fishing rights was taken into use. In the 1970s, then, *allemansrätten* was an established and commonly used concept in Finland. It appeared in the political debates of the decade, but mainly *internally*, as something at the centre of attention itself: a 'national heritage' that was discussed and defined by the different national political groups. In the 1990s, the uses of *allemansrätten* had expanded to various legislative debates. With the normalisation of the concept, *allemansrätten* could be used *externally*, to convey meanings related to national values outside the sphere of access rights to nature. In the context of European integration in the early 1990s, it was used to defend a particular Nordic way of life in contrast to European practices of ownership. It is this kind of national symbol, how it is understood (or felt) by the public, which is presented to foreign visitors and used in the branding of the Nordic countries today.[48]

In general, the digitised parliamentary data opens up a new research horizon on the public matters of the 20th century. The data complements the digitised national newspapers, which are available comprehensibly for the first three decades of the century only. Yet, the Finnish case presents shortcomings that can render digital historical research cumbersome and uninviting: the parliamentary data is not easily accessible through the current web user interface of the Finnish Parliament.[49] By their nature, parliamentary documents are structured according to time, theme and speaker, and basic search tools and filters that enable the use of these features would satisfy the needs of most historians.[50] In this chapter, I did not use the web interface, but applied textual analysis methods on the parliamentary data. These methods are applicable by historians with basic computational skills; however, a significant amount of data work is necessary when using such non-structured and partly weak quality data. It seems to me, therefore, that digital historians should pay extra attention to the workload and the trade-off related to the new digital sources: how much can be done 'easily' with the existing resources by the historian, and what data and development work can and should be left for broader cooperative projects? Moreover, this also implies that historians should actively partake in the digitisation processes of the key historical sources and the development of the related user interfaces.

Notes

1 Sandell 1997; Husa, Nuotio & Pihlajamäki 2007: 25–26. For everyman's rights in Finland generally, see Matilainen 2019: 34–35.

2 Wiktorsson 1996.

3 La Mela 2014; La Mela 2016; Sténs & Sandström 2016.

4 Pekonen 2014; La Mela 2016.

5 Quinn et al. 2010; King 2016; Abercrombie & Batista-Navarro 2018.

6 La Mela 2016.

7 Ihalainen & Palonen 2009.

8 Ihalainen, Ilie & Palonen 2016. For a list of the available parliamentary corpora by CLARIN, see https://www.clarin.eu/resource-families/parliamentary-corpora.

9 Apilo 2018.

10 Pekonen 2014.

11 Valtiopäivien 2006.

12 Pekonen 2014: 181–225; Voutilainen 2016.

13 The Documents are the main collection of the parliamentary documents (government proposals and committee statements, for instance), and the Annexes contain the motions of the MPs.

14 See, e.g., Riksdagshandlingarna 2012.

15 Digitoidut valtiopäiväasiakirjat 1907–2000, http://avoindata.eduskunta.fi/digitoidut/.

16 For example, the speakers' surnames are spelled in the Minutes with spaced text, which the search engine is unable to interpret. MP Koivisto's speaking turn appears in the text as 'Ed. K o I v I s t o:'.

17 XpdfReader, https://www.xpdfreader.com/about.html.

[18] For example, page numbers were removed and text column recognition errors corrected.

[19] Linguistic Analysis Command-Line Tool, version 1.5.15, https://github.com/jiemakel/las.

[20] Mäkelä 2016.

[21] Kettunen & Pääkkönen 2016.

[22] Finnish NGO 2018.

[23] Sandell 1997.

[24] Kardell 2004: 234.

[25] La Mela 2016.

[26] The keywords used in the search were *jokamie** and *joka mieh**, which capture both written forms of the term *allemansrätten* in Finnish: *jokamiehen oikeus* and *joka miehen oikeus*.

[27] La Mela 2014: 271–272; La Mela 2016: 218–219.

[28] Jokamiehen —ja joka naisen —viikkolehti. No. 3 (19 October 1907).

[29] 'Minä tahtoisin sanoa: puolustuskysymys on meillä joka miehen kysymys. Jokaikisen terveen Suomen miehen on otettava puolustuskysymys omakseen ja omalta osaltaan vastattava siitä.' Minutes of the Parliamentary Session of 1935 (Minutes 1935 II). Helsinki: Valtioneuvoston kirjapaino, 1936, p. 1623.

[30] Brofeldt 1943.

[31] '... elintarviketilanne ei vielä ole korjautunut sellaiseksi, että voisimme kieltää jokamieskalastajilta mahdollisuuden omalla työllään ansaita itselleen vähäisen särpimen lisän.' Minutes 1945 II, p. 2187.

[32] 'Minun nähdäkseni kalastusoikeus pitäisi saada vakiinnutetuksi, ei ainoastaan poikkeukseksi, vaan yleiseksi laiksi, että kaikilla kansalaisilla olisi kalastusoikeus.' Minutes 1945 II, p. 2189.

[33] 'Tosin on vanhastaan katsottu, että maantavan mukaan on olemassa ns. jokamiehen oikeus kulkea toisen maalla ilman omistajan lupaa.' Documents of the Parliamentary Session of 1964 (Documents 1964 V), Question no. 67, p. 2.

[34] Legal scholar V. K. Noponen was already using variants of *allemansrätten* in Finnish in his work on public and private roads in the 1940 and 1950s. Noponen also refers to concepts developed by the legal scholar S. Ljungman, who was among the first to present this 'newly-found catchphrase with legal value', *allemansrätten*. La Mela 2016: 216.

[35] Laki yksityisistä teistä. Helsingin Sanomat, no. 264 (30 September 1962), p. 31.

[36] See, e.g., Sandell & Svenning 2011.

[37] The AntConc corpus analysis tool is used for concordance searches and file views. The concordance search was used to detect keywords in the data and study their uses on sentence level. See http://www.laurenceanthony.net/software/antconc/.

[38] The selected law projects from the 1990s regard: state outdoor recreation area in Teijo, natural protection act, remuneration of environmental damage and the fishing law.

[39] A range of 10 words before and after the term was used to study collocation.

[40] Blei 2012.

[41] See, e.g., Weingart & Meeks 2012; Wehrheim 2018.

[42] MALLET toolkit, http://mallet.cs.umass.edu/.

[43] A different number of topics were tested manually. The number of topics did not affect the clear distinction between topics presented in Figure 11.3. A larger number of topics was preferred for producing more nuanced topics.

[44] 'Mitä tällä jokamiehen oikeudella tarkoitettaneenkaan, niin näyttää siltä, että jokainen pyrkii sitä tulkitsemaan omalla tavallaan, monet hyvinkin laajasti.' Minutes 1973 II, p. 1454.

[45] 'Mielestäni Suomessa nykyisin on pidettävä arvossa sitä oikeutta, mikä suomalaisilla on hyvin laajasti, eli jokamiehenoikeutta, jota ei muissa eurooppalaisissa valtioissa siinä mittakaavassa ole kuin Suomessa.' Minutes 1996 II, p. 1700.

[46] Minister of Agriculture Eemil Luukka on the law proposal on temporary fishing rights: '... jokamieskalastajat tästä lähtien saavat harjoittaa pyyntiään vain vakinaisen tai tilapäisen asuinpaikkansa lähivesistössä. Tämän rajoituksen kautta on tahdottu estää sellainen kulkurikalastajien toiminta, joka juuri on osoittautunut kaikkein haitallisimmaksi paikallisten asukkaiden kalanpyynnille, olkootpa he sitten kalastusoikeutta omaavia tai sitä vailla olevia.' Minutes 1945 II, p. 2187.

[47] La Mela 2016.

[48] Mission for Finland 2010; Tuulentie & Rantala 2013.

[49] Happily, the situation is improving. The research consortium "Semantic Parliament", which aims to produce a linked open data and research infrastructure on Finnish parliamentary data, started its work in January 2020. See https://seco.cs.aalto.fi/projects/semparl/en/.

[50] The digitised Canadian parliamentary debates webpage provides a very balanced and user-friendly interface for searching and browsing the parliamentary debates. See http://www.lipad.ca/. See also Beelen et al. 2017.

References

Abercrombie, G., & Batista-Navarro, R. (2018, May). *'Aye' or 'no'? Speech-level sentiment analysis of Hansard UK parliamentary debate transcripts.* In Proceedings of the Eleventh International Conference on Language Resources and Evaluation (LREC 2018). Miyazaki, Japan (pp. 4173-4180). European Language Resources Association (ELRA). Retrieved from https://www.aclweb.org/anthology/L18-1659.pdf

Apilo, A. (2018, May). *Digitized documents in Finnish Parliament.* Presentation at Aalto DH Pizza seminar, Otaniemi, Finland.

Beelen, K., Thijm, T. A., Cochrane, C., Halvemaan, K., Hirst, G., Kimmins, M., Lijbrink, S., Marx, M., Naderi, N., Rheault, L., Polyanovsky, R., & Whyte, T. (2017). Digitization of the Canadian parliamentary debates.

Canadian Journal of Political Science, 50(3), 849–864. DOI: https://doi.org/10.1017/S0008423916001165

Blei, D. M. (2012). Topic modeling and digital humanities. *Journal of Digital Humanities, 2*(1).

Brofeldt, P. (1943). *Jokamiehen kalastusoikeus ja muut poikkeukselliset kalastusmääräykset.* Helsinki: Otava.

Documents of the Parliamentary Session of 1964.

Finnish NGO (2018, 1 October). *Finnish NGO nominates 'everyman's right' for UNESCO heritage list.* YLE News. Retrieved from https://yle.fi/uutiset/osasto/news/finnish_ngo_nominates_everymans_right_for_unesco_heritage_list/10432231

Husa, J., Nuotio, K., & **Pihlajamäki, H.** (Eds.) (2007). *Nordic law: between tradition and dynamism.* Antwerp: Intersentia.

Ihalainen, P., Ilie, C., & **Palonen, K.** (2016). Parliament as a conceptual nexus. In P. Ihalainen, C. Ilie & K. Palonen (Eds.), *Parliament and parliamentarism: a comparative history of a European concept* (pp. 1–16). Oxford and New York, NY: Berghahn Books.

Ihalainen, P., & **Palonen, K.** (2009). Parliamentary sources in the comparative study of conceptual history: methodological aspects and illustrations of a research proposal. *Parliaments, Estates and Representation, 29*(1), 17–34.

Kardell, L. (2004). *Svenskarna och skogen.* Vol. 2: *Från baggböleri till naturvård.* Jönköping: Skogsstyrelsens förlag.

Kettunen, K., & **Pääkkönen, T.** (2016, May). *Measuring lexical quality of a historical Finnish newspaper collection—analysis of garbled OCR data with basic language technology tools and means.* In Proceedings of the Tenth International Conference on Language Resources and Evaluation (LREC 2016). Portoroz, Slovenia (pp. 956–961). European Language Resources Association (ELRA). Retrieved from http://www.lrec-conf.org/proceedings/lrec2016/pdf/17_Paper.pdf

King, L. (2016). Future citizens: cultural and political conceptions of children in Britain, 1930s–1950s. *Twentieth Century British History, 27*(3), 389–411. DOI: https://doi.org/10.1093/tcbh/hww025

La Mela, M. (2014). Property rights in conflict: wild berry-picking and the Nordic tradition of allemansrätt. *Scandinavian Economic History Review, 62*(3), 266–289. DOI: https://doi.org/10.1080/03585522.2013.876928

La Mela, M. (2016). *The politics of property in a European periphery: the ownership of books, berries, and patents in the Grand Duchy of Finland 1850–1910* (doctoral dissertation, European University Institute, Florence). DOI: https://doi.org/10.2870/604750

Matilainen, A. (2019). *Feelings of psychological ownership towards private forests* (doctoral dissertation, University of Helsinki, Faculty of Agriculture and Forestry). Retrieved from http://hdl.handle.net/10138/300433

Minutes of the Parliamentary Sessions of 1935, 1945, 1973, 1996.

Mission for Finland. (2010). Mission for Finland: Country brand report 25.11.2010. Final report of the Country Brand Delegation. Retrieved from http://www.maakuva.fi/wp-content/uploads/2011/06/TS_Report_EN.pdf

Mäkelä, E. (2016). LAS: an integrated language analysis tool for multiple languages. *Journal of Open Source Software, 1*(6), 35. DOI: https://doi.org/10.21105/joss.00035

Pekonen, O. (2014). *Debating 'the ABCs of parliamentary life': the learning of parliamentary rules and practices in the late nineteenth-century Finnish Diet and the early Eduskunta.* Jyväskylä: University of Jyväskylä.

Quinn, K. M., Monroe, B. L., Colaresi, M., Crespin, M. H., & **Radev, D. R.** (2010). How to analyze political attention with minimal assumptions and costs. *American Journal of Political Science, 54*(1), 209–228.

Riksdagshandlingarna. (2012). *Riksdagshandlingarna det finländska parlamentstrycket: handledning* [A guide to the Finnish parliamentary documents]. Library of the Parliament of Finland. Retrieved from http://www.eduskunta.fi/SV/tietoaeduskunnasta/kirjasto/aineistot/eduskunta/valtiopaivaasiakirjat-tietopaketti/Documents/Handledning-riksdagshandlingarna.pdf

Sandell, K. (1997). Naturkontakt och allemansrätt: om friluftslivets naturmöte och friluftslivets tillgänglighet i Sverige 1880–2000. *Svensk geografisk årsbok, 73,* 31–65.

Sandell, K., & **Svenning, M.** (2011). *Allemansrätten och dess framtid: utredning om allemansrätten.* Stockholm: Naturvårdsverket.

Sténs, A., & **Sandström C.** (2014). Allemansrätten in Sweden: a resistant custom. *Landscapes, 15*(2), 106–118.

Tuulentie, S., & **Rantala O.** (2013). Will free entry into the forest remain? In D. K. Müller, L. Lundmark & H. Raynald (Eds.), *New issues in Polar tourism* (pp. 177–188). Dordrecht: Springer.

Valtiopäivien. (2016). *Valtiopäivien alkamis- ja päättymisajat* [The beginning and closing dates of the parliamentary seasons]. Retrieved from http://www.eduskunta.fi/thwfakta/yht/ohje/valtiopaivat.htm

Voutilainen, E. (2016). Tekstilajitietoista kielenhuoltoa: puheen esittäminen kirjoitettuna eduskunnan täysistuntopöytäkirjoissa. In L. Tiittula & P. Nuolijärvi (Eds.), *Puheen kirjallisen esittämisen alueita, keinoja ja rajoja* (pp. 162–191). Helsinki: Suomalaisen Kirjallisuuden Seura.

Wehrheim, L. (2018). Economic history goes digital: topic modeling the *Journal of Economic History. Cliometrica.* DOI: https://doi.org/10.1007/s11698-018-0171-7

Weingart, S. B., & **Meeks, E.** (2012). The digital humanities contribution to topic modeling. *Journal of Digital Humanities, 2*(1).

Wiktorsson, G. (1996). *Den grundlagsskyddade myten: om allemansrättens lansering i Sverige.* Stockholm: City University Press.

CHAPTER 12

Evolving Conceptualisations of Internationalism in the UK Parliament

Collocation Analyses from the League to Brexit

Pasi Ihalainen and Aleksi Sahala

Introduction[1]

While the history of the diplomatic events and institutions of 20th-century international politics has been comprehensively explored,[2] macro-historical and long-term computer-assisted analyses of conceptualisations of the 'international' have not yet been attempted. With the increasing availability of digitised parliamentary debates, such an analysis of the everyday language of politics has become possible. In the conceptual history of internationalism, focus on Parliament is particularly pertinent in the British case, as the country has been one of the most active agents in the field of international cooperation while regarding Parliament as *the* forum of ideological debate. Parliament has had a say in foreign policy, too, regarding membership in international organisations.

After having previously analysed parliamentary debates with more conventional close-reading methods of the history of political discourse,[3] we turn here to text analysis programmes to explore their benefits for conceptual history.

How to cite this book chapter:
Ihalainen, P., & Sahala, A. (2020). Evolving conceptualisations of internationalism in the UK Parliament: Collocation analyses from the league to Brexit. In M. Fridlund, M. Oiva, & P. Paju (Eds.), *Digital histories: Emergent approaches within the new digital history* (pp. 199–219). Helsinki: Helsinki University Press. https://doi.org/10.33134/HUP-5-12

Our goal is to reconstruct meanings assigned to international issues in the UK Parliament in the long 20th century: How has the 'international' been experienced, understood, conceptualised, constructed, debated and redefined? How and why has the 'international' been given meaning and implicitly defined through its use in a variety of (ideologically motivated) political arguments, particularly in connection with membership in international organisations? To what extent and when, how, why and with what consequences has this attribute turned into an 'ism'?

We argue that the distant reading of extensive series of digitised UK parliamentary debates by the means of a collocation analysis helps to extend and deepen conceptual analysis so that previously unnoticed ways to discuss international cooperation can be discovered and the close reading of sources is more effectively focused. We supplement the analysis of parliamentary discourse at macro level with collocation analyses of particular debates and contextualised conceptual analyses in concrete speaking situations. The latter correspond with the criteria of historical research for understanding meaning created in specific contexts and provide checks to premature conclusions drawn on the basis of computer-assisted distant reading. In this exploration, conclusions of the distant reading remain suggestive so that problems rising from decontextualised interpretations can be pointed out. Thus, our investigation provides an example of interaction between text analysis programmes and an analytical mind familiar with the genre and discourses of the primary sources.

While doubts about the application of collocation analyses to intellectual history have by no means been overcome,[4] in corpus linguistics they have been used productively.[5] For sociolinguists, collocation is 'an accepted, linguistically meaningful measurement'[6] referring to 'the co-occurrence of two words within a pre-specified span, when the frequency of the co-occurrence is above chance, taking into account the frequencies of the "node" (the word in focus), its collocates, and the collocation itself'.[7] Applications thus far include a diachronic analysis of UK parliamentary speaking on Ireland,[8] an analysis of a parliamentary debate on the climate change[9] and an analysis of adjective collocates qualifying capitalism. Foxlee has aimed at combining more semantically and more pragmatically oriented versions of conceptual history with computer-assisted text analysis.[10] Guldi has demonstrated how word counts and text mining produce indices of historical change.[11] Lähdesmäki and Wagenaar have used collocation analysis to explore discourses of diversity within the Council of Europe by grouping the key terms in semantic fields (collocation networks) and measuring the frequencies of those fields in order to reveal how concepts were produced as policy.[12] The current authors share such an understanding of politics as primarily discursive and of the need to focus on conceptual innovations and active uses of language aimed at affecting policies.[13]

The Hansard Corpus (https://www.english-corpora.org/hansard/) contains nearly every speech given in the UK Parliament between 1803 and 2005,

1.6 billion words in total, and allows researchers to search on parliamentary debates, including collocation searches. While the scanned records have been proofread and optical character recognition (OCR) is not an issue, something like 5% of the debates have not been included in the Historic Hansard database (https://api.parliament.uk/historic-hansard/index.html) from which the data originates, which causes some uncertainty with search results. We started our distant reading with a collocation analysis of the noun collocates of 'internationalism' based on the tool of the Hansard Corpus, quoting selected examples from Historic Hansard to give more concrete content to the discernible trends. We then proceeded to collocation analyses of the entire vocabulary of 'international' in a selection of Commons (HC) and Lords (HL) debates concerning British membership in international organisations.

For the collocation analysis, we used a measure called PMI^2,[14] which is a less low-frequency sensitive improvement of the Church and Hanks' word association measure built around the idea of Pointwise Mutual Information (PMI).[15] The core idea of the PMI-based measures is to divide the corpus into forward-looking or bi-directional windows of fixed size, which define the maximum distance between the keywords and their possible collocates. The keywords are paired with each word that can be found within the defined window size, and the actual joint probability of each pair is compared to the expected probability of those words co-occurring independently. *The maximum score of 0* indicates that the words are only found together, and the minimum of $-\infty$ that the words never co-occur within the given window size. For calculating the scores, we used a Python script called *pmizer*, which is an open source script for calculating different PMI-based association measures from tokenised text.[16] We did not lemmatise our data, as we wanted to preserve singular and plural forms separately. To avoid our data being overcrowded with conjunctions, prepositions and pronouns, we filtered most of these out by using a simple stop-word list.

For the analysis of membership debates, there was no need to limit search terms as single debates varying from one to a few days were in question, and hence all references to the 'international' could be considered. A broad collocation window of 10 words both ways was used to discover every politically significant noun associated with the 'international'. The scores calculated with PMI^2 are reported below in the form '(number of collocates within the span of ten words both ways/score/distance)'.

Politically interesting collocates picked from result lists that ranked the closeness of the collocations on the basis of their score were grouped into collocation networks and their relative importance in both Houses discussed. While collocations are usually considered statistically significant when they appear in the corpus at least twice, individual combinations of words also deserve attention as politically potentially meaningful innovative speech acts. The next analysis is primarily based on distant reading, though some general context is introduced to support interpretation. A close reading of some findings will follow.

'Internationalism' in the UK Parliament, 1803–2005

As the Hansard Corpus is so extensive and as the use of 'international' is often technical rather than ideological (referring to aviation, for instance), our distant reading focused on collocations of 'internationalism'. The total number of co-occurrences of 'internationalism' in the Hansard Corpus with a nine-word collocation window is 1,542, with an emphasis on the 20th century and especially in the interwar period and the 1970s and 1960s. This leads to a manageable amount of results, even if ones that focus on the 'extreme' forms of international thinking that are expressed as an 'ism' word.

The noun collocates of 'internationalism' that were considered politically meaningful were divided into 13 loose semantic fields (groups of related terms, topical sub-categories or collocation networks), namely nationalism, party, socialism/labour, spirit, peace, democracy, imperialism, cosmopolitanism, globalism, collaboration, institutions, supra-nationalism and capitalism. The diachronic frequencies of the six most important of these semantic fields are visualised in Figure 12.1. The grouping of the terms was intuitive, building on previous empirical analyses of discourses on internationalism. Bringing in the historian's subjective mind in this way helped in discerning relevant topics among diversified discourses.

The diachronic frequencies point at the centrality of discourses on patriotism and nationalism for conceptualisations of internationalism. As Clavin and

Table 12.1: The number of collocations of 'internationalism' in UK parliamentary debates according to the Hansard Corpus.

1870s	4
1880s	8
1890s	0
1900s	8
1910s	38
1920s	132
1930s	188
1940s	202
1950s	129
1960s	99
1970s	317
1980s	204
1990s	130
2000–2005	83

Source: Author.

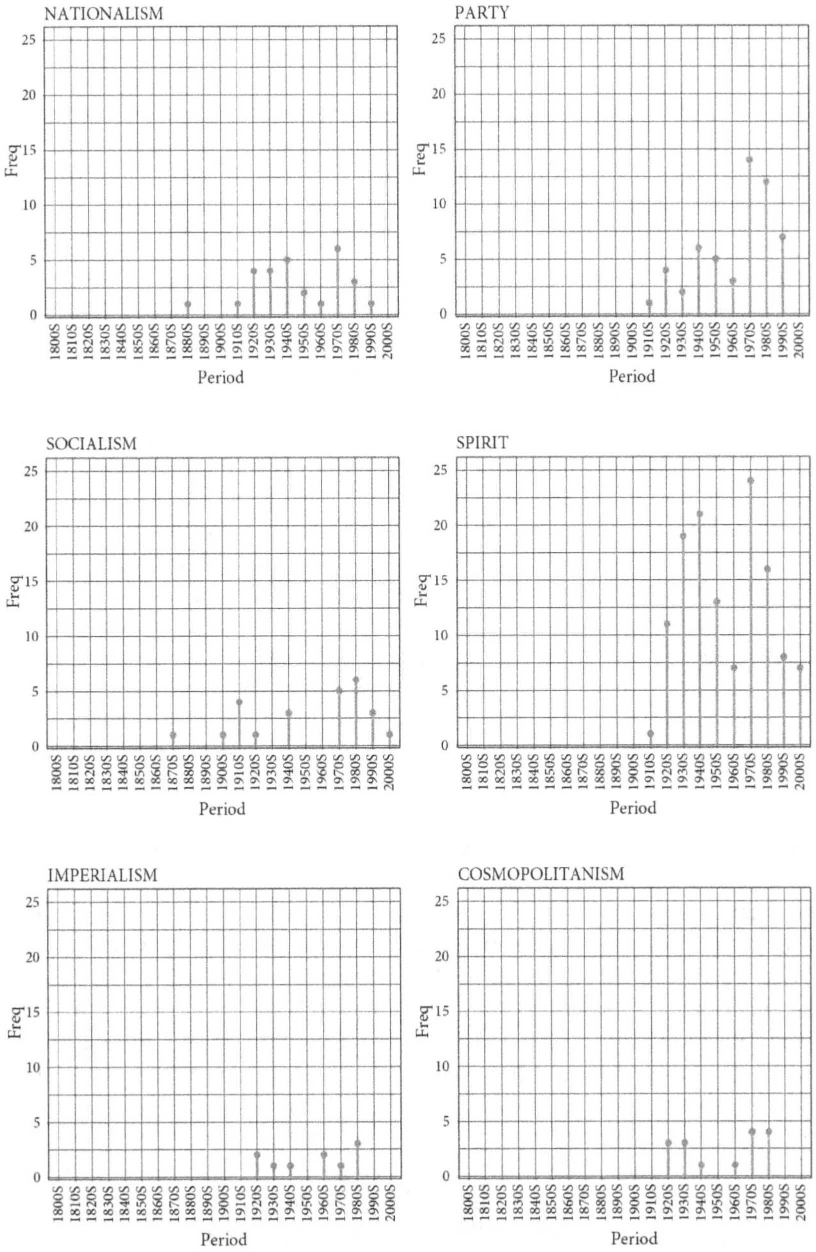

Figure 12.1: Politically significant collocate groups of 'internationalism' in the Hansard Corpus: nationalism, party, socialism (including the vocabulary of labour), spirit, imperialism, and cosmopolitanism. The visualisations were made by Kimmo Elo. Source: Author.

Sluga have argued, for much of the 20th century, internationalism was unthinkable without nationalism; nationalism was the basic premise, not a mere counter-concept of internationalism.[17] The vocabulary of patriotism contrasted with socialist internationalism in the British parliament already in 1882 as P. J. Smyth (Home Rule Party) criticised Irish agitation of 'the substitution of a vague, sickly, and godless internationalism for the manly patriotism' (*HC Deb. 9 March 1882 vol. 267 c524*; the references from now on are to volume and column numbers (c) in accordance with the conventions of British parliamentary debates). Patriotism or nationalism and internationalism (59 collocations) became increasingly associated after the First World War as the promoters of the League of Nations tried to reconcile these ways of thinking. Yet, J. D. Rees (Conservatives), a former colonial administrator, pointed at tensions between patriotism or nationalism and (socialist) internationalism, concluding that '[i]nternationalism means the negation of patriotism and the abnegation of everything of which we should be proud. Instead of extending internationalism I long myself to see it abolished completely off the face of the earth' (*HC Deb. 1 November 1920 vol. 134 c106*). Internationalism could only be based on nationalism, as Goronwy Owen (Liberals) put it: 'I have no sympathy at all with the people who preach internationalism as such … The basis of a proper internationalism is a good nationalism …' (*HC Deb. 27 April 1928 vol. 216 c1285*). Morgan Jones (Labour), a pacifist, agreed in the early 1930s as every European state was developing 'not towards a growing internationalism but towards essential nationalism' (*HC Deb. 10 May 1932 vol. 265 c1837*). Doubts about internationalism continued after the Second World War, especially among non-socialists: Ralph Rayner (Conservatives) was ironical when pointing out that 'Russia is still internationalist in so far as internationalism will serve her nationalism' (*HC Deb. 20 February 1946 vol. 419 c1192*).

Only from the mid-1950s can we find Conservatives conceptualising internationalism in more positive terms. Peter Smithers, a British delegate for the Council of Europe, believed that '[a] nationalist war today is a physical impossibility; and economically and socially the temptations of the benefits of internationalism are so great that nationalism in itself is no longer a very attractive proposition' (*HC Deb. 27 July 1955 vol. 544 c1288*). More radical challenging of nationalism dated from the time of the EEC membership as the young David Owen (Labour) declared: 'When I talk about European unity, I am talking in part about our concept of nationalism and internationalism. I find that one of the most dangerous facets of modern life and, indeed, of our history over the last 50 years is the scar of nationalism. I believe in internationalism as an article of faith' (*HC Deb. 26 October 1971 vol. 823 c1634*). By 1981, even the former Conservative MEP Hugh Dykes argued that 'Britain has always been internationalist in its nature. We changed the orientation of our internationalism by entering the Community in 1973. I wish that new, modern internationalism and Europeanism to continue, for the benefit of future generations' (*HC Deb. 8 April 1981 vol. 2 c1000*). Such positive associations between integration and internationalism, though interesting with hindsight, were not mainstream in the 1970s and 1980s either.

Conservative and liberal suspicions about internationalism had traditionally risen from its associations with socialism, as is revealed by 52 collocations of party vocabulary and internationalism, especially in the 1910s and 1920s, but still in the 1970s and 1980s as well. Party perspectives include associations between internationalism and socialism/socialist(s) (20), workers (10), labour (7), revolution (1), Marxism (1), bolshevism (1) and communism/communist(s) (2). Socialist or labour internationalism had emerged in the mid-19th century with the First International,[18] came up in the British parliament in the 1870s and was welcomed by 1911 as Josiah Wedgwood (Liberals) observed how '[i]nternationalism is spreading rapidly, not only the internationalism of capital but the internationalism of labour' (*HC Deb. 14 December 1911 vol. 32 c2625*). The founding of the International Labour Organisation (ILO) in 1919 activated this discourse, although typically the political rivals attacked the internationalist background of the Labour Party. By 1950, Joseph Kenworthy, a Labour peer, nevertheless declared that 'the future of mankind lies in internationalism: That word "internationalism" is a word we do not hear nearly often enough to-day: Real internationalism properly applied would have avoided the terrible catastrophes of the world wars of this century and have raised the standard of life of the whole of humanity' (*HL Deb. 28 June 1950 vol. 167 c1186*). Philip Russell Rea, a Liberal peer, also came up with ideas about 'more internationalism, some relinquishment of national sovereignty' as 'necessary in the modern world' (*HL Deb. 2 November 1960 vol. 226 c52*). Ronald Leighton, too, believed in internationalism, but added in line with the interwar prioritisation of nation states: 'The word "inter" means between: Instead of supra-nationalism, I want to see a group of independent, self-governing countries co-operating together' (*HC Deb. 21 May 1984 vol. 60 cc730–731*).

The spirit of internationalism (the fourth most common collocate of internationalism) had been discussed before the First World War as Philip Snowden (Labour), an anti-capitalist trade unionist, declared that 'we believe in the spread of a spirit of internationalism' and urged Britain to lead 'a great international league of peace' (*HC Deb. 15 March 1910 vol. 15 c308*). The vocabulary of this discourse included collocations with spirit (24), principle(s) (22), idea(s) (17), sense (10), ideal(ism) (10), word(s) (13), belief/believer (12), concept (11) and values (7), as well as thought, thinking, theories, enthusiasm, vocabulary and term. There would seem to have been a slight rise in the 'idea' of internationalism between the 1920s and 1940s and again in the 1970s and 1980s, as in the general intensity of internationalism discourse. The 'spirit' of internationalism peaked from the 1930s to the 1950s, 'principles' peaked in the 1950s. Critique against the 'idealism' of internationalism appeared between the 1920s and the 1950s and again in the 1970s, in the same period as 'values' were discussed. 'Sense' and internationalism were co-textualised a few times from the 1920s to 1940s and again since the 1970s, but with diminishing frequencies.

Explicit references to the spirit of internationalism were not so many as could be expected on the basis of Britain's role as a herald of liberal internationalism. In the aftermath of Hitler's accession to power, James Henderson Stewart (National Liberals), a supporter of Anglo-American cooperation, nevertheless assured that the British government had done more than any other 'to establish the spirit of internationalism' (*HC Deb. 27 April 1933 vol. 277 c366*). After the Second World War, the British spirit of internationalism was emphasised every now and then. In 1956, Lord Rea demanded that 'international questions must be handled with international, and not with national, mentality' and that 'we must recognise this spirit of internationalism much more than we have done in the past' by joining European organisations (*HL Deb. 15 March 1956 vol. 196, cc461–462*). Reginal Prentice (Labour) welcomed development aid as a way of 'building up a spirit of internationalism which can be a factor towards world peace' (*HC Deb. 25 April 1961 vol. 639, c303*).

Internationalism has customarily been associated with peace. This discourse emerged with the League of Nations and peaked in the 1930s. Dennistoun Burney (Conservatives), an aviation expert, summarised the logic of internationalism from the point of view of national, European and imperial security: '... if you are to have peace you must have internationalism, and if you are to have internationalism, you can only have it by abrogating to some extent the sovereign rights of each nation and at the same time restricting the freedom of the elective assembly of each national Government' (*HC Deb. 7 March 1929 vol. 226, c670*). By the 1930s, the problem was, according to Seymour Cocks (Labour), that Germany 'removed pacifism and internationalism from her vocabulary' (*HC Deb. 13 November 1933 vol. 281, c665*) so that, for Ralph Rayner (Conservatives), it already appeared as 'extremely dangerous to teach pacifism, internationalism, and the brotherhood of man' (*HC Deb. 14 June 1937 vol. 325, cc112–113*). Discourse on the spirit of internationalism nevertheless emerged in the interwar era, peaked with the creation of the United Nations and became again rarer in the 1950s and 1960s. After EEC membership, the UK Parliament appeared quantitatively at its most 'internationalist'; thereafter, collocations between spirit and internationalism have declined. Democracy was associated with internationalism in the parliamentary context mainly in the 1930s and 1940s, although Francis Pym (Conservatives), a former foreign secretary who opposed Thatcherism, argued boldly in 1987 that '[t]he world is interdependent, and internationalism must be nurtured in every democracy' (*HC Deb. 7 April 1987 vol. 114, c196*).

International issues could be conceptualised in further alternative ways. The British parliamentary elite had seen the League of Nations as supportive of the interests of the Empire.[19] They often discussed imperialism/imperialist(s) (commonwealth, empire, colonialism) and internationalism in the same context, with a break in the 1950s when decolonisation had started, reflected on the topic occasionally from the 1960s to the 1980s, and then dropped it from their vocabulary. Cosmopolitan ideals of internationalism—consisting of a variety of notions ranging from brotherhood, altruism, solidarity, humanitarian issues, aid and assistance to friendship, neighbourliness, fellowship and reciprocity—were also defended between the 1920s and 1940s. After the Second World War, this discourse became marginal, only to peak in the 1970s and 1980s in a rising internationalist atmosphere supportive of development and humanitarian aid, and losing popularity from the 1990s onwards. This period saw the emergence of a normative discourse on cosmopolitan democracy in political science, but such theories did not find their way to Parliament. The 1990s did see the emergence of the alternative discourse on globalisation, but only in three collocations with internationalism.

A discourse on collaboration (1) or cooperation (1) as internationalism surfaced by the end of the century, but as the low frequencies show, remained surprisingly marginal. Conventions on human rights, including that of the Council of Europe, appeared to Oliver McGregor, an economic historian, as 'the most remarkable features of recent history, a triumph for reason, co-operation and internationalism' over nationalism (*HL Deb. 16 December 1987 vol. 491, c729*). EEC membership supported discourse on systems, organisations, institutions and associations on the one hand and internationalism on the other. Yet, such debate withered away by the early 2000s, which may be reflective of the lack of commitment to the institutions of the community. The membership gave rise to entirely new debates on the relationship between integration (3), union (6), community/ies (11), Europeanism (3), supra-nationalism (4) and internationalism as well, but not to any great extent. In the meantime, the membership does not seem to have made such a great difference in associations between internationalism and markets (including trade(s)/trading, capital/capitalism/capitalist(s), economy, finance, growth and competition), a discourse that had existed before the First World War and been on a higher level in the interwar era. The global free trade visions of British politicians do not seem to have changed much with the post-Second World War economic integration: the EEC, too, was mainly conceptualised as a question of markets.

Debates on Membership in International Organisations

Next, we shall complement the above distant reading of trends in discourse on internationalism with analyses of collocates of the 'international' in entire parliamentary debates that concerned the British membership in international organisations—as key moments of discourse on the 'international'. The collocation analyses enabled a type of 'topic modelling' of the contents of the debates so that the results were not determined by previously selected search terms such as 'internationalism' only.

The selected membership debates concerned the League of Nations (LoN, in the Commons on 21 July 1919, in the Lords on 24 July 1919), the United Nations (UN, in both Houses on 22 August 1945), the Council of Europe (CoE, debated only in the Commons on 13 November 1950), the European Economic Community (EEC, several days in February 1972 in the Commons and in July 1972 in the Lords) and the European Union (EU, a couple of plenaries in September 2017 in the Commons and in January 2018 in the Lords). A further possibility might have been membership in NATO, but the defence alliance differed in its character from the other more general forms of international cooperation. It is also debatable whether these are the most representative occasions and whether the EU should be seen as a mere 'international organisation' or rather as a project of transnational integration. Debates on the EEC/EU in particular had several stages, and in principle all of these could have been analysed, but for the sake of consistency only *the second readings* of the related bills were considered. The second reading is typically the stage of deliberative decision-making when most extensive ideological contributions to the debate are made and competing arguments presented, reflecting much of what had come up in other parliamentary discussions and the public debate.

The Commons debates on the LoN membership on 21 July 1919 was a key moment in the history of British internationalism.[20] It took place in the aftermath of the signing of the treaty of Versailles that not only concluded the First World War with tough peace terms on Germany, but also introduced the League Covenant. The collocation analysis suggests that internationalism surrounding the League was conceptualised by the MPs to a great extent through the general concept of 'international law', as could be expected on the basis of the British role in drafting the Covenant and the inclusion of the International Court in it. The 'international' in the context of the League was about 'court' (4/-1184/2.75), 'legislation' (2/-1238/2.0), 'regulation' (1/-1238/1.0), 'justice' (4/-1271/2.75) and 'law' (1/-1571/1.0). Yet, for a trading nation, the 'international' also stood for finances, as reflected by nine close collocations of 'international' and 'finance' (9/-1029/1.0) and two more with 'financiers' (1/-1338/1.0) and 'financial' (1/-1655/1.0). 'Labour' had numerous close collocates with 'international' (10/-1220/2.2) due to the connected founding of the ILO, aimed at appeasing revisionist Western socialists under the alternative of the Communist International.[21] As an entirely new international organisation was being constructed, its institutions were discussed with terms such as 'bureau' (1/-1238/2.0) and 'machinery' (3/-1312/1.0). Discourses on 'experiment' (2/-1355/5.0), 'opportunity' (3/-1367/5.3) or 'cooperation' (1/-1397/3.0) and 'international' surfaced, but only rarely. Out of these findings, 'opportunity' will be analysed in more detail below.

The Lords paid plenty of attention to the moral aspects of the League, associating 'morality' (6/-800/1.0) tightly with 'international' and connecting 'morals' (1/-1059/3.0) and 'sanctity' (1/-1059/4.0) with it as well. The League was about 'treaties' (2/-1059/6.0), 'jurisprudence' (1/-1159/1.0), 'court' (2/-1178/1.0), 'sanction' (1/-1217/1.0), 'justice' (2/-1259/1.0), 'code' (1/-1259/1.0), 'rules' (1/-1259/6.0), 'law' (1/-1391/1.0) and 'treaty' (1/-1611/5.0), the total number of legal collocates rising to 13. Reflective of the more value- than interest-directed discourse (different from the down-to-earth approach of the Commons) is talk about 'international spirit' (2/-1117/1.5), which was reinforced by synonymous collocates such as 'friendship' (1/-1059/7.0) and 'reconciliation' (1/-1159/4.0). A major difference was the lack of debate on 'finances' and 'labour', which shows how economic and social issues were left for the lower house to deal with, appearing as less relevant in the social context of the peers.

The League was generally regarded as a drastic failure after the Second World War, and the British government then agreed with the United States and the Soviet Union on the founding of a new international organisation.[22] The Commons debated the UN membership in August 1945, in the aftermath of a victory over Nazi Germany and in the shadow of the first military use of the atomic bomb in Japan. Despite dissatisfaction with the League, British understandings of the 'international' had not changed much since 1919: the UN was likewise conceptualised through law, labour and institution. Next-door collocations of 'international' and 'court' (5/-1076/1.0), 'justice' (6/-1097/2.7), 'law' (4/-1228/1.0) and 'lawyers' (1/-1382/1.0) dominated, and collocations with 'conventions' (2/-1182/2.0) can be added to this discourse on international law. Associations with 'labour' (9/-1080/1.7) and 'workers' (1/-1582/7.0) continued to feature, which shows not only that the interests of the working class were central to the current Labour government, but also highlights a reaction to the strengthened international status of the Soviet Union and the connected need to appease the working classes of the West. Discourse on the institution focused in 1945 distinctly on 'control' (10/-1126/2.6), 'security' (5/-1476/3.2), 'machinery' (2/-1490/1.0) and 'peace' (4/-1544/1.0). 'Economic' (3/-1500/5.0) had rather loose connections with 'international' in comparison with the post-First World War situation. Collocates deserving further exploration include 'collective' and 'security'.

The Lords viewed the UN much like the Commons, emphasising law and justice on the one hand and the functioning of the institution aimed at collective security on the other. The peers associated 'international' and 'justice' (3/-1156/1.0), 'treaties' (1/-1292/5.0) or 'law' (1/-1509/1.0) and produced collocations of 'international' with 'supervision' (2/-1192/-1292/1.0), 'guards' (1/-1192/3.0), 'operation' (2/-1292/3.0), 'security' (5/-1341/3.6), 'peace' (4/-1386/1.0) and 'machinery' (1/-1573/1.0). Noteworthy are close associations between 'international' and 'collaboration' (2/-1151/1.0). Comments on 'patriotism' (1/-1292/9.0) and the 'commonwealth' (1/-1473/3.0) were also made.

Also at the formation of the CoE in 1950, the Commons drew predominantly from conceptualisations of the international law. 'Tribunal' (1/-1170/1.0) and 'court' (4/-1202/1.0) had several close collocations with 'international', and collocations with 'justice' (3/-1085/2.3) and 'jurists' (1/-1170/9.0) appeared. Associations between 'labour' (4/-1228/3.25) or 'workers' (1/-1370/2.0) and 'international' remained part of the discourse. Loose associations between 'international' and 'continental' (1/-1540/4.0), 'Brussels' (1/-1540/7.0) and 'federal' (1/-1634/4.0) were emerging, which may be indicative of a tendency to locate the 'international' out there in Europe. Economy or trade (1/-1578/9.0) had a marginal role in the CoE debates, nor do democracy or human rights feature,[23] which is surprising given the later role of the organisation, and associations between 'peace' (1/-1609/6.0) and 'international' were weak as well. The CoE appeared as a further body applying international law. Yet, it might have powerful tools of 'international pressure' (2/-1070/1.0, the strongest discovered association) in its possession, to which we shall return below.

The EEC, by contrast, was conceptualised in 1972 much less through law than economy. For the Commons, the EEC was about markets, trade, business and companies—*not* about law—which suggests a lack of dedication to common legislation as an aspect of the European integration. Associations between 'international' and 'companies' were exceptionally strong (7/-1022/1.0), but the 'international' was also associated with 'monetary' issues (6/-1171/2.0), 'trade' (5/-1345/2.6), 'fund' (3/-1362/2.0), 'trading' (2/-1442/1.0), 'firm' (1/-1515/9.0), 'business' (1/-1553/1.0) and 'growth' (1/-1659/5.0). An association between 'international' and 'continent' (1/-1529/4.0) can be found, but interesting is the remaining considerable semantic distance between 'international' and 'Europe' (2/-1781/6.5) or 'European' (1/-1971/5.0), 'community' (2/-1903/5.0) or even 'British' (1/-1933/3.0). The integration was not that much about partnership, with 'partners' only passingly associated with 'international' (1/-1383/9.0). Some associations with 'scientific' (2/-1215/6.0) aspects of integration appeared, while the defence aspect of the EEC was mentioned only in passing (1/-1622/2.0). At first sight, some concern on being located in an 'international periphery' (1/-1283/1.0) would seem to have been expressed, but close reading will lead to opposite conclusions.

The Lords talked much less about law than in connection with previous memberships. While 'international law' (1/-1732/1.0) was mentioned, 'rights' (1/-1505/4.0) and 'rules' (1/-1543/8.0) had few and relatively weak associations with 'international'. The economic aspect was less distinct than in the Commons—associations with 'companies' (1/-1432/7.0), 'capital' (1/-1443/2.0), 'monetary' (1/-1512/1.0) and 'trade' (1/-1704/1.0) appearing, but those with 'economic' (1/-1727/5.0) and 'market' (1/-1799/9.0) being much weaker. Associations with 'mobile' (1/-1073/1.0), 'cohesion' (1/-1173/3.0) and 'standards' (1/-1454/1.0) reflect an understanding of the ideas of the economic community, although a need for 'protecting' (1/-1073/2.0) would suggest the opposite view. 'International partnership' (1/-1419/1.0) as an expression made an appearance. The semantic distance between both 'British' (1/-1779/6.0) or 'community' (1/-1926/2.0) and 'international' is observable, just as in the Commons. Worth close reading is an occasional association between 'European' and 'internationalist' (1/-1638/3.0), for instance.

Debates since the Brexit referendum of June 2016 have been complex and are far from completed at the time of writing (August 2018/2019), which means that the following remarks necessarily remain provisional. The early Commons debates reflected a considerable concern about 'development' (4/-990/2.25) in the field of international questions and addressed international 'obligations' (4/-1042/1.5) to an exceptional degree. The latter way of speaking can be seen as an aspect of the traditional legal discourse on 'treaties' (3/-1209/1.0) and law (3/-1657/1.0), which seems stronger at the time of a prospective exit from the EU than during entrance negotiations. Yet, the Commons continued to understand the EU overwhelmingly through 'trade' (9/-1144/1.7, though this result is overemphasised by the title 'International Trade Secretary'), and the prospective withdrawal gave rise to questions about 'tax' (1/-1368/1.0), 'taxation' (1/-1442/4.0) and 'customs' (1/-1690/8.0). 'United Kingdom' (2/-1518/5.5), 'nation' (1/-1534/5.0) and 'UK' (2/-1712/4.5) were viewed as only slightly more 'international' than in the 1970s, and 'union' (2/-1750/8.0) and 'European' (2/-1988/5.5) continued to be dissociated from 'international'. The British MP refrained from conceptualising the EU which they were about to leave as 'international'.

The Lords, known for their more pro-integration stands, were likewise dedicated to 'international obligations' (3/-1243/1.0) and 'international treaty/treaties' (4/-1371/-1482/1.0), but also to the 'international reputation' of Britain (2/-1371/1.0). Like the Commons, they felt some concern about international 'development' (2/-1440/3.0). Discourses on international addressed economic issues with 'monetary' (1/-1301/1.0), 'trade' (6/-1432/2.3), 'fund' (1/-1460/2.0), 'manufacturing' (1/-1571/1.0), 'bank' (1/-1591/9.0) and 'financial' (1/-1794/1.0), but this was by no means the dominant discourse. Legal discourse played a more diversified role than at the time of joining the EEC, seen in association with 'divorces' (2/-1101/1.0), 'crime(s)' (2/-1360/-1518/1.0 -4.0), 'law' (7/-1516/3.6), 'rules' (2/-1582/6.5), 'court' (2/-1644/1.0), 'standards' (1/-1718/1.0), 'regulatory' (1/-1760/1.0), 'justice' (1/-1763/3.0) and 'rights' (1/ -2060/2.0). Noteworthy is the use of the metaphor 'divorce' to describe Brexit, with an emotional connotation side by side with concrete legal discourse. An exceptional intervention addressing 'internationalist heritage' (1/-833/1.0) has been chosen for closer reflection below. 'National' (2/-1597/2.0), 'nation' (1/ -1763/6.0) or 'UK' (2/-1877/8.0) had not become any more 'international' than in the membership debates, and there was really not anything 'European' that would appear as 'international' either (2/-1916/5.5). In the context of Russian interventions in Western elections in general and the British referendum in particular, 'international' found an association in 'cyberattacks' (1/-1201/3.0) as well. Otherwise, the British debates on Brexit show considerable trajectories in the prioritisation of economy and the rise of legal discourse as a consequence of the membership.

Individual Speech Acts Surrounding the 'International'

The third and final step of our analysis proceeded as close and contextualising reading of some discovered collocations. Potentially interesting collocates were pointed at in the above debate analysis. They were now located in their textual context in the House of Commons Parliamentary Papers database (Hansard 1803–2005 and, for the EU case, Hansard Online of the UK Parliament). This phase allowed some checking of the functioning of the collocation analysis programme and our preliminary conclusions. The quotations were analysed as individual speeches in which politicians defined the 'international' by the active use of language in political action in particular contexts. These could only be reconstructed on an exemplary basis in the confines of this report. While general trends of thought on internationalism (such as the centrality of law and economy) become obvious on the basis the macro-level collocation analysis and need no extensive discussion here, some peculiar points deserve attention as they demonstrate the importance of context in determining what exactly was done politically in Parliament, also revealing shortcomings in mere distant reading.

As the Commons debated the League Covenant, two Labour MPs came up with 'opportunities' opened up by it: for international relations in the spirit of the optimistic expectations of British internationalists, and for social reform central for the Labour Party. J. R. Clynes, a leading trade unionist and the deputy chairman of the Labour Party, welcomed the League '[a]s an instrument for providing, through the medium of International Courts and international action, an opportunity for considering differences as they arise' (*HC Deb. 21 July 1919 vol. 118, c961*). George Barnes, a former Labour leader who represented in 1919 the pro-coalition National Democratic and Labour Party and had been one of the British negotiators in Paris, encouraged social reform in the spirit of labour internationalism by pointing that 'for the first time Governments have put a chapter of Labour into an international Treaty [ILO] and made labour conditions a matter of international agreement', which constituted an 'opportunity' for workers worldwide (*HC Deb. 21 July 1919 vol. 118, c976*). These quotes exemplify the high leftist expectations for international cooperation during the post-First World War reconstruction.

Liberal and Conservative internationalists in the Lords were, in the name of the government, also predominantly optimistic. James Bryce, a respected constitutional lawyer, member of the International Court at The Hague and Liberal politician, viewed the League as based on 'the feeling that the world has now become one one in a new sense never dreamed of before' surrounding 'the belief that the community of the world requires that a new spirit should prevail in international relations—a spirit which seeks to substitute friendship for enmity' (*HL Deb. 24 July 1919 vol. 118, c1019*). George Curzon (Conservatives), a major imperialist (as former Viceroy of India) and acting Foreign Secretary, echoed this belief in rising internationalism, stating, 'the international spirit, the kind of idea that the future unit is not to be the race, the community, the small group, but is to be the great world of mankind, and that in that area you try and induce a common feeling, you try and produce co-operation which will be a better solvent of international difficulties …' (*HL Deb. 24 July 1919 vol. 35, c1029*). The League was basically welcomed by all political groups in the British parliament, even if questioning its effectivity was also widespread.

Doubts about weaknesses in organisation were equally present as the UN was formed in 1945. Prime Minister Clement Attlee, the leader of a Labour majority government, then forcefully advocated the concept of 'collective security' as the foundation of the UN Security Council 'where the policies of the States … could be discussed and reconsidered … especially when they showed signs of such divergences as to threaten the harmony of international relations. Collective security … is active co-operation to prevent emergencies occurring' (*HC Deb. 22 August 1945 vol. 413, c665*). Captain David Gammans (Conservatives), a former diplomat, was one of several MPs to question the definition of the UN as a provider of 'collective security', suggesting that such a concept should not be used at all (*HC Deb. 22 August 1945 vol. 413, c734*). The required unanimity of the permanent members, after all, would constitute a major limitation to the functionality of the world organisation. In the Lords, Robert Cecil, the key planner of the League, a leader of the League of Nations Union and a Nobel Peace Prize winner (1937), consistently assured that 'every attempt ought to be made, and must be made, to secure peace by international collaboration' (*HL Deb. 22 August 1945 vol. 413, c133*), bridging two major projects of British internationalism.

The debate on the CoE in 1950 provides a good reminder of the need for close reading and contextualisation. While a swift reading of the collocation results might suggest that 'international pressure' by the CoE was welcome, a closer analysis shows that the contrary was the case. Major Harry Legge-Bourke (Conservatives) was opposing restrictions to national or parliamentary sovereignty when arguing: 'I am in favour of the Council of Europe, but I am in favour of it only on one set of terms, and that is that it remains as a council and does not become an international pressure group. There seems to be very real danger of it becoming an international pressure group.' What particularly worried Legge-Bourke was a 'desire for the institution of a European Political Authority' (*HC Deb. 13 November 1950 vol. 480, c1479*).

Caution with far-reaching conclusions based on collocations is needed also in the case of the EEC membership. The MP who referred to 'international periphery' did not imply that Britain would become somehow peripheral outside the Community, but was concerned about the potential loss of sovereignty. Ronald King Murray (Labour), a leading Scottish lawyer, reacted to a suggestion that membership in the UN and NATO already implied a loss of national sovereignty and relativised the radicality of an EEC membership by pointing out that:

> … it was sovereignty in a peripheral sphere, the international periphery of our being which did not involve the heart of our domestic constitutional being as the Bill unquestionably does. We are surrendering a portion of the inner core of our sovereignty because we are dealing

> with two aspects of the constitution, first with an economic aspect and secondly with one which is more properly constitutional. (*HC Deb. 15 February 1972 vol. 831, c363*)

While general international or defence cooperation did not challenge national sovereignty, the economic and political aspects of the EEC did—a conclusion that has dominated much of the British press discourse ever since. Arguments in favour of membership won in 1972, although hardly in the extreme form presented by Frank Beswick (Labour), a former voluntary in the Spanish Civil War and a current party whip: 'My own approach to this Bill is that of an internationalist. I have always been ready to surrender sovereignty in those areas where individual and national dignity and wellbeing are not impaired' (*HL Deb. 26 July 1972 vol. 333, c1368*). Confrontations were even tougher in the Brexit debates. The supporters of 'leave', emphasising British national identity as distinct from the Continent, considered the vocabulary of the 'international' useless. 'International' was an attribute of the 'remain' side and often of backbenchers with limited political influence. An exceptional association between 'international' and 'European' was made by Liz Saville Roberts (Plaid Cymru), who emphasised the significance of the EU for British foreign relations as a whole: 'Beyond the single market and customs union, there are upward of 40 pan-European agencies that form the basis of our international relations across a range of policy areas' (*HC Deb. 7 September 2017, c422*). A suggestion that the government was acting against national values was heard in Helen Hayes' (Labour) declaration that Brexit impacted negatively 'our British values of tolerance, diversity and internationalism' (*HC Deb. 11 September 2017, c574*). Roger Liddle, a former researcher, adviser of Prime Minister Tony Blair and of the President of the European Commission and a think-tank chairperson, contributed to an intra-Labour dispute on Brexit. He appealed both to the trajectory of British internationalism and to the tradition of labour internationalism to persuade his party fellows to oppose Brexit: 'Europe is in a category of its own in terms of its impact on future generations … I want our party to lead, to seize this opportunity to demonstrate that, in contrast to this wretched Government, we can live up to our national responsibilities and our internationalist heritage' (*HL Deb. 31 January 2018, c1534*). Not only the Brexiteers but also their opponents were on the move, fighting on definitions of internationalism also with history-political arguments.

Results and the Added Value of Digital Methods for Conceptual History

This computer-assisted analysis combining the collocation tool of the Hansard Corpus, the collocation analysis of membership debates and a contextual analysis of instances of political speaking has provided us with an overview of the evolving discourse on internationalism in the UK Parliament, while also revealing innovative speech acts of potential political significance. Both expected and more surprising general trends were demonstrated, specificities of associations of the 'international' in the context of decisions on membership in international organisations pointed out and some peculiar arguments by individual MPs reconstructed.

The concrete findings include the dominance of discourses on international law in the founding of international organisations other than the EU. Parliamentary discourse, rather than contributing much to the creation of its first major international institution, turned more internationalist as a consequence of the founding of the League of Nations. The first, rather weak, wave of British internationalism lasted from 1919 to the founding of the UN in 1945. Internationalism remained relatively weak during the Cold War, with the exception of a few internationally oriented politicians, advocates of the EEC membership and expressers of global solidarity in the 1970s, when the second wave of British internationalism peaked. Once the EEC membership had become a reality, the parliamentary elite lost its enthusiasm about internationalism, especially with reference to European cooperation, and anti-European rhetoric rose during Thatcher's governments. Economic debate dominated and the legal discourse was set aside as Britain joined the EEC, only to be restored with Brexit when especially the trajectory of discourse on national sovereignty versus internationalism resurfaced. Early 20th-century discourses on labour internationalism have mostly withered away with the rise of non-socialist internationalism, with some revival in the 1970s and 1980s and during the Brexit crisis. Several factors indicate that internationalism was in decline well before Brexit, starting in the 1980s, and that trends in public discourse had implications for followed policies. Our conclusions correspond with Glenda Sluga's suggestion that the 'global seventies' of new international society and international public sphere were followed by the 'post-international' 1990s,[24] but the British turn to post-international discourse clearly deserves more attention.

Computer-assisted collocation analyses can contribute to conceptual history in at least two ways:[25] First, the analysis produces quantitative data on associations between political concepts that enable us to estimate trends in political attitudes the reconstruction of which with traditional methods would not be possible. Second, distant reading reveals original political points that would have gone unnoticed in close reading or in full-text keyword searches. Such arguments must be subjected to close reading and contextual analysis so that premature conclusions based on distant reading can be corrected. Revealed peculiarities in argumentation frequently turn out to originate from leading politicians attempting to influence the course of policy, which warns against low frequency thresholds.[26] All in all, the collocation analysis of discourse on internationalism in Parliament works well, enabling a more efficient locating of meaningful speech acts, although their meanings can only be properly understood with close reading and appropriate contextualisation.

The collocation analysis could be extended on many levels: In distant reading, it would be important to proceed beyond the 'extreme' concept of 'internationalism', with its inherited associations of socialism and pacifism, and to include concepts such as the world, humanity, universal, global, Empire, Commonwealth, cosmopolitan, supranational, multinational, transnational, Europeanism and trans-Atlantic, for instance. The global (imperial) dimension has remained central for Britons also in the days of European integration, and the joint natural language with the United States has supported discourses of isolationism against internationalism. At the level of membership debates, synonyms and counter-concepts of the 'international' (foreign, abroad, domestic, national, etc.) could be considered. At the level of individual speech acts, the dynamics between political parties in arguing about internationalism would deserve more attention. A more extensive reconstruction of the temporal contexts of the arguments on the basis of digitised newspapers and other forums of political debate would be helpful then. Furthermore, now that the sub-themes of the discourse on internationalism in the UK Parliament have been identified, the analysis of the dynamics between nationalisms and internationalisms in other parliaments and transnational interconnections between these debates could be explored.

Notes

1 Pasi Ihalainen was alone responsible for the planning of the research setting, analysis and the written report. Digital analysis method specialist Aleksi Sahala created the program script that enabled the distant reading of particular membership debates. Kimmo Elo produced the visualisations of the results of digital distant reading.
2 Yearwood 2009; Laqua 2011; Mazower 2012; McCarthy 2012; Sluga 2013; Clavin & Sluga 2017.
3 Ihalainen & Palonen 2009; Ihalainen & Matikainen 2016; Ihalainen 2017; Holmila & Ihalainen 2018; Ihalainen 2018.
4 Edelstein 2016.
5 Baker et al. 2008.
6 Baker, Brezina & McEnery 2017: 105.
7 Gabrielatos & Baker 2008: 11.
8 Baker, Brezina & McEnery 2017.
9 Willis 2017.
10 Foxlee 2018: 77, 80.
11 Guldi 2019.
12 Lähdesmäki & Wagenaar 2015: 16.
13 Ihalainen 2006; Halonen, Ihalainen & Saarinen 2015; Ihalainen & Saarinen 2015; Steinmetz & Freeden 2017; Ihalainen & Saarinen 2019.
14 Daille 1994.

[15] Church & Hanks 1990.
[16] The technical description of the analysis program has been written by Aleksi Sahala. See https://github.com/asahala/Collocations.
[17] Clavin & Sluga 2017: 5–6; Sluga 2013, 3, 5.
[18] Sluga 2013: 4.
[19] Holmila & Ihalainen 2018.
[20] Ibid.
[21] Ibid.
[22] Ibid.
[23] Cf. Häkkinen 2018.
[24] Sluga 2013: 6–7, 9.
[25] Cf. Steinmetz & Freeden 2017: 32, who are uncertain as to how to interpret semantic data rising from digital humanities.
[26] See also Kim 2014: 233.

References

Baker, H., **Brezina V.**, & **McEnery T.** (2017). Ireland in British parliamentary debates: plotting changes in discourse in a large volume of time-series corpus data. In T. Säily, A. Nurmi, M. Palander-Collin & A. Auer (Eds.), *Exploring future paths for historical sociolinguistics* (pp. 83–107). Amsterdam: John Benjamins.

Baker, P., **Gabrielatos, C.**, **Khosravinik, M.**, **Krzyzanowski M.**, **McEnery, T.**, & **Wodak, R.** (2008). A useful methodological synergy? Combining critical discourse analysis and corpus linguistics to examine discourses of refugees and asylum seekers in the UK press. *Discourse & Society, 19*(3), 273–306.

Church, K. W., & **Hanks, P.** (1990). Word association norms, mutual information, and lexicography. *Computational Linguistics, 16*(1), 22–29.

Clavin, P., & **Sluga, G.** (2017). *Internationalisms: a twentieth century history.* Cambridge: Cambridge University Press.

Daille, B. (1994). *Approche mixte pour l'extraction automatique de terminologie: statistiques lexicales et filtres linguistiques* (PhD dissertation, Université Paris 7).

Edelstein, D. (2016). Intellectual history and digital humanities. *Modern Intellectual History, 13*(1), 237–246.

Foxlee, N. (2018). Pivots and levers: political rhetoric around capitalism in Britain from the 1970s to the present. *Contributions to the History of Concepts, 13*(1), 75–99.

Gabrielatos, C., & **Baker, P.** (2008). Fleeing, sneaking, flooding: a corpus analysis of discursive constructions of refugees and asylum seekers in the UK press, 1996–2005. *Journal of English Linguistics, 36*(1), 5–38.

Guldi, J. (2019). The measures of modernity: word counts, text mining, and the promise and limits of present tools as indices of historical change.

International Journal for History, Culture and Modernity, 7. DOI: https://doi.org/10.18352/hcm.589

Halonen, M., Ihalainen, P., & Saarinen, T. (2015). Diverse discourses in time and space: historical, discourse analytical and ethnographic approaches to multi-sited language policy discourse. In M. Halonen, P. Ihalainen & T. Saarinen (Eds.), *Language policies in Finland and Sweden: interdisciplinary and multi-sited comparisons* (pp. 3–26). Bristol: Multilingual Matters.

Holmila, A., & Ihalainen, P. (2018). Nationalism and internationalism reconciled: British concepts for a new world order during and after the World Wars. *Contributions to Conceptual History, 13*(2), 25–53.

Häkkinen, T. (2018). British parliamentary attitudes towards a supranational parliament and the Consultative Assembly of the Council of Europe, 1948–1949. *Parliaments, Estates & Representation, 38*(1), 63–75.

Ihalainen, P. (2006). Between historical semantics and pragmatics: reconstructing past political thought through conceptual history. *Journal of Historical Pragmatics, 7*(1), 115–143.

Ihalainen, P. (2017). *The springs of democracy: national and transnational debates on constitutional reform in the British, German, Swedish and Finnish parliaments, 1917–1919*. Helsinki: Finnish Literature Society. DOI: http://dx.doi.org/10.21435/sfh.24

Ihalainen, P. (2018). Internationalization and democratization interconnected: the Swedish and Finnish parliaments debating membership in the League of Nations. *Parliaments, Estates and Representation, 39*(1), 11–31. DOI: https://doi.org/10.1080/02606755.2018.1483998

Ihalainen, P., & Matikainen, S. (2016). The British parliament and foreign policy in the twentieth century: towards increasing parliamentarisation? *Parliamentary History, 35*(1), 1–14.

Ihalainen, P., & Palonen, K. (2009). Parliamentary sources in the comparative study of conceptual history: methodological aspects and illustrations of a research proposal. *Parliaments, Estates & Representation, 29*(1), 17–34.

Ihalainen, P., & Saarinen, T. (2015). Constructing 'language' in language policy discourse: Finnish and Swedish legislative processes in the 2000s. In M. Halonen, P. Ihalainen & T. Saarinen (Eds.), *Language policies in Finland and Sweden: interdisciplinary and multi-sited comparisons* (pp. 29–56). Bristol: Multilingual Matters.

Ihalainen, P., & Saarinen, T. (2019). Integrating a nexus: the history of political discourse and language policy research. *Rethinking History: The Journal of Theory and Practice, 23*(4), 500–519. DOI: https://doi.org/10.1080/13642529.2019.1638587

Kim, K. H. (2014). Examining US news media discourses about North Korea: a corpus-based critical discourse analysis. *Discourse & Society, 25*(2), 221–244. DOI: https://doi.org/10.1177/0957926513516043

Laqua, D. (Ed.) (2011). *Internationalism reconfigured: transnational ideas and movements between the World Wars*. London: I. B. Tauris.

Lähdesmäki, T., & **Wagener, A.** (2015). Discourses on governing diversity in Europe: critical analysis of the White Paper on Intercultural Dialogue. *International Journal of Intercultural Relations, 44*(January), 13–28. DOI: https://doi.org/10.1016/j.ijintrel.2014.11.002

Mazower, M. (2012). *Governing the world: the history of an idea, 1815 to the present.* New York, NY: Penguin.

McCarthy, H. (2012). *The British people and the League of Nations: democracy, citizenship and internationalism, c.1918–45.* Manchester: Manchester University Press.

Sluga, G. (2013). *Internationalism in the age of nationalism.* Philadelphia, PA: University of Pennsylvania Press.

Steinmetz, W., & **Freeden, M.** (2017). Introduction: conceptual history: challenges, conundrums, complexities. In W. Steinmetz, M. Freeden & J. Fernández-Sebastián (Eds.), *Conceptual history in the European space* (pp. 1–46). Oxford and New York, NY: Berghahn.

Willis, R. (2017). Taming the climate? Corpus analysis of politicians' speech on climate change. *Environmental Politics, 26*(2), 212–231.

Yearwood, P. J. (2009). *Guarantee of peace: the League of Nations in British policy 1914–1925.* Oxford: Oxford University Press.

CHAPTER 13

Picturing the Politics of Resistance

Using Image Metadata and Historical Network Analysis to Map the East German Opposition Movement, 1975–1990

Melanie Conroy and Kimmo Elo

Introduction: Networks of the East German Opposition

This chapter shows how network graphs and analysis can be used to shed light on the structure and dynamics of the geospatial social networks of segments of the East German opposition movement between 1975 and 1990. What new knowledge can we uncover about a well-studied historical phenomenon if we combine the use of non-traditional source material, in this case metadata from an image database catalogue, with a non-traditional historical methodology, namely, social network analysis? This chapter studies the network of East German dissidents as reflected in the photographic database on the East German Opposition, which archives photos from the 1970s until the fall of the Berlin Wall.

In this chapter, we examine graphs of East German dissident networks, as well as sub-networks filtered by date and by place. We then discuss the general

How to cite this book chapter:
Conroy, M., & Elo, K. (2020). Picturing the politics of resistance: Using image metadata and historical network analysis to map the East German opposition movement, 1975–1990. In M. Fridlund, M. Oiva, & P. Paju (Eds.), *Digital histories: Emergent approaches within the new digital history* (pp. 221–235). Helsinki: Helsinki University Press. https://doi.org/10.33134/HUP-5-13

principles of social network analysis and historical network analysis. Finally, we consider how network analysis could be further improved for historical purposes. The primary tool we use is Palladio, a suite of tools for the visualisation of historical networks developed in the Humanities + Design Lab at Stanford University. Unlike many tools for creating network graphs, Palladio was designed for humanists to visualise data without the need for a designer.[1] Palladio can be used to visualise historical datasets and discover patterns in the data that researchers may choose to analyse using network analysis or other means, including examining the original historical sources.

An Unconventional Source Material: Metadata of an Image Database

The photographic database maintained by the Robert Havemann Society in Berlin as part of its archive on the East German Opposition consists of approximately 60,000 digitised photos with a relatively rich metadata providing information, including the date the photo was taken, the photographer, a descriptive title, keywords, regional/geographical tags and information about the persons to whom the photo is related.[2] The sample used in this chapter consists of photos featuring selected prominent figures of the East German dissident scene with a connection to the city of Jena. These individuals included academics, artists and intellectuals of diverse socio-economic backgrounds, who were part of a range of movements, from youth movements to peace activism to environmental movements, during the period from 1975 to 1990. In most cases, the photos were taken to document opposition action and activities and used as illustrations in underground magazines, bulletins and leaflets. We should, however, keep in mind that since the German Democratic Republic (GDR) was a dictatorship, photographing these kinds of illegal actions was closely bound with the risk of becoming subject to counter-measures by the security authorities. From this perspective, the photos also document the courage of the people involved in oppositional activities.

In the history of the East German opposition, Jena and Berlin were the two most important regions when it came to the structure, means, motives and dynamics of the opposition groups in the GDR. In Jena, the discrepancy between democracy and dictatorship often led to open conflicts, making this city the primary region of political opposition in the GDR. Jena was also called the secret capital of the GDR opposition, reflecting the complex domestic conflict between the state apparatus, church and opposition in the GDR.[3] The temporal focus of this chapter is the period between 1975 and 1990, a period heavily shaping the range of political action for the opposition and resistance groups. One key event was the Conference on Security and Cooperation in Europe (CSCE), held in Helsinki in August 1975, which caused the East German political leadership to become increasingly concerned with the destabilising impact of the CSCE.[4] As a consequence, the *Sozialistische Einheitspartei Deutschlands* (SED), the communist monopoly party of the GDR, took numerous repressive actions against dissidents and opposition groups, seeking to scatter the resistance and opposition by eliminating their leading personalities.[5] To what extent can we see the repressive actions of the SED in the networked relations of Jena-linked figures of the opposition?

One of the main components of the Jena-based opposition movement was the Jena Peace Community (*Jenaer Friedensgemeinschaft*), established in March 1983 as one of the first major opposition communities outside the protective walls of the Evangelical church. The local Peace Community was a dissident platform of short duration, but of long-lasting impact. Its founders were disillusioned with the reluctant resistance of the Evangelical church against state repression and, hence, sought to establish a new, independent platform under the umbrella of the European Peace Movement. The community itself was short-lived, because by the spring of 1983, the security authorities had already decided to destroy the Jena Peace Community once and for all. But, because the security police did not achieve its main goal (a complete destruction of Jena's opposition), the community had a long-lasting impact, causing Jena to remain an unsettled city and one of the most important places for political opposition between 1983 and 1989.[6] Members included Uwe Behr, Manfred Hildebrandt, Mario Dietsch, Edgar Hillmann, Michael Rost and Frank Rub, and non-church-members Roland Jahn and Petra Falkenberg. As we shall see, many of the members and allies of the Jena Peace Community remained active in the opposition movement in Jena for years after the crackdown.

The data culled from the database catalogue combine many of the elements of historical research which can be profitably analysed and give us an opportunity to study a network that is relatively circumscribed in both time and place. Further, the connections between individuals are consistent since they all represent co-occurrences in photos. Knowing the boundaries of the network and having an understanding of what the underlying data represent are fundamental to creating a data model and visualisations which contribute to a research problem rather than merely illustrating an archive. The individuals who appear most frequently in the data are known historical figures, many of whom were instrumental in the creation of the archive: Matthias Domaschk, Jürgen Fuchs, Roland Jahn, Robert Havemann, Katja Havemann, Bettina Wegner, Carlo Jordan, Gerd Poppe, Bärbel Bohley and Tom Sello.[7]

Many of these photos are of protests and actions by the opposition; other photos are casual portraits and group shots not obviously related to any political action. The photographers are recorded (where they are known) by the archivists; the photos were, for the most part, taken by members of the group and their acquaintances. We see one example of a group photo (Figure 13.1) taken at Ulrike and Gerd Poppe's home in Woltersdorf. In this photo, we see Robert Havemann, Ulrike Poppe and others who are gathered for a reading of

Figure 13.1: Reading at Ulrike and Gerd Poppe's property, photo by Gerd Poppe, courtesy of Robert-Havemann-Gesellschaft, 27 June 1981. Source: Robert-Havemann-Gesellschaft/Gerd Poppe/RHG_Fo_HAB_09781.

the works of Gert Neumann on 27 June 1981, after the release of Havemann from police custody.

In this photo, we see the conviviality of the opponents of the regime who are drinking wine and enjoying one another's company despite the serious circumstances. This is a rather typical example from the photo collection documenting activities of East German opposition. At the same time, since photos like this successfully document social actions taken by individuals, they offer a reliable source to reconstruct historical social networks.

An Unconventional Method: Why Network Analysis?

Social network analysis has been used since at least the 1940s in the social sciences.[8] Network analysis has only more recently been adopted within historical disciplines.[9] Networks are a powerful analytical tool for understanding the structure of groups, especially at scale or when there are complex interrelations between large numbers of individuals. While the network is a 20th-century concept, social relations that could be described as networks have existed in all historical periods and in all societies.[10] Whether we can profitably examine one particular social group through the lenses of network analysis is a reflection of how much we know about the internal structure of that group, the research question being asked and the completeness of the historical documentation that could be used to reconstruct the network.[11] Historical network analysis (HNA) is deeply rooted in social network analysis (SNA), using the same basic structures and metrics. But HNA must engage with questions of historiography and the use of sources in a way that is different from sociological methods. In this chapter, we show how network graphs and analysis can be used to shed light on the structure and dynamics of the geospatial social networks of segments of the East German opposition movement between 1975 and 1990. This chapter's exploration of dissident networks serves as an example of how scholars can discover connections between individuals and sub-groups that might track the spread of dissident thought between people, as well as between geographical regions.

SNA allows us to study the meaning and importance of relationships in great detail and, thus, offers a promising tool to examine past communities in the aggregate:

> With SNA, we are only interested in individuals as part of a much bigger whole. In fact, one advantage to the technique is that SNA helps us view an entire community and figure out which individuals we should be truly interested in and which ones were perhaps less significant. When we study past relationships systematically as SNA allows, the method will prevent us from misunderstanding the function of an individual's relationships or exaggerating the distinctiveness of those relations.[12]

In our eyes, the true power of HNA lies in its capability to untangle complex social interaction patterns by way of graphical visualisations, thus making those patterns easier to perceive and analyse. The limit of network analysis is in researchers reducing social relations to those patterns and potentially losing track of the ways in which the network abstracts from the source material. For this reason, HNA should be practised with a keen awareness of the source material and the cultural and historical context of the networks at hand.

Using Network Graphs to See the Big Picture

One of the difficulties in creating network graphs is to create legible diagrams which show the structure of the entire network. Many of the most famous network diagrams are both complex and vast. Such diagrams are often referred to derisively as 'hairball' graphs due to their illegibility.[13] As we shall see, using a combination of complex graphs of the whole network and smaller, more precise graphs of network segments is an easy way to overcome this problem. Figure 13.2 shows the network as a whole. The cleaned-up and corrected database contains 841 records (photographs) with 171 unique person references. There are a total of 1,843 co-occurrences of these individuals in photographs documented in the database.

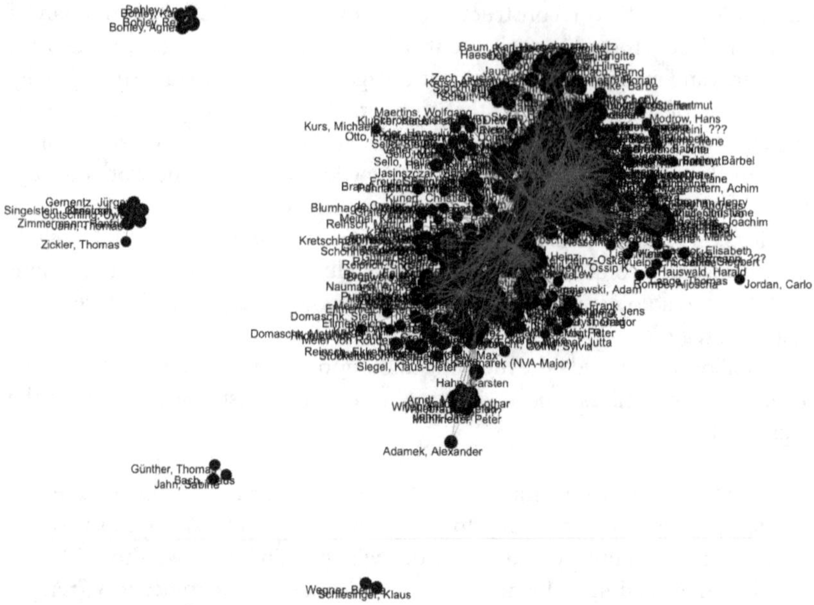

Figure 13.2: Network graph of GDR dissidents linked to Jena in photographs, 1975–1990. Source: Authors.

This network graph was created in one step in Palladio and was not modified, so it is relatively difficult to read, but it gives us a 'quick and rough' overall view of the network. There are many tools available for creating network diagrams which can make use of colour, refine the design and change the spacing and layout.[14] A network is a set of nodes (in this case, people) linked by edges (in this case, photo co-occurrences); in this graph, the nodes are labelled with the name of the person and sized based on the number of photos that person appears in.

It is apparent in Figure 13.2 that the majority of people who appear in the photos appear together. Figure 13.2 evidences the existence of a core social network of densely connected people, in network terms, the giant component. Outside this core component there are four distinct yet very small social groups. These sub-networks emerge from photographs taken in apartments or in the outdoors, apparently just documenting daily events and activities and people involved in these. In fact, such photographs form a large part of the giant component as well, despite the repressive political circumstances in the late 1970s and the 1980s, which meant that taking photos documenting members of underground and dissident groups was a rather risky business.

One way to make network graphs more legible to humanities scholars is to combine graphs with other types of diagrams with which they may be more familiar.[15] Palladio can be used to make maps, galleries and tables which can complement network graphs.[16] In this case, we can use the same dataset to produce a map which shows the approximate number of photos taken at each location. In order to obtain geographical data, we processed the keyword entries and collected all recognised geographical names and sub-regional information like street names or city districts which could be used to determine the city (for example, Berlin, Jena, Bad Frankenhausen). Almost three-quarters of the photographs included in our analysis could be connected with a geographical location. In the last step, we automatically geocoded these locations, finding latitude/longitude coordinates for all recognised locations for purposes of geospatial analysis. Figure 13.3 shows the locations of the photographs of individuals associated with Jena; the size of the circles represents the number of photos at that location. The green circles represent photos taken in East Germany and the red circles represent photos taken in West Berlin.

It is apparent in Figure 13.3 that Berlin and Jena are the most important regions and are strongly linked. We know from analysing the temporal distribution of these photographs that Jena remains the most important region until 1984, thus confirming previous studies stressing the importance of the Jena region for the East German dissident community. From 1985 onwards, Berlin gains in importance and becomes the most frequently referenced region in our data. This change is well in line with the overall course of events during the second half of the 1980s. A good example of how this change is connected to specific places are photographs referring to the *Umweltbibliothek* (Environment Library) in East Berlin. The library was founded in 1986 in the cellar rooms of the *Zionsgemeinde* and rapidly became one of the central communities of the East German dissident movement. What is not so clearly visible in the network graph (Figure 13.2) or the map (Figure 13.3) but evidenced by the dataset itself is that the core social network of East German opposition was rather small, revolving around certain key figures who were rather mobile. These central figures account for connections to some of the smaller towns. A good example of this phenomenon are the towns Fürstenwalde (Spree) and Grüneheide, both loosely connected to Robert Havemann (1910–1982), an intellectual and dissident sentenced to house arrest in 1976. A remarkable portion of photographs taken between 1975 and the early 1980s document Havemann's life under house arrest and the people visiting him.

Freezing Networks: Snapshots in Time and Local Networks

Just as giving researchers a view of the whole is important, it is helpful to visualise the network in specific places and at specific times. We can do that easily by filtering by place in Palladio and visualising only the nodes and edges associated with one place. Figure 13.4 shows the Jena-associated people who appear in photographs taken in West Berlin. West Berlin is a locus for individuals who were deported from East Germany but continued to be of interest to the East German government, such as Jürgen Fuchs and Roland Jahn. We can see that the network in West Berlin is much smaller, but still contains very important figures.

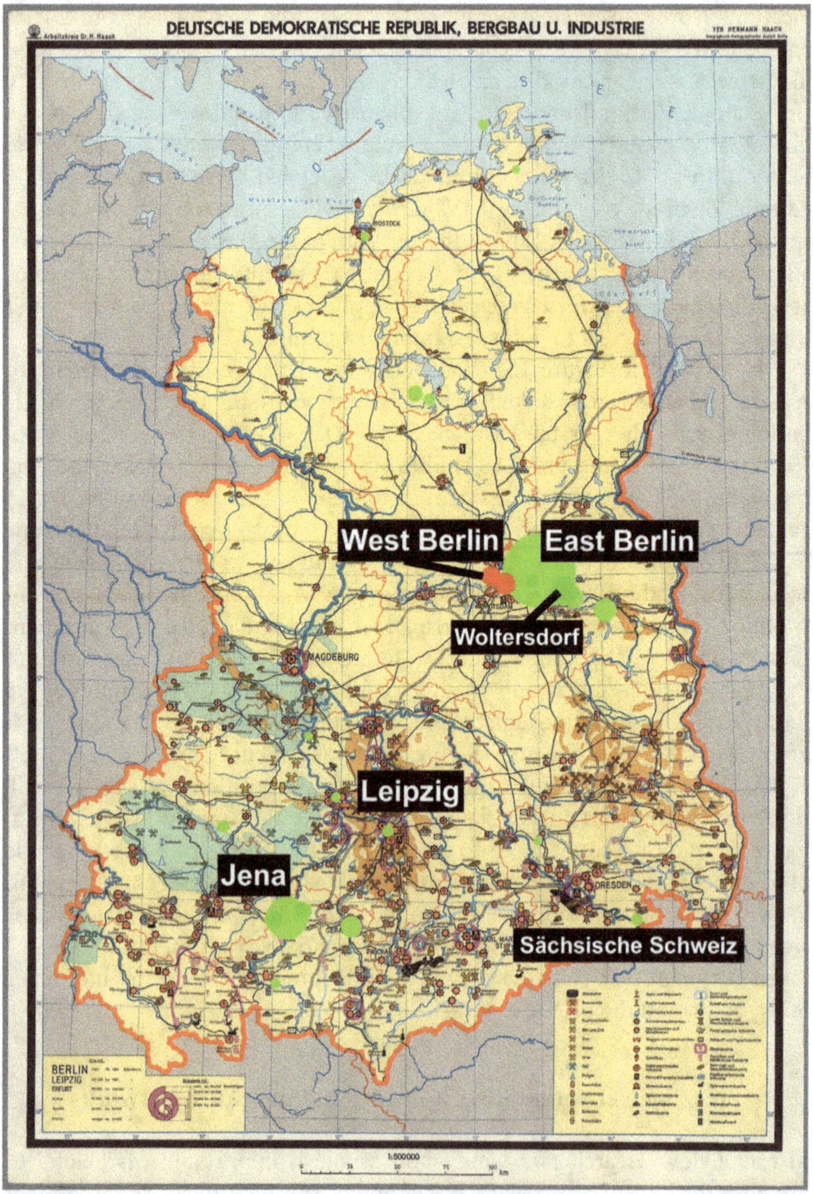

Figure 13.3: Map of photographs of GDR dissidents linked to Jena, 1975–1990, basemap. Courtesy of the David Rumsey Collection. Source: Authors; basemap Haack 1965.

Roland Jahn was an active member in the Jena dissident community, who engaged himself as a young university student in protest actions from the mid-1970s onwards. Jahn was ex-matriculated from the University of Jena in

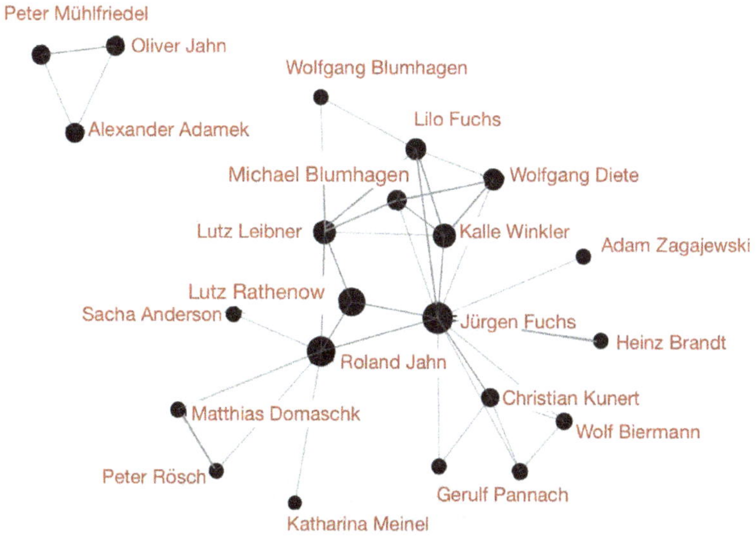

Figure 13.4: Network graph of GDR dissidents linked to Jena in photographs taken in West Berlin, 1975–1990. Source: Authors; data from the Robert-Havemann-Gesellschaft.

1977, arrested again in the early 1980s, and finally expelled to West Germany in May 1983. However, even after his expulsion, Jahn continued to support the East German opposition movement. Jürgen Fuchs, in turn, had already been expelled to West Germany in 1977, but he remained involved in the East German dissident community until 1990, especially via Lutz Rathenow, another strong figure in the network visualised in Figure 13.4.[17] Figure 13.4 shows that the networks of Fuchs and Jahn were, indeed, interconnected and formed the core of the network in West Berlin. There are other sub-networks (for example, the sub-network without a clear hub) of which Lilo Fuchs, Wolfgang Diete and Lutz Leibner were members. Despite appearing in a similar number of photographs as Jahn, Fuchs connects more individuals and more disparate parts of the network.

Similarly, making network graphs of specific moments, or 'snapshots', of the network at various times can be highly informative in understanding the evolution of the network and disentangling connections made in different periods.[18] Whereas Figure 13.2 is a static network that displays all of the nodes and connections in the period from 1975 to 1990, Figure 13.5 shows only the nodes and edges present in 1981. Tom Sello, the construction worker from Großenhain, is central to one network here, despite his relative youth at 24 years of age.

The dataset was filtered to the year 1981 to produce Figure 13.5; the graph shows two clusters of dissidents and their associates who appear in photos together. The first cluster is centred on Tom Sello and six other people in Sächsische Schweiz. The second is a larger set of individuals in a tightly clustered network located in Woltersdorf and centred on the trio of Reinhard Weißhuhn,

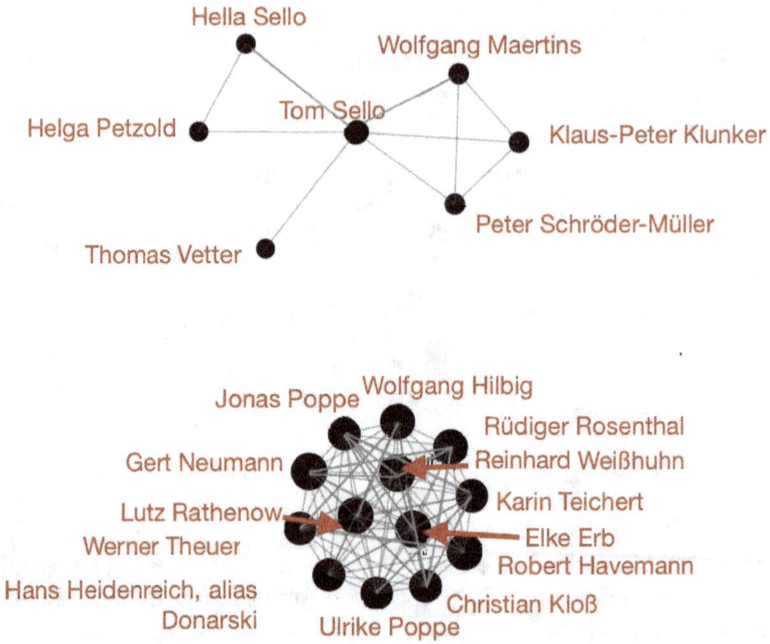

Figure 13.5: Network graph of GDR dissidents linked to Jena in photographs taken in 1981. Source: Authors; data from the Robert-Havemann-Gesellschaft.

Lutz Rathenow and Elke Erb. The high clustering shows that this group often appeared in many photos together. In fact, you may recognise this horizontal network of people with many connections to one another from the photo of the reading at Ulrike and Gerd Poppe's house on 27 June 1981 (Figure 13.1). This group appears in multiple photos together at the Poppe residence, which accounts for their high degree of association in the data. Unlike the photos of Tom Sello and his associates, these photos document a large and important gathering of leading figures from the movement in the same space.

Clarifying and Simplifying Network Graphs

Another way of cleaning up network graphs to make them more legible is to remove nodes that fall below a certain threshold in connection to the core of the network. In the case of Figure 13.2, we observed that the giant component comprised the majority of the nodes and edges, but was difficult to analyse due to its density. In order to focus on this giant component, which forms the core of the network, we removed the nodes which were not connected to the giant component and then graphed that network using Gephi. Figure 13.6 shows this network core.

By focusing only on the central component of the network, we can make out more of the network structure. For instance, we can see which nodes function

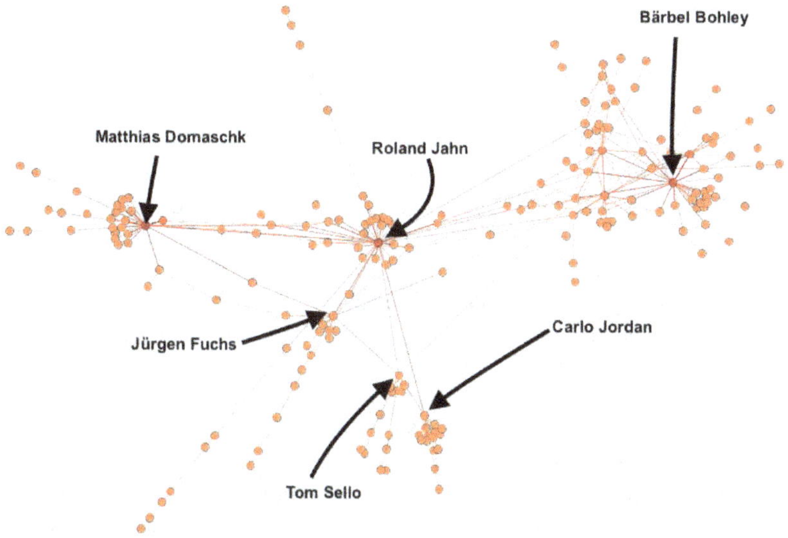

Figure 13.6: Network graph of GDR dissidents linked to Jena in photographs, 1975–1990. Source: Authors; data from the Robert-Havemann-Gesellschaft.

as hubs, having a number of connections that far exceeds the average number per node; we can also see which nodes function as connectors, tying together different sub-networks. Within this network, the centrality of Roland Jahn derives from the high number of individuals with whom he appears in photos, which makes him a hub; it is also significant that he connects the various communities, or cliques, we see in this graph. Other hubs include Bärbel Bohley, Mattias Domaschk and Carlo Jordan, all of whom appear in a large number of photos with other individuals. Many of the individuals who appear in photos with Domaschk and Jordan do not appear in photos with many (or any) others. Mattias Domaschk was active in Jena, including in the *Junge Gemeinde Jena-Stadtmitte*, but his contacts mostly only appeared in photos with him. Jordan was primarily active in the Berlin region, where he went on to become a leader in the green movement. Jürgen Fuchs and Tom Sello both have significant numbers of connections with otherwise isolated nodes, but they also have more connections to the broader network.

Comparing these observations to our lists of the presumed core members of the Jena group, especially Matthias Domaschk, Jürgen Fuchs, Bärbel Bohley and Tom Sello (see above), we can see the group was strongly connected through Roland Jahn, at least in terms of co-appearances in photographs. We can also readily observe that the women in the group, specifically Katja Havemann, Bettina Wegner and Petra Falkenberg, play less of a central role in tying together the network of photographic co-occurrences than do the major male figures. The relative absence of female figures from the core of the network makes the centrality of the artist Bärbel Bohley that much more striking, especially in the latter years when she is highly central. Figures like Mattias Domaschk were photographed with others in the opposition movement who did not appear elsewhere in photos, much as we saw earlier with Tom Sello, suggesting that he was bringing many people into the movement or associating with non-opponents of the regime. On the other hand, Bärbel Bohley is part of a sub-network that has many more co-occurrences among its members and has no clear hub. Again, it is worth investigating whether this photographic pattern has any reflection in real-world relationships or if it is an artifact of the photographic record, as was the case with the clique centred on the Poppe residence in Woltersdorf. Jürgen Fuchs, Carlo Jordan and Tom Sello are each connected to their own small 'clique' of people together with whom they appear in photos, although these cliques are more cut off from other sub-networks, as well as being smaller. The most significant mystery remains why the sub-network containing Bärbel Bohley is more diffuse and 'leaderless' than the rest of the sub-networks. When we examine the photos in which she appears, we see that she appears in many photos with crowds and figures who are not otherwise in the database, including, for example, the Dalai Lama. It would appear that Bohley brought many new people into the movement and connected dissidents to a broader world of activists than earlier 'hubs'.

Conclusions

HNA can make use of the tools of SNA to understand the structure of social relationships, whether in smaller networks or at scale. While some of the tried and tested techniques, like large 'hairball' graphs, may be limited in their use value for historians, network graphs which reflect real research questions, such as the shape and size of a network in a particular year or in a particular place, can easily be created when one is familiar with how information has been captured and structured.[19] These graphs are not mere illustrations of previously known relations, but a way of exploring segments of a large dataset to find new patterns and new questions: how, for example, the GDR opposition movement changed in relation to events like deportation to Berlin or the release of a member from detention. We have seen that the changes in the network following such events are not always predictable, such as when the movement held a very large and semi-public reading at Woltersdorf following Havemann's release or when Bärbel Bohley's very public events sometimes led to photographs depicting fewer documented members of the movement. For this reason, it is fundamental to consider what the graph is depicting (in this case appearances together in photos) and not to use the graphs in a naïve fashion to represent all real connections between individuals.

This chapter sought to exemplify how HNA could be used to explore and analyse personal and geospatial connections and ties behind a real historical phenomenon, the East German dissident movement. The networks reconstructed and analysed in this chapter fit quite well with the historical facts about the East German opposition, although we need to note that we cannot estimate how much data is missing or whether a larger sample would have affected our results differently. Nor can we know to what extent patterns in the photographic co-occurrences reflect relationships outside of photographs. Network analysis is known to be quite sensitive to missing data,[20] but applying network analysis can reveal discrepancies, such as when a group gains members or loses them, or when the structure of a group changes from tighter to looser, as the Jena-linked dissidents often did when they were deported or arrested. Network analysis can also reveal when group members like Tom Sello or Bärbel Bohley introduce many new people to the network. Despite these pitfalls, we are hopeful that our chapter could convince its reader that HNA could help scholars to gain new insights into the way in which social networks reflect political pressures in sometimes unexpected ways (for example, by growing or becoming more public in response to crackdowns). Although not impossible, such insights can be difficult to gain through the traditional methods of historical research.

Notes

1 Conroy 2019.

2 Robert-Havemann-Gesellschaft e.V., Archiv der DDR-Opposition, Bildarchiv.

3 The security authorities' operation 'Counter-strike' is documented in BStU 2013.

4 See, e.g., Schroeder 1998: 233ff; Gieseke 2008.

5 Veen 2000: 27–29.

6 Neubert 1998: 488.

7 Matthias Domaschk was a young political activist, who died on 12 April 1981 in Gera in a pre-trial detention of the East German security service after 13 hours of continuous interrogations. Tom Sello, in turn, engaged himself in several dissident groups in the GDR, especially in the 1980s. He also wrote for several underground publications (*Samisdat*) and was repeatedly attacked by the security service. Bettina Wegner was an East German songwriter and lyricist. In 1983, she was threatened with prison and forced to leave the GDR for West Berlin. Gerd Poppe was a political activist who fought for human rights in the GDR. He was also actively engaged in the publication and dissemination of several illegal underground publications (*Samisdat*). Poppe was subject to the Stasi's intensive observation and repressive activities. Bärbel Bohley was an East German opposition activist and artist. She was one of the co-founders of the Initiative for Peace and Human Rights (1985) and of *Neues Forum* (1989). For a detailed description of the other people mentioned, see Elo 2018.

8 For a history of the development of SNA within the social sciences, see Prell 2012: 19–50.

[9] On how HNA differs from SNA more generally, see Düring and von Keyserlingk 2015.
[10] Lemercier 2015.
[11] Ibid.
[12] Morrissey 2015: 69–70.
[13] Nocaj, Ortmann & Brandes 2015.
[14] Some of the most commonly used are Gephi, Cytoscape and R.
[15] Conroy et al. 2020.
[16] Conroy 2019.
[17] See further Elo 2018; Neubert 1998.
[18] Conroy et al. 2020.
[19] Drucker 2011.
[20] Wetherell 1998: 125.

References

BStU. (2013). *Aktion 'Gegenschlag': die Zerschlagung der Jenaer Opposition 1983*. Berlin: BStU.

Conroy, M. (2019). *Visualizing historical networks with Palladio*. White paper, Humanities Commons. DOI: http://dx.doi.org/10.17613/785h-s253

Conroy, M., et al. (2020). *Visualizing historical networks using graphs and matrices*. White paper, Humanities Commons. DOI: http://dx.doi.org/10.17613/jcd0-vt59

Drucker, J. (2011). Humanities approaches to graphical display. *Digital Humanities Quarterly, 5*(1), 1–21.

Düring, M., & von Keyserlingk, L. (2015). *Netzwerkanalyse in den Geschichtswissenschaften: Historische Netzwerkanalyse als Methode für die Erforschung von historischen Prozessen*. Berlin: Springer.

Elo, K. (2018). Geospatial social networks of East German opposition (1975–1989/90). *Journal of Historical Network Research, 2*(1), 143–165. DOI: https://doi.org/10.25517/jhnr.v2i1.45

Gieseke, J. (2008). East German espionage in the era of detente. *Journal of Strategic Studies, 31*(3), 395–424.

Haack, H. (1965). *Deutsche Demokratische Republik, Bergbau u. industrie*. Arbeitskreis VEB Hermann Haack, Geographisch Kartographische Anstalt Gotha (Wirtschaftskarte: Deutsche Demokratische Republik. MDI d. DDR nr. 7579/62).

Lemercier, C. (2015). Formal network methods in history: why and how? In G. Fertig (Ed.), *Social networks, political institutions, and rural Societies* (pp. 281–310). Turnhout: Brepols Publishers.

Morrissey, R. M. (2015). Archives of connection. *Historical Methods: A Journal of Quantitative and Interdisciplinary History, 48*(1), 67–79.

Neubert, E. (1998). *Geschichte der Opposition in der DDR 1949–1989: Forschungen zur DDR-Gesellschaft*, Berlin: Ch. Links.

Nocaj, A., Ortmann, M., & Brandes, U. (2015). Untangling the hairballs of multi-centered, small-world online social media networks. *Journal of Graph Algorithms and Applications: JGAA, 19*(2), 595–618.

Prell, C. (2012). *Social network analysis: history, theory and methodology.* London: Sage.

Robert-Havemann-Gesellschaft e.V., Archiv der DDR-Opposition. *Bildarchiv*. Retrieved from http://www.havemann-gesellschaft.de/archiv-der-ddr-opposition/bildarchiv/

Schroeder, K. (1998). *Der SED-Staat: Geschichte und Strukturen der DDR.* Munich: Bayerische Landeszentrale für politische Bildungsarbeit.

Veen, H.-J. (Ed.) (2000). *Lexikon Opposition und Wiederstand in der SED-Diktatur*. Munich: Propyläen.

Wetherell, C. (1998). Historical social network analysis. *International Review of Social History, 43*(1), 125–144.

CHAPTER 14

The Many Ways to Talk about the Transits of Venus

Astronomical Discourses in *Philosophical Transactions*, 1753–1777

Reetta Sippola

A Popular Astronomical Event

In the 1760s, one of astronomy's rarest predictable phenomena, the so-called Transit of Venus, was calculated to take place twice: in 1761 and in 1769. This phenomenon, when the planet Venus passes across the Sun, from the Earth's vantage point, was not only extremely rare, as the previous transit had taken place in 1639 and the next was to follow in 1874, but also very valuable scientifically, as observing this kind of transit would make it possible to determine the distance between the Earth and the Sun more accurately than before. This could in turn make it easier to improve a number of practical issues relying on astronomical knowledge, foremost among them to improve the accuracy of calculating locations at sea, which at this time was at best inaccurate, often resulting in costly and deadly accidents. Thus, the two Transit of Venus events and the astronomical information that could be derived from observing them enjoyed wide interest among both scientific professionals and the general

How to cite this book chapter:
Sippola, R. (2020). The many ways to talk about the Transits of Venus: Astronomical discourses in *Philosophical Transactions*, 1753–1777. In M. Fridlund, M. Oiva, & P. Paju (Eds.), *Digital histories: Emergent approaches within the new digital history* (pp. 237–257). Helsinki: Helsinki University Press. https://doi.org/10.33134/HUP-5-14

public. The scientific interest in the transits during the 18th century was represented through a large number of news items and scientific reports in the scientific literature, especially in scientific periodicals, such as the *Philosophical Transactions of the Royal Society of London*. In short, there was a large and varied scientific discourse talking about the Transits of Venus. This chapter explores what new historical knowledge about science in the 18th century we can derive from using digital methods to study such scientific discourse related to a particular scientific phenomenon.

However, alongside the natural philosophical news and reports, many broader perspectives towards early modern knowledge and the early modern world itself were also communicated in the scientific journals. By using digital history methodologies to analyse the qualitative meanings and quantitative amounts of the common topics and themes in a scientific periodical, I suggest in this chapter that there were simultaneously nine different ways of talking, or discourses, about astronomy and the two Transits of Venus of the 1760s.

Astronomy has been one of the main ways for scientists to explore explanations about our place in the universe, but astronomical knowledge has also been used for other more practical applications in economy, politics and transportation. This combination of pursuing natural philosophy endeavours both for knowledge and for practical applications was also central for the Royal Society of London, established in 1660 in England for improving the knowledge of nature and mankind, as articulated in their full official name. To serve astronomical practice, the Society funded two large expeditions to make observations of the 1760s Transits of Venus, but at the same time and partly through these expeditions they also took part in the larger and wider transformation of how the natural sciences were understood in the 17th and 18th centuries, by creating a communal and public space for circulating the new knowledge. The Society circulated a newsletter that disseminated and shared the new scientific information coming from collecting and observing abroad on scientific voyages and commercial encounters, as well as through experiments at home. The letter soon turned into the form of a periodical, entitled *Philosophical Transactions Giving some Account of the present Undertakings, Studies, and Labours of the Ingenious in many considerable parts of the World*, established in 1665 and published as the Society's official journal from 1752. From the mid-18th century onwards, *Philosophical Transactions* was a journal publishing scientific correspondence that had been selected and reviewed by the fellows of the Society. The journal also had a much wider readership than just natural philosophers.[1] Its topics included news about the latest innovations and discoveries and reports on geography, natural scientific specimens and natural and man-made phenomena, such as weather and electricity. Even the work of amateur experimenters was published, whereas many professional reports sent to the Royal Society were rejected and put to one side with a note 'not to be printed'.[2]

In the mid-1700s, many nations participated in a race for the knowledge, prestige and power that could be gained through successful observations of the two predicted Transits of Venus. National and international networks of knowledge invested a significant amount in astronomy research, and the importance of succeeding in observing the Transits of Venus has often been compared to the Cold War space race of the 20th century. Central in this were the observation instruments which were carefully collected and arranged for transportation to judiciously planned observation locations.[3] The Transits of Venus were then widely discussed in various contemporary printed periodicals, as well as in the general press. It was understandably a prominent topic in periodicals such as *Philosophical Transactions* reporting on the latest news within natural philosophy. The emphasis was on the conducted experiments and the reporting and theorising of the events. However, at the same time, the Royal Society's public communications also conveyed other more elusive and implied perspectives on the philosophical inquiries to their wide group of readers. In this light, this chapter uses the reporting of the Transits of Venus in *Philosophical Transactions* to critically discuss what kind of view of 'scientific' inquiry was offered to its readers: What was actually discussed about astronomy in particular and the new science in general among the texts that succeeded in being printed in *Philosophical Transactions* during the late 18th century? The guiding hypotheses behind the study is that the general values of 18th-century British society and the philosophical environment have been repeated directly and indirectly in the texts. By re-reading this discourse with the digital methods, we can access the underlying thoughts, paradigms (such as a shared model of the universe) and practices related to experimental science that existed at this time.

Topic Modelling the Publication of New Science

The historical meanings of the editing and peer reviews of *Philosophical Transactions* has been studied by Ellen Valle in particular, and subsequently by Julie McDougall-Waters, Noah Moxham and Aileen Fyfe.[4] My research continues their work by applying the use of 'machine reading' and the method of topic modelling for finding the underlying patterns and values that have influenced the public writing about new scientific knowledge. By comparing statistical amounts of various topics in *Philosophical Transactions* at different times, topic modelling reveals temporal changes in scientific approaches in the many ways of talking about the process and of the degrees of certainty within the emergent sciences. This could be a major contribution to the history of early scientific communications because this kind of temporal change has not been discussed in the earlier scholarship, which has only applied manual reading of these resources. The digital methodology of topic modelling provided a way to examine the large amount of texts in *Philosophical Transactions* and to reveal the changing patterns in the ways in which the two transits were discussed. It located the internal relations inside the 'big data', comprising all the words in the texts, and teased out their shared and underlying meanings.

I have focused on 1753–1777 as a period of 25 years containing the important astronomical events (the two Transits of Venus in 1761 and 1769). This period also covers the time after the Society had formally taken over the journal in 1752 and begun editing the articles communally via the so-called Committee of Papers, and before it changed into a new period of knowledge circulation in 1778 when Joseph Banks took on the presidency of the Royal Society. The time frame also contains the collection of new data during world-changing voyages of exploration, such as those of Captain Wallis in 1765–1768 and Captain Cook in 1768–1780, both supervised by the Royal Society.

The selected corpus of texts from *Philosophical Transactions* consists of a set of 1,421 documents relating to the transits, which represents a collective public discourse on scientific discoveries, innovations and experimental routine (a typical genre of texts published in the journal). The texts of the corpus were generated by optical character recognition (OCR) of a digitised version of *Philosophical Transactions* provided for research purposes by JStor, and I used a temporal selection of the *Royal Society Corpus*[5] which had been collected and pre-processed in a previous linguistics project headed by Elke Teich.[6] Their pre-processing included the transformation of data into a standardised format, cleaning of data (for example, OCR errors) and derivation and annotation of metadata.[7]

The research process consisted of three stages, which combined statistical and computational quantitative methods with qualitative analysis of the texts. During the first stage, I applied topic modelling to the corpus to create lists of probable keywords describing the themes existing within the data corpus. To operate with the topic modelling algorithm, I prepared a so-called 'stop list' of very common words (such as *the*, *is*, *as*, etc., as well as prepositions and conjunctions) to be filtered out and excluded in the analysis of the corpus. I also arranged the processing of the corpus temporally by dividing it into five-year sets (1753–1757, 1758–1762, 1763–1767, 1768–1772, 1773–1777) and then ran these through the topic modelling algorithm implemented in the MALLET software application. The output was a list of various topics or themes of interconnected keywords co-occurring throughout the articles. As a preliminary analysis, I used MALLET to produce a varying number of topics from the corpus and concluded that the best and most realistic fit, in terms of what from the keywords appeared to be relevant and meaningful topics that were not too general or too narrow, was when the number of topics was 50. Following this, I grouped the topics along semantic similarities in their keywords in order to locate their relations to the scientific contexts in which the original texts of the corpus were created. This was a crucial part of the research; while a 'topic' to the computer is merely a list of words that occur together in statistically meaningful ways,[8] in the following manual analyses by the researcher these lists are shown as a semantically meaningful string of keywords which need to be sewn together with a larger thread of historical context and interpreted in order to provide a meaningful label that refers back to the historical context. Therefore, the historical work of contextualising the English 1700s science discourse was ongoing throughout the entire research process.

In summary of the above, I programmed MALLET to create a list of 50 topics, each consisting of 20 keywords, and entered these into a spreadsheet which showed the number of these topics during the chosen years. The keywords represent co-occurrence patterns in the data corpus and probabilistic appearances of a particular theme. I located keywords that signified general trends and particular themes, such as those that concerned instruments in observation and experiments. After examining and labelling all the topics which were present in 2% or more of the text mass, I grouped the topics according to their semantic similarities. This revealed that the common topics in the data could be roughly grouped according to 'polite correspondence style', 'astronomy', 'chemistry', 'weather' and 'instruments and their use'. In actual fact, it was not until this stage that the processing of the data highlighted the most fruitful research questions warranting further investigation.

As mentioned above, Teich's linguistics team had already carried out research that applied topic modelling to the first two centuries of *Philosophical Transactions*. Their visualisations enable us to see topical trends in the corpus, in particular in terms of discipline formation and specialisation, that there is a growing separation of individual scientific disciplines over time and that the discourse became increasingly specific over time.[9] Aiming at different perspectives on the proposed material and research questions, I thus designed the commands and continued to fine-tune my topic modelling less towards general themes stretching over large time periods, and more towards more specific themes connected to my more focused period and scientific developments. As a result, this is an example not only of applying a fresh perspective on an already known resource, but, importantly, also of a collaboration among experts which is characteristic for contemporary digital humanities.[10] Teich's team identified 24 different topics in *Philosophical Transactions* which indicated the development of scientific sub-disciplines (including Chemistry, Mechanics and Reproduction, among others). This research was an excellent starting point for my inquiries, in which I used an alternative approach to examine the periodical and which found 25 topics that were theoretically visible, as they each referred to more than 1% of the amount of text. Our two approaches to the same data differ in the close reading perspectives, and the comparison has led me to notice other wider perspectives. In the following section, I will problematise what else can be depicted from the results of a computer-assisted distant reading of the periodical from the perspective of the cultural history of science.

Thematic Trends of the Discussion

When beginning to discuss the quantitative results of the topic modelling, it is indeed no surprise that the keywords and their frequencies show a notable rise in astronomical topics around both transits. They are visible during most years as a relatively large number of texts on astronomy, with the text mining revealing keywords such as 'transit', 'June' and 'Venus', where 'June' was the month when the 1761 transit occurred. Astronomy and its related practices and techniques were commonly mentioned, but in the researched time span, *Philosophical Transactions* also discussed a few non-astronomical topics. However, these also helped to locate relevant aspects of the scientific ways of talking also within astronomy, as I will demonstrate below when discussing the case of systematising observation results. In particular, these non-astronomical topics have a specific value as they can vividly illuminate what is *not* part of other discussions.

Shared discourses, split viewpoints

The remainder of this chapter will analyse the astronomical ways of talking by contextualising and connecting the prevalent topics in the published scientific communications (for example, in *Philosophical Transactions*) to the making of early modern knowledge. I begin with a thematic analysis of the text-mining results and then conclude with a summary of the approaches and temporal appearances of the nine ways of talking about science. Keywords of all of the discussed topics are listed in Appendix 14.1.[11]

The data shows that the discourse on the first transit (1761) circulated around various viewpoints concerning reliability and the structure of the solar system. The common themes consisted of exactness, measuring, relating and belonging (to the universe), which also reflect the excitement of using the enthusiastically approved, state-of-the-art instruments in making observations of the first transit. Instead of describing causal chains, the observations were communicated as indicating the values of various connecting sets of rules and theories. The observations were thus not neutral, but became charged with rules and theories.

The lists of observation data were apparently published as they had been recorded, and were then consequently explained through the use of mathematical algebraic reasoning (the topic 'Astronomical distance' with 11%), as a system of heavens that could be revealed ('Rules of the stars' topic with 5%) and how it related to the solar system ('Appliances' topic with 8%).[12] The first two topics were only present in 1758–1762, while 'Solar system' was an ongoing topic, although notably only at the beginning, as it almost disappeared (1% to 2%) around the second transit. In 1763–1767, the theme seems to split into two topics, as a similar topic 'Heavenly bodies' shortly appears at this point. However, it differs somewhat, as this topic focuses on the planetary system and its parts (which are described in a similar manner as the reports would talk about the human body, possibly in a 'plain' style), while the topic 'Solar system' discusses what can be achieved on Earth by using those heavenly bodies:

for example, '*latitude*' and '*degree*' are among its keywords, which could often signify the calculation of the location at sea. These distinctions already show that the discourse on the transits addressed many separate views on the topic, varying talk which not only promoted causal theories and mathematical reasoning or arranging raw data 'plainly', but also offered discussions on more social factors, such as the extent of trust and belief that could be placed in astronomical calculations.

There might be some skewing of this topic, as a large number of its keywords might be brought about by one single lengthy paper (23 pages in print) in *Philosophical Transactions* by the Astronomer Royal Nevil Maskelyne, on observations and methodological rules he developed following the 1761 transit. By collecting and comparing the data received from various observations at St. Helena about the Transit of Venus, Maskelyne formulated a set of theoretical rules about the skies and the use of astronomical instruments.[13] During this time, if the transaction discourse is representative, apparently a rather small part ('Rules of the stars' topic with 5%) of the astronomical interest concerned astronomy's theoretical system. This theoretical discourse topic also existed at the time of the second transit in 1769, meaning that Maskelyne's ideas continued to be referred to or discussed after his paper's initial 1761 publication. However, as the topic decreased from 5% to 2%, this indicates an increasing emphasis on other perspectives, such as a dispute on the relative importance of causal versus mathematical evidence. That Maskelyne's article constituted a dominant part of the topic could easily be identified through a keyword search in the dataset, and it is worth emphasising that it is both important as well as useful to also apply close reading to enable closer study and control the content of themes that arise from the distant reading of the text-mining results.

One alternative to using theories and mathematics to explain astronomical measurements was through empirical means (namely, repeated experiments or observations). This is demonstrated by the topic 'Distance measuring process' being continuously very strong (9–12%) throughout the period, thus representing scientists' interest in the general process of experimentation, while the keywords of the 'Astronomical distance' topic point towards explanations and mechanisms based on the laws of physics, physical circumstances and entities, such as velocity and distance. Apart from 'glass' (a reference to a material most likely indicating the lens of a telescope or an experiment tube), the keywords of the 'Distance measurement process' topic ('distance', 'degrees', 'line' and 'places') primarily point towards intangible concepts connected to very tangible experiments, of measuring and of practically producing new observational data. Interestingly, its keywords of 'appearance', 'means' and 'method' give this discussion various kinds of unsure, unsettled and dynamic connotations and, furthermore, the topic contained discussions about particular location-specific, probable or 'apparent' aspects.

The topic 'Astronomical distance' was discussed only once, in the 1758–1762 segment, with a sudden 11% spike, in which the observations of the heavens (and the astronomical signified keywords of [moon/sun's] limb, sun, star and wheel) were linked with the data in the tables (measure, feet, foot, inches) and algebra (cos, distance, wheel). This and the 'Distance measurement experiments' topic both mention the word 'distance', but the other keywords indicate a clear difference in meaning between the two, as the topics reveal how 'distance' was to be observed, depending on whether it addressed celestial distances or distances on Earth. In comparing these two topics, I claim that the topic modelling algorithm has revealed a very important temporal change: it has located a mainly shared discourse about the practices of deciding on the distance, but it has split this theme into two. Their separate keyword lists initially differ between practical experimentality and understanding the physical theories of the phenomena, but after this, both topics also share similar passages about the use of instruments and theorising the measurements.[14] Both topics discuss various means to measure distance, and the shared keywords of *measure*, *distance* and [the method of heaven's] *wheel*, which all appear in both of the discussed topics, capture a broader, shared discussion. This is the value of topic modelling: by using machine-reading and locating shared but slightly variable topics, the nuances of the discussions can better come to light.

The examination of these topics indicates that there were two profoundly different ways of what was considered to be the reliable way to find data. The first transit in particular allowed plenty of interest (11%) in making arguments through calculations, but for the second transit the frequencies indicate that the mathematics were no longer a primary worry. There is only a short temporal change within the statistics that could, however, exemplify a dramatic change in the paradigm. It appears that a more general perspective about measurements was developing and that means other than mathematical results had become increasingly relevant in the early modern search for reliability and 'truth'.

Following Newton's formulation of mathematical laws of nature, in the 18th century it was usually considered sufficient to settle an astronomical dispute if one could arrive at a successful set of mathematical calculations.[15] At a time when logical causalities became less interesting to the scientists, the large number of words indicating probability in my data raises questions about reliability, the meanings of eye-witnessing and the capabilities of the human mind and senses. These topics can also indicate that there was a split discourse according to the two schools of realists: one consisting of mathematical realists, including those who thought mathematics could provide the real motions of celestial bodies; the other comprising the group of physical realists who held that a mathematical model of the real structure of the heavens should be based on physics.[16]

Another example of transitions within the paradigm can be noted in the texts written in Latin. A few data and observation reports were received and published in Latin, including the transit observations from Uppsala in Sweden.[17] However, this kind of discourse was narrow and concentrated into two topics: 'Solar system Latin' and 'Transit and Latin'. The two topics were both most popular around the first transit, and while they both circulated the calculations for longitude, they differed in their perspectives. The first described the observations plainly, while the other seems to have emphasised the materiality of the observation process. This means that in Latin there were at the time in question two ways of discussing astronomy: first, as descriptions of the solar system; and, second, in the form of the actual process of making observations of the solar system. It also appears that during this period both Latin topics started to disappear. This decline of Latin had also been noted in passing by the previously mentioned linguistics researchers when stating that some non-thematic topics, including texts written in Latin, reached their peak in the early 18th century.[18] However, as we can observe in the keyword list, Latin was still used in the late 18th century in publishing accounts concerning the heavens and the solar system. The topic 'Solar system Latin' was popular between 1758 and 1767, with a 6% to 8% share of all discussions, but then almost disappeared (1% to 2% in the subsequent decade), while the 'Transit and Latin' topic was visible throughout the entire transit decade, but only with a 2% to 5% share.

The host of Latin words in 'Transit and Latin', '*vero*', '*inter*', '*hoc*', '*enim*' and '*hujus*', are all abstract, frequent words. 'Vero' is the fascinating one, as it means 'truly, indeed, to be sure, certainly'. In fact, among the 500 keywords in the other topics, there are many that indicate a continuous interest towards the 'true', such as in addition to 'true', also 'purpose', 'order', 'error', 'anemones', 'effect', 'probability' and 'rules'. And deriving from the keywords 'apparent' and 'error', the 'Telescope observations' topic can be seen as promoting an openness towards the meanings of the results and how changing circumstances could affect the observations, although the task in question seemed to be regarding some precise measurements, including 'minutes' and 'seconds'.

Taken together, these topics discuss a contemporary science culture that was seen as being open-ended and constantly recreated by various actors.[19] In particular, the certainty of probabilities and the transparency about practical choices when making observations seem to be continuing themes in the various discourses.

Talking about the weather

The external conditions of the observations were and are a central issue to astronomers. It especially appears to be the main way to talk about the astronomical observations in one topic which, due to its huge number of weather keywords, has been labelled 'Astronomer's weather'. This was a strong topic during its time: although it only existed during the 1768–1772 period, the topic arrived with a notable 14% of the volume of text published in *Philosophical Transactions*. The first words in this topic are 'ditto', 'air' and 'limb [of the moon or the sun]' which apparently refer to astronomical observation tables. These keywords were also accompanied by 'June' and by as many as five words describing weather.

Throughout the years in question, the weather was continuously discussed, but there is some increase in the latter 10 years of the studied period, during which the second Transit of Venus took place. This sudden rise in the topic modelling chart is understandable in the light of the unfortunate event of not having been able to make successful observations of the transit on the first attempt in 1761 due to difficult weather. It is therefore no surprise that we can find some discussion about the conditions already before and after the 1761 transit: it was anticipated that clouds could obscure visibility at the vital moment, as they had so often done when Edmond Halley had been observing a similar transit almost a century earlier.[20] The unpredictability of weather was just one of the several reasons why there was a need to simultaneously observe the Transit of Venus from many different and varied places on Earth. Beside cloud cover, Halley had already in 1716 pointed out in his observation advice the importance of arranging coverage from northern and southern latitudes, as both the ingress and the egress could not be observed from all the locations. Thus, to avoid a similar fate, a large-scale operation was connected to the Transits of Venus in order to coordinate several international observations and, as had been suggested by Halley, to arrange multiple observatory tents to be set up around the globe by British, Austrian and French observers.[21] The more observations that were made from many different and widely separated vantage points, the more accurate the ultimate results were likely to be.[22]

Weather was also employed in other discourses. In the topics 'Environmental circumstances' and 'Travel narrative', weather figures in the form of the blame and complaints that often figured in early modern observation accounts. These often served very practical purposes, as a failure to conduct an experiment could often be more easily accepted due to bad weather. Simultaneously, these topics address the practice and materiality of the observation process in the form of broken instruments, successful delivery of the instruments and other aspects affected by bad weather. In this, the topics provide valuable tangible insights into early modern scientific practice.

The topics concerning the weather were used in particular around the second transit (1769). The topic 'Telescope observations' appears to mention the weather during both transits, but only moderately, with a few percent (2% to 4% during the 1758–1772 period), while the main emphasis is on discussing the way in which the new more advanced instruments could create or diminish the observation errors. Nevil Maskelyne wrote a letter to the Royal Society in 1761 which discussed at length various contextual influences on the use of the instruments. Before listing the transit observation results, Maskelyne wrote about 'the observations themselves, and mention[ed] some cautions concerning them',[23] which among others included the exact practical adjustment of the quadrant (a navigational instrument used for angle measurements).[24,25] The context in which the instruments were used, then, was important to the narrative and the manner in which they were discussed.

On the other hand, the failure to produce consistent and certain results during the scientific voyages of observation connected to the 1760s transits has been blamed not just on bad weather, but also on other external or material conditions that affected the voyage, such as war, illness and, above all, inexperience in observing the phenomenon in question.[26] The quantitative distant reading of results through topic modelling provides a new opportunity to investigate how strong the pattern has been to make arguments about the failure (and at times success) of experiments through referring to external circumstances. Such talk about instruments and circumstances that affected the observation process attracted a wider group of readers among scientists besides astronomers. In the texts, therefore, such talk can also be seen as functioning as a way of elevating the experimenter's status as a scientist, or as mirroring the scientist's thoughts or search for reinforcement from other scientists; namely, to write down the observations in a punctual manner was entangled with a deeper purpose that made visible the discourse of complimenting others or showing evidence of their mistakes and failures. Reid even called this kind of performative behaviour 'playing the astronomer', as the astronomer was in a precarious position on an expensive voyage as he was likely the first one among the crew to be seen as less important and as excess weight.[27]

In this light, it is interesting to examine how instruments and bodies were referred to, as this reflects the general values that kept being repeated in the accounts. Simon Schaffer has suggested that the states of disrepair in observation reports or travel narratives refer simultaneously to the tools and to the humans that interact with them and with one another.[28] As he wrote, the states of disrepair helped distribute responsibility across cultures and spaces, offering resources to defend some reputations and damn others.[29] From this perspective, the referral to the external conditions and the others who contributed in the making of the observations were part of the pattern of this way of distributing the responsibility for scientific success and failure.

Referring to the sources and collaborators was also a matter of reliability. According to the semantic arrangement of the keywords in the topics 'Astronomer's weather', 'Environmental circumstances' and 'Travel narrative', the materiality of objects was closely linked with the circumstances of observing. Maskelyne's previously mentioned 1761 lengthy report was careful to mention and honour the builders and senders of the equipment,[30] and in a similar fashion while on a state-sponsored exploration voyage, another astronomer in his journal listed the people who had built or fixed the instruments he used.[31] If no observation was possible due to fog or a broken instrument, their role in the experiment or its possible failure was at least taken into consideration in the description of the event. Hence, the keyword 'wood' is interesting. This might indicate the 'honouring' often offered the makers of the instruments used in the observations, as such compliments were written with full description of the types of materials used in building them and thus the quantitative data also indicates the epistemological importance of the astronomical equipment.

Talking about the weather could also be an instrument of politics, as the making of science was, and is, very political. In the corpus, the weather was at times discussed in a text with what can be described as politeness or plain style. This structured a discourse which proposed openness towards the various possibilities and active influencing on the observer's circumstances. The impact of weather could not be controlled, but it could be understood by systematisation;[32] and as it affected the success of observations and experiments, it was used as both an explanation and a weapon by scientists in the political game of making knowledge and acquiring more funding. Royal Society funding affected the discourse and the attempts to increase the natural history knowledge, and while only a nominal part of the Society's funding came from the king, the results and communications of scientific results needed to please the funders. John Henry has pointed out that this meant that the funders would wish to gain practical applications from the experiments and developments of science. As a result, the Society had to be very apologetic and have its value clearly propagandised in its attempts to demonstrate the usefulness of science to the state.[33] In order to maximise the attention within the administration, the importance and rarity of the observations of the singular 1761 and 1769 Transits of Venus would have given a reason to report the events with such care. It was a good opportunity to emphasise the relevance of the expensive astronomical observations, which was brought up wherever and whenever the transits were mentioned.

The final topic featuring the weather was 'Travel Narrative', consisting of plain or technical descriptions of weather, geography and exploration events. The topic was very frequent and steadily present by 6% to 9% throughout the period, but was at its largest at the turn of the 1770s. As weather has been proved to be an important part of spatial descriptions of 'new' regions, which were especially discussed around this time, it is most likely that there was a correlation between talks of weather and such new areas with promises for imperial and scientific explorations.

Having so many obviously different kinds of weather topics at the same time means that, simultaneously, many and varied aspects were considered. If some discussion has been very small (or unimportant) in its scale, it would not be visible in this kind of topic modelling of 1,421 articles.

Talking about instruments

Regarding the importance of various disciplines within astronomy, before 1758 and between the transits, there was according to the statistical results more room for showing interest in chemistry, whereas at the end of the 25-year period, the data indicates a turn towards widening discussions about the use of experiments and optical instruments. This was connected to experiments of measurable phenomena such as air pressure, distance and microscopic life forms, and was influenced by technological developments (besides telescopes) that also led to increased use of three observation instruments in the form of the thermometer, the barometer and the hygrometer.

These were notable topics. The talk about the instruments and their particular use each received 6% to 10%, respectively, of the space of the published texts. However, the discussion was not fully diverted from astronomical topics, as the development of the instruments is linked to weather discourses. In fact, as the three new instruments became available to more observers, it was possible to collect much larger amounts of data of local and global weather patterns, so they could be systematised and understood not just as weather, but as climates. The influence of the political interests involved in producing the 'facts' of far-afield weather should not be underestimated either. Morgan Vanek has suggested that the actual reason why 18th-century literature is saturated with the rhetoric of meteorological science lies in seeing the topic as a prominent and productive term in the public debate about Britain's imperial obligations. She claims that 18th-century writers amplified the threat of environmental influence to justify a British right to govern all over the world, as with their governance the British could improve living conditions in the 'new' harsh regions.[34]

Finally, the last approach to astronomy is quite different from the others as it addresses a rather different mindset. Interestingly, together with the perspectives on the influences of various circumstances, at the time of the 1769 transit there was also the topic 'Ancient tradition' (with 6% of the text mass), which linked the new observational data with ancient calculations and beliefs. This might indicate the astronomers' certainty of the coming success in observing the second transit and their enthusiasm in comparing their innovations with other foundational theories. This could also discuss the many stages in which the rational thinking could be influenced when the collection of new knowledge in 17th- and 18th-century Europe was largely a cooperation among various specialised actors, where some collected field data and others depicted and analysed it. According to Francis Bacon, the different investigators (observers, experimenters and theoreticians) were in this required to be on guard against 'the idols', the profound and sometimes erroneous ideas created in one's mind, as well as the defective sensations of any particular individual.[35] Indeed, it sounds like a difficult business to create reliable knowledge navigating the circumstances of observation, various investigators and possible mindsets.

Conclusion: Nine Ways of Talking about Astronomy

In summarising the critical analysis of the topic modelling results, I suggest that during the third quarter of the 18th century *Philosophical Transactions* communicated astronomical topics in at least nine different ways. The actual events surrounding the two significant Transits of Venus and other aspects of astronomy naturally dominated the discussions in the years 1758–1762 and

1768–1772 and, connected to this, the periodical contained 24 topics that were common enough to be meaningful in the text-mining results. I located five ways of talking about astronomy that existed as temporal trends, emphasised only during the transit of 1761 or 1769.

The first two ways were especially common around the 1761 transit. These sub-themes explored *the meanings given to the systematisation of data*: they denoted the practical ways of describing raw data and the systematisation of results (and in fact ended up publishing the long lists of various observation results), or attempted *to reveal a system of the universe by theorising* the heavenly bodies. This reveals the emerging new natural philosophical ways of thinking about the universe.

The next three ways of talking in astronomical topics were particularly common around the 1769 transit. In the 1770s, both the instruments and circumstances of experimentation seem to have been included in a wide way of talking about observation, such as *how the surroundings and weather can influence the observing process*. The third way of talking then points to the lived experience of the field practices of astronomical observation. The fourth astronomical discourse addressed weather and geographical locations *as evidence for the technological advances and greatness of the empire that used them despite the environment and conditions*. The material conditions offered a strong rhetorical explanation to success and failure: honouring and complaining was linked to collaboration between the makers and users of the materials and also to accepted rules of polite communication. These two ways of talking also connect to Steven Shapin's research on the role of actorship in early scientific practice and my data suggests that it would be relevant to further explore the language and style of how one communicated one's research in early modern scientific networks. The fifth discourse linked events to their *tradition* and could be seen to guard the human senses against erroneous input.

The above five ways of talking were temporal trends that existed only during a part of the research period in question. There were also four continuous sub-themes that were observed in the data. According to the statistical appearance of topics, these four discourses were dynamic and their perspective might have changed over time, but nevertheless they continued in some notable form. These aspects were pointed out first and foremost via the digital method, although in retrospect it is easier to see and contextualise them as a part of the data.

The search for *reliable means of observation* was another theme that was characteristic in the entire period around the two Transits of Venus. The sixth astronomical way of talking concerned *the materiality of instruments, their use, and the practice of experiments*. The processes of observing and measuring would in this discourse be linked to trusting the results made through material objects, including the instruments, senses and the human body.

The seventh discourse also concerned the search for reliability and indicates that there continued to be some difference in the ways of making arguments through *mathematical or physical causal reasoning*. While generally the quest between the causal and mathematical evidence for new knowledge is visible in many topics, the nuances or sub-themes appeared in temporal turns. For example, the topic 'Rules of the skies' lessened towards the end of the studied period, whereas experimentality seems to have become more common. In the two topics that concerned the measuring of distance, the discourse was split into two subsequent practices, with a different focus on the means of obtaining reliable measurements. In other words, this study revealed a temporal variability in what means of observation were seen as reliable.

The eighth perspective suggests that the Royal Society's interaction with its public in the form of its periodical typically proposed some flexibility and openness for developing knowledge, primarily through further experiments. The *openness to probabilities* indicates a structurally designed outlook on knowledge and aligns with the Society's values that everyone should themselves test the reliability of accepted truths through using thorough experiments. In 1758–1762, the astronomical topics tackled reliability issues with algebra and by systematising of results: the way to do this was through collecting large amounts of data and systematising them, which according to the results was a popular method regarding the first transit. At the end of the decade, in 1768–1773, the process of measuring and observing seems to have been more cautious in that is was giving more attention to probabilities, which indicates easier acceptance towards new open-ended scientific hypotheses and continuously *ongoing experimentation*. During the second transit, the tables and the raw observation data had still been published, but now with less importance than before, as the data lists are nowhere near as visible when compared to earlier observations. This means that the mechanical approach to systematise raw data into thematic lists was no longer a remarkable approach. Instead, the natural laws and mathematics were emerging as a more reliable explanation for proving the validity of the experiments.

And, finally, the ninth way reveals the publication of the scientific reports to have been entangled with *accepted social manners*. It illuminates the importance of the language in communicating about one's research.

Regarding the various individual topics, eight were discussed continuously across the whole period and only one of these (the 'Distance measuring process' topic) concerned astronomy. These topics displayed more general talk about the making of scientific knowledge through collecting and observing in the form of various 'plain' descriptions: the travel location ('Travel narrative'), the events and collected specimens ('Events, history, specimens'), events in a polite style ('Events supposing politeness'), 'new' species ('Species') and observation reports ('Reports'), the last two accounting for up to 5% of the temporal change, although usually being less. The descriptions of these 'standard' observations continued to be presented in mostly stable amounts throughout the period. Among the continuous topics, the relationally biggest temporal change from a large amount (6% or 8%) to virtually nothing took place with regard to the most specific topics (relating to the states of substances and environmental circumstances). These findings about the ways of talking are also supported by the findings of Teich's linguistics team, who noticed, interestingly, that some of the major changes occur for non-thematic topics, as the method brought out 'the hows' of the discourses.[36] However, he non-thematic 'hows', by which I mean the values and themes inside the discussions, are the most interesting results. These 'hows' describe the ways of doing or speaking (for example, through polite language or by expressing caution towards various probabilities).

Many results in this study were 'exactly what one would expect'[37] according to the research literature. Hence, it was pleasing to begin the analysis with those results as they seemed to confirm that the topic modelling had been carried out correctly. While the results in this way often confirm an earlier hypothesis, the real value of topic modelling is, however, in generating new ways of examining our materials, to deform them.[38] I see this as an opportunity to remove all the expected details and to reveal what surprising new findings are left. It is in this way that this study has shown how a well-known but manually too large research material can present different historical insights when interrogated through computational distant readings of digitised sources, thus illuminating the underused methodological opportunities for historians. The power of topic modelling really emerges when we examine change of the thematic trends across the entire text collection. This means that the temporal changes become visible as the topics are listed at intervals in a longer period.[39] As the case of the talk of 'distance' demonstrated, the comparison of two topics of the same theme resulted in noticing both a general discourse and located particular themes and also different ways to talk about them.

The temporal change of the paradigm was not seen directly in the results sheet produced by running the data corpus through MALLET, but became visible when interpreting the results through their contextualisation as a part of the well-known events within the history of science. As a list of words, composed statistically by an algorithm which knows nothing about the context of the study, the keywords per se are not the conclusion to our research questions. Rather, the key is the joint participations of the results and the researchers' insights and contextualisation, which is the approach that produces the hidden underlying meanings of the texts in *Philosophical Transactions*. Examining my familiar sources with this new method has, in other words, been beneficial to help me better understand the big phenomenon of the new emerging practice of science, which is a result that is much more important than just creating a general understanding of how scientists were talking in different ways about Venus.

Appendix 14.1: The Topic Labels and Keywords

Environmental circumstances: observations side air light difference lower years rain observation circumstances acid diameter set table latitude height scale electric force highest

Heavenly bodies: water sun parallax comet eclipse event it's wheel earth greenwich crystals cos axis chance coins square moon's nerves orbit lungs

Astronomical distance: feet limb observations sun foot cos inches velocity star measure est distance meteor modes cum electrified mercury black diapason wheel

Ancient tradition: birds venus transit clear blood ancient quadrant spot satellite vesuvius highest morning density roman horizon dist rest instrument charcoal observatory

Transit and Latin: longitude light contact weight vero transit clouds inter hoc contained servant primarytopic enim tab south city happen sky vapours hujus

Solar system: side quae moon vel stone observation clear degree read fpage earth sed height sin solis corpusbuild letter lpage latitude quod

Rules of the stars: venus ditto clock center moon's system veneris vertical solar miles column atque wood maskelyne mons sun's horizontal egress meridian quidem

Astronomer's weather: ditto air limb wind fluid sun time cloudy amp part clock salt june lowest contact bird matter clouds fixed north

Distance measuring process: distance experiment made experiments glass case great appears give proper state means degrees small method observation general appearance line places

Ancient manuscripts: observations inscription greek appears word fig hours inscriptions pag urine birch cliff emperor lead spindle steam tumor cells things father

Telescope observations: sun's parallax apparent cape telescope pro paris error wire power west etiam rev minutes issn etruscan rest centers april seconds

Travel narrative: made equal water observed body called half surface good kind sur place weather fpage received inches force white ground plate

Events, history, specimens: water large likewise issn days manner strong thing william inches red applied increase place easily larger numbers discovered cut history

Events supposing politeness: time found great day letter part parts matter title amp;c bodies proportion difference present mentioned till vol suppose power fire

Species: number quantity small fig air philosophical heat sun feet appeared considerable fla iron species corpusbuild lpage sea true end long

Reports: part point amp;c greater manner parts sir put end primarytopic years london left observed june substance observe order lightning animal

Hygrometer measurements French: temperature qui une proportion inch conductor form lgs hygrometer mountains luc's cette nous anemones deux open general aug sides temperatures

Thermometer, electricity and effects: heat des thermometer degree electricity column surface series instrument effect inches heights birds electrical torpedo boiling hill columns top common

Barometer measurements French: air les quicksilver barometer height tube experiments dans hath pour metal sur point fish ball density expansion shock ces par

States of substances with jargon: motion colour common form earth read kind sir learned bottom stones mercury spirit james measure england head lib miles proved

Notes

1 Moxham 2016: 469.

2 Byrch 1761; Dunn 1761, The L&P V: 102–103.

3 See, e.g., the correspondence regarding the transport and arrival of the instruments by Maskelyne in 1760.

4 See Valle 2006; McDougall-Waters, Moxham & Fyfe 2015; Moxham & Fyfe 2018.

5 Kermes, Degaetano, Khamis, Knappen & Teich. 2016a.

6 I wish to express my gratitude to them for generously allowing me to use the data corpus that they had pre-processed in their project 'Information Density and Scientific Literacy in English: Synchronic and Diachronic Perspectives of the Collaborative Research Centre SFB 1102'.

7 Kermes, Degaetano, Khamis, Knappen & Teich 2016b: 1929.

8 Shawn, Weingart & Milligan 2013.

9 Fankhauser, Knappen & Teich 2016: 498.

10 Their project has already been finished and I have not collaborated in the research, but I was later permitted to use their open data. On another view upon collaboration, Matthew Kirschenbaum described the cooperation as also being 'a social undertaking. It harbors networks of people who have been working together, sharing research, arguing, competing, and collaborating for many years.' See Kirschenbaum 2016.

11 In addition to the 20 discussed topics (see Appendix 14.1), there were five topics (making 25 topics in total) that were unrelated to astronomical issues, and were therefore excluded from this study. The excluded six topics focused on medical knowledge, nutrition, mortality rates, paleontological finds and geographical events such as earthquakes.

12 In this topic occurs the keywords *fpage, corpusbuild* and *lpage*, which derive from terms used for the metadata included in the JStor text files and not from the original articles. This error originates in the pre-processing of the data: had it been noticed earlier in the research process, the corruption of the topic could have been avoided by including these terms in the stop word list. The topic has, however, been accepted as a part of the analysis in its partly erroneous form, as it was not considered to skew it considerably based on the reason that the keywords did not appear in the earliest part of the topic but as the 10th, 16th and 18th in the order of appearance. In topic modelling with MALLET, the earliest keywords have more significance in the analyses of the topic's meaning than the later ones in the list.

[13] Maskelyne 1761.
[14] My depiction was guided by a similar analysis as in Mohr & Bogdanov 2013: 554.
[15] Henry 2017: 168.
[16] See Çimen 2018.
[17] Topic 'Transit and Latin' uses keywords like 'servant', which indicates polite letter writing and, in the case of the Royal Society, very probably a set of observations sent to them.
[18] Fankhauser, Knappen & Teich 2016: 498.
[19] Golinski 2017: 181.
[20] Jardine 1999: 141.
[21] Halley 1716: 246; Leverington 2003: 143.
[22] Gascoigne 2000.
[23] Maskelyne 1761: 562.
[24] Turner & Turner 1998: 30.
[25] Maskelyne 1761: 563.
[26] Galison & Daston 2008: 316.
[27] Reid 2008: 172.
[28] Schaffer 2011: 708.
[29] Ibid.: 709–710.
[30] Maskelyne 1761: 560.
[31] Wales 1777: 73.
[32] Hooke 1663; cf. Daston 2015.
[33] Henry 2017: 174.
[34] Vanek 2016: ii–iii.
[35] Sargent 2012, 83.
[36] Fankhauser, Knappen & Teich 2016: 498.
[37] Blevins 2010.
[38] Shawn, Milligan & Weingart 2013.
[39] Blevins 2010.

References

Primary sources

Byrch, W. D. (1761). *Of the late transit of Venus, with obsns or help from Mssrs Sic, Ridout and Dean*. The Letters and Papers V, p. 102.

Dunn, S. (1761). *Of the late transit of Venus*. 1-page letter to Dr. Morton, read 8 June. Not printed. The Letters and Papers V, p. 103.

Halley, E. (1716). A new method of determining the Parallax of the Sun, or his distance from the Earth. *Philosophical Transactions, XXIX*, 243–249.

Hooke, R. (1663). *For the making a more accurate history of the changes of weather*. Royal Society, Cl.P/20/24.

Kermes, H., Degaetano, S., Khamis, A., Knappen, J., & Teich, E. (2016a). The Royal Society Corpus.

Maskelyne, N. (1761). A letter from the Rev. Nevil Maskelyne, M. A. F. R. S. to the Rev. Thomas Birch, D. D. Secretary to the Royal Society: containing the results of observations of the distance of the moon from the Sun and fixed stars, made in a voyage from England to the Island of St. Helena, in order to determine the longitude of the ship, from time to time; together with the whole process of computation used on this occasion. *Philosophical Transactions, 52*, 559–581.

Wales, W. (1777). *The original astronomical observations, made in the course of a voyage towards the South Pole, and round the world, in H.M.S. Resolution and Adventure, in the years MDCCLXXII, III, IV, and V*. London: printed by W. and A. Strahan.

Secondary sources

Blevins, C. (2010). Topic modeling Martha Ballard's diary. Retrieved from http://www.cameronblevins.org/posts/topic-modeling-martha-ballards-diary/

Çimen, Ü. (2018). On saving the astronomical phenomena: physical realism in struggle with mathematical realism in Francis Bacon, Al-Bitruji, and Averroes. *HOPOS: The Journal of the International Society for the History of Philosophy of Science, 9*(1), 135–151. DOI: https://doi.org/10.1086/701058

Daston, L. (2015). Supervision: weather watching and table reading in the early modern royal society and Académie Royale des Sciences. *Huntington Library Quarterly, 78*(2), 187–215.

Fankhauser, P., Knappen, J., & Teich, E. (2016). *Topical diversification over time in the Royal Society Corpus*. Digital Humanities 2016: Conference Abstracts (pp. 496–500). Kraków: Jagiellonian University and Pedagogical University.

Galison, P., & **Daston, L.** (2008). Scientific coordination as ethos and epistemology. In H. Schramm, L. Schwarte & J. Lazardzig (Eds.), *Theatrum scientiarum—English edition*, Vol. 2: *Instruments in art and science*. Berlin and Boston, MA: De Gruyter.

Gascoigne, J. (2000). Exploration, enlightenment and enterprise: the motives for Pacific exploration in the late eighteenth and early nineteenth centuries. Retrieved from https://web.viu.ca/black/amrc/index.htm?home.htm&2

Golinski, J. (2017). Enlightenment science. In I. R. Morus (Ed.), *The Oxford illustrated history of science 1* (pp. 180–210). Oxford: Oxford University Press.

Henry, J. (2017). The scientific revolution. In I. R. Morus (Ed.), *The Oxford illustrated history of science 1* (pp. 143–179). Oxford: Oxford University Press.

Jardine, L. (1999). *Ingenious pursuits: building the scientific revolution*. New York, NY: Doubleday.

Kermes, H., Degaetano, S., Khamis, A., Knappen, J., & **Teich, E.** (2016b). *The Royal Society Corpus: from uncharted data to corpus.* Abstract book. Proceedings of the LREC 2016. Portoroz, Slovenia. Retrieved from http://www.lrec-conf.org/proceedings/lrec2016/summaries/792.html

Kirschenbaum, M. (2016). *What is digital humanities and what's it doing in English departments?* Retrieved from http://dhdebates.gc.cuny.edu/debates/text/38

Leverington, D. (2003). *Babylon to Voyager and beyond: a history of planetary astronomy.* Cambridge: Cambridge University Press.

McDougall-Waters, J., Moxham, N., & **Fyfe, A.** (2015). *Philosophical Transactions: 350 years of publishing at the Royal Society (1665–2015).* Retrieved from https://royalsociety.org/~/media/publishing350/publishing350-exhibition-catalogue.pdf

Mohr, J. W., & **Bogdanov, P.** (2013). Introduction—topic models: what they are and why they matter. *Poetics, 41*(6), 545–569.

Moxham, N. (2016). Authors, editors and newsmongers: form and genre in the philosophical transactions under Henry Oldenburg. In J. Raymond & N. Moxham (Eds.), *News networks in early modern Europe* (pp. 445–492). Leiden and Boston, MA: Brill.

Moxham, N., & **Fyfe, A.** (2018). The Royal Society and the prehistory of peer review 1665–1965. *Historical Journal, 61*(4), 863–889.

Reid, F. L. (2008). William Wales (ca. 1734–1798): playing the astronomer. *Studies in History and Philosophy of Science, 39*, 170–175.

Sargent, R.-M. (2012). From Bacon to Banks: the vision and the realities of pursuing science for the common good. *Studies in History and Philosophy of Science, 43*(1), 82–90.

Schaffer, S. (2011). Easily cracked: scientific instruments in states of disrepair. *Isis, 102*(4), 706–717.

Shawn, G., Milligan, I., & **Weingart, S.** (2013). The historian's macroscope: big digital history. An experiment in writing in public, one page at a time. In *The historian's macroscope—working title.* Under contract with Imperial College Press. Open draft version. Retrieved from http://themacroscope.org

Shawn, G., Weingart, S., & **Milligan, I.** (2013). Getting started with topic modeling and MALLET. In *The historian's macroscope—working title.* Under contract with Imperial College Press. Open draft version. Retrieved from http://themacroscope.org

Turner, G. L'E., & **Turner, A.** *Scientific Instruments, 1500-1900: An Introduction.* University of California Press, 1998.

Valle, E. (2006). 'Reporting the doings of the curious': authors and editors in the *Philosophical Transactions* of the Royal Society of London. In B. Nicholas (Ed.), *News discourse in early modern Britain: selected papers of CHINED 2004* (pp. 71–90). Bern: Peter Lang.

Vanek, M. E. (2016). *Changeable conditions: British writing about the weather in Canada, 1700–1775* (PhD thesis, University of Toronto).

CHAPTER 15

The Many Themes of Humanism

Topic Modelling Humanism Discourse in Early 19th-Century German-Language Press

Heidi Hakkarainen and Zuhair Iftikhar

Introduction

Topic modelling is often described as a text-mining tool for conducting a study of hidden semantic structures of a text or a text corpus by extracting topics from a document or a collection of documents.[1] Yet, instead of one singular method, there are various tools for topic modelling that can be utilised for historical research. Dynamic topic models, for example, are often constructed temporally year by year, which makes it possible to track and analyse the ways in which topics change over time.[2] This chapter provides a case example on topic modelling historical primary sources. We are using two tools to carry out topic modelling, MALLET and Dynamic Topic Model (DTM), in one dataset, containing texts from the early 19th-century German-language press which have been subjected to optical character recognition (OCR). All of these texts were discussing humanism, which was a newly emerging concept before mid-century, gaining various meanings in the public discourse before, during and after the 1848–1849 revolutions. Yet, these multiple themes and early interpretations of humanism in the press have been previously under-studied. By

How to cite this book chapter:
Hakkarainen, H., & Iftikhar, Z. (2020). The many themes of humanism: Topic modelling humanism discourse in early 19th-century German-language press. In M. Fridlund, M. Oiva, & P. Paju (Eds.), *Digital histories: Emergent approaches within the new digital history* (pp. 259–277). Helsinki: Helsinki University Press. https://doi.org/10.33134/HUP-5-15

analysing the evolution of the topics between 1829 and 1850, this chapter aims to shed light on the change of the discourse surrounding humanism in the early 19th-century German-speaking Europe.

The concept of humanism (*Humanismus*) was first coined by Friedrich Immanuel Niethammer (1766–1848) in German-speaking Europe in 1808.[3] The concept was originally used in the pedagogical debate concerning education, especially in the *Gymnasium*. This pedagogical debate between humanist and philanthropist (realist) education was related to 19th-century educational reforms and especially to the school reform in Bavaria, which preceded the Prussian school reform between 1809 and 1819.[4] However, in addition to these pedagogical debates, the concept of humanism spread more widely in the 1830s and 1840s, and in this gained new meanings and interpretations.

However, as the previous studies have focused on the early 19th-century pedagogical debates, this wider dissemination and popularisation of the new concept in the printed press has not been under an extensive close study.[5] There exist a large number of printed publications discussing humanism already in the first part of the 19th century, which makes an inquiry on press debates a challenging task for historians.[6] In order to tackle this challenge of the vast size of potential source material, this chapter uses the quantitative method of computer-based 'topic modelling' to assist the qualitative analysis.

By topic modelling a set containing almost 100 key texts from the years between 1829 and 1850, this chapter recovers several of those multiple discourses connected to humanism before, during and after the outburst of the 1848–1849 revolutions. By combining and comparing topic modelling with MALLET with Dynamic Topic Modelling (DTM), this chapter seeks to map and analyse what kinds of topics were related to humanism before 1850 and how these topics changed and evolved over time. During 21 years, humanism appeared in various contexts from education to philosophy, religion and politics. Where the MALLET, as the most well-established topic modelling tool within the field of digital history,[7] is used in detecting the most prominent themes in the discussion on humanism, DTM makes available a finer look into the topics at the temporal level and, in this case study, provides a new kind of insight into the growing importance of temporality within the German-language humanism discourse between the early 1800s and the mid-century.[8]

In contrast to temporally ambitious research on huge corpuses, this chapter focuses on a rather small text corpus, which allows more exploration of the possibilities of cross-reading the material with methods of close and distant reading. This study of the discussion surrounding humanism before 1850 thus provides a reasonably manageable but rich investigation of some of the ways in which newspapers and periodicals addressed topical issues and transferred concepts and new ideas across political borders within the lands of the German Confederation.

At the same time, we seek to explore what kinds of methodological benefits and risks are involved in the topic modelling of historical sources. The technique of topic modelling decides what constitutes a topic on an algorithm that creates a statistical model of word clusters. It is thus not a fixed schema, but a variable probabilistic model that should also be treated as such. We will demonstrate how various forms of cleaning and filtering of the data can have drastic results on the output of the topic model. We also present and compare outputs from different methods of topic modelling, using the MALLET application and DTM, and address various methodological concerns related to topic modelling.

Topic Modelling with MALLET

The first essential step in describing the 19th-century German-language press discourse on humanism was to identify its various individual themes or topics using the quantitative method of topic modelling. Topic modelling has its roots in information retrieval, natural language processing and machine learning. This probabilistic tool has attracted attention among historians, because it enables detecting underlying thematic structures behind a large corpus of documents, as well as surprising connections between individual texts. A topic comprises a distribution of words. A single document is assumed to contain words about multiple topics within the whole dataset. Each word is drawn from those dataset topics. The study used two topic modelling tools where the first is called MALLET (Machine Learning for Language Toolkit, version 2.0.8.), which is an open source Java-based software package for natural language processing using Latent Dirichlet Allocation technique (LDA).[9]

Before using MALLET and in pre-preparation, the machined encoded OCR German-language press texts were cleaned and corrected manually (especially the recurring problem with some Unicode characters). In some cases, this included shortening the texts by excluding clearly irrelevant sections.

The model was then made with the 'optimise-interval' command, which sets each topic's probabilistic Dirichlet parameter that indicates the topic's proportion in the whole dataset, and gives a better fit to the data by allowing some topics to be more prominent. In addition, the number of topics to be identified by MALLET is set beforehand as there is no 'natural' number of topics in a corpus, but this part requires manual evaluation and iteration by the researchers.[10] Both MALLET and the DTM tool only mechanically detect topics and assign them numeric values, whereas identifying and naming the topics (that is, determining and labelling the thematic categories found by the machine reading) is something the human researcher has to carry out using manual reading. And this is an act of interpretation.

Topic Modelling with DTM

Within probabilistic topic modelling, LDA is a frequently used technique and its MALLET implementation has traditionally been the most popular tool to analyse historical corpuses. Ever since topic modelling was first introduced in the early 2000s, there have been new extensions that help to model temporal relationships. One shortcoming of the LDA method is that it assumes that the order of documents is irrelevant. But if we – as historians are often prone to – want to discover the evolution of topics over time, then we have to take the time sequence into account. DTM attempts to overcome this shortcoming and captures the dynamics of how topics emerge and change over time.[11]

DTM is designed to explicitly model the ways in which topics evolve over time and to give qualitative insights into the changing composition of the source material. However, it is not the only such tool available and it has also been subjected to critique for penalising large changes from year to year.[12] The DTM is a probabilistic time series model, which is designed to track and analyse the ways in which latent topics change over time within a large set of documents. For example, David M. Blei and John D. Lafferty demonstrated the functioning of DTM by investigating topics of the journal *Science* between 1880 and 2000.[13] Our case study is based on a small source corpus, which, as we will soon see, was one important factor in the output from the dynamic topic modelling. Because of the small size of the dataset, cleaning and filtering the data had a major impact on DTM's output. The more historical sources were pre-processed, the more stable the model became.

As mentioned above, few but not all text files were reviewed for common mistakes and in a few instances some mistakes were manually corrected. Python's Natural Language Toolkit (nltk) library was used for the pre-processing and filtering of the texts. Prior to passing on the text data to DTM tools, the text was processed using the following pre-processing pipeline:

1. **Punctuation and numbers removal.** Punctuation characters within and around all the words were deleted and all the other characters except alphabetic characters were removed.
2. **Stop words removal.** This is a common operation when processing text in any domain. The list of German stop words was initially taken from the nltk library and MALLET tool. This list was extended by reviewing the texts and some words deemed to be useless were then added to the list. Any words in the stop words list were removed in pre-processing.
3. **Stemming and lemmatising.** Stemming is the process by which a word is reduced to its base form and all the inflectional forms of a word are reduced to a single base stem. Using language dictionaries, lemmatisation converts a word to its base lemma. This is the word from which all the inflectional forms are derived. The base stem is then used by the lemmatisers to find the base lemma, which is then kept in the text.
4. **Classification.** The words were then classified into different parts-of-speech with the goal being to keep various nouns and verbs identified in the input texts. Words which belong to other parts-of-speech were removed.
5. **Rare words.** As a final step, the words which appear only once in the whole input corpus were also removed.

We then used Gensim (Python library) to run the DTM tool. After creating various outputs of models with 5 to 20 topics, as for the previous analysis using MALLET, we decided to limit the number of topics to 10. Like MALLET, DTM also gives keywords (that is, a cluster of words relevant to the topic), which help to identify the topic.

Source Material

The source material used in this study is a sub-dataset from the digital corpus Austrian Newspapers Online (ANNO), provided by the Austrian National Library (at http://anno.onb.ac.at). The digital ANNO collection contains around 20 million pages of German-speaking newspapers and periodicals that are available for full text searches.[14] The Austrian National Library at their ANNO-portal provides an OCR tool for machine encoded optically recognised text which, although not totally reliable and contains errors, can be used for the digital analysis.

According to the full text search engine of the ANNO portal, the word *Humanismus* (humanism) was mentioned 326 times in the press between 1808 and 1850.[15] Because the old German *Fraktur* typeface is challenging for OCR, the results should not be interpreted as entirely reliable, but as giving an indication of the scale of use, how much this word was circulated in the press. In some texts, humanism appeared only once in passing, while in others it was mentioned several times and discussed explicitly. Based on their relevance, length and readability, we have selected 95 key texts for topic modelling analysis (see Appendix 15.1). These texts include book reviews, articles, news, feuilleton writings and political reports, while reprints, short notices, adverts and obituaries have been excluded.

Figure 15.1 illustrates the publishing centres and various publications that make up the dataset. The graph is made with the Gephi visualisation application and it aims to depict the source material in a visually conceivable way. Moreover, Gephi is a frequently used software tool for network analysis, because it enables the portrayal and analysis of relationships or interaction between persons, entities and objects, such as geographical places or publications.[16] The objects (nodes) and their relationships (edges) can be presented in many different ways. In this case, the layout was made manually instead of choosing one of the most popular layout algorithms such as Force Atlas or Fruchterman Reingold. The nodes and edges tables were imported to Gephi as CSV files and in the edges table the connection between a publication and its place of publishing gained 'weight' in accordance to the amount of texts discussing humanism in that particular publication during the period between 1829 and 1850. The more humanism was mentioned, the thicker the line between a newspaper or a magazine and the city in which it was published. Accordingly, the strength of connections indicates which were the most important publishing centres

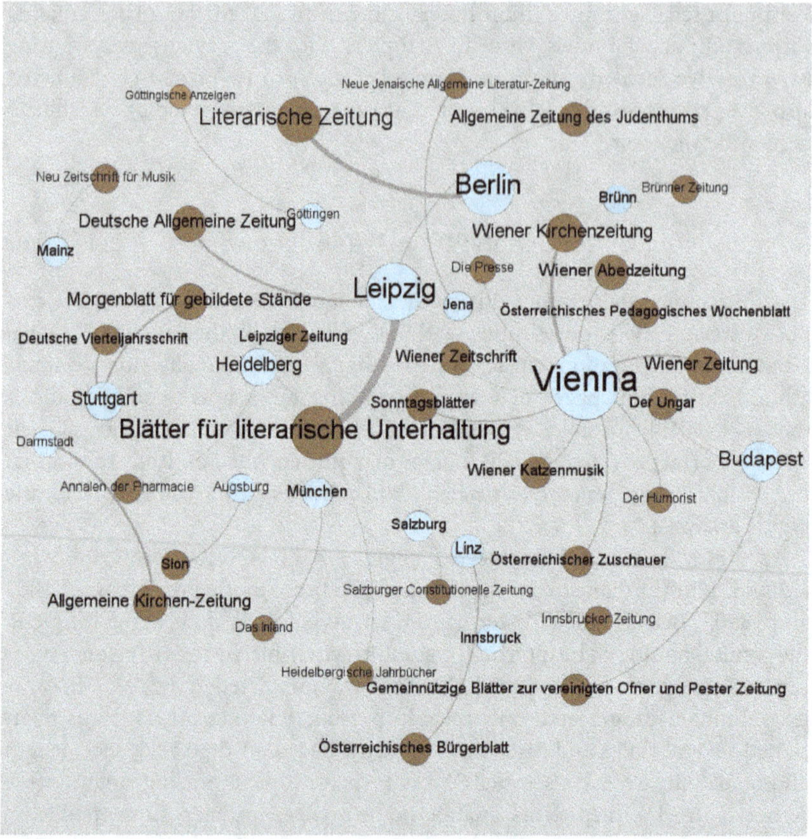

Figure 15.1: Network diagram of publications and publishing centres of the dataset. Source: Authors.

and highlights publications that most extensively dealt with humanism in this dataset. Even though the ANNO source corpus is partial and dominated by Austrian newspapers and magazines, Figure 15.1 shows that the early 19th-century discussion on humanism surpassed political borders within the German Confederation spreading in the area of fragmented German lands and German-speaking parts of the Habsburg Empire. Vienna, Leipzig and Berlin were the most important publishing centres and the literary journals *Blätter für literarische Unterhaltung* and *Literarische Zeitung* dealt with the topic most extensively, although the publications dealing with humanism ranged from daily newspapers to religious magazines and satirical journals.

German Humanism According to MALLET Topic Modelling

Initial details about MALLET are summarised in the previous section. Below are the eight topics in order of prevalence with their top words as discovered by MALLET when asked to determine the 10 most prevalent topics and as labelled (education, reformation, etc.) by us. The number of topics was chosen after experimenting with different kinds of models and 10 topics were chosen as a best way for modelling the source corpus, which was small and fragmented. Topic modelling usually involves filtering away so-called stop words, non-informative frequently appearing words such as articles, particles and pronouns. However, especially when it comes to creating a model with a small number of topics, pre-processing the data has a danger of compromising the results as the researcher makes decisions on removal of stop words according to her or his pre-understanding, thus projecting into the data certain presuppositions regarding what is important in the corpus.[17] Accordingly, in this model, no pre-filtering of stop words was carried out before the analysis, but two topics that contained only stop words were filtered out after creating the model. See Appendix 15.2 for the whole model.

Religion: fich menschen gott religion find juden zukunft religiösen gottes humanismus mensch christenthum christliche niht darum demokratie humanität christlichen christen theorie

Education: erziehung schulen lehrer sprache bildung seyn gymnasien unterricht realismus sprachen realschulen schüler jugend individuum wissenschaften anstalten schrift realschule

Revolution: wurde freiheit volk stadt wurden berlin revolution kammer bald volkes völker waren heute republik straßen preußen fast macht bürgerwehr haufen

Philosophy: fich philosophie ruge find nationalismus princip paris jahrbücher literatur preußen geschrieben briefe socialismus anfichten brief patriotismus rage artikel principien staatsanwalt

Reformation: kirche fich universitäten luther reformation staat lehre staats reform gemeinden schottischen glaubens bloß kirchen verfassung staate theologen lehrer wissenschaft hervor

Death penalty: todesstrafe sei abg verbrechen strafe habe amendement antrag könne man dieß gesetze redner verbrecher abgeschafft jury wolle abschaffung angenommen gegen

Press debate: dafs christlichen philologie gegner muss zeitung liberalismus sache sinne bedeutung gesinnung jedenfalls artikel presse giebt philologen meinung klassischenmonarchischen christliche

Social issues: fie the fich hamburg euch gesehen zigeuner habt bey ift diefe wiffen feine sprachen stadt armen glück schüler jhr their

The output from MALLET provides eight topics with different keywords. In the 'Education' topic, words like *Erziehung* (education/upbringing), *Schulen* (schools), *Lehrer* (teacher) and *Sprache* (language) are clustered together with such difficult-to-translate German concepts like *Bildung* and *Gymnasien*, which indicate that this topic is related to the educational debates about the role of humanism in the modern schooling system that were a very important issue in the era of comprehensive school reforms. After all, the concept of

Humanismus (humanism) was, as mentioned above, first coined as a pedagogical concept, fostering classical education and the study of classical languages.[18] The 'Reformation' topic, on the other hand, contains words like *Kirche* (church), *Universitäten* (universities), *Luther* (Luther) and *Reformation* (reformation), which give reason to believe that this topic deals with humanism historically in relation to Martin Luther and the reformation era.

However, in addition to these highly obvious and clear results, there are also topical word clusters which show a completely different kind of interpretation of humanism. The topic 'Philosophy', for instance, contains words like *Philosophie* (philosophy), *Ruge* (Ruge), *Nationalismus* (nationalism), *Princip* (principle) and *Paris* (Paris). All of these words are connected to the philosopher Arnold Ruge (1802–1880), who was also a political writer, associated with the Young Hegelians and Karl Marx, and known for his radical ideas that religion should be separated from politics and intellectual thinking. Ruge was one of the main figures who in the 1840s introduced a new interpretation of humanism as a political concept and his ideas were highly debated in the press.[19] For Ruge, humanism meant political emancipation from the old *ancien régime*. He incorporated humanism in democratic-republican ideology, which combined social critique with critique towards religion and growing nationalism. Humanism meant political, religious and social freedom, which was universal for the whole of mankind and superseded national borders. Accordingly, in *Geschichtliche Grundbegriffe*, Ruge's interpretation of humanism is called *kosmopolitischer Humanismus* (cosmopolitan humanism).[20]

This radical new political meaning of the concept of humanism is also visible in topics that dealt with social problems and political issues like the death sentence and the 1848–1849 revolution. For example, the topic labelled 'Social issues' contains keywords like *Zigouner* (gypsies), *Armen* (the poor), *Stadt* (city) and *Glück* (happiness). Again, the topic 'Death penalty' is clustering together words like *Todesstrafe* (death penalty), *Verbrechen* (felony), *Strafe* (punishment) and *Amendement* (amendment), which are all related to the debates around abolishment of the death penalty, which was a topical issue especially in Austria around 1849. Moreover, topic modelling of the dataset reveals a topic relating explicitly to the European revolutions in 1848–1849. This topic labelled with the title 'Revolution' contains the following keywords: *wurde* (came), *Freiheit* (freedom), *Volk* (people), *Stadt* (city), *Berlin* (Berlin), *Revolution* (revolution), *bald* (soon), *heute* (today), *Republik* (republic) *Straßen* (streets), *Macht* (power), *Bürgerwehr* (militia) and *Haufen* (pile). This topic, especially, indicates how humanism became a political concept in the 1840s when both early socialists and liberals adopted humanism in their political language as they demanded political emancipation from the old regime.[21]

This result demonstrates the diversity of the meanings given to humanism in the early 19th-century press. In addition to educational debates, humanism also appeared in the discussions surrounding social and moral issues, law and politics. In fact, the extremely diverse topics of humanism indicate a pervasive reorganising of ideas related to the human being and his or her place in the universe in the post-Napoleonic era, in which the liberal bourgeoisie was gaining a new foothold in society at the same time that the Church and absolutist power were challenged in the aftermath of the French Revolution. This transformative era created new interpretations on how politics, religion, education and philosophical thinking should be organised in modern secularising society, and, despite the practices of censorship especially in Prussia and Austria,[22] the press played a major role in circulating these ideas among a growing readership.

Consequently, the vast processes of secularisation and modernisation help us to understand why the 'Religion' topic was the most dominant theme in the early 19th-century press discussion on humanism. This most prevalent topic contains many interesting keywords indicating how discourses surrounding religion, morality and politics were actually significantly entangled in the early 19th-century discussion on humanism. The clustering of words like *Menschen* (human being), *Gott* (god), *Religion* (religion), *Juden* (Jews), *Zukunft* (future), *Humanismus* (humanism), *Christenthum* (Christianity), *Demokratie* (democracy), *Humanität* (humanity) and *Theorie* (theory) is a good example of the interpretative challenges that take place when identifying and labelling topics that are not cohesive but multifaceted and extremely complex. We will examine the 'Religion' topic closer below using DTM. But first, we will locate which years this topic emerged most dominantly between 1829 and 1850.

Following the task of identifying topics, it is vital to also explore them and their meanings in the historical context in which they came to life. In other words, it is essential to acknowledge the temporality of the topics and study them from in a dynamic historical perspective. For example, the volume of the press was very different in 1829 and in 1850. Furthermore, the new Young Hegelian philosophical ideas and growing interest in social issues was part of the intellectual and social landscape of the 1840s and it goes without saying that the outbreak of the revolutions in 1848 was clearly a major historical event that impacted on the public discourse surrounding humanism.

Without additional programming, MALLET does not present the topics in relation to time. Yet, it is possible to inspect the dynamic temporal aspect of the topics by organising the dataset chronologically.[23] Accordingly, the files of the dataset were numbered from the oldest, in this case 1829, to the youngest, here 1850. This means that it is now possible to study how topics emerged and changed over time (Figure 15.2). In Figure 15.2, the two stop word topics are filtered out, presenting only the eight relevant topics.

We can now see the thematic trends and how the topic patterns change over time. The figure above indicates that before 1840 'Education' and 'Social issues' were important topics in relation to humanism, but in 1848 the topic 'Revolution' became dominant. In 1849, it was replaced as the leading topic by 'Death penalty', with 'Religion' following in prevalence. The 'Religion' topic gained importance especially immediately after the revolution, which could indicate a reaction to the turbulence and violence in 1848–1849. Yet, despite

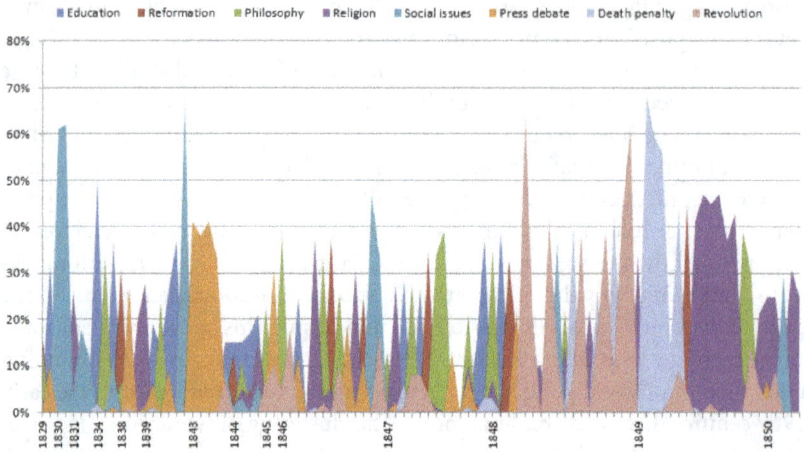

Figure 15.2: Annual allocation of topics. Source: Authors.

the chronological aspect, MALLET's results are always compressed and cannot give any further insight into the dynamics within the topics that have been discovered. In the next section, we will further analyse how dynamic topic modeling (DTM) can make it possible to gain insight about the dynamics within one singular topic.

Discovering Temporalisation of German Humanism with DTM

Preliminary details about DTM and text pre-processing details are mentioned above. The cleaning of the data had a major impact on the output of the model. At first, the results were very similar to the MALLET analysis and many topics seen before persisted. For example, humanism continued to emerge in relation to the topic of 'Religion' ['menschen', 'humanismus', 'humanität', 'zukunft', 'ste', 'stch', 'religion', 'wahrheit', 'bloß', 'demokratie', 'christenthum', 'recht', 'gegenwart', 'fich', 'wohl']. Also, the topics 'Education' ['bildung', 'mehr', 'erziehung', 'zeit', 'lehrer', 'jugend', 'realschulen', 'find', 'wissenschaft', 'sache', 'neuen', 'immer', 'gymnasien', 'zweck', 'mittel'], 'Death penalty' ['sei', 'verbrechen', 'abg', 'könne', 'redner', 'schon', 'antrag', 'amendement', 'angenommen', 'staat', 'dieß', 'abgeschafft', 'ab', 'be', 'abschaffung'] and 'Revolution' ['wurde', 'macht', 'völker', 'volk', 'geschichte', 'bald', 'freiheit', 'berlin', 'volkes', 'revolution', 'werk', 'wurden', 'je', 'regierung', 'tage'] were remarkably similar. However, there were also changes. Social issues and debates around Ruge's interpretation of humanism were more in the background and there was more than one category relating to religion and education.

Furthermore, with DTM, we had more fine-tuned results as the source corpus was divided into different time frames and keywords were arranged year by year. As the keywords appeared in a list from most important to least

1829	'menschen',	'humanismus',	'humanität',	'zukunft'
1830	'menschen',	'humanismus',	'humanität',	'zukunft'
1831	'menschen',	'humanismus',	'humanität',	'zukunft'
1832	'menschen',	'humanismus',	'humanität',	'zukunft'
1833	'menschen',	'humanismus',	'humanität',	'zukunft'
1834	'menschen',	'humanismus',	'humanität',	'zukunft'
1835	'menschen',	'humanismus',	'humanität',	'zukunft'
1836	'menschen',	'humanismus',	'humanität',	'zukunft'
1837	'menschen',	'humanismus',	'humanität',	'zukunft'
1838	'menschen',	'humanismus',	'zukunft',	'humanität'
1839	'menschen',	'humanismus',	'zukunft',	'humanität'
1840	'menschen',	'humanismus',	'zukunft',	'humanität'
1841	'menschen',	'zukunft',	'humanismus',	'humanität'
1842	'menschen',	'zukunft',	'humanität',	'humanismus'
1843	'menschen',	'zukunft',	'humanität',	'humanismus'
1844	'menschen',	'zukunft',	'humanität',	'humanismus'
1845	'menschen',	'zukunft',	'humanität',	'humanismus'
1846	'menschen',	'zukunft',	'humanität',	'humanismus'
1847	'zukunft',	'menschen',	'humanität',	'humanismus'
1848	'zukunft',	'menschen',	'humanismus',	'humanität'
1849	'zukunft',	'menschen',	'humanismus',	'humanität'
1850	'zukunft',	'menschen',	'humanismus',	'humanität'

Figure 15.3: Output from the DTM before data cleaning, including the four first keywords. Source: Authors.

important, it was possible to detect the ways in which the order of these keywords changed within one singular topic. The most striking new discovery with DTM was that there were cases in which words with temporal meaning such as *Zeit* (time) or *Zukunft* (future) became increasingly important towards mid-century. This discovery resonates strongly with the conceptual historian Reinhart Koselleck's famous argument that the early 19th century was a *Sattelzeit*, a period in which the notion of time changed radically and concepts became increasingly abstract and more future-oriented. Koselleck suggested that as modern concepts became more entangled with historical time, being associated increasingly with the past, the present and the future, the phenomena which previously were seen as static and unchanging became conceived as dynamic processes.[24]

To give an example, in Figure 15.3 we have the four most important words for the topic 'Religion', containing words like *Menschen* (human being), *Humanismus* (humanism), *Zukunft* (future), *Humanität* (humanity), *Religion* (religion), *Wahrheit* (truth), *Demokratie* (democracy), *Christenthum* (Christianity), *Recht* (justice) and *Gegenwart* (present), which are very similar to those words seen in the most prevalent 'Religion' topic in the MALLET results.

However, here the topic seems to be relating more to human beings and morality rather than religion. In addition, the meaning of the word *Zukunft* (future) is of special interest here, as its position changes radically between

1829	'menschen',	'gott',	'religion',	'humanismus',	'zukunft',
1830	'menschen',	'gott',	'religion',	'humanismus',	'zukunft',
1831	'menschen',	'gott',	'religion',	'humanismus',	'zukunft',
1832	'menschen',	'gott',	'religion',	'humanismus',	'zukunft',
1833	'menschen',	'gott',	'religion',	'humanismus',	'zukunft',
1834	'menschen',	'gott',	'religion',	'humanismus',	'zukunft',
1835	'menschen',	'gott',	'religion',	'humanismus',	'zukunft',
1836	'menschen',	'gott',	'religion',	'humanismus',	'zukunft',
1837	'menschen',	'gott',	'religion',	'humanismus',	'zukunft',
1838	'menschen',	'gott',	'religion',	'humanismus',	'zukunft',
1839	'menschen',	'gott',	'religion',	'humanismus',	'zukunft',
1840	'menschen',	'gott',	'religion',	'humanismus',	'zukunft',
1841	'menschen',	'gott',	'religion',	'humanismus',	'zukunft',
1842	'menschen',	'gott',	'religion',	'humanismus',	'zukunft',
1843	'menschen',	'gott',	'religion',	'humanismus',	'zukunft',
1844	'menschen',	'gott',	'religion',	'zukunft',	'humanismus',
1845	'menschen',	'gott',	'religion',	'zukunft',	'humanismus',
1846	'menschen',	'gott',	'religion',	'zukunft',	'humanismus',
1847	'menschen',	'gott',	'religion',	'zukunft',	'humanismus',
1848	'menschen',	'gott',	'religion',	'zukunft',	'humanismus',
1849	'menschen',	'gott',	'religion',	'zukunft',	'humanismus',
1850	'menschen',	'gott',	'religion',	'zukunft',	'humanismus',

Figure 15.4: Output from the DTM after data cleaning, including the five first keywords. Source: Authors.

1829 and 1850. Figure 15.3 shows the output from the DTM before data cleaning, including the four first keywords. In post-cleaning, the letters 'ste' were filtered out.

However, this striking change did not appear in all the outputs, but the more we removed stop words and filtered the data for better results, the more stable the topic appeared (Figure 15.4). In addition, the word God (*Gott*), which is missing in the first output together with religion (*Religion*), is now continuously the second most important word after human being (*Mensch*). The information about the proposition of each word within the topic indicates that changes were so minor that altering the script by removing stop words and removing words that appeared only once changed and stabilised the model to the extent that changes could no longer be seen in the order of the keywords.[25]

Yet, to give another example, the word *Zeit* (time) became increasingly important in another topic that included keywords such as *Wissenschaft* (science/knowledge) and *Erziehung* (education/upbringing). The change is visible both before and after filtering stop words. The Dirichlet parameter indicates that the weight of the word *Zeit* did not increase, but the growing importance resulted from the fact that the importance of the word *Wissenschaft* decreased radically around 1846.[26] This was a modest change, but it persisted in the outputs made before and after removing the stop words and carrying out other data filtering, such as removing words that appeared only once.

1829–1850
Philology
Church history
Philosophical tendencies
Revolution & Distribution of power
Political debate
Philosophy of science
Education of the Jews
Education
Religion, Morality & Relationship to God
Study of languages

Figure 15.5: Topics detected by the DTM tool after data cleaning. Source: Authors.

In the end, after data cleaning and filtering the historical sources, the DTM tool provided a list of the 10 most prevalent topics in the early 19th-century press (Figure 15.5). Yet, because of the short timeline and small size of the source corpus, the final output provided very static results and only very small changes within these topics were able to be discovered.

However, it is important to bear in mind that the dataset used in this case study was small. A larger dataset together with a potentially longer timeline would probably make it possible to detect and analyse more drastic changes over time. In any case, both of these examples illustrate that topic models are first and foremost probabilistic models providing estimates of the most salient discourse topics. Semantic changes are related to probabilistic proportional changes (in topic word list) and examining the probability distribution parameters (values associated with topic words in the output) is vital for understanding how these models work in practice.

Conclusions

This study has investigated the early 19th-century German press discourse on humanism, which has been an under-researched area to date. In this chapter, we have modelled the topics of humanism in the early 19th-century German-language press with MALLET and DTM. By analysing the evolution of the topics between 1829 and 1850, this chapter has explored the change of the discourse surrounding humanism in early 19th-century German-speaking Europe. Both topic modelling applications detected different topics among the text corpus and recognised different semantic categories in the early 19th-century German-language source material without any understanding of the substance or context of these texts.

Topic modelling contains various methods, which can be used for different purposes. As we have shown, topic modelling can provide assistance for historical research as a tool for analysis and interpretation. In this study, we created different topic models of a dataset that was relatively small and could be closely read in addition to distant reading. Both MALLET and the DTM tool not only enable us to identify thematic categories (that is, topics within the dataset), but they also make it possible to trace these topics back to file level. The outputs produced detailed results on how each topic appeared in each of the 95 texts of the dataset, which makes it possible to trace topics back to the level of individual articles for close reading analysis. If one is especially interested in, say, 'Revolution' as a press topic, one could select and read all the news articles and other texts in which this topic appeared during the time frame of 1829 to 1850. This kind of assistance is invaluable for mapping and assessing sources, which is often laborious and time-consuming.

At the same time, our study also sheds light on the potential benefits and risks of topic modelling within historical research. From a methodological perspective, it is important to bear in mind that although topic modelling might produce highly compelling results, the analysis of these results demands time, skills and caution. One has to remember that results can vary depending upon the input topic number, size of the dataset, specific tool used for topic modelling, data cleaning and methods of filtering. Topic modelling provides assistance for historical research as a tool for analysis and interpretation, but the output of a topic modelling process is not a result in itself and needs to be studied further for reliable conclusions. Topic modelling results can answer a historian's intuitive questions by providing focus and direction to the analysis of historical corpuses through traditional methods of historical inquiry, source criticism, close reading and contextualisation. Perhaps even more importantly, topic modelling has the potential to challenge established patterns of thought and underlying presumptions by providing a completely different angle on historical sources.

Appendix 15.1: Dataset

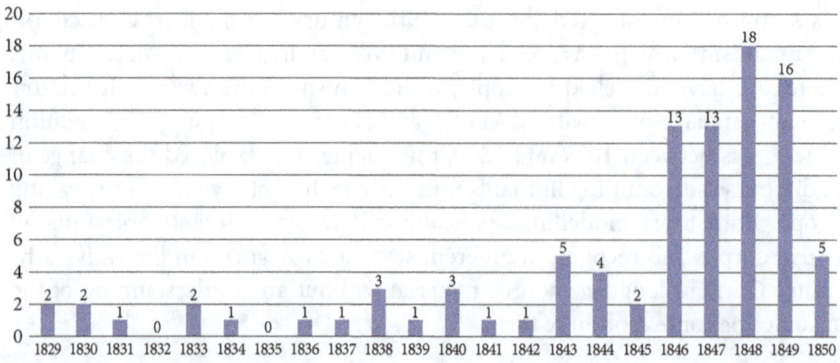

Appendix 15.2: MALLET Tool

Topic ID	Topic label	Dirichlet parameter	Keywords
0	[EDUCATION]	0,12609	erziehung schulen lehrer sprache bildung seyn gymnasien unterricht realismus sprachen realschulen schüler jugend individuum wissenschaften anstalten schrift realschule
1	[REFORMATION]	0,07934	kirche fich universitäten luther reformation staat lehre staats reform gemeinden schottischen glaubens bloß kirchen verfassung staate theologen lehrer wissenschaft hervor
2	[PHILOSOPHY]	0,09784	fich philosophie ruge find nationalismus princip paris jahrbücher literatur preußen geschrieben briefe socialis-mus anfichten brief patriotismus rage artikel principien staatsanwalt
3	[RELIGION]	0,18337	fich menschen gott religion find juden zukunft religiösen gottes humanismus mensch christenthum christliche niht darum demokratie humanität christlichen christen theorie
4	[SOCIAL ISSUES]	0,05893	fie the fich hamburg euch gesehen zigeuner habt bey ift diefe wiffen feine sprachen stadt armen glück schüler jhr their
5	[STOP WORDS]	1,43466	mit aber nur man hat noch diese zeit welche haben mehr gegen denn selbst uns alle ohne ihm sondern leben
6	[PRESS DEBATE / CONTROVERSY	0,06722	dafs christlichen philologie gegner muss zeitung liberalismus sache sinne bedeutung gesinnung jedenfalls artikel presse giebt philologen meinung klassischen monarchischen christliche
7	[LAW / DEATH PENALTY]	0,07172	todesstrafe sei abg verbrechen strafe habe amendement antrag könne man dieß gesetze redner verbrecher abgeschafft jury wolle abschaffung angenommen gegen
8	[REVOLUTION]	0,11352	wurde freiheit volk stadt wurden berlin revolution kammer bald volkes völker waren heute republik straßen preußen fast macht bürgerwehr haufen
9	[STOP WORDS]	0,07725	fich ift find feine fein diefe diefer feiner fei fondern nnd felbfi ihm nichts zwifchen diefem fchon lehre fehr wol

Appendix 15.3: DTM Tool

10 topics found by DTM after data cleaning:

Philology: philologie alterthums wissenschaft studien zeit bedeutung artikel klassischen richtung gymnasien weise zeigt damals gewinnen darauf
Church history: kirche deutschen humanismus ganz zeit Deutschland große ruge macht geschichte staat bald reformation freiheit princip hätte jahrhunderts
Philosophical tendencies: tendenz so deutfchen bey welt bildet herr wißen vermögen gerade briefe feuerbach menfchen diese
Revolution & Distribution of power: schon geht volk bleibt freiheit berlin verbrechen hand viele ersten fall davon gut
Political debate: mittel freien entwickelung liberalismus gemacht monarchischen indessen ganz bedeutung zeit glaubens weder regierung
Philosophy of science: geist denen idee lebens welt einzelnen vielmehr leben einzelnen philosophie schule recht staat partei
Education of the Jews: schon juden wenig sinne schule allgemeinen mag allerdings beziehung irgend sagen christlichen öffentlichen wenigstens
Education: bildung zeit erziehung schon humanismus schüler leben lehrer immer seyn kraft besonders deutsche ganz wohl allein aufgabe
Religion, Morality & Relationship to God: got zukunft humanität menschlichenleben wahre christenthum mensch freiheit demokratie wahrheit religiösen sagen gewalt welt politik
Study of languages: sprache sprachen zeit realschulen gesehen welt bildung amburg jugend schulen find gymnasien erfahrung habt werke neuen element

Notes

1 See further Erling 2014: esp. 58–59, and Jacobi, Atteveldt & Welbers 2015.
2 Blei & Lafferty 2006.
3 The concept of *Humanismus* was coined in 1808 when Niethammer used it in his book *Der Streit des Philanthropinismus und Humanismus in der Theorie des Erziehungs-Unterrichts unsrer Zeit*. However, the tradition of German humanism dates back to the 15th and 16th centuries, when the ideas of Italian renaissance humanism spread across Europe. Accordingly, such concepts as *humanitas* and *studia humanitatis* are much older origin, dating back to antiquity.
4 See further Bollenbeck 1994: 142–155.
5 In addition to Georg Bollenbeck's book, the most extensive studies discussing 19th-century German humanism are by Landfester 1988 and van Bommel 2015.
6 The book industry and the press were both growing in volume in the first part of the century, expanding even more dramatically as the 19th century neared its close. See further Erling & Tatlock 2014. Cf. St. Clair 2004.

[7] See further Brauer & Fridlund 2013: 159.
[8] Cf. Steinmetz & Freeden 2017: 2, 5.
[9] LDA (Latent Dirichlet allocation) was developed by David Blei and others in 2003 and MALLET (MAchine Learning for LanguagE Toolkit) was written by Andrew McCallum. For more information, see http://mallet.cs.umass.edu/about.php. See also *The Programming Historian* tutorial on MALLET, Graham, Weingart & Milligan 2012.
[10] The model provides as output three different files: topic 'state' assigning each word in the text to a topic, 'topic keys' consisting of the top words for each identified topic and the topic 'composition' consisting of allocation of percentage of every topic in each of the 95 files that were included in the analysis.
[11] DTM, Blei & Lafferty 2006.
[12] Hall, Jurafsly & Manning 2008: 364.
[13] Blei & Lafferty 2006.
[14] See ANNO webpage.
[15] See further, Hakkarainen 2020: 27–28.
[16] See further, e.g., Cordell 2015.
[17] Cf. Schonfield, Magnusson & Mimno 2017.
[18] See further Bollenbeck 1994: 142–155; van Bommel 2015.
[19] See, e.g., Anon. 1846; Anon. 1 & 4 August 1847; Anon. 1848.
[20] Bödeker 1982: 1123–1124.
[21] Ibid.:1121–1126. See also Hansson 1999: 77–106.
[22] See further Dussel 2011: 25–34; Stöber 2014: 141–142.
[23] Cf. Blevins 2010.
[24] Koselleck 1985. See also Steinmetz & Freeden 2017: 2, 5.
[25] However, even after filtering there was a minor increase in the percentage. In 1829, the proportional number for the word '*Zukunft*' was 0.010673; in 1850, it was 0.016537.
[26] In 1829, the proportional number for the word '*Wissenschaft*' was 0.01164-2238616473554; in 1850, it was 0.006096759758556382.

References

Anon. (1846, 7 January). Arnold Ruge und sein neuester Standpunkt. *Blätter für literarische Unterhaltung.*

Anon. (1847, 1 August). Arnold Ruge: Politischer Bilder aus der Zeit. *Blätter für literarische Unterhaltung.*

Anon. (1847, 4 August). Arnold Ruge: Politischer Bilder aus der Zeit. *Blätter für literarische Unterhaltung.*

Anon. (1848, 11 January). Polemische Briefe von Arnold Ruge: Reihe von 'Offenen Briefen zur Vertheidigung des Humanismus'. *Blätter für literarische Unterhaltung.*

ANNO – Austrian Newspapers Online (Austrian National Library). Retrieved from http://anno.onb.ac.at/faq.htm

Blei, D. M., & Lafferty, J. D. (2006, 25–29 June). *Dynamic Topic Models.* Paper presented at the ICML '06 Proceedings of the 23rd international conference on machine learning (pp. 113–120). Pittsburgh. Retrieved from https://mimno.infosci.cornell.edu/info6150/readings/dynamic_topic_models.pdf

Blevins, C. (2010). *Topic modeling Martha Ballard's diary.* Retrieved from https://www.cameronblevins.org/posts/topic-modeling-martha-ballards-diary/

Bollenbeck, G. (1994). *Bildung und Kultur: Glanz und Elend eines deutschen Deutungsmusters.* Frankfurt am Main: Insel.

Brauer, R., & Fridlund, M. (2013). Historizing topic models: a distant reading of topic modeling texts within historical studies. In L. V. Nikiforova & N. V. Nikiforova (Eds.), *Cultural research in the context of 'digital humanities': proceedings of international conference 3–5 October 2013, St Petersburg* (pp. 152–163). St. Petersburg: Herzen State Pedagogical University and Publishing House Asterion. Retrieved from https://matsfridlund.files.wordpress.com/2014/04/publ2013brauerfridlundconf.pdf

Bödeker, H. E. (1982). Menschheit, Humanismus, Humanität. In O. Brunner, W. Conze & R. Koselleck (Eds.), *Geschichtliche Grundbegriffe: Historisches Lexikon zur politisch-sozialen Sprache in Deutschland*, Vol. 3: *H-Me* (pp. 1063–1128). Stuttgart: Klett-Cotta.

Cordell, R. (2015). Reprinting, circulation, and the network author in antebellum newspapers. *American Literary History, 3*(27), 417–445. DOI: https://doi.org/10.1093/alh/ajv028

Dussel, K. (2011). *Deutsche Tagespresse im 19. und 20. Jahrhundert.* 2nd edn. Berlin: Lit Verlag.

Erling, M. (2014). The location of literary history: topic modelling, network analysis, and the German novel, 1731–1864. In M. Erling & L. Tatlock (Eds.), *Distant readings: topologies of German culture in the long nineteenth century* (pp. 55–90). New York, NY: Camden House.

Erling, M., & Tatlock, L. (2014). Introduction: 'distant reading' and the historiography of nineteenth-century German literature. In M. Erling & L. Tatlock (Eds.), *Distant readings: topologies of German culture in the long nineteenth century* (pp. 1–25). New York, NY: Camden House.

Graham S., Weingart, S., & Milligan, I. (2012). Getting started with topic modeling and MALLET. *The Programming Historian* tutorial on MALLET. *The Programming Historian, 1.* Retrieved from https://programminghistorian.org/lessons/topic-modeling-and-mallet

Hakkarainen, H. (2020). Contagious humanism in early nineteenth-century German-language press. *Contributions to the History of Concepts* 3(15), 22–46. DOI: https://doi.org/10.3167/choc.2020.150102

Hall, D., Jurafsly, D., & Manning, C. D. (2008). Studying the history of ideas using topic models. In *EMNLP '08 Proceedings of the Conference on Empirical Methods in Natural Language Processing* (pp. 363–371). Honolulu, Hawaii. Retrieved from https://dl.acm.org/citation.cfm?id=1613763

Hansson, J. (1999). *Humanismens kris: Bildningsideal och kulturkritik i Sverige 1848–1933*. Stockholm: Brutus Östlings Bokförelag Symposion.

Jacobi, C., van Atteveldt, W., & Welbers, K. (2015). Quantitative analysis of large amounts of journalistic texts using topic modelling. *Digital Journalism,* 1(4), 89–106. DOI: https://doi.org/10.1080/21670811.2015.1093271

Koselleck, R. (1985). *Futures past: on the semantics of historical time*. Translated by K. Tribe. Cambridge, MA: MIT Press.

Landfester, M. (1988). *Humanismus und Gesellschaft im 19. Jahrhundert*. Darmstadt: Wissenschaftliche Buchgesellschaft.

Schonfield, A., Magnusson, M., & Mimno, D. (2017). Pulling out the stops: rethinking stopword removal for topic models. In *Proceedings of the 15th Conference of the European Chapter of the Association for Computational Linguistics*, Vol. 2: *Short papers*. Retrieved from http://aclweb.org/anthology/E17-2069

St. Clair, W. (2004). *The reading nation in the Romantic period*. Cambridge: Cambridge University Press.

Steinmetz, W., & Freeden, M. (2017). Introduction: conceptual history. In W. Steinmetz, M. Freeden & J. Fernández-Sebastián (Eds.), *Conceptual history in the European space* (pp. 1–46). New York, NY: Berghahn Books.

Stöber, R. (2014). *Deutsche Pressegeschichte*. 3rd edn. Munich: UVK Verlagsgesellschaft Konstanz.

van Bommel, B. (2015). *Classical humanism and the challenge of modernity: debates on classical education in 19th century Germany*. Berlin: De Gruyter.

CHAPTER 16

Manuscripts, Qualitative Analysis and Features on Vectors

An Attempt for a Synthesis of Conventional and Computational Methods in the Attribution of Late Medieval Anti-Heretical Treatises

Reima Välimäki, Aleksi Vesanto, Anni Hella, Adam Poznański and Filip Ginter

Introduction

Authorship and originality were tricky things in medieval literature and documents. They were written in a culture of imitation rather than originality. The Latin word *auctoritas* could mean both an author and their authority, usually both combined. *Auctoritas* had initially meant the quality by which a person can be trusted. Consequently, it came to mean the authoritative status of a person and further that of their writings.[1] So, the 'author' was not just any writer whose texts were read, but the modern equivalent to their status would be something like that of Judith Butler in gender studies or Max Weber in sociology. Often, only writers meriting the status of *auctoritas* were explicitly cited, others

How to cite this book chapter:
Välimäki, R., Vesanto, A., Hella, A., Poznański, A., & Ginter, F. (2020). Manuscripts, qualitative analysis and features on vectors: An attempt for a synthesis of conventional and computational methods in the attribution of late medieval anti-heretical treatises. In M. Fridlund, M. Oiva, & P. Paju (Eds.), *Digital histories: Emergent approaches within the new digital history* (pp. 279–301). Helsinki: Helsinki University Press. https://doi.org/10.33134/HUP-5-16

silently borrowed and, in modern terms, plagiarised. Thus, it is not uncommon to find late medieval theological treatises where long passages are copied from other high and late medieval works, but only patristic sources and the most important medieval theologians such as Bernard of Clairvaux are named. As the 'authorship' in medieval discourse was more related to responsibility over content than style or form, we can find very original literary works written under the term 'compilation'.[2] Some of these compilations circulated under the name of an authoritative figure, such as Augustine, and were generally considered to convey his thoughts, even if the actual content contained very little of his original works. Furthermore, scribes and secretaries were often employed in the actual composition of the final work, creating a further layer of stylistic authorship in a text.[3] Due to these characteristics, the scholarship of medieval literature has for a long time recognised that the role of a compiler and even copyist was often comparable and at times surpassed that of an *auctor*.[4] Finally, many texts circulated anonymously or under an early modern misattribution.

In this chapter, we discuss one such complicated case of medieval authorship, an anti-heretical treatise known as the *Refutatio errorum*, written in the 1390s in German-speaking Europe. It has many of the characteristics described above. It is of compilatory nature, containing passages from different sources, very few of which are named in the text itself. It has no prologue or comparable section, where someone would claim their authorship over the text. Instead, the whole treatise is very practical, intended to provide information, but not to flaunt with rhetorical abilities of its composer. For a long time, the treatise was considered anonymous, until R. Välimäki provided contentual, structural and codicological evidence linking the treatise to the inquisitor Petrus Zwicker, who also authored a more famous anti-heretical work entitled *Cum dormirent homines*.[5] As is usually the case with reattribution of a medieval work, the conclusions are not based on single evidence, but on a combination of mutually enforcing pieces of evidence (described below). The purpose of this chapter is to add a new element to the analysis: computational authorship attribution using a Support Vector Machine (SVM). We discuss the results of the computer classification in relation to qualitative analysis of the text. The aim is to find out if computational methods provide added value to conventional authorship attribution of a medieval text. Or, could one claim that the computational methods are to be regarded as superior to qualitative interpretation by an expert human reader?

Computational authorship attribution can be considered a sub-category of style-based document authentication (*Echtheitskritik*),[6] and the first attempts to apply computational methods in the attribution tasks of Latin literature were in the 1970s.[7] After that, there was a lull in computational study of classical and medieval literature with a few exceptions,[8] but since the late 1990s and especially in the past five years several studies have demonstrated that computational authorship attribution can be a powerful tool in the recognition of classical and medieval authors.[9] As perhaps symptomatic to the whole field of digital humanities, the first publications of this new wave of computational authorship studies have concentrated on developing the methodology itself, and results have been published mainly in digital humanities journals. At the same time, the attribution of new texts to classical and medieval authors goes on with little regard to the results of computational stylistics,[10] and some recent publications even claim that statistical stylometry has fallen out of favour.[11] Although such a claim betrays lacking knowledge of one's research field, digital humanities scholars are not entirely blameless. Very few publications have tried to bridge the gap between discussions on authorship in the fields of literature studies and history, and in the computational linguistics respectively. Remarkable exceptions are Jeroen de Gussem's recent article on trails of Nicholas of Montiéramey's secretarial style in Bernard of Clairvaux's writings, as well as Mike Kestemont and colleagues' study on collaborative authorship of Hildegard of Bingen and Guibert of Gembloux.[12]

Consequently, computational analysis can raise suspicion among humanities scholars trained in qualitative methods. Machine learning or other branches of computational text classification may appear as radically new ways of analysing sources that bypass the human expertise (and are therefore terrifying). This they, however, are not. Although utilising computational capacity and handling amounts of data that far surpass the abilities of any human individual, the computational authorship attribution uses stylistic features that have been long since recognised as marks of authorship. A. Mutzenbecher prepared a new edition of Maximus of Turin's sermons at the beginning of the 1960s and defined 16 criteria (some with several sub-categories), which he divided into four slightly overlapping groups: (1) external evidence, (2) biblical quotations and their exposition, (3) style and (4) sources. Some of his criteria were primary, some secondary. An authentic sermon had to fulfil two primary criteria and several secondary criteria.[13]

For the purposes of this chapter, it is not necessary to explain what all of these were. It is sufficient to note that many of Mutzenbecher's criteria were purely qualitative, such as the theological topics Maximus typically discussed, but especially criteria for the introduction and exposition of the biblical citations (numbers 6 to 8) and criterion 13, linguistic-stylistic characteristics, include features that are similar to stylistic features used in computational authorship attribution: word uni- and bigrams formed of function words and other very common expressions (for example, *enim, ex quo, hoc est, quanto magis, sed dicit, ego dico, mirum est*).[14] Mutzenbecher was well aware that these stylistic features appeared in almost all other authors in addition to Maximus, and that none of them could individually constitute authorship, 'but if several of them support each other reciprocally, their relationship might express something typical.'[15] Computational authorship attribution does precisely that: it uses features that appear in almost all authors, but with different emphasis. To put it simply: it is the combination of all the significant stylistic features in comparison to their combination in other authors that determines authorship. A computer, however, is not limited to a few obvious stylistic features of an author, but can handle thousands and millions of these in a systematic and repeatable way.

The *Refutatio Errorum* and Its Redactions

The test case in this study is a text known as the *Refutatio errorum*. It is a polemical description of the Waldensians, a religious group persecuted as heretics by the Catholic Church in the Middle Ages and early modern period. In the 1390s, a series of inquisitions and other trials were directed against the group in German-speaking Europe,[16] and the *Refutatio* was written as part of the literary polemics accompanying the persecution. The treatise gives a view of Waldensianism very similar to that of the better known polemical treatise against the Waldensians, *Cum dormirent homines* (henceforth, CDH), written by one of the most important inquisitors of the late 14th century, the Celestine provincial Petrus Zwicker. The *Refutatio* is clearly a representative of the same era and state of knowledge about the Waldensians as the CDH. It has been commented on by scholars much less than the CDH, quite likely because the only available printed version, edited by Jacob Gretser together with the CDH (1613/1677), is obviously incomplete. It has 10 chapters, but the text stops abruptly in the middle of the tenth chapter.[17]

Among the scholars, there has been confusion rather than actual disagreement about the *Refutatio*'s authorship. For a long time, everyone was reluctant to make definite claims about its authors. In his groundbreaking studies on the CDH, P. Biller did not suggest any author or dating for the *Refutatio*, but seems to have held the view that the two treatises were *not* written by the same author, that is Zwicker. In fact, Biller uses the common manuscript tradition of the *Refutatio* and CDH as an argument against the attribution of the CDH to Peter von Pillichsdorf, the author suggested by Gretser in his 17th-century edition. The argument runs as follows: Gretser's misattribution was based on the now lost Tegernsee manuscript, which included the CDH and a short anti-Waldensian treatise by Pillichsdorf, who is the only author mentioned in the manuscript. This consequently led Gretser to propose Pillichsdorf as the author of both these treatises treating the same topic. According to Biller, this is a parallel case to that of the several manuscripts, including the CDH and the *Refutatio*. These too were two different treatises on the same subject, but were treated as one by both medieval scribes and modern compilers of manuscript catalogues. Biller did not state anything explicit concerning the authorship of the *Refutatio*, calling it and Zwicker's CDH only 'two tracts on similar material'.[18] They do indeed cover very much the same material, and because of this P. Segl has tentatively proposed that these two treatises originated from the same hand.[19] E. Cameron describes the treatise very vaguely, but evidently treats it as a product of the 1390s, at one point calling it 'a third treatise from Zwicker's circle'.[20] A. Patschovsky has also associated the *Refutatio* loosely with Zwicker, without making any definite claims about its authorship.[21] In other words, there has been a vague suspicion that Petrus Zwicker, or someone close to him, wrote the treatise.

To further complicate the study of this text, the only available printed editions are based on a text that is anything but representative of the manuscript tradition of the *Refutatio*. As noted, Jacob Gretser printed the tract in the 17th century from a manuscript that ends abruptly in the middle of Chapter 10. I. von Döllinger's 19th-century edition from the same manuscripts does not help, but adds further confusion, as the order of the chapters is mixed in the edition, and material not belonging to the *Refutatio* is inserted among the text.[22] An analysis of all the preserved 19 manuscripts of the work by Välimäki has demonstrated that the edited version of the texts does not concur with the main manuscript tradition, that is the most common and widely circulated medieval text. All in all, Välimäki found four different redactions of the *Refutatio errorum*. Of these, Redaction 1 is by far the most common, with 13 manuscripts. It is also the only redaction accompanying Zwicker's better known and more popular treatise, the *Cum dormirent homines*. The two texts appear together in eight manuscripts. In comparison, the text printed by Gretser in the 17th century is a late and incomplete redaction (Välimäki's Redaction 4) represented by only two medieval manuscripts.[23]

In addition to collation of the *Refutatio*'s manuscript tradition, Välimäki has also proposed that the treatise can be attributed to Petrus Zwicker. The two works present a very similar view on the Waldensians; they both follow similar structure of polemical refutation by presenting heretical propositions and Catholic counter-arguments, mainly based on biblical quotations. The most important pieces of evidence for the common authorship are the sources cited in these two works. In the CDH, Zwicker quotes almost exclusively the Bible in support of his arguments. The single exception to the rule is a reference to Boethius' *Consolation of Philosophy*. The same quote can be found in almost the exact same form in the *Refutatio errorum*. In addition, the author of the *Refutatio* had direct access to Moneta of Cremona's 13th-century anti-heretical treatise *Adversus Catharos et Valdenses*. The treatise was very rare north of the Alps, but Petrus Zwicker used it when composing the CDH. The final rare source implying the authorship of Zwicker is a misquotation of Ezekiel 33.12 in the *Refutatio*. The exact form of this quotation comes from the legal consultations on the case against the goldsmith Heynuš Lugner in the late 1330s or early 1340s, transmitted in two manuscripts, a Bohemian inquisitor's manual Linz MS 177, and another, St. Florian, MS XI 234, which is copied from the first manuscript. The Linz manual was once owned by Petrus Zwicker and the St. Florian manual was copied from his own inquisitor's manual. Ergo, the author of the *Refutatio* had access to a rare text, which has certain manuscript circulation only in connection to Petrus Zwicker.[24]

Texts for the Analysis and Pre-processing

Next, we analyse the two most important redactions of the *Refutatio* with computational classification in order to verify Zwicker's authorship. The redactions selected for the classification are the most common and longest Redaction 1 and Redaction 4 representing the version in Gretser's edition. The text of Redaction 4 is taken from a manuscript Augsburg, Universtitätsbiliothek MS 338 (TEST1) as well as Gretser's edition (TEST2). Redaction 1 is transcribed from the manuscript Vienna, Österreichische Nationalbibliothek (ÖNB), MS 1588 (TEST3). All texts are long enough for a reliable authorship attribution, from around 5,500 words in TEST2 to over 9,000 words in TEST3. We excluded Redactions 2 and 3, both extant in a single manuscript and not close to the original text. Neither of these redactions is representative of the medieval or modern reception of the work.

We trained the classifier with Petrus Zwicker's CDH (around 23,000 words). The text we used comes from the same Gretser's edition as one of the tested versions of the *Refutatio*. The reference corpus for training our classifier consisted of late ancient and medieval anti-heretical polemical treatises, which is the genre of both Zwicker's CDH and the *Refutatio*. In total, this training data has around 600,000 words. The emphasis is on medieval texts, and the corpus includes three works that are almost contemporary to Zwicker's texts: Wasmud von Homburg's *Tractatus contra hereticos*, an anonymous *Attendite a falsis prophetis* and the already mentioned Peter von Pillichsdorf's *Contra Pauperes de Lugduno*. In addition, the most important source and stylistic model for Zwicker's CDH, Moneta of Cremona's *Adversus Catharos et Valdenses*, is included. From Moneta's very long treatise, we selected only Book 5, where many of the anti-Waldensian arguments are presented. Alone, Book 5 has over 120,000 words, and including all 400,000 words from the whole treatise would have created an imbalanced reference corpus. The complete corpus with bibliographical information is in Appendix 16.1. The data is available at our GitHub page in masked form only to protect copyrights of recent editions used in the corpus.[25]

The dataset we use is far from easy and common in authorship attribution tasks. It is a mixed corpus of different edition and transcription standards, which is a problem for feature selection. Even though character n-grams are widely used as features in text classification, recent computational studies on the authorship of classical and medieval texts have preferred lemma-level approach and function word analysis over character n-grams or plain text.[26] This is partly due to the orthographical variation in medieval Latin. The effects of orthographical variation are more marked when the features used are a few dozen function words. However, as our classifications are based on a much more complex set of features, the effect of single 'bad' features for the end result is minimal. Using word uni- and bi-grams from plain text, as well as character n-grams, also has significant benefits in Latin. It gives access to stylistic solutions below the word level, such as the author's decision to use the subjunctive instead of the indicative.[27]

We solved the most common issues of different editorial principles and orthographical variation with simple normalisation rules:

u → v
j → i
y → i
ae → e
oe → e
char → car (to solve variation charitas vs. caritas)
wa → va (to solve variation ewangelium / evangelium and waldenses / valdenses)

These solve the majority of orthographical variation caused by editorial and scribal conventions and the differences of medieval and classical Latin without masking potentially significant stylistic features. In addition to orthographical normalisation, in the pre-processing phase we cleaned the texts from editorial additions such as page numbers and chapter titles (unless part of the original). Punctuation, numerals and single characters were removed. From early medieval texts, we naturally cleaned the references to bible books and verses (which were added by later editors), but in late medieval texts, most notably Zwicker's own treatise, these are part of the original and were thus preserved. The pre-processing was done automatically, but confirmed with sanity checks.

However, the transcripts from medieval manuscripts have much more variation than edited texts. While orthographical habits and grammatical mistakes of individuals are excellent stylistic features when one is dealing with autographs, in medieval manuscript culture such variation is noise in data. We are usually not interested in writing conventions of an individual scribe, but those of the author or compiler of the work. Even the usual orthographical variation of late medieval manuscripts is challenging to normalise without also masking potentially significant stylistic features.[28] Thus, in addition to solving the question of Zwicker's authorship, we experimented with the data in order to find a relatively effortless way to pre-process and analyse such a corpus with a computer. The expected results from our dataset are as follows:

1. If the pre-processing and feature selection are able to overcome the orthographical challenges, all test cases of the *Refutatio* should be classified in a similar way. We expect that they are classified as Zwicker's works together with the CDH (values over 0).
2. All other works should get values below 0 in the classification.
3. If Peter von Pillichsdorf's treatise from Gretser's edition is classified together with Zwicker's works, the early modern editorial solutions have more weight more than medieval authorship.

Computational Authorship Attribution: Methods

The puzzle we set out to solve is: Did Petrus Zwicker write the *Refutatio errorum*? In authorship attribution, this is called a verification problem: we do not have a closed set of candidates, but one suspected author.[29] We constructed the verification problem as a simple binary classification, where Zwicker's treatise forms one class and all other authors in the training material a second class. The classifier was trained with this material, and the versions of the *Refutatio* were presented as a test case. We use the two corpora combined as training data for the classifier, while the test cases form the test data. The different redactions of the *Refutatio* are each treated as a separate test case.

Here, we present an overview of the methods. For technical details and code, please consult our project repository.[30] For the classification, we use a linear SVM, which is a simple yet effective classifier and has traditionally been applied in text classification tasks.[31] The SVM works by learning a weight for every feature from the training data, so as to maximise the decision margin between the two classes. The weight being positive or negative is an indication of which class the feature is potentially associated with, although one needs to exercise caution when comparing features in isolation based on their weight. The features we use with the SVM are word unigrams and bigrams. In other words, we train the classifier with the training data to recognise the features typical and atypical of Petrus Zwicker's style. After that, the test cases are classified, and the output is a value indicating how much (positive) or how little (negative) the sum of weighted features in each test case resembles the class (Zwicker). The values are represented on a scale between −1 and 1.

The value and the decision are largely useless in isolation if we cannot be certain that the classifications are valid overall. Here, we apply the standard technique of cross-validation using the training data, which provides us with an estimate of the classification accuracy and therefore the reliability of our results on the actual test documents.[32]

The classifier we use is by nature undiscriminating when it comes to the features. It does not care which features are used, as long as they increase the training accuracy. In authorship attribution tasks, this would ideally be features that describe the author's way of writing, such as the usage of function words. Even within a single genre as in our training data, however, the particular topic of each text affects the results. We run the classification to unmasked data, and among the 10 strongest positive features five included 'Waldensians' in some form.[33] A classification from such features is based only partly on an author's style, and the topic of the texts heavily distorts the results. Therefore, we must mask topic words so as to not let the classifier focus purely on the topic of the texts instead of the author's style. To this end, we calculated the thousand most common words in post-classical (Christian) Latin.[34] Any word not in the calculated word list will be masked. This has been shown to drastically increase the accuracy of cross-genre classifications, as it forces the classifier to learn author-specific rather than topic-specific features.[35] This method does not completely remove topic words, but it only leaves the ones that appear regularly across different genres. In the following, we concentrate on results from the classification in the masked data.

Comparing the Results

The classification from the SVM using masked data is presented in Table 16.1 and in Figure 16.1.

The results were both expected and unexpected. First of all, the classification confirms that also from a stylistic perspective Petrus Zwicker is the author of the *Refutatio errorum*. All redactions, whether transcripts from manuscripts or the text from Gretser's edition, were classified as Zwicker's texts with a clear margin to other works. The exception here is the short treatise *Attendite a falsis*

Table 16.1: SVM Classification, masked data.

TEST2	Refutatio errorum R4b (Gretser)	1.0
Anon.	Attendite a falsis prophetis	0.953
Petrus Zwicker	Cum dormirent homines	0.926
TEST1	Refutatio errorum R4a	0.745
TEST3	Refutatio errorum R1	0.662
Durand of Huesca	Liber antiheresis	-0.062
Anon. of Passau	Tractatus de erroribus hereticorum	-0.212
Berthold von Regensburg	Sermones	-0.254
Wasmud von Homburg	Tractatus contra hereticos	-0.352
Anon.	Disputatio inter Catholicum et Paterinum hereticum	-0.357
Durand of Huesca	Liber contra Manicheos	-0.573
Petrus de Pillichsdorf	Contra Pauperes de Ludguno	-0.574
Moneta Cremonensis	Adversus Catharos et Valdenses, Book 5	-0.717
Alanus de Insulis	Contra haereticos	-0.807
Petrus Veronensis	Summa contra haereticos	-0.854
Johannes Cassianus	De incarnatione Domini contra Nestorium	-0.889
Hermannus de Scildis	Tractatus contra haereticos negantes immunitatem Ecclesiae	-0.953
Augustinus Hipponensis	Contra Faustum Manichaeum	-0.986
Augustinus Hipponensis	Contra epistulam Fundamenti	-1.0

Source: Authors.

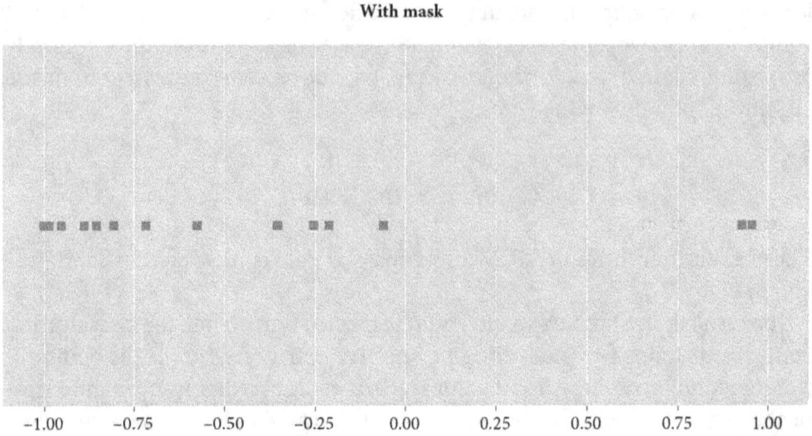

Figure 16.1: Green dots represent the test cases (*Refutatio*), red dots Zwicker's CDH and blue dots texts by other authors. Source: Authors

prophetis, discussed below. But if we exclude it, all other works from the reference corpus got values below 0, and Zwicker's texts were neatly classified between 0.662 and 1.0. Not surprisingly, the text from Gretser's edition got the highest value (1.0), in fact higher than the CDH. This appears contradictory at first, but the explanation is simple: the classifier first learns the weight of features from the whole text, but in cross-validation the text is divided into slices of 1,000 words, and the final value is the average of all the slices. Some of these got values below 1, weighting down the average. In other words, the *Refutatio*'s style is indistinguishable from Zwicker's style in the *Cum dormirent homines* in comparison to the reference corpus.

After pre-processing and masking, the features on which the SVM bases its decision pass the sanity check. In Appendix 16.2, there is a list of the 50 strongest positive and negative features. In both positive and negative class, these are function words or common content words, or bi-grams combining such common words with masked words. Among these, only one positive feature ('imo' 6.344) results from orthographical variation (imo vs. immo). All in all, a classification based on these features can be deemed reliable and non-dependable from topics.

The classifier was also able to distinguish authorial signature from both editions and manuscripts so that the editorial solutions or orthographical variation do not completely distort an author's style. This is confirmed not only by the consistent classification of the different versions of the *Refutatio*, but also by the value acquired by Peter von Pillichsdorf's *Contra Pauperes de Ludguno*. Despite being a tract on the same topic (Waldensians) as the CDH and the *Refutatio*, and from the same edition (Gretser) as the CDH and TEST2, it got a clearly negative value of –0.574. Six other texts got values nearer to the threshold, so Pillichsdorf's tract is very far from Zwicker's texts. The edition, of course, has an effect, as we can see from the very strong value TEST2 got.

The unexpected result was the *Attendite a falsis prophetis*. It got a very high value (0.953), and in the classification in the unmasked data, not presented here in detail, the result was consistent (0.559). This cannot be explained by the same topic, as the extremely high value is based on masked data. How should we interpret this? Do we have a new text attributed to Petrus Zwicker? This is a possibility, but the SVM's classification must be considered against the historical context, manuscript tradition and the contents of the text.

First, very little in the contents of the text contradicts Zwicker's views in the *Refutatio* or the CDH. In fact, the *Attendite* presents similar Waldensian propositions and Catholic counter-arguments to those of Zwicker. For example, the CDH, *Refutatio* and *Attendite* all begin by refuting the Waldensian claim of a legitimate lay ministry and proceed then to treat individual points of doctrine such as denial of Purgatory and oath-taking. P. Biller has already pointed out a certain similarity between the *Attendite* and the CDH.[36] There is a minor detail: the *Attendite* states that the Waldensians do not accept the books of Maccabees as parts of the biblical canon.[37] In the CDH, Zwicker stays silent about this and in fact uses the Maccabees to prove that the intercession on behalf of the dead had its foundation in the Bible.[38] This small divergence, however, can be explained by the development of Zwicker's argumentation. He desperately needed the Maccabees in order to maintain the principle of finding the foundation of Catholic doctrine and practices solely in the Bible, a principle that was only fully developed in his main work, the CDH. The author of the *Attendite* did not follow these guidelines: some of the arguments are supported by patristic quotes. Yet, this does not automatically deny Zwicker's authorship. Although Zwicker got rid of extra-biblical quotes almost completely in writing the *CDH*, he refers to patristic *auctoritates* several times in the *Refutatio*.[39] Solely based on the contents, the *Attendite* could be an early work of Petrus Zwicker. He was, after all, a man obsessed about the Waldensians and the threat they posed to the Church, and it is not out of the question that he wrote a third treatise against them.

The main doubt comes from the dating of the work. This is remarkably difficult, because the text is very general and does not refer to any specific persons or incidents. Nor does the author use any particular or rare sources. In principle, any late medieval author with access to anti-heretical treatises commonly circulating in Central Europe could have written the text. There have been two propositions about the author, one obviously mistaken, and another probably due to confusion with another text. Based on one manuscript (Wrocław, University library MS I F 230), R. Cegna misdated the text to the year 1399 and misattributed it to the Silesian inquisitor Johannes of Gliwice.[40] There are no grounds whatsoever for either the dating or the attribution,[41] and a few manuscripts predate the one used by Cegna. Older research attributes the treatise to the Bohemian reform preacher and troublemaker Conrad of Waldhausen, which would date the text to the 1360s.[42] The attribution might have resulted from confusion of this short tract with Conrad's sermon on the same Bible verse, given at some point in 1363 to 1369.[43] The manuscript transmission history points to Austria, Southern Germany, Bohemia and Silesia. P. Biller has proposed that the earliest possible dated manuscript of the *Attendite* is St. Paul im Lavanttal, MS 71/4, which has the year 1373 at folio 160va, referring to the composition date of a copy of a polemical letter from a converted Austrian Waldensian to Lombardian Waldensian Brethren.[44] Although the part with the *Attendite* (folios 144ra–146vb) belongs to the same fascicule with the letter, it is uncertain if 1373 is the production date of this particular exemplar. The manuscript MS 71/4 is a compilation with fascicules produced at different times in the late 14th and early 15th centuries.[45] The dating can only be confirmed through codicological analysis of the physical object itself, which is not possible within this study. The more secure dating comes from Klosterneuburg, MS CC 826, datable to 1391 and described by P. Biller.[46] With absence of a systematic study on the manuscript circulation of the *Attendite*, this is the most credible *terminus ante quem*. It means that the geographical distribution and dating of the manuscripts overlaps with the beginning of Petrus Zwicker's career as inquisitor of heresy, not excluding his authorship.

The final caveat comes from the credibility of the attribution itself. The text is only around 2,500 words long, making the attribution unreliable, as we are dealing with data with noise. In addition, the *Attendite* and the CDH (which is the material we used to train the computer for the class Zwicker) quote the same Bible verses. Although the quotations are not word-to-word identical, there is shared material in these two works. In the attribution of such a short text, it necessarily has an impact. Finally, we used a version of the text from a single manuscript, which we had in machine-readable format. There is a critical edition of the text by R. Cegna, but it too is mainly based on a single manuscript with variant readings in endnotes.[47] The final attribution of the *Attendite* is only possible when further study reveals the earliest redaction of the text and the manuscript dates are confirmed. From the earlier proposed authors, texts from Conrad of Waldhausen must be included in the classification as a possible author. At this point, we must be content to say that the *Attendite a falsis prophetis* is possibly attributable to Petrus Zwicker, but the attribution needs corroborating evidence from the manuscript tradition.

Conclusion: Additional Value of the Computational Analysis?

In the future, the computational authorship attribution should be taken into the toolbox of historians and philologists, who work with anonymous, pseudo and dubious texts. The classifiers developed for the analysis of modern literature or forensic purposes have been proved to be effective also in the study of ancient and medieval texts.

In our case study, the authorship of the *Refutatio errorum*, the computational methods produced both corroborating evidence and expected results, as well as radically new insights. The authorship of the *Refutatio* was confirmed as Petrus Zwicker through computational stylistics. Although there were previous, convincing pieces of evidence in support of this, the analysis is not without added value. A computer's decision is based on a completely different set of features than contents analysis and contextual evidence presented in the previous studies. Another important result was the classification of Peter von Pillichsdorf's treatise as clearly non-Zwicker. This not only confirms the earlier qualitative attribution, but demonstrates that our classifier can bypass the stylistic conventions of an early modern editor and detect the medieval author signature below.

The greatest added value of computational authorship attributions comes, however, from the unexpected results, from texts behaving in an anomalous way. In this classification, the *Attendite a falsis prophetis* did precisely this. Up until this point, nobody has really considered Zwicker's authorship, because the manuscript tradition points to a somewhat earlier treatise. Yet, when the classification gave a strong attribution to Zwicker, it forced us to reconsider the qualitative evidence. This, in turn, was revealed to be indecisive as well. Although we are not ready to declare the case closed and a new text attributed to Zwicker, the example demonstrates the true power of computational methods: it breaks the existing patterns of thought and demands re-evaluation of previous presuppositions.

Our chapter demonstrates that computational history cannot progress in isolation from the more conventional study of history, particularly the very basic archival study of sources. The attribution of the *Attendite a falsis prophetis* is to remain ambiguous until the existing manuscripts are surveyed in detail. The study of history depends on source criticism, and in order to date, attribute and localise sources with digital methods we have to take care that our metadata is up to standard.

Acknowledgements

This study has been funded by the Academy of Finland, Academy Programme DIGIHUM 2015-2019: consortium Profiling Premodern Authors (PROPREAU), project number 293024.

Appendix 16.1: Text Corpus

TEST1: Refutatio errorum, Redaction 4a
Source: Augsburg, Staats- und Stadtbibliothek, MS 338, fols. 159r–170r.

TEST2: Refutatio errorum, Redaction 4b
Source: Gretser, J. (Ed.). (1677). *Lucae Tvdensis episcopi, Scriptores aliqvot*

svccedanei contra sectam waldensivm. Maxima Bibliotheca Veterum Patrum, Et Antiquorum Scriptorum Ecclesiasticorum. Tom. XXV. Lvgdvni: Anissonios, 302G–307F.

TEST3: Refutatio errorum, Redaction 1
Source: Vienna, Österreichische Nationalbibliothek, MS 1588, fols. 191r–211v.

TRAINING DATA
Suspected author: Petrus Zwicker:
Text: Cum dormirent homines (CDH)
Source: Gretser, J. (Ed.). (1677). *Lucae Tvdensis episcopi, Scriptores aliqvot svccedanei contra sectam waldensivm*. Maxima Bibliotheca Veterum Patrum, Et Antiquorum Scriptorum Ecclesiasticorum. Tom. XXV. Lvgdvni: Anissonios, 277F–299G.

Other authors:
Author: Alanus de Insulis (Alain of Lille)
Text: Contra haereticos
Source: Patrologia Latina 210. Text from *Corpus Corporum*: http://mlat.uzh.ch/?c=2&w=AlDeIn.ConHae

Author: Anonymous
Text: Attendite a falsis prophetis
Source: St. Florian, MS XI 152, fols. 48v–50v.

Author: Anonymous
Text: Disputatio inter Catholicum et Paterinum hereticum
Source: Hoécker, C. (Ed.). (2001). *Disputatio inter catholicum et paterinum hereticum: die Auseinandersetzung der katholischen Kirche mit den italienischen Katharern im Spiegel einer kontroverstheologischen Streitschrift des 13. Jahrhunderts*. Tavarnuzze (Firenze): SISMEL edizioni del Galluzzo, 3–80.

Author: Anonymous of Passau
Text: Tractatus de erroribus hereticorum
Source: Nickson, M. A. E. (1962). *A critical edition of the treatise on heresy ascribed to Pseudo-Reinerius, with an historical introduction*. Queen Mary, University of London, 1–154.

Author: Augustinus of Hippo
Text: Contra Faustum Manichaeum
Source: Patrologia Latina 42. Text from *Corpus Corporum*: http://mlat.uzh.ch/?c=2&w=AugHip.CoFaMa

Author: Augustinus of Hippo
Text: Contra epistulam Fundamenti

Source: Corpus Scriptorum Ecclesiasticorum Latinorum (CSEL) 25.1. Text from *Corpus corporum*:
http://mlat.uzh.ch/?c=19&w=August.CoEpFunCSEL

Author: Berthold von Regensburg
Text: Sermones [XXIIII, XXVIII, XXVIIII, 'Sancti pre Fidem' and 'Dominica Duodecima']
Source: Czerwon, A. (2011). *Predigt gegen Ketzer: Studien zu den lateinischen Sermones Bertholds von Regensburg*. Tübingen: Mohr Siebeck, 203–233.

Author: Durand of Huesca
Text: Liber contra manicheos
Source: Thouzellier, C. (1964). *Une somme anti-cathare: le Liber contra Manicheos de Durand de Huesca*. Louvain: Spicilegium sacrum Lovaniense, 67–336.

Author: Durand of Huesca
Text: Liber Antiheresis
Source: Selge, K.-V. (Ed.) (1967). *Die ersten Waldenser: mit Edition des Liber antiheresis des Durandus von Osca* (Vol. 2). Berlin: De Gruyter, 3–257.

Author: Hermannus of Scildis
Text: Tractatus contra haereticos
Source: Zumkeller, A. (1970). *Hermanni de Scildis O.S.A.: tractatus contra haereticos negantes immunitatem et iurisdictionem sanctae Ecclesiae et Tractatus de conceptione gloriosae virginis Mariae*. Würzburg: Augustinus-Verl., 3–108.

Author: Johannes Cassianus
Text: De incarnatione Domini contra Nestorium
Source: Corpus Scriptorum Ecclesiasticorum Latinorum (CSEL) 17. Text from *Corpus Corporum*: http://mlat.uzh.ch/?c=19&w=Cassia.ConNesCSEL

Author: Moneta Cremonensis (Moneta of Cremona)
Text: Adversus Catharos et Valdenses, Liber V
Source: Moneta (Cremonensis). (1743). *Monetae Adversus Catharos et Valdenses: libri quinque*. T. A. Ricchini (Ed.). Romae: Ex Typographia Palladis, 389–560.

Author: Petrus de Pillichsdorf (Peter von Pillichsdorf)
Text: Contra Pauperes de Lugduno
Source: Gretser, J. (Ed.) (1677). *Lucae Tvdensis episcopi, Scriptores aliqvot svccedanei contra sectam waldensivm*. Maxima Bibliotheca Veterum Patrum, Et Antiquorum Scriptorum Ecclesiasticorum. Tom. XXV. Lvgdvni: Anissonios, 299E–302F.

Author: Petrus Veronensis (?)
Text: Summa contra haereticos
Source: Kaeppeli, T. (1947). Une somme contre les hérétiques de S. Pierre Martyr (?). *Archivum Fratrum Praedicatorum, 17*, 295–335

Author: Wasmud von Homburg
Text: Tractatus contra hereticos Beckardos, Lulhardos et Swestriones
Source: Schmidt, A. (Ed.) (1962). Tractatus contra hereticos Beckardos, Lulhardos et Swestriones des Wasmud von Homburg. *Archiv für mittelrheinische Kirchengeschichte, 14*, 336–386.

Appendix 16.2: The 50 Strongest Positive and Negative Features from the SVM Classification on Masked Data

Positive features:

tv xxxxxxxxx	6.895
imo	6.344
xxx item	5.824
sed dicis	5.234
xxx dixit	5.04
item xxxx	4.864
item xxxxx	4.389
item xxx	4.385
xxxxxxxx imo	3.262
semper xxxxx	3.081
nostri xxxx	2.793
non solvm	2.562
ecce xxxxxxxxx	2.517
xxxxxx ecce	2.459
svvm xxxxx	2.225
sanctorvm dei	1.919
dixit xxxxxx	1.833
dicis xxxxxxxx	1.729
dicentes xxxxxx	1.691
dicis	1.648
xxxxxx item	1.608
xxxxxxx item	1.493
ecce	1.435
xxxxx mea	1.397
adhvc in	1.346
item xxxxxx	1.303
vbi xxxxxxxxx	1.295

item xxxxxxxxx	1.287
nec qvidem	1.285
solvm	1.235
qvod angeli	1.143
sibi ipsis	1.129
domine xxxxx	0.953
mevm item	0.893
domini nostri	0.819
habes	0.812
discipvli	0.752
xxxxx domine	0.746
dominvs xxxxxxxx	0.744
nvnqvam	0.742
qvi venit	0.729
noster xxxxx	0.692
tva	0.672
vt videlicet	0.658
privs per	0.65
velvt	0.634
xxxxx nolite	0.614
habere xxxxxxxx	0.614
xxxxx ecce	0.606
xxxxx pro	0.595

Negative features:

ait	−11.246
apostolvs	−6.224
tantvm	−5.863
nec	−5.201
vt	−3.964
ei	−2.957
idest	−2.747
xxxxxxxx vt	−2.545
hvivs	−2.221
enim	−2.133
xxxxxxxxx vt	−1.95
qvod	−1.93
xxxxxxxxxxxxx xxxxxxxx	−1.705
deo	−1.642
ac	−1.619
qvomodo	−1.477
de	−1.415

dicitvr	−1.334
dicit	−1.321
nvllvs	−1.277
hoc	−1.275
est	−1.251
libro	−1.198
dicvnt	−1.187
qva	−1.177
cavsa	−1.173
xxxxxxx qvod	−1.166
si avtem	−1.125
xx	−1.105
secvndvm	−1.066
se	−1.052
sic	−0.999
ista	−0.929
non est	−0.905
dictvm	−0.894
facit	−0.825
xxxxxx qvia	−0.813
ab	−0.787
si	−0.739
xxxxxxxxxx	−0.718
xxxxxxxx	−0.714
potivs	−0.69
carnem	−0.684
itervm	−0.677
xxxxxxxxx	−0.661
et	−0.651
qvod xxxxxxx	−0.63
legitvr	−0.629
aliqva	−0.629
xxxxxx	−0.623

Notes

1 See, e.g., Levy 2012: 23–24.
2 Minnis 1988: 192–193, 196 and passim.
3 Kestemont, Moens & Deploige 2015; De Gussem 2017.
4 See, e.g., Johnson 1991; Williams-Krapp 2000; Minnis 2006; Conti 2012.
5 Välimäki 2016: 45–76; Välimäki 2019: 38–39, 48–49, 56–58, 61–64, 102.
6 Stover & Kestemont 2016a: 144.
7 Marriott 1979; one should also remember the pioneering work on statistical stylistics that precedes the computer era, Yule 1944.

[8] See, e.g., Clark 1987.

[9] Gurney & Gurney 1998; Tse, Tweedie & Frischer 1998; Tweedie, Holmes & Corns 1998; Forsyth, Holmes & Tse 1999; Kestemont 2012; Kestemont, Moens & Deploige 2015; Kestemont et al. 2016; Stover & Kestemont 2016a; Stover & Kestemont 2016b; De Gussem 2017.

[10] See, e.g., Weidmann 2015.

[11] Adams 2016: 202.

[12] Kestemont, Moens & Deploige 2015; De Gussem 2017.

[13] Mutzenbecher 1961: 202–219.

[14] Ibid.: 203–204, 207–209.

[15] Ibid.: 202.

[16] Kolpacoff 2000: 247–261; Modestin 2007: 1–12; Välimäki 2019: 30–37.

[17] Gretser 1677.

[18] Biller 2001: 252–253.

[19] Segl 2006: 185 n. 102.

[20] Cameron 2000: 140, 142–143.

[21] Patschovsky 1979: 27 n. 42.

[22] Döllinger 1890: 331–344.

[23] Välimäki 2019: 39–48.

[24] Välimäki 2016: 57–76; Välimäki 2019: 38–39, 48–49, 56–58, 61–64, 102.

[25] See https://github.com/propreau/zwicker.

[26] Kestemont, Moens & Deploige 2015; De Gussem 2017.

[27] Cf. Kestemont, Moens & Deploige 2015: 9–10.

[28] Such as variations -ci-/-ti- ; -mq-/-nq- ; -dq-/-cq- ; -mp- / -mn-, which cannot be normalised with simple replace rules without losing significant features in the text.

[29] Koppel, Schler & Argamon 2009; Koppel et al. 2012.

[30] See https://github.com/avjves/AuthAttHelper.

[31] Cortes & Vapnik 1995; Chang & Lin 2011. In particular, we used the scikit-learn implementation of SVM with L2 penalty and squared hinge as loss. The C-parameter of the classifier was set using cross-validation so as to avoid overfitting on the test data.

[32] In cross-validation, we only focus on our training data, ignoring the actual test texts. We remove one document at a time from the training data and consider it as a new test case. Our current training data now consists of all texts but the new test case, and using it we subsequently train the classifier and let it give a class and a value for the new test case. Since we know the actual authors of the texts included in the training data, these results show how accurately the classifier classifies data which it has not seen.

[33] 'heretici valdenses'; 'valdensis'; 'valdensis heretice'; 'valdensivm'; 'tv valdensis'.

[34] We calculated the word list from a corpus of 15 million words compiled for an attribution task of Augustine of Hippo's works. It is available at https://github.com/propreau/zwicker.

[35] Stamatatos 2017.

[36] Biller 1974: 365.
[37] St. Florian, MS XI 152, fol. 49v.
[38] Zwicker 1677: 288D–288E.
[39] Välimäki 2016: 77–114; Välimäki 2019: 61–62, 68–71, 73–85, 90, 94–98, 102–103.
[40] Cegna 1982.
[41] Patschovsky 1994: n. 15.
[42] Bartoš 1932: 32–33; Molnár 1989: 158 n. 29.
[43] Cf. Patschovsky 1979: 125–126.
[44] Biller 1974: 221. Biller cites MS 92/4, fol. 161va, but it is a mistake, the manuscript in question is MS 71/4. For the best overview of the manuscript tradition, see Biller 1974: 365–366.
[45] Glaßner 2002: Cod. 71/4 (olim 28.4.23).
[46] Biller 1974: 216–217, 365.
[47] Cegna 1982: 53–65.

References

Adams, J. (2016). *The revelations of St Birgitta: a study and edition of the Birgittine-Norwegian texts, Swedish National Archives, E8092*. Leiden: Brill.

Bartoš, F. M. (1932). Husitika a bohemika několika knihoven německých a švýcarských. *Vestník královské ceské spolecnosti nauk: Trída filosoficko-historicko-jazykozpytná, 5*, 1–92.

Biller, P. (1974). *Aspects of the Waldenses in the fourteenth century, including an edition of their correspondence* (doctoral dissertation, University of Oxford).

Biller, P. (2001). *The Waldenses, 1170–1530: between a religious order and a church*. Aldershot: Ashgate.

Cameron, E. (2000). *Waldenses: rejections of holy church in medieval Europe*. Oxford: Blackwell.

Cegna, R. (1982). La condizione del valdismo secondo l'inedito 'Tractatus bonus contra haereticos' del 1399, attribuibile all'inquisitore della Silesia Giovanni di Gliwice. In *I Valdesi e l'Europa* (pp. 39–66). Torre Pellice: Società di studi valdesi.

Chang, C.-C., & **Lin, C.-J.** (2011). LIBSVM: a library for support vector machines. *ACM Transactions on Intelligent Systems and Technology (TIST), 2*(3), 1–27.

Clark, F. (1987). *The pseudo-Gregorian dialogues*, Vol. 1. Leiden: Brill.

Conti, A. (2012). Scribes as authors, transmission as composition: towards a science of copying. In S. Ranković, I. B. Budal, A. Conti, L. Melve & E. Mundal (Eds.), *Modes of authorship in the Middle Ages* (pp. 267–288). Toronto: Pontifical Institute of Mediaeval Studies.

Cortes, C., & **Vapnik, V.** (1995). Support-vector networks. *Machine Learning, 20*(3), 273–297.

De Gussem, J. (2017). Bernard of Clairvaux and Nicholas of Montiéramey: tracing the secretarial trail with computational stylistics. *Speculum, 92*(S1), S190–S225.

Döllinger, J. J. I. von (1890). *Beiträge zur Sektengeschichte des Mittelalters: Zweiter Theil. Dokumente vornehmlich zur Geschichte der Valdesier und Katharer*. Munich: C. H. Beck.

Forsyth, R. S., Holmes, D. I., & Tse, E. K. (1999). Cicero, Sigonio, and Burrows: investigating the authenticity of the Consolatio. *Literary & Linguistic Computing, 14*(3), 375–400.

Glaßner, C. (2002). *Inventar der Handschriften des Benediktinerstiftes St. Paul im Lavanttal*. Retrieved from http://www.ksbm.oeaw.ac.at/stpaul/inv/index.htm

Gretser, J. (Ed.) (1677). Refvtatio Errorvm, Quibus Waldenses distinentur, incerto auctore. In *Lucae Tvdensis episcopi, Scriptores aliqvot svccedanei contra sectam waldensivm*, Maxima Bibliotheca Veterum Patrum, Et Antiquorum Scriptorum Ecclesiasticorum, Vol. 25 (pp. 302G–307F). Lvgdvni: Anissonios.

Gurney, P. J., & Gurney, L. W. (1998). Authorship attribution of the Scriptores Historiae Augustae. *Literary and Linguistic Computing, 13*(3), 119–131.

Johnson, L. S. (1991). The trope of the scribe and the question of literary authority in the works of Julian of Norwich and Margery Kempe. *Speculum, 66*(4), 820–838.

Kestemont, M. (2012). Stylometry for medieval authorship studies: an application to rhyme words. *Digital Philology: A Journal of Medieval Cultures, 1*(1), 42–72.

Kestemont, M., Moens, S., & **Deploige, J.** (2015). Collaborative authorship in the twelfth century: a stylometric study of Hildegard of Bingen and Guibert of Gembloux. *Literary and Linguistic Computing, 30*(2), 199–224.

Kestemont, M., Stover, J., Koppel, M., Karsdorp, F., & Daelemans, W. (2016). Authenticating the writings of Julius Caesar. *Expert Systems with Applications, 63*, 86–96.

Kolpacoff, J. M. (2000). *Papal schism, archiepiscopal politics and Waldensian persecution (1378–1396): the ecclesio-political landscape of late fourteenth-century Mainz* (doctoral dissertation, Northwestern University, Illinois).

Koppel, M., Schler, J., & **Argamon, S.** (2009). Computational methods in authorship attribution. *Journal of the American Society for Information Science and Technology, 60*(1), 9–26.

Koppel, M., Schler, J., Argamon, S., & **Winter, Y.** (2012). The 'fundamental problem' of authorship attribution. *English Studies, 93*(3), 284–291.

Levy, I. C. (2012). *Holy scripture and the quest for authority at the end of the Middle Ages*. Notre Dame, IN: University of Notre Dame Press.

Marriott, I. (1979). The authorship of the Historia Augusta: two computer studies. *Journal of Roman Studies, 69*, 65–77.

Minnis, A. J. (1988). *Medieval theory of authorship: scholastic literary attitudes in the later Middle Ages*. 2nd edn. Aldershot: Scolar Press.
Minnis, A. J. (2006). Nolens auctor sed compilator reputari: the late-medieval discourse of compilation. In M. Chazan & G. Dahan (Eds.), *La méthode critique au Moyen Âge* (pp. 47–63). Turnhout: Brepols.
Modestin, G. (2007). *Ketzer in der stadt: der Prozess gegen die Strassburger Waldenser von 1400*. Monumenta Germaniae Historica, Studien und Texte 41. Hannover: Hahnsche Buchhandlung.
Molnár, A. (1989). *Storia dei valdesi 1. Dalle origini all'adesione alla Riforma (1176–1532)*. 2nd edn. Turin: Claudiana.
Mutzenbecher, A. (1961). Bestimmung der echten Sermones des Maximus Taurinensis. *Sacris Erudiri: Jaarboek voor Godsdienstwetenschappen, 12*, 197–293.
Patschovsky, A. (Ed.) (1979). *Quellen zur böhmischen Inquisition im 14. jahrhundert*. Monumenta Germaniae Historica, Quellen zur Geistesgeschichte des Mittelalters 11. Weimar: Hermann Böhlaus Nachf.
Patschovsky, A. (1994). Ablaßkritik auf dem Basler Konzil: der Widerruf Siegfried Wanners aus Nördlingen. In J. Pánek, M. Polívka & N. Rejchrtová (Eds.), *Husitství—reformace—Renesance: Sborník k 60. narozeninám Františka Šmahela* (pp. 537–548). Prague: Historický Ústav.
Segl, P. (2006). Die Waldenser in Österreich um 1400: Lehren, Organisationsform, Verbreitung und Bekämpfung. In A. de Lange & K. Utz Tremp (Eds.), *Friedrich Reiser und die 'waldensisch-hussitische Internationale' im 15. Jahrhundert: Akten der Tagung Ötisheim-Schönenberg, 2. bis 4. Oktober 2003* (pp. 161–188). Heidelberg, Ubstadt-Weiher and Basel: Verlag Regionalkultur.
Stamatatos, E. (2017). Authorship attribution using text distortion. In *Proceedings of the 15th Conference of the European Chapter of the Association for Computational Linguistics*, Vol. 1: *Long papers* (pp. 1138–1149). Valencia: Association for Computational Linguistics. Retrieved from http://aclweb.org/anthology/E17-1107
Stover, J. A., & **Kestemont, M.** (2016a). The authorship of the Historia Augusta: two new computational studies. *Bulletin of the Institute of Classical Studies, 59*(2), 140–157.
Stover, J. A., & **Kestemont, M.** (2016b). Reassessing the Apuleian corpus: a computational approach to authenticity. *Classical Quarterly, 66*(2), 645–672.
Tse, E. K., **Tweedie, F. J.**, & **Frischer, B. D.** (1998). Unravelling the purple thread: function word variability and the Scriptores Historiae Augustae. *Literary and Linguistic Computing, 13*(3), 141–149.
Tweedie, F. J., **Holmes, D. I.**, & **Corns, T. N.** (1998). The provenance of *De Doctrina Christiana*, attributed to John Milton: a statistical investigation. *Literary & Linguistic Computing, 13*(2), 77–87.
Välimäki, R. (2016). *The awakener of sleeping men: inquisitor Petrus Zwicker, the Waldenses, and the retheologisation of heresy in late medieval Germany* (doctoral dissertation, University of Turku, Turku).

Välimäki, R. (2019). *Heresy in late medieval Germany: the inquisitor Petrus Zwicker and the Waldensians*. York: York Medieval Press.

Weidmann, C. (Ed.) (2015). *Augustinus: sermones selecti*. Corpus scriptorum ecclesiasticorum Latinorum 101. Berlin and Boston, MA: De Gruyter.

Williams-Krapp, W. (2000). Die überlieferungsgeschichtliche methode: Rückblick und ausblick. *Internationales Archiv für Sozialgeschichte der Deutschen Literatur, 25*(2), 1–21.

Yule, G. U. (1944). *The statistical study of literary vocabulary*. Cambridge: Cambridge University Press.

Zwicker, P. (1677). [Pseudo]-Petri de Pilichdorf contra Haeresin Waldensium Tractatus [Cum dormirent homines]. In J. Gretser (Ed.), *Lucae Tvdensis episcopi, scriptores aliqvot svccedanei contra sectam waldensivm, Maxima Bibliotheca Veterum Patrum, Et Antiquorum Scriptorum Ecclesiasticorum*, Vol. 25 (pp. 277F–299G). Lvgdvni: Anissonios.

CHAPTER 17

Macroscoping the Sun of Socialism

Distant Readings of Temporality in Finnish Labour Newspapers, 1895–1917

Risto Turunen

Introduction

> But in spite of all indifference, the sun of socialism has cast its first rays there. Even there, great and clear thoughts on the injustices of the present system are silently smouldering.[1]

The optimistic quote above was written in 1903, by a labour journalist outlining the preconditions of socialism in the eastern periphery of the Grand Duchy of Finland. Characteristic of the socialist discourse of the time, he used the phrase 'the sun of socialism'. It was one of the most important symbols of the Finnish labour movement in the early 20th century, figuring not only in newspapers, but also in poetry and red banners. Without doubt, there was something in the red sun of socialism that captured the contemporary proletarian imagination.

Many studies in social and cultural history have proven that symbols acting as 'simplified objectifications of ideologies' play a crucial role in the making

How to cite this book chapter:
Turunen, R. (2020). Macroscoping the sun of socialism: Distant readings of temporality in Finnish labour newspapers, 1895–1917. In M. Fridlund, M. Oiva, & P. Paju (Eds.), *Digital histories: Emergent approaches within the new digital history* (pp. 303–323). Helsinki: Helsinki University Press. https://doi.org/10.33134/HUP-5-17

of political movements.[2] The sun is the starting point for this chapter, for we believe that this symbol carries rich temporal information from a century ago. Thus, it can be used as a symbolic key to unlock socialist perceptions of the imagined past, present and future. The breakthrough of Finnish socialism has been analysed from a variety of perspectives,[3] but the focus has not been on 'temporality', that is, the way human beings experience time. There are some occasional comments on the socialist temporality in the previous research, mainly concentrating on the Marxian interpretation of history or on the future expectations in the form of socialist utopianism and eschatology.[4] The third dimension of time, the present, has largely escaped scholarly attention. For example, the sun of socialism has been seen in the context of the future, as a symbol for a better tomorrow and freedom.[5] The future-oriented meaning certainly existed, but we can add more interpretative depth to the investigation of the sun by also including the present in our analysis.

According to Reinhart Koselleck's thesis on temporality, the emergence of modernity, especially the unexpected rupture of the French Revolution of 1789, diminished the value of experience in forecasting the future.[6] While Koselleck's argument concerned the German-speaking world, we argue that the General Strike of 1905 had a similar effect in the Finnish context, expanding the gap between the experiences (of the past) and the expectations (towards the future) and, simultaneously, creating a new understanding of the present. The General Strike from 30 October to 6 November in 1905 was not only a direct result but rather an active extension of the 1905 Russian Revolution to the Grand Duchy Finland.[7] For the first time in Finnish history, workers momentarily seized a great part of political power, and this brief moment, a mere one week of imagined proletarian rule, meant that neither the old rules of politics nor old temporalities applied to the new situation. The General Strike led to a set of parliamentary reforms and to universal suffrage in 1906, and finally in 1907, just four years after the quote at the beginning of this chapter, Finland had the largest socialist party with parliamentary representation in Europe.[8]

This chapter has a threefold goal. First, regarding historical content, it constitutes a case study that tries to decipher the intriguing symbol of the rising sun and, thus, to broaden our understanding of the socialist temporality in Finland. The focus lies on the relation between the sun and the present, or more precisely, on how the sun illuminates the proletarian perception of their reality at the turn of the century. Second, methodologically speaking, we introduce 'macroscopic' approaches that allow historians to see something in the sources that is unavailable to the naked eye.[9] In practice, this means quantifying comparable word frequencies, collocates and key collocates. Third, we describe what it means to write digital history, by sketching a simple theoretical model, which sheds a new light on the intellectual journey the scholar undertakes on her way from original sources to historical wisdom.

Relative Word Frequencies: Counting the Heartbeats of Finnish Politics?

We begin our journey to the core of the socialist sun with an already well-established practice in digital history, that is, counting relative word frequencies over time. First, we download the dataset from the National Library of Finland: the raw text files of the biggest socialist (*Työmies*, '*The Working Man*'), conservative-nationalist (*Uusi Suometar*, '*New Finland*') and liberal-nationalist (*Helsingin Sanomat*, '*Helsinki News*', and before 1904 *Päivälehti*, '*The Daily Paper*') newspapers from 1900 to 1917.[10] Then, we find the words referring to the present in each year by using the search string 'nyky*', which covers the most common Finnish words denoting the present moment: 'nykyinen' ('present' as an adjective), 'nykyisyys' ('present' as a noun) and 'nykyisin' / 'nykyään' (adverbs for the present moment).[11]

Figure 17.1 shows a trend. The socialist newspaper *Työmies* has the highest frequency of 'the present' in 1900, but by the year 1904 the references to

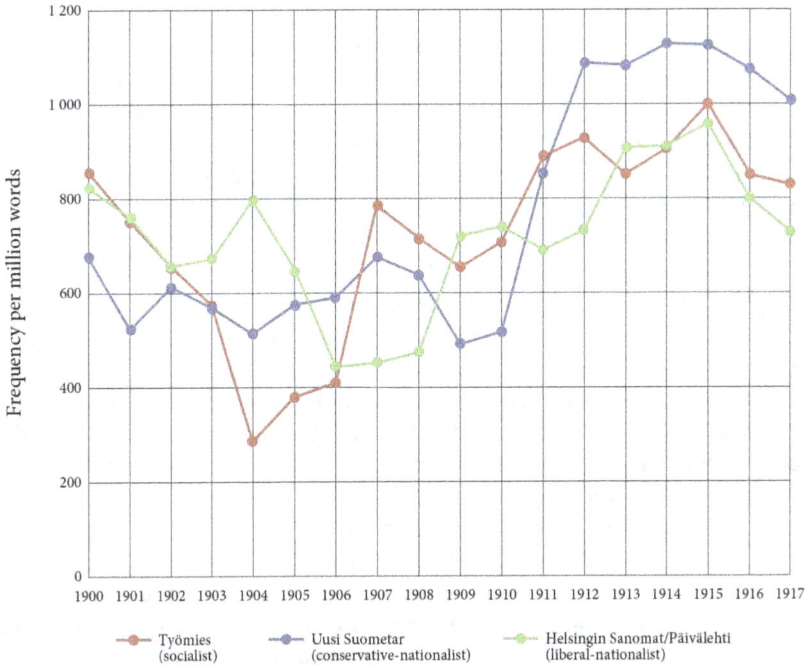

Figure 17.1: The relative amount of the present ('nyky*') in three newspapers, 1900–1917. Source: Raw text files of *Työmies*, *Uusi Suometar*, and *Helsingin Sanomat / Päivälehti*, distributed by the National Library of Finland, https://digi.kansalliskirjasto.fi/opendata.

the present have dropped far below the two bourgeois newspapers. What does this trend, this piece of information, mean? Based on previous research, censorship might lead us to the correct explanation. According to Antti Kujala, the censorship of the labour press in Finland became considerably tighter in 1903 when the Finnish Social Democratic Party officially adopted Marxism. Bans and warnings succeeded in silencing the most radical socialist discourse, for during the next year political commentary disappeared 'almost completely' from *Työmies*.[12] However, the General Strike of 1905 broke the silence on political matters as preventive censorship ended temporarily.

The renowned Finnish socialist poet Kössi Kaatra summarised the dramatic new temporality summoned by the strike in his poem *Suurina päivänä* ('*During the Great Days*') from 1906:

> It is great to be alive,
> when in a single day, in a night
> now we create more new things than in the work of many centuries.[13]

Reading Kaatra's words and focusing especially on the temporal marker 'now', it is not a surprise that we see a sharp rise in the socialist present, especially during 1907, which happens to be the year when Finland held the first parliamentary elections. Could the new political situation (electoral speculation, campaigns and aftermath) explain the peak of 1907? Based on both close and distant reading of *Työmies*, this seems to be the case. The words such as 'strike', 'government', 'nation, land', 'Duma' and 'senate' increase greatly in close proximity to the present after the General Strike.[14] Thus, the rise of the present means, in fact, the rise of the *political* present.

We could explain this finding in the light of Benedict Anderson's theory of 'imagined communities' which argues that between 1500–1800 technological innovations and the advance of print-capitalism profoundly changed our experience of time and space.[15] In the case of Finnish working people, these changes probably took place much later, beginning approximately from the mid-19th century onwards.[16] When looking at the date on the front page of the daily socialist newspaper, a Finnish worker could see with her own eyes that time was moving linearly forwards day after day. In addition, she could imagine that *meanwhile* there were thousands of other workers like just like her reading the very same edition, although she had never actually met them.[17] Using Anderson's theory to explain the dissemination of socialism instead of nationalism, as it has usually been applied, guides our analysis towards the close connection between temporalities and print media, or in our case, between the socialist interpretation of the present and the Finnish labour press. Because temporalities are always constructed, they can be manipulated. The leading socialist newspaper reacted to the changing political conditions after the General Strike by accelerating the flow of time, by repeating an imperative temporal message: the time to act is *now*.

One should not forget that there might be other alternative explanations for the peak of 1907. For example, there could have been more adverts in the socialist newspaper in 1907 than before, as the adverts of the early 20th century often referred to the present in order to sell their products better. The lack of information on what constitutes the peaks and valleys of word frequencies is not a trivial problem, but rather characteristic of word frequency charts in digital humanities. Far too often, they neglect variation inside a given corpus. Figure 17.1 is slightly better than the usual combination of a relative word frequency (y-axis) and time (x-axis) in the sense that it contains the extra dimension of political affiliation. However, the figure would be even better if it showed the frequency of 'the present' in different newspaper genres (editorials, foreign section, adverts, poems, letters to the editor, etc.) for each newspaper under investigation. The distribution of genres would show us in which journalistic context the present is discussed in each major political language of the time.

Despite the weaknesses, simple word frequency charts can reveal useful, low-level information to historians. In this case, it revealed above all that the amount of the socialist present varies strongly over time. The valley of 1904 is probably due to censorship, whereas the peak of 1907 is explained by the heated political situation. However, the general trend is that all the newspapers increase their references to the present with the passage of time. Does the trend reflect the increasing heartbeat of Finnish politics, or the rise of present-intensive advertising in all newspapers, or perhaps something completely different? We do not want to get entangled in that question in the context of this chapter, but we do want to highlight the importance of keeping an open mind when attaching meanings to the figures. As doctors know, if the heart beats faster than normal, the possible causes are many and varied.

Collocation: Mining the Semantic Structure of the Socialist Present

Historians inspired by conceptual history, discourse studies or the Cambridge school of intellectual history have for long been interested in the linguistic contexts in which their historical objects of interest (concepts, discourses, intellects) figure.[18] Nowadays, it is possible to quantify such linguistic contexts, given that the textual sources are in a machine-readable form. One approach to operationalise 'the linguistic context' is to define the context as all the words appearing in a window of x words to the left or right of the studied word. Since we are dealing with a highly inflected language, Finnish, it is important to lemmatise all the words in the text files, that is, to replace all word variations with their base form, before the actual analysis in order to get more reliable results.[19] In our case study, we could quantify all the words that exist in proximity of five words from the words referring to the present in the three biggest socialist newspapers. Why five words? There is no magic formula for defining the

Table 17.1: The most frequent words in a window of five words from the 'present' (search strings 'nykyi*' and 'nykyä*') in three socialist newspapers, 1895–1917.

RANK	WORD	TRANSLATION	FREQUENCY
1	olla	to be	60,941
2	ja	and	25,893
3	se	it, that	19,693
4	että	that	14,741
5	joka	which	14,673
6	ei	no	12,174
7	tämä	this	8,618
8	ne	they	6,348
9	kun	when	4,779
10	saada	to get	4,721

Source: Lemmatised raw text files of *Työmies*, *Kansan Lehti* and *Länsisuomen Työmies / Sosialisti*, 1895–1917, distributed by the National Library of Finland, https://digi.kansalliskirjasto.fi/opendata.

perfect window size. Historians must decide, usually through trial and error, which is the most appropriate selection for their own research questions.

As we can see in Table 17.1, the problem with this approach is that the most frequent words connected to the present are common words which do not reveal anything relevant from the historian's perspective. Fortunately, corpus linguists have developed a statistically more sophisticated method in collocation analysis that produces more meaningful raw information for historians to contemplate. Collocates are words that appear *more frequently than statistically expected* in close proximity to the search word.[20]

When looking at Table 17.2, one can immediately see that it contains useful information inviting a further human analysis. After close reading of the concordances, the list of examples of 'the present' as they occur in the socialist newspaper texts, we found three categories of technical errors: some collocates had, not surprisingly, OCR errors; some were lemmatised into a wrong base form; and some suffered from an incorrect word segmentation. We also increased the minimal frequency of collocation to a relatively high cut-off point of 200 instances, in order to filter out advertisements that plague all quantitative analyses of the Finnish newspaper corpus.[21] Then, after cleaning up Table 17.2 for errors and function words, we created a simple visualisation that is hopefully easier to understand for most historians.[22] Apart from absolute frequencies and Finnish originals, Figure 17.2 contains the same information as that in Table 17.2, but in a more accessible and user-friendly form. Figure 17.2 shows what could be poetically defined as 'the architecture of the concept'.[23] It is based on the principle that the human brain can intuitively understand: the closer the word is to the centre, the more strongly it is connected to the socialist present.

Table 17.2: The collocates of the present ('nykyä', 'nykyi*') in three socialist newspapers, 1895–1917, min. frequency 200.

RANK	WORD	TRANSLATION	FREQUENCY	MI-VALUE
1	yhteiskuntajär-jestelmä	societal system	354	10.29
2	tilanne	situation	1,460	9.91
3	järjestelmä	system	1,506	8.58
4	mallita	to prevail (OCR error)	448	8.44
5	vallita	to prevail	1,464	8.14
6	oleskella	to stay	404	8.11
7	yhteiskunta	society	2,026	8.11
8	tätä	this	282	7.56
9	olosuhteet	conditions	488	7.35
10	kapitalistinen	capitalist	394	7.32
11	kallis	expensive	587	6.95
12	pula	shortage	293	6.87
13	kurja	miserable	322	6.86
14	politiikka	politics	299	6.84
15	valtiollinen	state-	500	6.79
16	työttömyys	unemployment	452	6.76
17	muoto	form	801	6.68
18	asema	position, condition	3,547	6.64
19	olo	condition	1,731	6.63
20	kanta	view	897	6.56
21	kunnallinen	municipal	487	6.55
22	sota	war	1,415	6.55
23	taloudellinen	economic	658	6.53
24	vaikea	hard, difficult	295	6.52
25	käytäntö	practice	594	6.51
26	kehitys	progress, development	555	6.46
27	kurjuus	misery	280	6.42
28	säilyttää	to preserve, to save	323	6.39
29	epäkohta	grievance, shortcoming	307	6.36
30	mahdoton	impossible	485	6.35

Source: Lemmatised raw text files of *Työmies*, *Kansan Lehti* and *Länsisuomen Työmies* / *Sosialisti*, 1895–1917, distributed by the National Library of Finland, https://digi.kansalliskirjasto.fi/opendata.

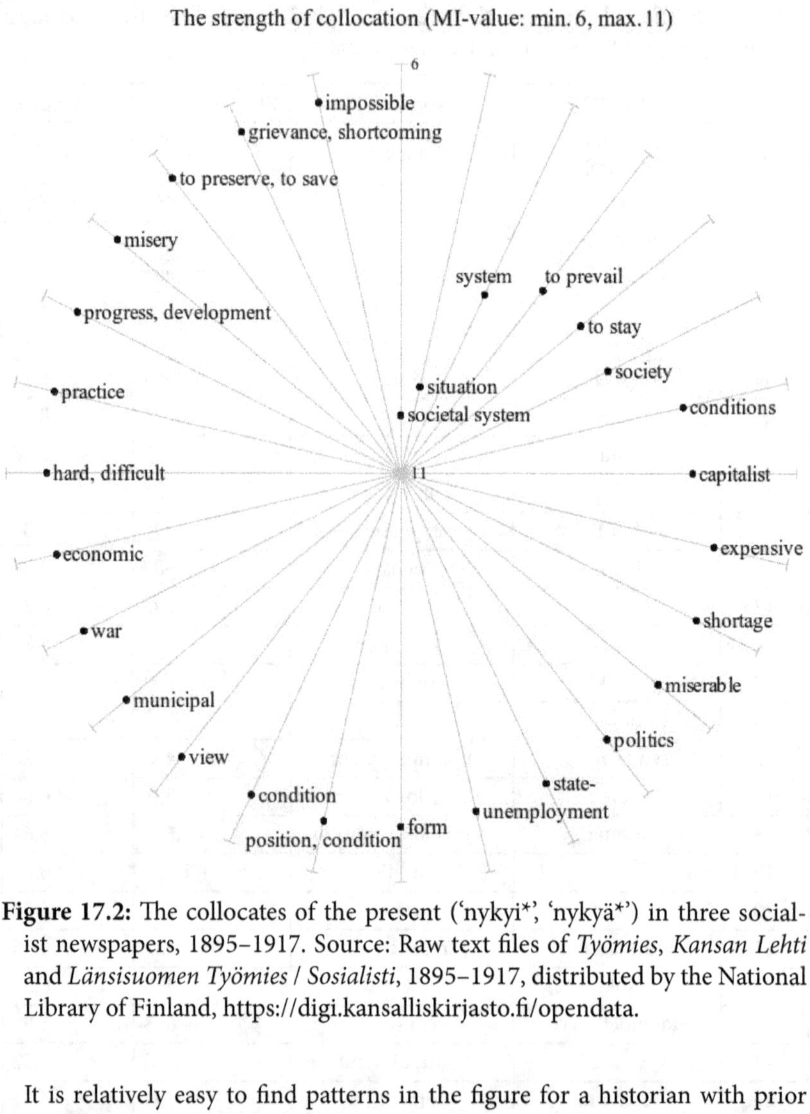

Figure 17.2: The collocates of the present ('nykyi*', 'nykyä*') in three socialist newspapers, 1895–1917. Source: Raw text files of *Työmies*, *Kansan Lehti* and *Länsisuomen Työmies / Sosialisti*, 1895–1917, distributed by the National Library of Finland, https://digi.kansalliskirjasto.fi/opendata.

It is relatively easy to find patterns in the figure for a historian with prior knowledge on the topic. First, the socialist present seems to attract phenomena that are considered to be negative, if not universally, at least as perceived by most people. In addition to the abstract concept of misery, the readers of the socialist newspapers were frequently introduced with the more concrete evils of 'shortage', 'unemployment' and 'war'. Negativity was enforced with the adjectives 'miserable' and 'hard, difficult', especially when talking about current 'conditions'. A close reading also reveals that current 'politics', referring to both tsarist repression and domestic bourgeois oppression, belong to the same negative semantic field.[24] The critique of 'politics' is understandable since the socialists, despite polling the most votes in every election, were not represented in the government until in the year 1917.[25] Of course, in the socialist understanding, their interpretation of the present was not negative in an exaggerated sense, but rather a realistic portrayal of the inherent problems in capitalism.

This leads us to the second feature worth highlighting in Figure 17.2: the misery of the socialist present was not accidental, but *systematic*. The words 'societal system', 'system' and 'society' in the figure hint at this socialist pattern of conceptualising the present. The everyday had a structure, and those great 'capitalist', 'state', 'economic' and 'municipal' forces shaping the present were not mystical nor divine, but explainable through a rational analysis. Let us take a quote from each of the three main socialist newspapers to illustrate the logic:

> The eyes of many workers have opened even here [in Eura] to see the misery into which the present system has brought our society.[26]

> The curse of the present system is precisely that the more satisfied the capitalists can be with their lives, the more miserable the life of the workers has become under the constraining conditions.[27]

> Everyday experience shows us that it is not possible to achieve sufficient improvements for the condition of the majority of the people on the grounds of the present bourgeois system ...[28]

Thus, socialists not only disapproved of the present with negative words, but they also tried to explain the causal mechanism behind it, by arguing that the present system was the root of all evil.

Although the present was in essence systematically bad, there was hope, or as the grand old man of Finnish labour history Hannu Soikkanen has argued in his seminal study *Arrival of Socialism in Finland* (1961), 'the present and future conditions were contrasted as starkly as possible'.[29] According to Soikkanen, this contrast was one of the main features of socialism that made it psychologically so attractive for the working people. The third pattern in Figure 17.2, visible to an experienced eye, refers to this connection between the present and the future, that is, to the words that imply changes and movement. 'The present situation' indicates a way of thinking that is not limited by eternal conditions created by God in the beginning of time. In addition, the phrase 'the prevailing conditions' is used regularly in the political language of Finnish socialism, in order to undermine the foundations of the present status quo:

> Modern socialism is thus a product of the prevailing economic and social conditions in the present.[30]

> Class struggle is rooted in the unsolvable conflicts between employers and employees. A collective agreement cannot remove the conflict, and neither can it abolish the hegemony of the capital over work in the prevailing conditions of the present.[31]

> Capital is accumulating in the hands of fewer and fewer people while the propertied class is not growing. Marx taught that the natural result is that the conditions themselves must change, there will be a fall of the prevailing system.[32]

Finally, the concept of 'progress' is fundamental to understanding the socialist temporality, for it tied together the past, present and future. If the present capitalist society was indeed a temporary product of a historical process, then society would surely change in the future too, or like one socialist journalist foretold: 'By the force of historical progress, the present system of oppression shall be once wiped from the stage, and its wretched henchmen shall get the reward they deserve.'[33]

We have seen that the collocation method, combined with different visualisation techniques (tables, figures), can produce a massive amount of low-level information on the semantic content of a concept in historical texts, in this case on the concept of the present in three leading socialist newspapers. It would have taken several years, perhaps a decade, to manually close read the more than 180 million words printed in these newspapers. However, a computational distant reading helped us to discover that the socialist present was (1) negative, (2) systematic and (3) changeable.

In the end, it always depends on the skills of a historian whether or not elementary quantitative information is successfully transformed into historical knowledge. Here, instead of limiting our critical thinking only to the meanings of preliminary 'results', we should also inquire into the presuppositions embedded in each quantitative method. For example, from a historian's point of view, the collocation method is lacking comparative contexts for it operates only within the political language of socialism. How do we know if these found features of the socialist present are unique, or if they belong to a more general discourse of the time?

Key Collocation: Placing the Socialist Present into the Contemporary Context

The collocation method shows the strength of mutual relation between two words. Another useful method historians interested in language could borrow from corpus linguistics is the keyness method, which can be used to show differences between two discourses. Keyness detects the words which appear more frequently than expected by pure chance in the text collection A ('target corpus') compared to the text collection B ('reference corpus').[34] Next, we combine the main ideas behind the two methods under the concept of key collocation, which aims to reveal semantic differences in the use of a certain historical concept.

First, as previously, we collect all the words appearing in a window of five words of the present (using search strings 'nykyä*' and 'nykyi*') in the socialist newspapers, and combine these words into one unified corpus. Then, we do exactly the same for the bourgeois newspapers, in this case for the biggest liberal-nationalist newspaper *Helsingin Sanomat / Päivälehti* and the biggest conservative-nationalist newspaper *Uusi Suometar*. Now we have two corpora, and we can utilise the keyness method in order to see which words appear more frequently in the socialist discourse on the present compared with the bourgeois discourse on the present.

Table 17.3 places our findings on the socialist present in the previous section into the wider context of the early 20th-century newspaper discourse. The only clearly negative word in the top 20 key collocates is 'unemployment'.

Table 17.3: The key collocates of the socialist present ('nykyä*', 'nykyi'), compared with bourgeois newspapers, 1895–1917.

RANK	WORD	TRANSLATION	KEYNESS	EFFECT SIZE
1	työläinen	worker	1,917	19.8
2	yhteiskunta	society	1,586	5.8
3	oma	own (OCR error)	900	2.1
4	kapitalistinen	capitalist	598	38.5
5	köyhälistö	proletariat, the poor	587	28.7
6	yhteiskuntajärjestelmä	societal system	546	53.8
7	liitto	union	539	3.1
8	torppari	crofter	524	5.6
9	työmäki	working people (OCR error)	505	13.6
10	työ	work	504	2.0
11	työväki	working people	448	4.2
12	tilanne	situation	432	2.3
13	järjestelmä	system	422	2.3
14	työttömyys	unemployment	420	6.8
15	työnantaja	employer	414	5.8
16	työmies	working man	390	3.2
17	palkka	wage	368	2.3
18	moida	can (OCR error)	366	2.8
19	järjestö	organisation	357	5.3
20	ammatillinen	occupational, vocational	321	33.7

Source: Lemmatised raw text files of *Työmies*, *Kansan Lehti*, *Länsisuomen Työmies / Sosialisti*, *Helsingin Sanomat / Päivälehti* and *Uusi Suometar*, 1895–1917, distributed by the National Library of Finland, https://digi.kansalliskirjasto.fi/opendata.

However, scrolling further down the list shows that socialists indeed use words such as 'misery' (ranked 24 by keyness value), 'miserable' (27), oppression (87) and 'hunger' (111) in close proximity to the present much more often than their contemporaries, leading us to the conclusion that the level of negativity in the socialist discourse on the present was extraordinary. Socialists imagined the worst possible present.

What about the systematic nature of the present we encountered when quantifying collocates? It exists also in Table 17.3 in the form of 'society', 'capitalist', 'societal system' and 'system'. In addition, we have strong supporting evidence of 'social order' (76), 'economic system' (80), 'production system' (86), 'class society' (205) and 'system of oppression' (359).

The third feature of the socialist present, changeability, seems to be the least unique to labour newspapers. Apart from 'situation', words referring to the *changing* and *changeable* nature of the present are missing from Table 17.3. Some of them can be found in the key collocation list: for example, 'reaction' (70) and its counter-concept 'progress / development' (900). However, looking at the whole list of key collocates, it seems that this feature of the socialist present does not stand out in the context of Finnish newspaper discourse. Perhaps all the major political languages of the time—from liberalism, conservatism and socialism to Lutheran Christianity—believed that the world was changing, but they had different interpretations of what exactly was changing, how fast and, above all, if these changes happening in the present were leading to a better or worse society in the future.

It can be intellectually satisfying to find confirmation of prior interpretations, but nothing compares to finding something new. What is new is that the socialist protagonists of the present differ starkly from the bourgeois ones. The socialist version is based on the antagonism between good ('worker', 'working people', 'working man', 'proletariat / the poor', 'crofter') and evil ('employer') actors. This fundamental feature of the present was not found in the traditional collocation analysis, for the antagonism is so deeply rooted in the overall socialist discourse that it does not specifically stand out in the context of the socialist present. This socialist tendency to construct political agency through a vigorous repetition of collective singulars, especially 'the working people' and 'proletariat / the poor', can only be invoked when comparing socialism to other political languages of the time, in this case with the help of the key collocation method. Correspondingly, the trade union jargon ('union', 'organisation') escapes the collocation analysis, but it is clearly visible in the list of key collocations.

While collocation concentrates on the architecture of a concept in isolation, within only one discourse, key collocation can reveal the uniqueness or generality of these historical conceptual architectures. In the case of the socialist present, the latter method seems to confirm most of the findings achieved in the collocation analysis. Nevertheless, we should also respect the fact that an opposite result was possible. For example, we know that a negative present is not a feature confined to the socialist discourse of the early 20th century (old people complained about present children and manners already in the days of Plato[35]), but the point is that key collocation gives us a comparative empirical context, against which we can measure how much (for example, 'negativity') is much. Constructing comparative contexts through traditional close readings is a labour-intensive task. Perhaps this is one reason why historical temporalities have been analysed based on a rather limited amount of sources.[36]

From Sources to Wisdom: DIKW for Digital Historians

In this final part before the concluding remarks and return to the sun of socialism, we rise from the empirical case study to a more abstract level, by providing a theoretical account of our intellectual journey so far with the help of the so-called DIKW pyramid, a concept that has been influential in the information sciences, knowledge management and systems theory for decades.[37] The pyramid describes the hierarchical relations between Data, Information, Knowledge and Wisdom. Although the pyramid has received criticism from several directions,[38] we believe that a slightly revised version of the pyramid can be useful for explaining not only the analytical process of this chapter, but also, more broadly, the idea and promise of distant reading in the context of digital history.

The vertical axis in the model represents what is usually described as 'connectedness'. Connectedness increases as we climb up the ladder towards wisdom.[39] The idea is not completely unfamiliar to historians, but we traditionally prefer the word 'context' when describing the process of historical analysis. In fact, the etymological root of context means weaving or joining together.[40] Thus, we can replace 'connectedness' with 'context' in the model without a bad conscience.

Then, we should add one layer below data, that is, historical sources.[41] The central difference between sources and data to digital historians is that the latter is machine-readable, and currently only a small part of historical sources is available for computational analysis as data. In the context of this chapter, physical historical newspapers are sources, whereas their digital representations—the PDF images and text files we downloaded from the National Library—belong to the category of data.

What is information, then? Here, we differ from general definitions of information as 'data + context', or 'data + meaning',[42] for the words 'context' and 'meaning' carry too much historical weight in the humanities. 'Information as processed data' is a more suitable definition for our purposes.[43] Examples of information would be simple word frequency time series (for example, Figure 17.1), word frequency tables (for example, Tables 17.1–17.3) or visualisations of words appearing close to one another (for example, Figure 17.2). In each of these examples, raw data has been computationally re-organised into low-level information.

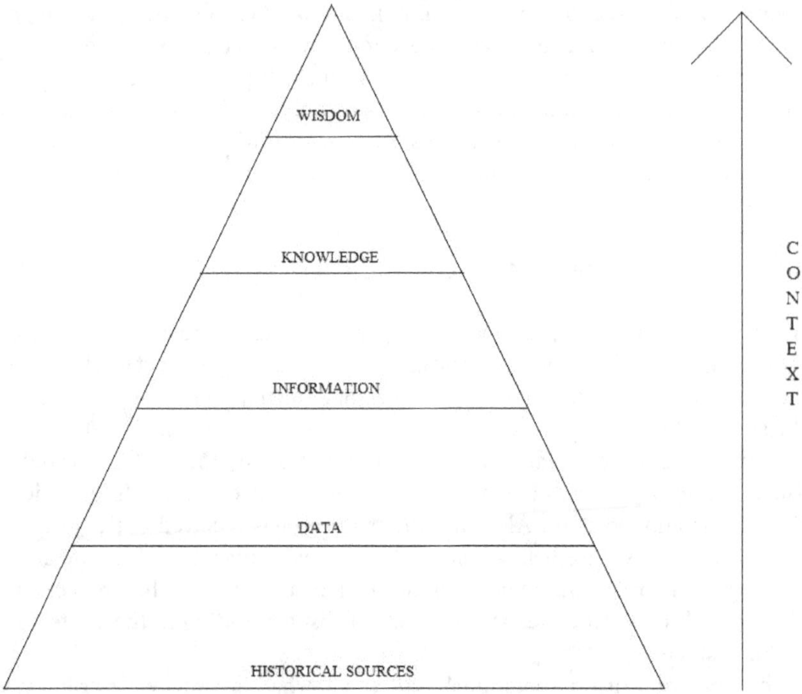

Figure 17.3: The revised version of the DIKW pyramid. Source: Author.

In our model, information does not include the historian's interpretation of information, which is located one step higher in the pyramid. Knowledge is information that is interpreted and contextualised by a human scholar. In this chapter, knowledge refers to assigning meaning to individual tables and figures, and then connecting these meanings not only to one another, but also to previous research—a difficult enterprise we undertook in the preceding pages.

The top of the pyramid is called wisdom, and it is the most controversial layer, for it escapes a clear definition.[44] Thus, it might be best to demolish it entirely. Russell Ackoff, often acknowledged as the founder of the pyramid, defined wisdom as evaluated understanding.[45] A historian could perhaps imagine wisdom as an ability to see which parts of the specific knowledge she has produced is relevant in answering the most complex questions of history. If knowledge means deciphering the meaning of the socialist sun, wisdom requires that a historian understands the meaning of this meaning under the aspect of eternity. (We have not reached an understanding this deep in this chapter.)

Now that we have reconstructed the pyramid, we can explain the point of distant reading in digital history. Distant reading aims at making the foundations of our historical explanations more solid, by piling up more stuff in the bottom of the pyramid. In other words, we want to increase the scale of historical sources, and this is possible as long as our sources are in a machine-readable form. A historian can hardly read 100,000 words per day, whereas a computer can 'read' more than billions of words a minute. Of course, such distant reading is not reading with an understanding, but rather finding connections between words on a more primitive level.

However, we should not underestimate the fact that distant reading techniques, already in their current premature phase, can produce information that cannot be produced by human cognitive abilities alone. It is then up to a scholar to make sense of this elementary information. When a seasoned historian criticises your digital history research for 'lacking context', he or she probably means that you have not reached the level of historical knowledge, in other words, you have not paid enough attention to connecting your preliminary findings to one another and to previous research. Data nor information interprets itself. Nowadays, it is already a cliché that distant and close reading methods are complementary. With the visual aid of the pyramid, we could rephrase this idea: in digital history, the goal is to shift our limited cognitive energy upwards.[46] We distribute the most monotonous part of our historian's craft to the machines, in order that they could find patterns and trends that need human explanations. Machines are fast, precise and tireless, in other words, good at refining data to information, but, at least by now, only humans are able to refine information to knowledge.

Conclusions

What have we learned from our distant readings of the present, from turning our macroscope towards the sun of socialism? First of all, as expected, the General Strike of 1905 seems to be a pivotal moment, a measurable rupture, in the history of socialist temporality. The words referring to the present increase rapidly after the strike. Metaphorically, the strike meant a mental earthquake that had long-term consequences. The strike reshaped the political environment so dramatically that old ideological maps lost much of their ability to explain contemporary reality. In this new situation, the political language of Finnish socialism turned out to be a temporary winner, gaining most votes in each of the post-strike elections. According to Hannu Soikkanen, socialism gave working people a coherent and solid world view which stood in sharp contrast to their unstable conditions.[47] We could specify this argument from the perspective of temporality by adding that a new understanding of time formed one important part in the breakthrough of the socialist world view. In those turbulent times, the political language of Finnish socialism offered the most believable interpretation of the present for the working people. As demonstrated by our collocation analyses, labour newspapers convinced their readers that the present misery was caused by the system, and this system could and should be changed.

Thus, based on our distant readings, we argue that the meaning of the socialist sun in the early Finnish labour movement was not limited to the temporal dimension of the future. The socialist sun affected the present too, by making it appear in a new, bad light. When one saw the red sun in the future, simultaneously the shackles of capitalism came out in the broad daylight of the present. We also learned that socialists did not see the present system as eternal or divine, but as historical and man-made. In fact, we could contrast the sun of socialism with the biblical sun which was the same for everyone, or in Jesus' words: 'He (Father in heaven) causes his sun to rise on the evil and good, and sends rain on the righteous and on the unrighteous.'[48] Our distant readings, especially the key collocation analysis, revealed that the socialist sun was shining exclusively for the 'working people', 'workers' and 'the proletariat', but not for 'the capitalist employers'. Thus, unlike the biblical sun that directed people's attention towards the hereafter, the red sun of socialism highlighted earthly problems.

If we wanted an even deeper understanding of the socialist sun and temporality, in other words, if we wanted to get closer to the top level of historical wisdom in the DIKW pyramid, these same analyses (comparable relative word frequencies, collocation, key collocation) should be performed for each dimension of the time: the past, present and future. In addition, we could broaden our quite narrow focus from word frequencies to richer forms of linguistic information. For example, experimenting with verb tenses (the socialist use of past, present or conditional forms) sounds reasonable when solving questions related to historical perceptions of time.

In the end, we could speculate for a moment: if the telescope and microscope changed the fields of astronomy and biology, will the macroscope, or computational methods in general, change our historical research?[49] We believe the answer is positive in the long term, but we are not quite there yet. According to Max Weber, a new 'science' emerges where new problems are pursued by new methods,[50] but in this chapter we have mainly answered old questions by using novel tools developed outside the community of historians. While not revolutionising the field, these tools can help us to improve our craft, in our everlasting quest towards historical wisdom.

Notes

1 'Työwäestön olosuhteista Karjalassa', *Työmies*, 21 August 1903, p. 1, https://digi.kansalliskirjasto.fi/sanomalehti/binding/728854?page=1.

2 The quote is from Korff 1993: 124. On political symbols in the context of socialist movements, see, e.g., Steinberg 2002: esp. 224–246; Hake 2017: esp. 100–119.

3 See, e.g., Soikkanen 1961; Haapala 1986; Ehrnrooth 1992; Suodenjoki 2010; Rajavuori 2017.

4 On Marxian interpretation of history, see, e.g., Soikkanen 1961: 30, 91–92, 231–232; on socialist utopianism, see Ehrnrooth 1992: 169–177; on socialist eschatology, see Huttunen 2010: 57–65.

[5] Kaihovaara 1986: 34–35; Kaihovaara 1991: 52.

[6] Koselleck 2004: 263–267.

[7] Tikka 2017.

[8] Alapuro 1988: 115–117; Eley 2002: 66, table 4.2.

[9] *Le Macrosope* was the title of Joël de Rosnay's classic introduction to systems theory (1975). Katy Börner reintroduced the concept in her often-cited article on plug-and-play macroscopes. See Börner 2011.

[10] Available at https://digi.kansalliskirjasto.fi/opendata?language=en. For more information on the historical newspaper collection, see Pääkkönen et al. 2016.

[11] The absolute numbers for the search string 'nyky*' in 1900–1917: 72,874 hits in 96,354,158 total words in *Työmies*; 121,473 times in 157,438,611 total words in *Uusi Suometar*; and 96,923 times in 135,166,576 total words in *Helsingin Sanomat / Päivälehti*. All the calculations in the chapter were performed using AntConc (3.5.7.), available from http://www.laurenceanthony.net/software.

[12] Kujala 1995: 42–53.

[13] Kaatra 1906: 4. Translation by the author.

[14] This analysis is based on comparing the words appearing in close proximity to the present before (1.1.1904–30.10.1905) and after (7.11.1905–31.12.1907) the General Strike of 1905 in *Työmies*. In practice, all the words appearing in a window of five words to the left or right of the search string 'nyky*' were collected into one 'post-revolutionary' mini-corpus, which was then statistically compared with all the 'pre-revolutionary' neighbouring words of the same search string. The method is explained more carefully in the section entitled 'Key Collocation'.

[15] Anderson 2006.

[16] Kokko 2016: 24–25, 44–45, 413–425.

[17] Anderson 2006: 24–26, 33.

[18] On conceptual history, see, e.g., Koselleck 2004; on discourse analysis, Baker 2006; on the Cambridge school, Skinner 2002.

[19] Finnish text files were lemmatised with the LAS command-line tool. See Mäkelä 2016.

[20] There are different collocation metrics. We have used mutual information (MI) which measures the probability of whether or not the relationship between the search word and its neighbouring word is likely to exist by mere chance. The higher the MI value, the stronger the link between two words.

[21] With the high cut-off point, many commercial adverts that contain words referring to the present 'drown' in the sheer mass of newspapers texts since not many of them circulate in each of the three chosen socialist newspapers. Thus, the ideological patterns of the socialist language use become more visible when the cut-off point is high.

[22] The visualisation was achieved with LibreOffice (5.1.6.2), available from https://www.libreoffice.org/.

[23] de Bolla 2013.

[24] On tsarist repression in the socialist newspapers, see, e.g., 'Suomen suhde Venäjään', *Sosialisti*, 5 December 1908, p. 2, https://digi.kansalliskirjasto.fi/sanomalehti/binding/717172?page=2; 'Wenäjä ja me', *Kansan Lehti*, 13 December 1909, p. 1, https://digi.kansalliskirjasto.fi/sanomalehti/binding/649887?page=1; 'Wirkaryssät uusia eduskuntawaaleja hommaa massa', *Työmies*, 23 October 1912, p. 1, https://digi.kansalliskirjasto.fi/sanomalehti/binding/1187961?page=1. On domestic bourgeois oppression, see, e.g., 'Suhteemme hallitukseen', *Kansan Lehti*, 4 July 1907, p. 1, https://digi.kansalliskirjasto.fi/sanomalehti/binding/645861?page=1; 'Työväen suojeluslait', *Sosialisti*, 6 April 1911, p. 2, https://digi.kansalliskirjasto.fi/sanomalehti/binding/1177250?page=2; 'Budjettikeskustelu eduskunnassa', *Työmies*, 23 April 1913, p. 2, https://digi.kansalliskirjasto.fi/sanomalehti/binding/1187515?page=2.

[25] Soikkanen 1975: 120–197.

[26] 'Euran Pohjoispäästä', *Sosialisti*, 27 April 1907, p. 3, https://digi.kansalliskirjasto.fi/sanomalehti/binding/702923?page=3.

[27] 'Länsi-Teiskosta', *Kansan Lehti*, 12 January 1912, p. 3, https://digi.kansalliskirjasto.fi/sanomalehti/binding/1238591?page=3.

[28] 'Miksi me vaadimme järjestelmän muutosta', *Työmies*, 23 December 1902, p. 2, https://digi.kansalliskirjasto.fi/sanomalehti/binding/739481?page=2.

[29] Soikkanen 1961: 29.

[30] 'Hiukan sosialismista', *Kansan Lehti*, 22 June 1911, p. 1, https://digi.kansalliskirjasto.fi/sanomalehti/binding/1238279?page=1.

[31] 'Kollektiiwiset työ- ja tariffisopimukset Englannissa ja Amerikassa', *Työmies*, 4 August 1909, p. 2, https://digi.kansalliskirjasto.fi/sanomalehti/binding/730033?page=2.

[32] 'Anarkia, pakkoluowutukset ja sosialidemokratit', *Sosialisti*, 28 September 1907, p. 2, https://digi.kansalliskirjasto.fi/sanomalehti/binding/703031?page=2.

[33] 'Sosialistin kirjapaino-osuuskunnan kirjapainon pakkokappaleasia', *Sosialisti*, 25 November 1913, p. 2, https://digi.kansalliskirjasto.fi/sanomalehti/binding/1178786?page=2.

[34] Baker 2006: 125–128. There are different keyness metrics. We have used the log-likelihood (four-term) test in order to measure statistical significance. In addition, we have measured effect size using ratio of relative frequencies.

[35] Quintelier 2007: 165.

[36] For example, the only monograph focusing on Finnish temporality in the late 19th century is based on a correspondence of one educated family in eastern Finland. See Ollila 2000.

[37] Rowley 2007.

[38] See, e.g., Tuomi 1999; Frické 2009; Jennex 2009.

[39] See, e.g., Bellinger, Castro & Mills 2003.

[40] Hyrkkänen 2009: 260.

[41] Perhaps we should add even one more layer to the very bottom of the pyramid, that is, life itself. People's rich lives leave only fragmentary sources for historians (and computers) to analyse.
[42] See, e.g., Worboys & Duckham 2004: 5; Floridi 2010: 20.
[43] Ackoff 1989.
[44] Hoppe et al. 2011.
[45] Bellinger, Castro & Mills 2003.
[46] This idea is taken from a very different academic field: plasma physics. See Carpenter & Cannady 2004: 4–6.
[47] Soikkanen 1961: 30.
[48] Matt. 5:45. On the many meanings of the sun in the Bible, see Patterson 2011.
[49] Graham, Milligan & Weingart 2015: 1–2.
[50] Franco Moretti made Weber's quote famous for digital humanists in his pioneering article on distant reading; see Moretti 2000.

References

Ackoff, R. (1989). From data to wisdom. *Journal of Applied Systems Analysis, 16*, 3–9.

Alapuro, R. (1988). *State and revolution in Finland.* Berkeley, CA: University of California Press.

Anderson, B. (2006). *Imagined communities: reflections on the origin and spread of nationalism.* London: Verso.

Baker, P. (2006). *Using corpora in discourse analysis.* London and New York, NY: Continuum.

Bellinger, G., Castro, D., & Mills, A. (2003, 7 May). *Data, information, knowledge and wisdom.* Retrieved from http://www.systems-thinking.org/dikw/dikw.htm

Börner, K. (2011). Plug-and-play macroscopes. *Communications of the ACM, 54*(3), 60–69.

Carpenter, S., & Cannady, J. (2004, July). *Tool for sharing and assessing models of fusion-based space transportation systems.* 40th AIAA/ASME/SAE/ASEE Joint Propulsion Conference and Exhibit, Fort Lauderdale, Florida. DOI: https://doi.org/10.2514/6.2004-3535

de Bolla, P. (2013). *The architecture of concepts: the historical formation of human rights.* New York, NY: Fordham University Press.

Ehrnrooth, J. (1992). *Sanan vallassa, vihan voimalla: Sosialistiset vallankumousopit ja niiden vaikutus Suomen työväenliikkeessä 1905–1914.* Helsinki: Finnish Historical Society.

Eley, G. (2002). *Forging democracy: the history of the Left in Europe, 1850–2000.* Oxford: Oxford University Press.

Floridi, L. (2010). *Information—a very short introduction.* Oxford: Oxford University Press.

Frické, M. (2009). The knowledge pyramid: a critique of the DIKW hierarchy. *Journal of Information Science, 35*(2), 131–142. DOI: https://doi.org/10.1177/0165551508094050

Graham, S., Milligan, I., & Weingart, S. (2015). *Exploring big historical data: the historian's macroscope*. London: Imperial College Press.

Haapala, P. (1986). *Tehtaan valossa: Teollistuminen ja työväestön muodostuminen Tampereella 1820–1920*. Helsinki: Vastapaino and Finnish Historical Society.

Hake, S. (2017). *The proletarian dream: socialism, culture, and emotion in Germany, 1863–1933*. Berlin: De Gruyter.

Hoppe, A., Seising, R., Nürnberg, A., & Wenzel, C. (2011, July). *Wisdom—the blurry top of human cognition in the DIKW-model?* Proceedings of the EUSFLAT conference, Aix-les-Bains, France.

Huttunen, N. (2010). *Raamatullinen sota: Raamatun käyttö ja vaikutus vuoden 1918 sisällissodan tulkinnoissa*. Helsinki: Finnish Literature Society & Finnish Society of Church History.

Hyrkkänen, M. (2009). All history is, more or less, intellectual history: R. G. Collingwood's contribution to the theory and methodology of intellectual history. *Intellectual History Review, 19*(2), 251–263. DOI: https://doi.org/10.1080/17496970902722932

Jennex, M. (2009, January). *Re-visiting the knowledge pyramid*. Proceedings of the 42nd Hawaii International Conference on Systems Sciences. Waikoloa, Hawaii. DOI: https://doi.org/10.1109/HICSS.2009.876

Kaatra, K. (1906). *'Suurlakkokuvia' ym. työväenlauluja*. Hämeenlinna: Boman & Karlsson.

Kaihovaara, P. (1986). *Juurella lipun punaisen: Työväenjärjestöjen liput—osa työväenkulttuuria*. Helsinki: Yhteiskunnallinen Arkistosäätiö.

Kaihovaara, P. (1991). Työväenliikkeen lippukulttuurin symboleista. In U. Peltonen & K. Stenvall (Eds.), *Myytit ja symbolit: Kirjoituksia suomalai sista kulttuuritulkinnoista* (pp. 47–61). Väki Voimakas 5. Tampere: Finnish Society for Labour History.

Kokko, H. (2016). *Kuviteltu minuus: Ihmiskäsityksen murros suomenkielisen kansanosan kulttuurissa 1800-luvun puolivälissä* (doctoral dissertation, University of Tampere, Tampere). Retrieved from http://urn.fi/URN:ISBN:978-952-03-0282-5

Korff, G. (1993). History of symbols as social history? Translated by H. Drost. *International Review of Social History, 38*(Supp. 1), 105–125.

Koselleck, R. (2004). *Futures past: on the semantics of historical time*. Translated by and with an Introduction by K. Tribe. New York, NY: Columbia University Press.

Kujala, A. (1995). *Venäjän hallitus ja Suomen työväenliike 1899–1905*. Helsinki: Finnish Historical Society.

Moretti, F. (2000). Conjectures on world literature. *New Left Review, 1*(January–February), 54–68.

Mäkelä, E. (2016). LAS: an integrated language analysis tool for multiple languages. *Journal of Open Source Software, 1*(6), 35. DOI: https://doi.org/10.1109/HICSS.2009.876 10.21105/joss.00035

Ollila, A. (2000). *Aika ja elämä: Aikakäsitys 1800-luvun lopussa*. Helsinki: Finnish Literature Society.

Patterson, R. (2011, 23 May). *Sun, light, and the Son*. Bible.org. Retrieved from https://bible.org/article/sun-light-and-son

Pääkkönen, T., Kervinen, J., Nivala, A., Kettunen, K., & Mäkelä, E. (2016). Exporting Finnish digitized historical newspaper contents for offline use. *D-Lib Magazine, 22*(7–8). DOI: https://doi.org/10.1045/july2016-paakkonen

Quintelier, E. (2007). Differences in political participation between young and old people. *Contemporary Politics, 13*(2), 165–180. DOI: https://doi.org/10.1080/13569770701562658

Rajavuori, A. (2017). *Esityksen politiikka: Sosialistinen agitaatio keskisuomalaisella maaseudulla 1906–1908*. Helsinki: Finnish Society for Labour History.

Rowley, J. (2007). The wisdom hierarchy: representations of the DIKW hierarchy. *Journal of Information Science, 33*(2), 163–180. DOI: https://doi.org/10.1177/0165551506070706

Skinner, Q. (2002). *Visions of politics: regarding method*, Vol. 1. Cambridge: Cambridge University Press.

Suodenjoki, S. (2010). *Kuriton suutari ja kiistämisen rajat: Työväenliikkeen läpimurto hämäläisessä maalaisyhteisössä 1899–1909*. Helsinki: Finnish Literature Society.

Soikkanen, H. (1961). *Sosialismin tulo Suomeen: Ensimmäisiin yksikamarisen eduskunnan vaaleihin asti*. Porvoo: WSOY. DOI: http://doi.org/10.31885/2018.00017

Soikkanen, H. (1975). *Kohti kansanvaltaa 1. 1899–1937: Suomen Sosialidemokraattinen Puolue 75 vuotta*. Helsinki: Suomen Sosialidemokraatinen Puolue, Puoluetoimikunta.

Steinberg, M. (2002). *Proletarian imagination: self, modernity, and the sacred in Russia, 1910–1925*. New York, NY: Cornell University Press.

Tikka, M. (2017). Strike in Finland, revolution in Russia: the role of workers in the 1905 General Strike in the Grand Duchy of Finland. In M. Hilson, S. Neunsinger & I. Vyff (Eds.), *Labour, unions and politics under the Northern Star: the Nordic countries, 1700–2000* (pp. 197–217). New York, NY: Berghahn Books.

Tuomi, I. (1999). Data is more than knowledge: implications of the reversed knowledge hierarchy for knowledge management and organizational memory. *Journal of Management Information Systems, 16*(3), 103–117.

Worboys, M., & **Duckham, M.** (2004). *GIS: a computing perspective*. 2nd edn. Boca Raton, FL: CRC Press.

PART IV

Conclusions

CHAPTER 18

The Common Landscape of Digital History

Universal Methods, Global Borderlands, *Longue-Durée* History, and Critical Thinking about Approaches and Institutions

Jo Guldi

In old-fashioned social history, the study of the 'common landscape' used to serve an index of social and cultural difference.[1] Take two regions, two neighbourhoods or two houses, side by side: their differences illuminate cultural ideas about hierarchy, the reality of divergent incomes, and separate relationships with the material world. Just so, the current volume invites us to conduct a survey of the 'common landscape' of digital history in all its variation.

'Field' though it might be in name, the domain of history as practised by scholars of different methodological and political orientations, geographical and temporal subjects of study, and institutions around the globe is really more of a patchwork of different fields and sub-fields, connected by an infrastructure of main-travelled roads and divergent footpaths that only precariously serve the whole. Some of these fields are closely guarded by an embattled elite, others plowed by an army of workers, still others remote provinces known only to a handful of toilers. Here and there, social historians and

How to cite this book chapter:

Guldi, J. (2020). The common landscape of digital history: Universal methods, global borderlands, *longue-durée* history, and critical thinking about approaches and institutions. In M. Fridlund, M. Oiva, & P. Paju (Eds.), *Digital histories: Emergent approaches within the new digital history* (pp. 327–346). Helsinki: Helsinki University Press. https://doi.org/10.33134/HUP-5-18

business historians have already harvested crops for generations. The bumper harvest of the future promised by new technology frightens some with its scale and lack of care, a question addressed by at least two chapters in this volume. In other places, however, tinkerers deploy the new algorithms to cottage-sized gardens of their own liking. Whether they garden with medieval heretics or parliamentary discourse, these cottage-gardeners are increasingly dabbling in some new technology—be it topic models, vectors or other tools found in this volume. Their work is just the garden. The landscape itself is changing as a result of these multiple efforts: it is a changing ecosystem, rebalancing in reaction to human labour, sometimes enclosed or guarded.

The landscape metaphor, to be sure, obscures strong forces of historical change. In Chapter 4 above, Mats Fridlund offers an oceanic image for history and its trends. Forces whence we know not where transform the discipline, moving everything with them. For Fridlund, technology is the wave: in the modern era, technology is the reigning factor. Even scholars who eschew quantitative methods depend upon the word processor, JSTOR articles and newspaper indexes that self-proclaimed non-digital historians depend upon. Using the analytical insights of the history of technology, Fridlund deconstructs the digital, and argues that, like nature, technology is always already with us.

Indeed, there is something elemental in the transformation of scholarship in the modern era. New work with algorithms potentially participates in such a tide, and what is thrilling about it is the sense that any scholar, anywhere in the world, might contribute to its movement. Approaches to the study of history developed by one cadre of researchers working on 19th-century Finland may rapidly translate to studies of 19th-century Britain, of the 20th-century United States, or of medieval China.

Yet, the diversity of different specialisations, periods and interests persists, despite the waves and winds that blow through from time to time. As the rich and diverse studies of this volume have demonstrated, digital history is not so much a field or sub-field in this rich and varied landscape, as a universal approach to history. The practices and methods of digital history are transforming plots here and there across the entire landscape: here a neural net, there a topic model, elsewhere a map or a social network, spanning the entire range of periods, geographies, orientations and institutions, such that no field of historical scholarship, however remote, is today too far away from some garden bed where some scholar has applied a computer-aided practice to their labours.

For proof of this intermingling diversity, one has only to look at the rich set of different algorithms and questions in this volume. Each chapter contributes a different orientation and algorithm, such that the volume as a whole surveys a wide variety of different times, places and orientations. Nonetheless, the neural nets used to study medieval heresy have been used elsewhere to analyse the history of photography, and the topic models used here to analyse German humanist discourse have been used elsewhere to study the history of British parliamentary debates about infrastructure and 20th-century American newspaper coverage of cities.

Surveying digital history thus implies looking over the whole of the rich landscape of spaces that constitute traditional history. All of its periods, geographies and intellectual orientations are being reworked according to collective investments, new approaches, and the questions and problematics opened up thereby.

But is a common set of approaches, shared between knowledge-workers, necessarily the same as a hegemonic project of empire? What is the difference between a 'universalising' set of common practices and a 'universal' history, a single narrative that is supposed to provide a final answer for all times and places? Will the oceanic wave of digital history drown out the lovingly cultivated diversity of the cottage farmer?

In this chapter, I will set out to answer these questions, exploring how the methods of the digital historians exemplified in this volume overlap with the universally applicable discourses of critical theory, how far the two are exclusive and where they are now collaborating together to forge a new set of critical approaches to the study of time. I will use the examples in this volume to test and refine earlier assertions about the trajectory of digital history with regard to the *longue durée*, microhistory, critical theory and politics. I will conclude that the imprint of the *longue durée* is clear; the political implications of practising digital history less so. Along the way towards answering those issues, this chapter will remark on several major features of the common landscape of history as it is now evolving.

This chapter will therefore raise questions about the institutional, national and geographic alignments that make 'doing digital history' possible, reflecting further on some of the themes of institutional investment covered in this book. It will raise questions about the future institutional geography of scholarship, drawing on the implications raised by this volume—one of the most methodologically and forward-thinking volumes on digital history at present—coming from a European nation whose sometime borderland status flags important changes in the geography of scholarship under the digital turn.

Finally, this chapter will look ahead to new trends in scholarship visible in the contributions from this volume, notably: a rise of methodological articles that model the 'bridge' between close and distant readings, the rising importance of scholarship that targets the 'fit' between questions and algorithms, and the increasing importance of international institutional collaboration. As the chapters in this volume demonstrate, digital history is well on its way to establishing theories and methodologies that satisfy these most critical criteria of scholarly investigation; in the years that follow, scholars who pay attention to these themes will have even more to look forward to.

The Universalism or Common Space of the Digital Humanities

The discussion of methods herein, one might say, offers a truly 'universal' tendency for scholarly exchange, and it is worthwhile pausing to understand what we mean by that. In another volume, the reader who specialises in medieval history might flip only to the chapter written by the medievalist. But it is a truism that in digital history, and the digital humanities more generally, to pass over the other sections would be an error. The methods developed for one sub-field will be relevant to the next sub-field tomorrow if they aren't already today.

We see in these critical reflections the shape of new standards for historical work as scholars puzzle over the fit between particular algorithms and questions. In Chapter 16, Välimäki and his co-authors (Reima Välimäki, Aleksi Vesanto, Anni Hella, Adam Poznański and Filip Ginter) used neural nets to confirm the authorship of the *Refutatio Errorum*, an anti-heretical treatise from Germany in the 1390s, establishing, in the process, a new standard for author detection. In Chapter 15, Heidi Hakkarainen and Zuhair Iftikhar prove that topic models are well-suited to engaging Koselleck's idea of concept history, linking concepts with temporality. The chapter describes a vast culture of experimentation and discovery, as scholars try out competing algorithms, testing the fit of each method to the scholarly questions independently identified as problematic in each field.

To dub such a capacity for common meeting 'universalism' is to underscore that anyone might play with any of the ideas at stake, even while an enormous pluralism existed of period, subject and political orientation. It would certainly not imply the universal applicability of any one fact or conclusion reached by the research, which is subject, as all historical research is, to the revisions of new discoveries, new archives and new approaches. Perhaps an even better term than 'universalism' for what we are investigating would be the 'common space' of the city that Hannah Arendt identified as a metaphor for the best strivings of both Enlightenment and democracy: that they could be accessed by anyone, that they enlivened and illuminated all lives that touched them.[2]

By employing the image of 'common space' in the city as a metaphor for a certain aspiration in discursive activity, Arendt underscored the question of access: since the European Enlightenment, the modern city was defined by spaces of equal access, spaces that didn't shut people out. We might say the same about digital history: whatever the critique from the outside, the practitioners of digital history have taken pains not to shut out any practitioners whomsoever, and many of them have worked at length to convert digital tools into material for critically inspecting empire, gender and race.[3]

What about the contention that digital history is itself imperial and *universalising* in nature, threatening to draw all history practitioners into a single method, problem of study and macrohistorical overview of the *longue durée*? A notorious example of universalising claims by biologist interlopers relates to a decade ago, and the haunting claim, made in the national media of the United States, that historians would be obviated by the coming of the computer.[4] As digital history is actually practised, we see very little of this. More relevant is a portrait of individual scholars or scholars in small units working together to execute some new perspectival opening onto their sub-field—medieval heresy, the Finnish Parliament, the Finnish borderlands or European humanists.

Not one chapter in this volume gestures towards a universalising macrohistory of the *longue durée* that would eliminate the perspective of workers or feminists beneath the triumph of the nation or empire. Not one chapter in the whole book even claims to dispense with or obviate the field of social history, biography, intellectual, cultural or political history, although most chapters build on aspects of other forms of history in some respect. To paint the common landscape of scholarship, the artist would truly have to recognise a thousand *digital histories*, not one digital history, stretching along the plain, informed by exchanges, building on works already in progress across the land.

Another version of the complaint against digital history as *universalising* and therefore coercive borrows an image from Lawrence Stone, who in the 1970s warned against quantitative enterprises of all kinds as commandeering graduate students into massive, pyramidal projects where their intellectual inquiry is dictated from above and individual initiative is squashed.[5] This, too, seems not to be the case. In the quarters of digital humanities where graduate students are enlisted, they are often featured as first-authors on projects that they were invited to craft with the skill and support of leaders in the field.[6]

Graduate students and early-career faculty in this volume, including Reetta Sippola and Matti La Mela, are particularly distinguished as early adopters and explorers of new technology, who have been willing to extend their training in some sub-fields to adopt new technologies, test a theory or explore a time period. The borrowing—from computer science, statistics, the digital humanities, linguistics or library science—means that these early adopters are fast at work in building up the discursive commons that Arendt so praised.

Whatever we call it, exchange between sub-fields has quite a bit going for it. Discursive commons, technological borrowing and other such scholarly programmes of exchange represent an instinct for common space or the universal that, according to science, has been waning of late in the academy. This tendency to narrow the study of the universal back to readings in one's subfield, we learn, is not merely a habit of the humanities, but can be quantitatively identified in the social sciences and sciences as well. According to the research of sociologists of knowledge such as James Evans, scholars today generally cite fewer readings directly outside their realm of concern than did scholars a generation ago. It seems to be the case that internet-enabled web catalogues have restricted universal reading habits of borrowing from nearby disciplines, whether for critical theory or for other inspiration. The sheer overwhelming scale of available knowledge left scholars paralysed by the task of keeping up with their nearest cohort.

History seems to indicate that information economies more generally are marked by a pulse of broadening the process of collecting information and refining the information thereby collected. This pulse of information analysis has been studied across decades-long exchanges about early-modern botanical knowledge, as well as on the personal scale of Darwin's notebooks.[7] What we are calling 'universal' moments or moments of 'common spaces' seem to be moments of expansion, when scholars looked to particular discussions as relevant for scholars who worked across a broad variety of periods and places.

Today, the digital humanities partake of a similar moment of universalism, in which scholars of 1980s online culture, 19th-century novels and Chinese medical texts regularly meet and compare notes, finding algorithms to borrow from one another. As a result, a discussion of methods offers a meeting ground on a broad scale, as well as an opportunity to compare notes across different sub-fields and disciplinary orientations.

There have been other moments of expansion on a theoretical level, where humanities disciplines are reforged through insights from without. Such, for instance, was the impact of the steady importation of continental philosophy and critical theory into the humanities since the 1970s. A Freudian reading of Augustine could be interesting to those contemplating the nature of the biographical subject during the American Revolution precisely because the *method* could be so easily transported and applied to other fields and subjects. By the same token, a Foucauldian reading of colonial India might, in theory, interest readers from the social history of industrialisation.

Indeed, it is possible that methodological moments of unification offer a necessary antidote to the paradigm of modern specialisation of knowledge, with its tendencies to mince fields into sub-fields and further sub-fields, with the concomitant risk of knowing more and more about less and less. The arrival of critical theory in the 1970s meant that the scholar of Virginia Woolf and of Classical Athens could find both a common meeting ground and a common language in terms of inclusiveness, femininity, the knowledge of the state and the construction of the individual.

At the same time, however, the digital humanities are beginning to see a moment of critical inward inspection, of the refinement of processes and pipelines. The 'universal' impulse in the digital humanities is thus giving way to another phase of information analysis—one predicated upon the close inspection and comparison of algorithms, the attention to metadata, and the examination of OCR errors and named-entity detection. As Kimmo Elo points out, this domain of attention is a necessary part of the process of refinement if the garden of earthly methodologies is to bear fruit. The labour of refinement and inspection will almost certainly be a domain of work that requires the labour of historians.

If building interoperable tools and applying them to great questions of history represents the universal access of the city square—liberating with its sense of wide access and possible exchange—the work of refining metadata and inspecting tools is more like the garden plot of digital history, a place that requires focused attention and hard work to produce useful results. The metaphor is complete if we imagine that the garden of tool- and data-refinement produces useful results that can be taken back to the universal exchange of the city square. As Johan Jarlbrink points out, inspecting the results of metadata analysis through simple methods such as the 'tally' stands to help us unpack the 'black box' of digital learning.

A volume of the present kind offers a rare glimpse into how the entire breadth of history is shaped—in its temporal range, from studies in the history of Finnish feminism to medieval heretics to labour politics, and in its methodological range, from the prosecution of new frontiers with existing tools like topic modelling to the close attention to algorithms, metadata and tallies of OCR errors. The scholar who represents each period, place, theme and method has a separate body of texts and different methods, to be sure; indeed, the scholarship in question was in part selected so as to adequately represent the diversity of possible methods, approaches and statistical rigour practised across history as a whole.

In offering a meeting ground of methods and periods, a methodological volume offers an important service to the discipline as a whole. The scholar of medieval heresy may wind up later borrowing the tools from the scholar of humanism or labour politics, even if their data for the moment looks entirely different. Digital practices tend to lend themselves across formats, political interests, historiographical orientations, periods or geographies. Thus, digital tools draw historians back to a certain methodological universalism, even in the face of other kinds of plurality, insofar as they encourage practices of reading-across-boundaries, in the form of conferences or volumes, like this one, that reward the practice of rich learning in new directions.

The Pedagogical Role of Discourse

In order to enjoy knowledge as a commons, one mandate is that the experts of the commons must be motivated with an eagerness to explain, to render accessible the more difficult concepts that they have assembled for the use of others. In the era of critical theory, difficult writers from Marx to Heidegger got interpreters who translated their concepts into ready-to-wear essays: 'Benjamin for Historians', the beginner's guide.[8] Digital humanities can only claim to be a 'commons' accessible to all sub-fields of history insofar as it too has been equipped with multiple translation projects, rendering difficult statistics and algorithms within the grasp of the total novice.

The present volume is a monument to the pedagogical impulse of digital history. The writers assembled here have taken pains to draw down the abstractions of algorithms, statistics and databases into language of period, inquiry and method familiar (or at least tractable) for traditional historians. Each chapter introduces its method, algorithm and dataset in careful detail, presuming little prior acquaintance with historical method. Writers test and explore the possibility of 'false positives' raised by misinterpreting topic models. They ask about the bridge between macroscopic 'overviews' of the material and 'close reading', and how an overview can or should guide the reader back to individual texts or episodes. They seek to open up the 'black box' of digital analysis, to unpack and critique its workings, and to thus devise a new machine for critical analysis of the past. The result is a series of essays that are pedagogically precise: an instructive model about how to describe a new process for the use of other scholars. These are the tactics that historians of the future should recognise as a new standard for how openly, precisely and clearly we write—for what a truly 'universal' or 'common' practice of historical reasoning looks like.

The authors of the individual chapters of this volume have taken the editors' direction for clarity, instruction and critical thinking to heart. In Chapter 9 on feminist history in Finland, the question under investigation is the correct approach to take, and Heidi Kurvinen playfully offers her own experiences of success and failure as an example for other scholars venturing onto this unpredictable frontier of knowledge, where the rules of adequate preparation are not entirely spelled out as yet. In Matti La Mela's Chapter 11 on the freedom to roam in Finnish parliamentary debates, he walks the reader through a step-by-step recreation of the process, suitable to educating historians with no prior use of the algorithms or techniques at stake. In Chapter 16 by Välimäki and colleagues, the authors critically explore the use of each part of their data (the examples of anti-heretical texts with known authors used to train the neural net, the authors proposed by other scholars) and each algorithm (the Support Vector Machines used to detect authorship, the vector machine used to clean the data). Computational author detection, they urge, should become the new currency of the discipline, amplifying other criteria of authorship detection such as structure, manuscript tradition and argumentation.

The writers in this volume have also shouldered the burden of offering their own interpretation of the new approaches necessary to digital history. From the 'tensor history' of Timo Honkela's foreword to the 'resource criticism' of Mats Fridlund's Chapter 4, their inquiries point to the importance, as history adopts new methodologies, of adequately spelling out the limits of an inquiry, the sources of the data, the silences and limits of each inquiry and the possibilities opened by particular algorithms.

I read the theoretical trajectory of this volume as a powerful demand that each historical encounter explicitly renders obvious its limits, both in terms of sources and in terms of methods. And if that seems like something that historians have already done in carefully describing their paper archives and theoretical baggage, consider this: what if every historical study that leans, in part or in whole, on secondary sources, newspapers, parliamentary debates or other digitised corpora considered not only the limits of the micro-archive, but also the limits of the macro-archive? We would have to choose forms of analysis that allow us to form an overview of the archive as a whole, for the purposes of both *longue-durée* analysis and acknowledging the historical situatedness and inherent bias of each archive. In essence, we are being invited into a new age of historical criticism, one that brings the 'capital/periphery' critique of post-colonial studies home in the sense of recognising the limits of data and critique, acknowledging the way in which our source-base and view of history has been shaped by power and limited all along.

The Universal Borderlands of the Digital Humanities

One token of the universalism of the digital humanities is that the contributions of a group of historians stationed mainly in Finland (rather than Britain or the United States) could dare to claim for itself so vast a title as *Digital Histories*, as if aiming to define the new field. Nor is the volume bound by an exclusive orientation to Finnish history: the subjects of this volume range across Europe. Perhaps because of the 'universal' tendency of digital humanities research outlined above, digital humanities research in Finland is, indeed, as diverse as the historical discipline in Finland. The present volume represents an earnest attempt to define the historiographical range of questions presented by historians working with digital techniques, to cover the range of algorithmic and metadata practices used by our colleagues, and to introduce new scholars to best practices and techniques that merit attention from scholars of any time period or geography.

The digital humanities provide an arena of study that is 'universal' in that it incorporates broad engagement with international currents in intellectual and cultural history, feminist history and the history of science. The topics herein contained range from medieval studies of authorship among Waldensian heretical texts to the popular reception of scientific astronomy in the 18th century. Far from being rigid and inflexible, the chapters here show off an astonishing variety of methods, each the mirror of a historical problem with its own historiographical legacy stretching back over decades. The research projects in question demonstrate something of the expansiveness of interest and time period that could be found within most national traditions.

International sharing of methods and data has been intense over the last decade, among historical practitioners, and this international intensity has raised a number of new international capitals for digital humanities research—among them digital humanities centres and nodes of excellence in Umeå, Uppsala, Venice, the Max Planck Institute Berlin, the Dutch national research infrastructure CLARIAH, the University of Sussex, the Language Bank of Finland, the University of Helsinki and the University of Turku. On a global level, digital humanities researchers in Singapore, Taiwan, China and Latin America are producing significant demonstrations of new methods. The map of digital history practitioners on the avant-garde of methodology is both more international and marked by the presence of younger universities and research institutes than a more traditional map of excellence in the humanities. With all respect to the digital humanities summer institutes that introduce many scholars to the techniques of DH, this is simply not a field of which one gains mastery by a single visit to a great master at Oxford, Cambridge or Harvard: the field is moving too quickly, with nodes of excellence developing in seemingly improbable places.

The conditions for international participation in digital history are set by trajectories that have something to do with the existence of national traditions of history in all of those places, as well as the rise of an international information economy over the lifetime of the authors of the present volume. As Paju's Chapter 2 explains, historical researchers in Finland have experimented with digital techniques since the 1960s, much as American researchers trace their roots back to experimentations with punch cards and Latin codices in the 1950s. Like universities around the world, Finland has a national tradition of historical research with centres of excellence of teaching and learning. Finnish scholars, building on generations of institutional development, have had the opportunity to theorise important questions about statistical measures and AI, close reading and distant reading, and the role of learned societies in building and maintaining the intellectual infrastructures of today.

As such, the volume represents an event horizon within the global practice of historical scholarship which marks the rise of institutional 'borderlands' that are less well-established than the Ivy League or the ancient universities of Western Europe. Finland's distinctiveness within the digital humanities thus offers a paradigmatic path for other national bodies of researchers who wish to vie for distinction on the frontiers of interdisciplinary knowledge-making. Like many other economies in the developed world, and many in the developing world as well, Finland is heir to the information economy with all of its perquisites. Like many privileged departments in Europe, Canada, North America and Australia, Finland's history departments, libraries and language banks have benefited from an aggressive institutional programme of digitisation and support. These three preconditions—a tradition of historical study, participation in the international information economy and institutional development funded on a national or international level—make it possible for scholars and universities to mark themselves out for distinction within the space of digital history research.

The 'universal' power of the digital humanities has thus established an arena where newer institutions and national traditions of historical research can play, on equal terms, with the oldest and most distinguished universities in the world. The present volume demonstrates how scholars from a European borderland have harnessed this power to demonstrate their engagement with new methods, tools and critiques.

Digital Directions: The *Longue Durée,* Identity, etc.

Critical readers will want to know whether the digital histories of this volume are closing out or displacing other kinds of inquiry. By implication, they wonder whether departments that choose to invest in digital research are necessarily thereby foreclosing on other kinds of research strategy. The rationale behind fears such as these are located in the real, historical experience of intellectual 'turns' in the academy: one meeting ground sometimes displaces another, and this was true of critical theory. Topics of study inherited by the 20th-century humanities from the 19th century and classical precedents included the existence of 'genres' in fiction, the search for ideal character in the genre of biography, the ideal of succeeding generations of 'reform' in the study of political regimes and the history of progress through a cascading series of perfections (whether in the form of intellectual history, the history of science or the history of technology).

As scholars came to understand the past with the aid of critical theory, old categories of research (genre, character, reform and progress) each held within them a doctrine that was itself a historical construct. What critical theory did for the liberal conscience of the university was to create a series of substitutions where a former doctrine was broken open in favour of a series of new research questions. Many of those questions were informed by politics (for example, jettisoning the doctrine of empire's beneficence in favour of a series of critical questions). Rather than taking the 19th-century agenda of matters for historical investigation as a given, it was possible to subject each of them to deconstruction and historical analysis. In the process, a new set of research questions emerged: instead of character, there was agency, and with it the question of under what conditions it became possible for an individual or a certain group to exert change over their fate or the course of collective experience. Instead of technology as the progress of inventions from one generation to the next, the history of science and technology was reborn as a series of questions about the ideology of science and technology; their affiliation with empire, masculinity and capital; the institutions that support them; and the illusion of forward progress. Critical theory buried the naïve liberal scholarship that came before it, replacing it with a series of new research questions.

Just as critical theory pushed out the set of uncritical liberal targets of research that came before it, so, it might be expected, will the new goals of digital history displace some of the focus of the scholarly record before them. It is too soon to tell what the subjects of replacement will be; the relationship between digital history and earlier generations of history is still in formation. Moreover, the number of digital history papers that directly counters an extant historical theory is very small, in comparison with those in digital literature, where scholars such as Ted Underwood and Andrew Piper have explicitly taken on some of the mainstream conclusions of the field and shown how digitally produced knowledge overturns received wisdom about, say, the idiosyncrasy of Flaubert.

While digital history remains, as yet, immature, the field as a whole is guided by theories of when, how and whether digital history will call for a revision of lasting tropes in the discipline. In *The history manifesto*, my co-author and I pushed the strongest possible case for a revolution in critical thinking abetted by access to digital tools, and we sought to describe what that might look like: in brief, we conjectured that *longue-durée* timescales of 100 years or more would displace microhistory on the scale of the human life or shorter. We advanced some related claims about the political crises of the present and the new *longue-durée* inquiries that they might provoke (shifting attention to climate change and economic inequality over identity politics). How have those prophesies held up when it comes to the writing of 'digital history' five years later?

One of our guesses was the renewed importance of *longue-durée* perspectives, given the fact that digital research made trivial the repetition of cultural-studies-type analytics on long time scales using scales of material that would be impossible for the traditional reader. Just such an approach is represented, in the current volume, by several uses of newspaper corpora. In Chapter 15, Heidi Hakkarainen and Zuhair Iftikhar prove that, over 21 years, the language of Austrian newspapers demonstrates the growing importance of historicist thought. They chart the succession of disciplines through which ideas of humanism spread, a modelling of ideas like a contagion, a transition from education to the reformation to revolution and later the death penalty. They reveal how newspapers gradually connected the human, the spiritual, democracy and the future, a new language evidenced by the increasing importance of the terms *Zukunft* (future) and *Zeit* (time) to the definition of humanism. In Chapter 11, Matti La Mela uses the Finnish parliamentary debates to investigate the freedom to roam over a century. On an even longer time span, in Chapter 12, Pasi Ihalainen (with the help of Aleksi Sahala) identifies several kinds of discourse about internationalism since the founding of the League of Nations, including internationalism typically opposed to (but sometimes arising from) *nationalism*; variants of *party* and *labour* internationalism; the *spirit* of nationalism linked to ideas and values; and the promise of *peace* and *democracy* arising from internationalism, especially after 1930. A revised chronology of internationalism shows a peak in the 1970s, followed by a period of frustration.

New findings that draw from long timescales can border on the breathtaking. Perhaps the most surprising finding in Ihalainen and Sahala's investigation of long-term discourses of internationalism was the longevity of ideas. Ihalainen found that down to the 'leave' side of Brexit, many of the ways of describing the promise and threat of internationalism remained unchanged since discussions of the League of Nations in the interwar period, on both the left and the right.

Much of the work that was once carried out by the 'close reading' of the cultural turn in the 1980s and 1990s can now be achieved with greater precision and efficacy by algorithms designed to discern, and to measure, similarities and differences of expression and sentiment, allowing the tight comparison of decades, institutions, political parties and individuals. The work in this volume aptly demonstrates that the work of the cultural and linguistic turns—concerned with the shift of lexicons and the insight this provides about historical identities and communities—are now, on their cutting edge, digital in method.

There are real challenges facing the prosecution of the *longue durée* as well. In Chapter 3, Jari Eloranta, Pasi Nevalainen and Jari Ojala point to the overwhelming scale of the archives that still await digitisation in their domain, that of the modern business history of Finland. They cite the archives of Finland's 20th-century government administration since the 1970s, now held in the National Archives: 'roughly 200 shelf-kilometres' of documents essential to understanding the history of the welfare state and neoliberalism. These archival materials would have to be scanned first before they were analysed by digital means, and they are not scheduled for digitisation. A more practical approach, for the moment, is the kind of sampling recommended by Claire Lemercier and Claire Zalc in their *Quantitative methods in the humanities*.[9] The facts of this dynamic raise challenges to archival institutions, grant-writing bodies in the humanities and the institutions of democracy themselves. A survey *could* be conducted by sampling documents out of that 200 kilometres of shelves, but what would be left out? Surely citizens of each region in Finland deserve the tools to monitor the history of how changes in government organisation affected their own landscape. Serving citizens requires an infrastructure and the building of tools. If such an infrastructure needs to be built for other purposes, and the archives need to be digitised, then historians can rise to the challenge of asking questions about the *longue durée* of that 200 kilometres of shelves and its analysis. Indeed, it is possible, as Ted Underwood has lately argued, that trends otherwise invisible on the short *durée* would emerge from such an analysis.[10]

Some of the guesses hazarded by *The history manifesto* went against the actual course of scholarship, in particular the continuing importance of research into gender, race and class. Prognostications that identity politics would be displaced by a larger, shared concern over economic inequality proved short-sighted in the face of the rise of right-wing movements around the world and the renewed relevance of identity-based activism. To counter those movements, scholars, journalists, lawyers, artists and ordinary citizens have returned to the *longue durée* of injustice in a powerful way; for instance, through the demands for reparations for slavery in Britain and America, or in the public controversy over monuments to confederate generals across the American South. Indeed, until racism, sexism and nationalism are abolished, historians are bound to ask questions about where they came from.

Thus, what we see in the new practice of digital history is not so much the displacement of critical theory by digital history, as the integration of the questions posed by critical theory on longer time spans, addressed with methods that allow the historian to fully integrate the methods of the cultural, social and linguistic turns. The natural outgrowth of these dynamics is a kind of digital history that fixes on identity and empire as its subject, exemplified by the many projects gathered and reviewed in Roopika Risam's *Postcolonial digital humanities* (2019). The present volume gathers studies in the history of Karelian borderlands and Finnish feminism. It is unsurprising that any cultural or political event could be traced at scale and in depth by digital means.

Implications and Future Directions

What are the implications of such a study for other scholars, if not to mark out a definitive set of algorithms or revisions for others? I would argue that the output of such a volume as this is significant in that it sketches out the computational best practices of a moment. It also speaks frankly to some of the challenges ahead. It is to the work of coming challenges that I will write for the remainder of this conclusion.

The need for theorising the bridge between distant and close readings

The possibility of informing close reading with the power of synthetic tools is one of the major promises of digital history. Of his century-long examination of collocation in parliamentary discourse, Ihalainen explains, 'distant reading reveals peculiar political points that might have gone unnoticed in mere close reading or full-text keyword searches of the same documents'.

While a few of the chapters in this book begin with distant reading and end by examining particular documents, there are few examples today of historical or literary practice that moves from the distant overview down to the level of authors or other categories and into particular passages in the book, critically examining the results of a search based on the close reading of the page. Like much of the work in the contemporary digital humanities, results of distant reading are frequently given in a summary chart or single finding. Two notable exceptions offer a meditation on the 'bridge' between the distant and the close, and provide historians with a way forward. In a rich meditation on the history of close reading among historians of women, in Chapter 9, Heidi Kurvinen draws a contrast between the tools she studied in her training and the topic modelling she applied to a study of Finnish suffragettes; in the process, she offers her reflections on using the topic model as an index of different episodes, and compares some of the findings of close and distant reckoning. Similarly, in Chapter 7, Johan Jarlbrink descends from a project that surveys the effects of media on cities to critically examine the sample of cities recognised by the computer. Bridging close and distant reading becomes, for Jarlbrink, an opportunity to recognise problems in the measurements supplied by algorithmic tools on 'dirty' data. As we can see from the two examples above, the practice of distant and close reading is evolving, and new hybrids are being forged that unlock insights in the archives and highlight shortcomings in the technology.

Future approaches to the bridge between close and distant reading may do well to follow the pattern set by Andrew Piper in his recent survey of modern literature, *Enumerations*, which proceeds from distant readings of the themes and trends across poetry and the novel, down to particular authors, poems and passages, as guided by the tools of distant reading.[11] After all, the same tools that draw our attention to words can be used to compare individual speakers as well as parties, and indeed to draw attention to the particular paragraphs and sentences that the computer discerns to be the most exemplary cases of a particular concept and collocation pattern. That is, where a scholar learns that an important collocate of 'internationalism' is 'nation', it would be useful to learn next which individual speaker in Parliament pairs the two words together most frequently, and the individual speech in which those concepts are juxtaposed the most. Additional measures such as these may lend confidence that particular sentences given as examples of collocation are not merely cherry-picked for their familiarity, but actually offered foundational instances of the making or re-use of the concept.

More to the point, as historians engage in moving from the small example to the big question, and from the big overview back to individual speech acts, the process of movement itself is open to methodological argument, questions of interpretation and over-interpretation. It is important that historians begin to describe their choice of exemplary passages. Thick description of the process of extraction affords an opportunity to articulate the work of human interpretation and machine contextualisation. As we examine this frontier, we will begin to understand better the application of distant reading to work on different scales, including the scale of the corpus, the author, the work, the paragraph and the word.

Theorising the difference between AI and statistical measures

In the work here, the terms 'mutual information' and 'neural nets' appear on the same page. Their basis could not be more different, however. The former is statistical and can be described, mathematically, at every step; the latter has been developed mainly from computer-science departments aiming to mirror human processes, and essentially represents a black box of pattern recognition. Some scholars in the computer sciences herald a day where autonomous intelligence will obviate human supervision in most domains, including education. Colleagues in other parts of the university are more skeptical, arguing that AI, in most cases, relies on the labour-intensive hand-tooling of research questions to algorithms. More precise and transparent answers, they suggest, are to be had from old-fashioned statistics.

Humanists are far from the centre of these debates, but our testing of algorithms and our successes and failures have implications beyond our own discipline. As Eloranta and his colleagues point out, business and economic historians have a long history of critical engagement with statistical measures such as regression and event analysis that could easily contribute to a rigorous comparison between statistical measures and unsupervised machine learning. Elsewhere, in Chapter 16, Välimäki and his colleagues rely on neural networks (the epitome of unsupervised, black-box AI), while another advances a preference for mutual information: the epitome of advanced statistics, where equally useful clusters are formed on the basis of a relatively transparent clustering formula. Because we know our textual corpora and their historical context so well, as the scholars' research on authorship illustrates, historians are often in a better position to 'train' and 'test' the scripts of AI and to comment on how well they work. These findings could usefully be published in the *Papers of the National Academy of Sciences* or *Science*, to the edification of other disciplines and the credit of our own.

To the degree to which historical methods border on questions of the success of AI or a preference for transparent statistics, historians have an opportunity to theorise about the stakes of one choice over another. As the discipline of digital history becomes more advanced, we should expect more work of this kind.

Transparent documentation of the choice of algorithm, text and result in the practice of critical search

Elsewhere, I have argued that scholarly engagement, both traditional and digital, in general tends towards the critical examination of the choices that inform a research project.[12] Whether the choices made in an archival visit are informed by the reading of critical theory, or whether political interest in the *longue durée* drives a scholar towards particular algorithms, critical thinking about the motives and limits of particular kinds of research is always being called upon to inform the constraints of the research process. I generalised the digital research process into a pattern I called 'critical search', and I characterised major opportunities for critical thinking inherent in any research process. Instances of critical search in an article might include discussing the choice of keywords and algorithms and how initial choices reveal and conceal aspects of a corpus later disclosed by adjustments to the initial search. The point, in any case, is that these are forms of critical reflection that scholars are prone to in general, and through these critical reflections, the entire community of readers comes to consensus about the uses of particular algorithms, the multiple dimensions of digital archives and the interpretative questions that govern digital research.

The chapters in this volume offer freely evolved examples of critical search, in the sense that they reflect upon the process of creating knowledge with digital tools. In their search for how 19th-century Austrian newspapers described the emergent principle of humanism, Hakkarainen and Iftikhar describe multiple iterations of different kinds of topic models, configurations, with or without stop words, and how they ultimately decided on a combination of topic models with a corpus little prepared for analysis. The process of curation, decision-making and interpretation is shown to be at the heart of scholarly digital work.

In Chapter 12, Ihalainen and Sahala explain their persuasive use of information theory's concept of 'mutual information' to examine lexical change over time. They use pointwise mutual information (PMI) to identify the most regular combinations of words used to describe the international, the global and the transnational in British parliamentary debates in the 20th century. Their method begins with computational work, but traces back digital findings to the text, excerpting compelling passages illustrating the rising tide of interwar optimism about international relations.

We should expect more critical engagement with the search process in the future. As a community, we are learning how to better highlight the distance between *interpretive* work and *computational* work in each research process. In making the choices behind an algorithmic deployment transparent, digital scholars acknowledge that an algorithm isn't a toaster oven, into which a neophyte puts texts in order to achieve an automatic result. Rather, the process of curation, critical inquiry, secondary reading and interpretation remain at the heart of scholarly inquiry.

Engagement with new standards of scholarship from the institutions of historical and cultural knowledge-making

Several of the chapters in this volume implicitly call for a deeper level of participation by historians and their national and international societies in following standards of data preservation, sharing and transparency. In Chapter 10, Maiju Kannisto and Pekka Kauppinen offer a detailed description of copyright issues that had to be overcome for data analysis and sharing in the domain of contemporary media analysis. In Chapter 5, Jessica Parland-von Essen argues that the institutions of cultural analysis should take care to preserve, describe and make accessible multiple layers of data, including its mark-up, analyses, tools, descriptive metadata, consent, rights and attributions of labour. In the process, she describes a potential mountain of cultural labour to be executed by the libraries, archives and IT centres of the world.

Parland-von Essen's chapter suggests a precise charge to the meetings of national historical associations and other learned societies. All of our meetings should have not merely panels for presenting new work in the digital humanities, but also panels for discussing the standards of data presentation, annotation and interoperability.

Cultural institutions (for instance, the Swedish and Finnish literary societies) have a particular role to play in setting out standards for data that is transparent and accessible. Were they to engage the questions raised in this book, in meetings, pamphlets, conferences and hiring, they would have the opportunity to shape how the caretakers of data document the many kinds of labour that have shaped the collection, as well as how practising scholars indicate that they have used data with origins elsewhere. National and international historical meetings offer an important opportunity for inviting cultural institutions and providers of data, from our museums to the private Elseviers of the world, to cooperate with scholars in following these mandates.

On the one hand, directives from national historical associations and conferences are profoundly needed. Even high-profile infrastructure initiatives such as Europeana do not currently provide workflows suited to historians' needs. On the other hand, groups of historians concerned with these issues have already assembled over generations. Petri Paju's Chapter 2 discovers a long-standing tradition for digital-historical institutions and collaborations: for example, the

Helsinki Corpus of English Texts with its origins in the 1980s, the Association for History and Computing, and the Electronic Center for History Research (later Agricola), launched in 1996 by scholars, librarians and archivists; and later the Helsinki Centre for Digital Humanities, or HELDIG, was established at the University of Helsinki in 2016. If these institutions have historically had little influence over mainstream practice, then a new generation of national historical associations and other learned societies could usefully mine the affiliates list of the digital centres for faculties already invested in the important issues of data preservation, documentation and accessibility.

International collaborations and tool sharing

The beauty of computational research is its interoperability: once a technique has been discovered for author attribution in medieval Latin, it should work nearly as well on any early Latin texts whatsoever. The same is true for parliamentary discourse: the collocate machine described by Ihalainen and Sahala should apply to any modern body of text, and the particular tactics for engaging party-political differences of lexicon should be immediately applicable to digitised records of the French *débats*, the debates of the European Union, the Canadian and Australian Hansards and the debates of the City Council of New York City, to name a few active projects. Despite these opportunities, however, there are relatively few examples of international collaborations that take advantage of the astonishing interoperability of algorithms by drawing together scholars working on similar genres of texts.

One initiative that successfully crosses these boundaries is the Oceanic Exchanges project,[13] to which six nations (including Finland, represented by Hannu Salmi at Turun Yliopisto) contribute their historical newspapers and their technical expertise. In the case of newspapers, text-recognition technology applied in one nation can rapidly be adopted to newspapers elsewhere, so the international collaboration represents a massive virtuous cycle of exchanges. All of these efforts contribute to making the international infrastructure of future research, such that one day soon, we should expect that high-school students of history in Finland, America and Mexico will be able to keyword search the newspapers of their national traditions and compare debates about democracy and markets across nations over 200 years.

It is harder to explain why there is not such an international collaboration for the novel, for debates of democratic bodies, for the records of courts of law, for religious texts, for plays, for musical notation, for stylometric authorship attribution and for other genre-specific questions where scholars have similar questions related to form: comparing authors and chapters of the novel, for instance; comparing speakers, parties and constituencies in democratic debate; comparing kinds of charges, prosecution and defence; or judges, juries and defendants in the courts of law. In each of these genres, an international pooling of technical expertise could result in the rapid creation of new knowledge about best methods for turning raw visual images into readable text, for turning text into data annotated with appropriate metadata categories and for deriving meaning over time. The only bar against such collaborations is one of organisation, effort and collegiality: creating useful partnerships depends on planning for international visits, sharing plans of work and the willingness to engage in a process of mutual discernment about where grants and research projects overlap.

The benefits of such collaborations are, of course, tremendous: they can result in the pooling of common goals and strategies, the most efficient use of grant money, the joint discovery of new methodologies and even the joint funding of new infrastructure that makes clean, accessible data available to all.

Notes

1 Stilgoe 1982.
2 Arendt 1973 [1958].
3 Risam 2019.
4 Michel et al. 2011.
5 Stone 1979.
6 Klingenstein, Hitchcock & DeDeo 2014; Barron et al. 2018; Kraicer & Piper 2019.
7 Blair 2010; Murdock, Allen & DeDeo 2017.
8 Weeks 1982; Gay 1986; Schwartz 2001; Brown 2013.
9 Lemercier & Zalc 2019.
10 Underwood 2019.
11 Piper 2019.
12 Guldi 2018.
13 The website of the project is https://oceanicexchanges.org/.

References

Arendt, H. (1973 [1958]). *The human condition*. Chicago, IL: University of Chicago Press.

Barron, A. T. J., Huang, J., Spang, R. L., & **DeDeo, S.** (2018). Individuals, institutions, and innovation in the debates of the French Revolution. *Proceedings of the National Academy of Sciences, 115*(18), 4607–4612. DOI: https://doi.org/10.1073/pnas.1717729115

Blair, A. (2010). *Too much to know: managing scholarly information before the modern age*. New Haven, CT: Yale University Press.

Brown, C. G. (2013). *Postmodernism for historians*. London: Routledge. DOI: https://doi.org/10.4324/9781315836102

Gay, P. (1986). *Freud for historians*. Oxford: Oxford University Press.

Guldi, J. (2018). Critical search: a procedure for guided reading in large-scale textual corpora. *Journal of Cultural Analytics*. DOI: https://doi.org/10.22148/16.030

Klingenstein, S., Hitchcock, T., & **DeDeo, S.** (2014). The civilizing process in London's Old Bailey. *Proceedings of the National Academy of Sciences, 111*(26), 9419–9424. DOI: https://doi.org/10.1073/pnas.1405984111

Kraicer, E., & **Piper, A.** (2019). Social characters: the hierarchy of gender in contemporary English-language fiction. *Journal of Cultural Analytics*. DOI: https://doi.org/10.22148/16.032

Lemercier, C., & **Zalc, C.** (2019). *Quantitative methods in the humanities: an introduction*. Charlottesville, VA: University of Virginia Press.

Michel, J. B., Shen, Y. K., Aiden, A. P., Veres, A., Gray, M. K., Google Books Team, Pickett, J. P., Hoiberg, D., Clancy, D., Norvig, P., Orwant, J., Pinker, S., Nowak, M. A. & **Lieberman Aiden, E.** (2011). Quantitative analysis of culture using millions of digitized books. *Science, 331*(6014), 176–182. DOI: https://doi.org/10.1126/science.1199644

Murdock, J., Allen, C., & **DeDeo, S.** (2017). Exploration and exploitation of Victorian science in Darwin's reading notebooks. *Cognition, 159*, 117–126. DOI: https://doi.org/10.1016/j.cognition.2016.11.012

Piper, A. (2019). *Enumerations: data and literary study*. Chicago, IL: University of Chicago Press.

Risam, R. (2019). *New digital worlds: postcolonial digital humanities in theory, praxis, and pedagogy*. Evanston, IL: Northwestern University Press. Retrieved from http://www.jstor.org/stable/10.2307/j.ctv7tq4hg

Schwartz, V. R. (2001). Walter Benjamin for historians. *American Historical Review, 106*(5), 1721–1743.

Stilgoe, J. R. (1982). *Common landscape of America, 1580 to 1845*. New Haven, CT: Yale University Press.

Stone, L. (1979). The revival of narrative: reflections on a new old history. *Past & Present, 85[11]*, 3–24.

Underwood, T. (2019). *Distant horizons: digital evidence and literary change*. Chicago, IL: University of Chicago Press.

Weeks, J. (1982). Foucault for historians. *History Workshop, 14[3]*, 106–119.

Index

Page numbers in **bold** indicate tables and in *italic* indicate figures.

A

Aalto University 57
Academy of Finland 26, 34, 98
accessible data 90
Ackoff, Russell *316*
administrative metadata 97
Adversus Catharos et Valdenses 283, 284, **287**
Agricola network 31
AI
 see artificial intelligence.
Alatalo, Mikko **169**, 171
allemansrätten in parliamentary sources 181
 collocation analysis 188
 emergence of concept in 20th century *185–186*
 Finland's EC membership 189
 fishing rights 187, 192
 mapping shifts in discursive environments 188, *191*
 quantity and quality of parliamentary documents 183, *185*
 topic modelling 190–*191*
Anderson, Benedict 166, 306
Andræ, Carl Göran 116, 117
angle readsearch 81
Annales School of historians 30
anti-heretical treatises
 see medieval anti-heretical treatises.
Aquinas, Thomas 115
archives
 Central Archives for Finnish Business Records 55, 58
 Finnish National Archives 32, 33, 55, 56, 58
 impacts of digitisation on 75

archives *(Continued)*
microfilming 32
paper 58
Swedish National Archives 54
see also Living Archive audio-visual archives.
Arendt, Hannah 330
artificial intelligence 33, 49, 60, 341
MetaSignal/MetaAlert project 45, 58
Association for History and Computing (AHC) 29
astronomical discourses in *Philosophical Transactions* 237
nine ways of talking about astronomy 249
shared discourses, split viewpoints 242
talking about instruments 246, 248
talking about the weather 245
thematic analysis 241
topic modelling 239
Attendite a falsis prophetis 284, **287**, *288*–289, 291
Attlee, Clement 213
auctoritas 280
audio-visual archives
see Living Archive audio-visual archives.
Augustine 280
Austrian National Library 263
Austrian Newspapers Online (ANNO) collection 263, *264*
authorship attribution
see medieval anti-heretical treatises.
automation 113
Aydelotte, William 5

B

Bacon, Francis 249
Baltic trade data 52
Bang, Nina Ellinger 53
Banks, Joseph 240
Barnes, George 212
Behr, Uwe 223
Benson, Allen 104
Bernal, Martin 72
Bernard of Clairvaux 280–281
Berridge, V. 156, 159
Berry, D. M. 58
Bessette, Jean 151
Beswick, Frank 214
big data 78
in economic and business history 47
Biller, P. 282, 289, 290
bioinformatics 34, 91
Blei, David M. 262
Blevins, Cameron 5
Boethius 283
Bohley, Bärbel 223, *231*
born-digital materials 31, 59, 79, 106
Brexit 210, 214, 215
British Parliament
see internationalism in UK parliament.
Broadberry, Stephen 49
Bryce, James 212
Bryggari, Tuomas 187
Burney, Dennistoun 206
Busa, Roberto 5, 115, 117
Bush, Vannevar 115
business strategy research 49

C

Cameron, E. 283
canonisation 165
causal relationships 49
Cecil, Robert 213
Cegna, R. 289–290
Central Archives for Finnish Business Records 55, 58
Centre for Microfilming and Conservation, Mikkeli, Finland 32

Centro per L'Automazione dell'Analisi Letteraria 117
Chandler, Alfred, Jr. 49
Charmantier, Isabelle 122
checksums 97
Church, K. W. 201
citations 75, 92, 95
citizen science 48
CLARIN (Common Language Resources and Technology Infrastructure) collaboration 168
CLARIN-ERIC 100
Clavin, P. **202**
Clio-Infra database 52
cliometric methods 48
Cliometric Revolution 48, 71
close reading 30, 33, 80, 108, 119, 153, 156, 340
Clynes, J. R. 212
Cocks, Seymour 206
Cohen, Daniel J. 4
Cohen, I. Bernard 72
Colliander, Christian 156
collocation analysis
  allemansrätten in parliamentary sources 188
  Finnish labour newspapers 307, **308**, **309**, *310*
  see also internationalism in UK parliament.
computational authorship attribution 280, 286–*288*
Computational History and the Transformation of Public Discourse in Finland, 1640–1910 project 34
Computer technology for family research (Sukutietotekniikka) 29
concordance searches 189
Conference on Security and Cooperation in Europe (CSCE), Helsinki 223
Conrad of Waldhausen 290
Conrad, Alfred 48
Consolation of Philosophy 283
content drift 91
Continuation War 130, 132, 172
  see also Karelian evacuees, Finland.
Contra Pauperes de Lugduno 284, 285, **287**, 289
copyright *93*, *96*, 100
corpus linguistics 29, 200, 312
Council of Europe 200, 204, 207
  British membership debates 208, 209, 213
counterfactual modelling 50
critical search 342
critical theory 332, 333, 337
crowdsourcing metadata 106
cultural history 30
cultural institutions 343
Culturomics project 79
Cum dormirent homines 280, 282–283, **287**, *288*, 289
Curzon, George 212

D

Dalai Lama 232
Danish Sound data 52
DARIAH-EU 100
Dasu, Tamraparni 114, 115
data cleaning 78, 91
  see also manual labour.
data management
  see digitisation of sources; research data management.
de Figueirêdo, X. 107
de Gussem, Jeroen 281
descriptive metadata 97
DHN conference series 35
Diete, Wolfgang *229*
Dietsch, Mario 223
digital history 1.0 74
digital history 1.5 79
digital history 2.0 76
digital history, defined 4

Digital History of Telco and Exchanges in Finland and Sweden consortium 57
Digital Humanities Academy Programme 34
Digital Humanities in the Nordic Countries 35
digital images
lack of metadata 108
quantities of 78, 108
see also East German opposition movement.
digital newspaper collections 32, 34, 78, 80
increase in citations 75
manual labour involved in research 118
Named Entity Recognition (NER) project 120, *121*
semi-automatic text extraction 80
women's suffrage movement 153, **158**
see also Finnish labour newspapers; humanism discourse in early 19th-century German-language press.
digital noise 34
digital publications 79
digital resource criticism 13, 81
digital source criticism 13, 34, 97
digitisation of sources 11, 104
digital newspaper collections 32
gender sensitivity 152
history of 32
impacts on archives 75
microfilming 32
PDF document collections 107, 108
see also digitising economic and business history; metadata.
digitising economic and business history 45
big data 47
born-digital documents 59
business history 54
databases and their challenges 52
event data analysis 50
further challenges 57
MetaSignal/MetaAlert project 45, 58
paper archives 58
quantitative and qualitative methods 49, 60
DIKW pyramid 315, *316*
Diplomatarium Fennicum database 33
distant reading 6, 30, 80, 108, 119, 153, 340
DOI identifiers 91
Döllinger, I. von 283
Domaschk, Matthias 223, *231*, 232
DTM
see Dynamic Topic Modelling.
Dykes, Hugh 204
Dynamic Topic Modelling, humanism discourse in early 19th-century German-language press 261, *268*, *269*, *270*, *271*

E

Early English Books Online (EEBO) 5, 80
East German opposition movement 221
map of photographs *226*, *228*
network graphs 225, *226*, 227, *229*, *230*, *231*
photographic database 222, *224*
snapshots in time and local networks 227, *229*, *230*
temporal distribution of photographs 227
using historical network analysis *224*
using image metadata 222, *224*
econometric tools 48, 50
economic history 25, 35
see also digitising economic and business history.

Economy and History 27
Edelstein, D. 106
Edoff, Erik 120
EH-net databases 52
Electronic Centre for History Research in Finland 30
Ellison, John W. 5
Elo, Kimmo 168
Emergency Settlement Act, Finland 131
emerging digital historical practices 69
 everyday digital impacts on research 74
 normal digital history 74
 paradigmatic digital history 76
 scientific revolutions theory 70, 77, 83
 semi-automatic digital history 79
Ennen ja nyt (Then & Now) 31
Enoch, Jessica 151
Environment Library, East Berlin 227
Erb, Elke *230*
European Commission 98
European Open Science Cloud (EOSC) 100
European Union/European Economic Community
 British membership debates 204, 207, 208, 210, 213, 215
 Finnish membership 174, 189
Europeana cultural heritage portal 99, 100
Eurovision Song Contests 172, 175
Evans, James 331
event data analysis 50
everyman's right
 see allemansrätten in parliamentary sources.

F

factor analysis 24
Fagerjord, A. 58
FAIR Data concept 90
Falkenberg, Petra 223, *231*
Feitosa, H. 107
feminist digital history research 149
 feminism and digital analysis 150
 first steps in digital humanities research 152
 importance of search words 155
 women's suffrage movement 153, **158**
Fickers, Andreas 81
FIN-CLARIN consortium 168
findable data 90
Finna.fi search portal 92, 99
Finnish Academy
 see Academy of Finland.
Finnish audio-visual heritage
 see Living Archive audio-visual archives.
Finnish historical national accounts 49
Finnish labour newspapers 303
 collocation analysis 307, **308**, **309**, *310*
 DIKW pyramid 315, *316*
 keyness method 312, **313**
 relative word frequencies over time *305*
Finnish National Archives 32, 33, 55, 56, 58
Finnish National Library 33, 118, 153, 188, *305*
Finnish Parliament 183
 quantity and quality of parliamentary documents 183, *185*
 see also allemansrätten in parliamentary sources.
Finnish rule-based named-entity recogniser (FiNER)
 see Living Archive audio-visual archives.
fishing rights 187, 192
Fogel, Robert 48, 50
forced migration
 see Karelian evacuees, Finland.

Foxlee, N. 200
Friberg, Maikki 157
Fridlund, Mats 153
From Roadmap to a Road Show project 153
Fuchs, Jürgen 223, 227, 229, *231*, 232
Fuchs, Lilo *229*
full-text search 81, 117
fuzzy set Qualitative Comparative Analysis (fs/QCA) 51
Fyfe, Aileen 239

G

Gammans, David 213
gender history
see feminist digital history research.
genealogists 29
General Strike 1905, Finland 304, 306, 317
generic research datasets 95, *96*
Geographic Information System (GIS) 5, 33
Gephi network analysis tool 119, *230*, 263
Ghadially, Rehana 150
Global Price and Income History database 52
Globe and Mail 75
Gold, Matthew K. 149
Google Books 78, 80, 114
Google Ngram Viewer 79
Gopher-based internet pages 30
Gretser, Jacob 282, 283, 284, *288*
Gripenberg, Alexandra 156
Groningen University 48
Guibert of Gembloux 281
Guldi, J. 200
Gutman, H. G. 47

H

Hadenius, Stig 116
Halley, Edmond 246
Halonen, Tarja 170, 171
Hanks, P. 201
Hansard Corpus 201
Haukka, J. 131
Havemann, Katja 223, *231*
Havemann, Robert 223, *224*, 227, *230*
Hayes, Helen 214
Heikkilä, Tuomas 34
HELDIG 35
Helsingin Sanomat 153, **158**, 188, *305*, **313**
Helsinki Centre for Digital Humanities (HELDIG) 35
Helsinki Corpus of English Texts 29
Helsinki Finite-State Toolkit 168
Henry, John 248
HFST-SweNER 120, 168
Hildebrandt, Manfred 223
Hildegard of Bingen 281
Hillmann, Edgar 223
histoGraph project 106
Historiallinen Aikakauskirja 23, 24, 27, 28
historical economics tradition 48
historical linguistics 29
historical national account series 48
historical network analysis *224*
see also East German opposition movement.
History in the digital age 5
history of computer-assisted history research in Finland 21, **37**
developments in 2000s and 2010s 33
digital newspaper collections 32, 34
digitisation of sources 32
internet 29, 30
late 1960s 23
microcomputers 28
microfilming 32
research projects in 1970s 26
text processing 28

Hjerppe, Riitta 49
HNA
  see historical network analysis.
Hollinger, David 72
Homburg, Wasmud von 284, **287**
Huistra, Hieke 156
human rights conventions 207
humanism discourse in early 19th-century German-language press 259
  Death penalty topic 265, 266, 267, *268*
  Dynamic Topic Modelling 261, *268*, *269*, *270*, *271*
  Education topic 265, 266, *267*, *268*
  MALLET topic modelling 261, *264*, *268*
  Philosophy topic 265, 266, *268*
  Press debate topic 265, *268*
  Reformation topic 265, 266, *268*
  Religion topic 265, 267, *268*, *269*, *270*
  Revolution topic 265, 266, *267*, *268*
  Social issues topic 265, 266, *267*, *268*
  source material 263, *264*
  stop words removal 262, 265, *270*
Huttunen, Pertti 23, 24
H-verkko email list 30
Hyvönen, Eero 35

I

Ice Hockey World Championship 174
images
  see digital images; East German opposition movement.
imagined communities theory 166, 306
Index Thomisticus 115
infrastructures and services 98
inquisition
  see medieval anti-heretical treatises.
intellectual property rights *93*, *96*, 100
international collaborations 344
International Labour Organisation (ILO) 205
internationalism in UK parliament 199
  Brexit debates 210, 214, 215
  Council of Europe membership debates 208, 209, 213
  EEC/EU membership debates 204, 207, 208, 210, 213, 215
  Hansard Corpus 201
  individual speeches 211
  League of Nations membership debates 208, 212, 215
  trends in discourse on internationalism **202**, *203*
  United Nations membership debates 208, 209, 213
internet
  everyday impacts on research practices 74
  introduction of 29, 30
interoperability 92, 94, 344
interoperable data 91

J

Jahn, Roland 223, 227, 229, *231*
Jarlbrink, Johan 34, 156
Järvinen, Pertti 24
Jena Peace Community 223
Jockers, Matthew 5
Johannes of Gliwice 289
Johansen, Hans Christian 53
Johnson, Theodore 114, 115
jokamiehenoikeus
  see allemansrätten in parliamentary sources.
Jokela school shooting, Finland 174
Jones, Morgan 204
Jordan, Carlo 223, *231*, 232
Journal of American History 4, 5
Jutikkala, Eino 24

K

Kaarna, Mikko *191*
Kaatra, Kössi 306
Kahk, Juhan 27
Kansan Lehti **308**, **309**, *310*, **313**
Kardell, L. *185*
Karelian evacuees, Finland 129
  Emergency Settlement Act 131
  forced migrations from Karelia 130, 131, 132, 138
  further migration after Continuation War 133, **140**, **142**, **143**, 144
  Land Acquisition Act 133
  material and methods 133, **136**
  official resettlement plans 131, 133
  return to Karelia during the Continuation War 130, 132, **136**, 137, 138, 139, **140**, 141, **143**
Kauhajoki school shooting, Finland 174
Kaukiainen, Yrjö 27
Kekkonen, Urho 168, **169**, 170
Kenworthy, Joseph 205
Kero, Reino 24, 26
Kestemont, Mike 281
keyness method 312, **313**
Kilpi, Kalevi 187
Kleemola, Olli 168
Koivuniemi, Paula **169**, 170
Kompare, Derek 166, 175
Kone Foundation 6
Korst, Knud 53
Koselleck, Reinhart *269*, 304
Koski, Markku *191*
Krajewski, Markus 115
Kramer, Michael J. 176
Kranzberg, Melvin 21, **37**
Kuhn, Thomas 70, 75, 77, 83
Kujala, Antti 306
Kultala, Kalle **169**

L

labour movement
  see Finnish labour newspapers.
Lafferty, John D. 262
Lagoze, Carl 118
Lähdesmäki, T. 200
Lahti, Leo 11
Land Acquisition Act, Finland 133
Language Bank of Finland 99
Länsisuomen Työmies **308**, **309**, *310*, **313**
Lappalainen, Jussi T. 28
Lappalainen, Vesa 28
LAS language analysis tool 184, 189
Latent Dirichlet Allocation (LDA) technique 261, 262
layered PDF format 107, 108
Le Roy Ladurie, Emmanuel 3, 16
League of Nations 204, 206
  British membership debates 208, 212, 215
Legge-Bourke, Harry 213
Leibner, Lutz *229*
Leighton, Ronald 205
lemmatisation 262
Letters of 1916 Digital Edition project 106
Levenshtein distance 118, 119
Liddle, Roger 214
linguistics 29, 200, 312
link rot 91
Linneus, Carl 122
Living Archive audio-visual archives 165
  Eurovision Song Contests 172, 175
  journalists **169**, 171
  Kauhajoki school shooting 174
  limits and possibilities of interpretation 175
  metadata and FiNER analysis 167
  musicians **169**, 171

Myrskyluodon Maija (television series) *173*
nationally significant periods 172, *173*
people most frequently mentioned 168, **169**
presidents 168, **169**, 170
sports events 172, 174
under-representation of women 171
wars 172
longue durée 329, 330, 337
Lothian, Alexis 151
Lounasmeri, Lotta 170
Lugner, Heynuš 283
Lund University 117
Luther, Martin 266

M

Maccabees, book of 289
machine-readable data 90
Maddison Project database 48, 52
Maddison, Angus 48
MALLET (Machine Learning for Language Toolkit) software
allemansrätten in parliamentary sources 190
astronomical discourses in *Philosophical Transactions* 240
humanism discourse in early 19th-century German-language press 261, *264*, *268*
women's suffrage movement 154, **158**
Mannerheim, Carl Gustaf Emil **169**, 170
manual labour 113
coding work 116
history of 115
Named Entity Recognition (NER) project 120, *121*
newspaper database research 118
Mårtenson, Lasse **169**, *173*
Maskelyne, Nevil 243, 246, 247
Maule, Frances 151
Maximus of Turin 281
McDougall-Waters, Julie 239
McGregor, Oliver 207
medieval anti-heretical treatises 279
Adversus Catharos et Valdenses 283, 284, **287**
Attendite a falsis prophetis 284, **287**, *288*, 289, 291
auctoritas 280
computational authorship attribution 280, 286, **287**, *288*
Contra Pauperes de Lugduno 284, 285, **287**, 289
Cum dormirent homines 280, 282, 283, **287**, *288*, 289
Refutatio errorum 280, 282, **287**, *288*, 291
text pre-processing 284
medieval sources 34
Mellink, Bram 156
metadata 90, 95, 97, 103
administrative 97
challenges for digital history 106
checksums 97
crowdsourcing 106
defined 104
descriptive 97
layered PDF format and 107, 108
non-textual materials and 108
ontological model 105
problems with creation process 12, 105
selection of research material and 108
structural 97
technical 97
see also Living Archive audio-visual archives.

MetaSignal/MetaAlert project 45, 58
Meyer, John 48
microcomputers, introduction of 28
microfilming 32
Microsoft Excel 115
migration
see Karelian evacuees, Finland.
MiKARELIA database 133
Miles, Josephine 5
mobile phones 31
Mold, A. 156, 159
Moneta of Cremona 283, 284, **287**
Mons, Barend 94
Moretti, Franco 6, 30, 33
Morrissey, R. M. 225
Moxham, Noah 239
Müller-Wille, Staffan 122
multidisciplinary teamwork 78
Murray, Ronald King 213
Mussell, Jim 78
Mutzenbecher, A. 281
Muuttoliikeprojekti (Migration Project) 27
Myrskyluodon Maija (television series) *173*

N

Named Entity Recognition 120, *121*, 122
see also Living Archive audio-visual archives.
National Archives, Finland 32, 33, 55, 56, 58
National Archives, Sweden 54
National Library of Austria 263
National Library of Finland 33, 153, 188, *305*
National Library of Sweden 118
NATO 208
natural language processing 33, 35
see also MALLET (Machine Learning for Language Toolkit) software.
Neitzel, Sönke 76
NER
see Named Entity Recognition.
network analysis *224*
see also East German opposition movement.
Neumann, Gert *224*, *230*
New York Times 45
newspaper collections
see digital newspaper collections.
Nicholas of Montiéramey 281
Niethammer, Friedrich Immanuel 260
Niitemaa, Vilho 26
NLP
see natural language processing.
Nokia 31
non-textual materials 108
see also digital images, lack of metadata.
North, Douglass C. 48
not invented here syndrome 91
Nurmio, Yrjö 32
Nyberg, Arto **169**, 171

O

Obama, Barack 174
OCR
see optical character recognition.
Oiva, Mila 154, 157
Old Bailey records, UK 78
OPEDAS (Other People's Existing Data and Services) 94
Open Archival Information System (OAIS) standard 97
Open Data 90
open data portals 35
Open Science and Research Initiative report 98
optical character recognition 32, 34, 107, 117, 122, 153, 184, 240
ORCID identifiers 91

Owen, David 204
Owen, Goronwy 204

P

Päätalo, Kalle 28
Päivälehti 153, **158**, *305*, **313**
Pajala, Mari 166, 172, 175
Palladio software 222, *226*, 227
paper archives 58
paradigmatic change in sciences 70, 77, 83
paradigmatic digital history 76
parliamentary debates
  see allemansrätten in parliamentary sources; internationalism in UK parliament.
parliamentary reform, Finland 183
Patschovsky, A. 283
PCs (personal computers), introduction of 28
PDF document collections 107, 108
Pearce-Moses, Richard 104
pedagogical role of discourse 333
persistent identifiers 90, 91, 95, 97, 100
personal data 97, 100
Phillips, Amanda 151
Philosophical Transactions
  see astronomical discourses in *Philosophical Transactions.*
Pillichsdorf, Peter von 282, 284, 285, **287**, 289
Piper, Andrew 337, 340
Pitkänen, Kari 28
PMI-based measures 201
Poppe, Gerd 223, *224*
Poppe, Ulrike *224*, *230*
Posner, M. K. 150
Prentice, Reginal 206
Project Gutenberg 5
provenance of digital sources 97
Provinssirock festival 174
Psychological Association of Finland 25
PTL Tele/Sonera 55, 56
public access rights to nature
  see allemansrätten in parliamentary sources.
Pym, Francis 206

Q

quantification of research 70
quantitative history research 24, 30, 35

R

Rainio, Kullervo 25
RAND laboratories 46
Rasila, Viljo 5, 23, 24, 25, 26, 27, 152
Rathenow, Lutz *229*, *230*
raw data publishing 94
Rayner, Ralph 204, 206
Rea, Lord 206
Rea, Philip Russell 205
readsearch methodologies 80
Rees, J. D. 204
refugees
  see Karelian evacuees, Finland.
Refutatio errorum 280, 282, **287**, *288*, 291
regression analysis 50
Reid, F. L. 247
Reilly, S. K. 109
Renvall, Pentti 24
Republic of Letters project 106
research data management 89, 104
  checksums 97
  citations 92, 95
  content drift 91
  copyright *93*, *96*, 100
  dataset types 95, *96*
  digital source criticism 13, 34, 97
  documentation 91, 97, 98
  FAIR Data concept 90
  infrastructures and services 98

research data management *(Continued)*
link rot 91
persistent identifiers 90, 91, 95, 97, 100
personal data 97, 100
provenance 97
publishing raw data 94
research data life cycle 92, *93*, *96*
version control 95, 98
wiki technology 100
see also digitisation of sources; metadata.
research infrastructures 98
re-usable data 91
rights of access to nature
see allemansrätten in parliamentary sources.
Rikardsson, Gunnel 117
Risam, Roopika 339
Robert Havemann Society 222
Roberts, Liz Saville 214
Roman brick stamps 23
Roman social history 24
Rosenzweig, Roy 4
Rost, Michael 223
Royal Society Corpus 240
Royal Society of London
see astronomical discourses in *Philosophical Transactions.*
Rub, Frank 223
Ruge, Arnold 266

S

Salmi, Hannu 174
Sampo series 35
Sanoma Digital Archives 188
Sarvimäki, M. 131
Savela, Juho 154
Schaffer, Simon 247
Scheltjens, Werner 53
school shootings 174
Schumpeter, Joseph 70
Science 262
scientific revolutions theory 70, 77, 83
search
critical 342
full-text 81, 117
importance of search words in topic modelling 155
search engines 80, 107
everyday impacts on research practices 74
readsearch methodologies 80
selection of research material and 108
Second World War
see Karelian evacuees, Finland.
Segl, P. 282
Sello, Tom 223, *229*, *230*, *231*, 232
semi-automatic digital history 79
semi-automatic text extraction 80
set-theoretic relations 51
Sluga, Glenda **202**, 215
Smithers, Peter 204
Smyth, P. J. 204
SNA
see social network analysis.
Snickars, Pelle 34, 156
Snowden, Philip 205
Social background of the civil war (Rasila) 24
social network analysis *224*
social science history 47, 48
socialist sun
see Finnish labour newspapers.
Soikkanen, Hannu 311, 317
Solberg, Janine 151, 153, 154
Sosialisti **308**, **309**, *310*
Soundtoll Registers Online (STRO) compilation 52
source criticism, digital 13, 34, 97
Sozialistische Einheitspartei Deutschlands (SED) 223
spearfishing readsearch 81
Statistical methods in history research (Rasila) 26

statistical significance measures 50
stemmatological analyses 34
stemming 262
Stewart, James Henderson 206
Stockholm School of Economics 57
Stone, Lawrence 331
stop words removal 262, 265, *270*
structural metadata 97
Studia Historica series 24
Studia Stemmatologica 34
style-based document authentication
  see computational authorship attribution.
Sukutietotekniikka (Computer technology for family research) 29
Sulkunen, I. 159
Sumiala, Johanna 170
sun of socialism
  see Finnish labour newspapers.
Suomen Latu 185
Support Vector Machine (SVM)
  see computational authorship attribution.
Swedish Genealogical Association 54
Swedish historical monetary statistics 52
Swedish National Archives 54
Swedish National Library 118
Swedish Seamen's House enrolment database 52, 54

T

tally sticks 120
Tampere University 23, 24, 25, 27, 45
technical metadata 97
TEI (Text Encoding Initiative) standard 94
Teich, Elke 240, 241
temporality
  see Finnish labour newspapers.
Tepora, Tuomas 170
text mining 107
  see also topic modelling.
text processing 28
text segmentation 118
textblocks 118
textual analysis 29, 33, 35
  see also manual labour.
Then & Now (Ennen ja nyt) 31
Thomas Aquinas 115
Tilly, Charles 47
Tolonen, Mikko 11, 35
tombstone pages 95
tool sharing 344
topic modelling 33, 117
  allemansrätten in parliamentary sources 190, 191
  importance of search words 155
  Latent Dirichlet Allocation (LDA) technique 261, 262
  women's suffrage movement 153, **158**
  see also humanism discourse in early 19th-century German-language press.
Toronto Star 75
Torppa, Jorma 23
Transits of Venus
  see astronomical discourses in *Philosophical Transactions.*
trawl readsearch 81
Työmies *305*, 306, **308**, **309**, *310*, 313

U

UK Parliament
  see internationalism in UK parliament \b.
Umrani, Farida 150
Umweltbibliothek, East Berlin 227
Underwood, Ted 80, 81, 337
UNESCO *185*
United Nations, British membership debates 208, 209, 213
universalism of digital humanities 329, 335

University of Helsinki 25, 27, 28, 168
University of Jyväskylä 45, 46, 52, 53
University of Oulu 24
University of Turku 24, 26, 27, 28
URN identifiers 91
Uusi Suometar *305*, **313**

V

Välimäki, R. 280, 283
Valle, Ellen 239
van Tielhof, Milja 53
Vanek, Morgan 249
Venus
see astronomical discourses in Philosophical Transactions.
version control 95, 98
Virén, Lasse *173*
Virrankoski, Pentti 27

W

Wagener, A. 200
Waldensians 282, 283, 289
Waris, Heikki 24
Weber, Max 318
Wedgwood, Josiah 205
Wegner, Bettina 223, *231*
Weißhuhn, Reinhard *230*
Weller, Toni 76, 83
Welzer, Harald 76
Wernimont, Jacqueline 154
Wickham, Hadley 115
wiki technology 100
Winter War 130, 131, 172
Wirilander, Kaarlo 23
Women's Feminist Union, Finland 155, 159
women's suffrage movement 153, **158**
word processing 28

Y

Yle/Yleisradio
see Living Archive audio-visual archives.

Z

Zaagsma, Gerben 79
Zwicker, Petrus 280, 282, **287**, *288*

www.ingramcontent.com/pod-product-compliance
Lightning Source LLC
Chambersburg PA
CBHW051348290426
44108CB00015B/1926
* 9 7 8 9 5 2 3 6 9 0 2 0 2 *